Recreation and Resources

8
98

y

Recreation and Resources

Leisure patterns and leisure places

J. Allan Patmore

Basil Blackwell

First published 1983
Basil Blackwell Publisher Limited
108 Cowley Road, Oxford OX4 1JF, England

British Library Cataloguing in Publication Data
Patmore, J. Allan
Recreation and resources.
1. Recreation
I. Title
333.78′0942 GV75
ISBN 0-631-11551-X

Typesetting by
Katerprint Co Ltd, Cowley, Oxford
Printed in Great Britain by
Billing and Sons Ltd, Worcester

Contents

Acknowledgements

I must first acknowledge my deep indebtedness to the Social Science Research Council, whose award of a personal research grant (HR P7741/2) made the writing of this book feasible. Those thanks are far more than the conventional, for my interest in recreation was strongly encouraged by the erstwhile chairman of the Council's Human Geography Committee, Professor M.J. Wise, and by my colleagues when I served as a member of that Committee from 1973 to 1977. It led elsewhere to the creation of the Council's joint Panel on Leisure and Recreation Research with the Sports Council, and to the conscious nurturing of a more interdisciplinary approach to leisure research. This book is a deliberate reminder that, important though a wider approach undoubtedly is, the geographer's distinctive view remains a basic component of that wider understanding. Successive secretaries to the Human Geography Committee – Hilary York, Averil Cooper, John Edwards and Angela Williams – cheerfully translated enthusiasm into practicality as the wider leisure initiative of their committee developed. To Angela Williams I owe my particular thanks, for she encouraged me to write this geographical appraisal of the field and smoothed the inevitable administrative problems that arose. I am also extremely grateful to the University of Hull for permitting me to take study leave at short notice and to my departmental colleagues for readily shouldering the additional burdens created by my absence.

This book has numerous reminders that leisure ideals often succumb to leisure realities. Those reminders are the unconscious contributions of numerous friends in the world of practical leisure provision. To name them all would be tedious, but to the following I owe far more than they will ever know, or this book worthily reveal: from the Countryside Commission, Roger Sidaway (who taught in my stead at Hull for two terms), Mike Kirby, Ray Taylor and Sally Bucknall; from the North York Moors National Park Committee, successive chairmen Michael Foster and Martin Territt, the National Park Officer Derek Statham, Michael

Webster, Ian Crookall and Roy Brown; and from the Sports Council, the Chairman Dick Jeeps, the erstwhile Director-General Emlyn Jones, John Coghlan, John Wheatley and Cyril Villiers. To Michael Collins of the Sports Council, my thanks are especially heartfelt. His unstinting friendship, his bubbling enthusiasm, his encyclopaedic knowledge and his unerring grasp of ideas and concepts will leave me ever in his debt. He would have written a far more scintillating and informed book than I ever could, but his interest in (and patience with) my endeavours has been deeply appreciated. Many other academic friends have been a continuing encouragement: my particular thanks go to Bill Slater, Brian Rodgers, Terry Coppock and Gordon Cherry. None of these have any responsibility for what I have written, but their stamp remains – however well disguised – on all my thinking.

Many organisations have helped in providing material. Time and space did not permit all to be incorporated, but special thanks are due to Joan Gordon (Sports Council), Bryan Berryman (Scarborough Public Library), R. Davies (Department of the Environment), Peter W. Dove (Scarborough), David Gray (Walkers Studies, Scarborough), George Hallas (Yorkshire Dales National Park), Mike Ingham (Peak Park Joint Planning Board), John Miles (Transport and Road Research Laboratory), Shirley Penney (Nature Conservancy Council) and Ann Prosser (Welsh Office).

The importance of the maps in a book of this kind speaks for itself: their clarity and quality are entirely the result of Keith Scurr's ability to translate the roughest sketches into maps of elegance and meaning. I am especially grateful for his quiet forbearance when I monopolised so much of his time in a drawing office sadly depleted of staff. He was helped on some occasions by Andrew Bolton. Brian Fisher turned my slides into usable photographs effectively and speedily. (Except where specifically acknowledged, all the photographs are my own.) Stella Rhind deciphered my scrawl to make manuscript typescript with a speed and accuracy that arouses astonishment as well as gratitude. Joyce Bell, my secretary, served as memory, shield and helpmate with a patience and an efficiency I have long taken too much for granted.

My last but most important word of thanks is to my long-suffering wife and to Elizabeth. May their patience and forbearance one day be rewarded by the separation of work and leisure in our lives.

J. Allan Patmore
North Ferriby

Introduction

The explosion of leisure activities during the 1960s, and in particular the rapid growth of the use of the countryside for recreation, sparked an academic interest that closely paralleled the practical concern of planners with the phenomenon. Much of this interest came from geographers and led to several papers and texts of note in the late 1960s and early 1970s.[1]

Since 1975, however, a number of changes have tended to stifle this interest or change its direction. The rising cost of fuel and the periodic threat to the continuity of supplies brought a slackening in the growth of countryside recreation, while deepening recession and rising unemployment focused the attention of planners and politicians on more basic issues of work, housing and social deprivation. Academically, there was a growing recognition of the importance of leisure, but more because of its social implications than because of the spatial patterns of leisure activities and the use of land and water resources for recreation. This changing emphasis argued for the need to involve a much wider range of disciplines and to strengthen the work of isolated pioneers in the fields of sociology, social psychology, economics and education.

Better understanding of people's motivations, perceptions and satisfactions in the leisure field has not, however, lessened the importance of a clear understanding of the resulting patterns of activity and the complex demands on land and water resources that they generate. The present book seeks to fulfil this need. It deliberately emphasises the approach and the concerns of the geographer, but is designed for a much wider audience. While the basic theme has an intrinsic interest of its own, it may also serve to heighten the understanding of those whose prime allegiance is to other disciplines, or whose concern is practical provision rather than academic contemplation.

One further caveat is needed. Recreation patterns are strongly conditioned by national attitudes and are, equally, constrained by the particularities of national resources. Conceptual development in the geography of recreation remains relatively rudimentary,[2] and international comparisons may confuse rather than clarify.[3] It was decided, therefore, in a book of modest compass, to explore the situation as it exists in England and Wales alone. Scotland was omitted not only because of the striking differences of institutions, patterns and resources north of the border, but because it has already been well served by an earlier work.[4]

1 Leisure and Society

WORK AND LEISURE

> Many people suffer a lingering feeling that leisure is something of a luxury. As an escape from the commendable pursuit of earning a living and making a contribution to the national economy, leisure seems tainted. When carried to excess it is called idleness. But the Committee believe that it is time for this puritan view of leisure to be jettisoned. Leisure is as much a part of life as work and it plays an equally important part in man's development and the quality of his life.[1]

In 1973, when the House of Lords Select Committee on Sport and Leisure made its forthright testament of belief in the positive purpose and value of leisure, Britain was riding a rising tide of personal and national prosperity. Energy was relatively cheap, work relatively plentiful. Leisure might be 'something of a luxury', but it was a luxury that the great majority of people had increasing time and increasing means to enjoy. Nor was leisure purely a private and individual matter: the provision of leisure opportunities became a growing concern of the public as well as the private sector. The government, in responding to the Report of the Select Committee, could agree that 'recreation should be regarded as "one of the community's everyday needs" and that provision for it is "part of the general fabric of the social services".'[2] The value of leisure was unhesitatingly accepted: 'Where the community neglects its responsibilities for providing the individual with opportunities and choice in the provision of sports and recreational facilities, it will rarely escape the long-term consequences of this neglect. When life becomes meaningful for the individual then the whole community is enriched.'[3]

Events soon strengthened this view. As early as the mid-1970s, conditions in Britain's emerging post-industrial society were pointing to the need to re-examine the roles of work and leisure at individual and national levels, but it was the economic recession of the early 1980s that brought the issues into sharp and immediate focus. It may be unduly emotive to speak starkly of 'the collapse of work',[4] but there is no mistaking the underlying trend (figure 1.1). In the 1960s the unemployed accounted for less than one in fifty of the working population, but by early 1982 the proportion had risen to more than one in eight.

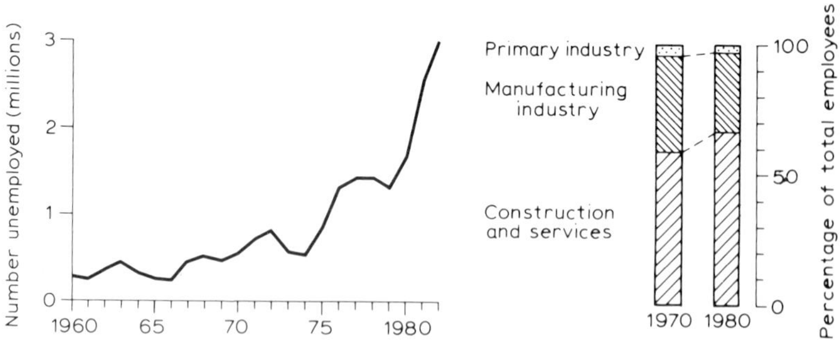

FIGURE 1.1 The number of registered unemployed in the United Kingdom, 1970-82 (left) and the distribution of employees in the United Kingdom by industry, June 1970 and June 1980 (right).
The data for unemployment relate to June each year, except for February in 1982.
Source: data from *Employment Gazette* (Department of Employment) and Central Statistical Office, *Monthly Digest of Statistics* (HMSO, March 1982)

As the figure shows, the rise in unemployment stems not just from a cyclical downturn in the economy, but also from an accelerating tendency in the last twenty years that transcends short-term fluctuations: mechanisation and automation, plus foreign competition, have steadily reduced the labour demands of primary and manufacturing industry. Until recently, however, that shrinkage had been balanced in large part by a growth in the service sector. Between 1961 and 1980, for example, employment in insurance, banking and finance increased from 0.7 to 1.3 million, in local government from 1.9 to 3.0 million and in the National Health Service from 0.6 to 1.2 million.[5] Now, employment in the service sector is also contracting, with electronic automation in particular enhancing productivity and reducing manpower needs. The net result is a growing shortage of jobs, a shortage that is generating new attitudes to the experience and the opportunity of work and, in counterpoint, to the enjoyment – or the endurance – of leisure.

These changes heighten the need for a fuller knowledge and understanding of leisure. This book's prime concern is with the geographical aspects of leisure – the patterns it generates and its impact on land and water resources. Wider issues – the human experience of leisure, its role in society and its economic worth – are the province of the social psychologist, the sociologist and the economist, but no geographical view would be complete without a brief consideration of the wider context; leisure is as much a social as a spatial concern and the questions raised by these concerns cannot be viewed effectively in the isolation of a single discipline. This introductory chapter looks therefore at some of the wider issues of leisure and society, at the structure of leisure institutions, and at leisure provision as a necessary setting for more geographical considerations.[6]

THE MEANING OF LEISURE

Leisure is more readily experienced than defined. The word itself is derived through the Old French *leisir* from the Latin *licere*, to be allowed or to be lawful. Words with the same root include 'licence', both in its meaning of leave or permission to do something and in its alternative implication of liberty of action, particularly when the liberty is excessive and borders on the 'licentious'.[7] These twin threads of freedom to choose and of social control, of social patterns within a moral or a legal context, are reflected in the meanings that the term 'leisure' has itself acquired.

The word can be used in three distinct contexts.[8] The first relates leisure to *time*, the residual time remaining when the needs of work and of basic human functions such as sleeping and eating have been satisfied. The leisure-as-'non-work' approach was adopted by the Countryside Recreation Research Advisory Group (CRRAG) in their glossary of terms, where leisure is defined as 'the time available to the individual when the disciplines of work, sleep and other basic needs have been met'.[9] But even this simple definition raises problems. Should the journey to work, for example, be counted as 'work' or 'non-work' time? Should eating for pleasure, even in the setting of the family at home, be equated with leisure or with a physiological 'discipline'?

The second approach links leisure to *activity*. Instead of the negative 'non-work' approach, leisure is defined positively as the time when leisurely activities are undertaken. These activities have varied functions. Simple relaxation brings recuperation, literal re-creation. Diversion brings new experiences, broadens knowledge or develops creativity. Social contact, within or beyond the family, yields the varied pleasures of human intercourse and develops personality. Recreation is often used as a term to describe leisure in this context of specific activity: to quote the CRRAG glossary again, 'recreation is any pursuit engaged upon during leisure time, other than pursuits to which people are normally "highly committed".'[10] The concept of 'highly committed' implies restriction on the freedom of choice of activity and includes, in the CRRAG definition, 'such things as optional shopping, overtime, secondary work, house repairs, car maintenance, further education, homework, child care, religion and politics'.[11]

The concept of commitment relates also to the third approach, leisure as an *attitude of mind*. In this context, leisure is a matter of the individual's perception rather than of rigid time-based or activity-based definitions. It is rooted in enjoyment and reflects degrees of pleasure and satisfaction. For some people, the boundary between work and pleasure is blurred, with work yielding the satisfactions that others find only in their non-work time and activities. Again, to some, house repairs or gardening are 'necessary chores' and scarcely seen as leisure while to others they give great pleasure and release creativity.

These differing concepts of leisure are important in any understanding of the role of leisure in society and in the life of the individual. For convenience, this book will use the convention that *leisure* relates to time, and the whole of non-work time in particular, and that *recreation* relates to the specific activities pursued in that leisure time. But the distinction is a convention, and its rigid application can occasionally stifle a full exploration of the values and the satisfactions of the leisure experience.

ATTITUDES TO LEISURE

The satisfactions of leisure are linked to the values and attitudes of society as well as to the perceptions of the individual. Historically, both values and attitudes have undergone great changes.[12] The first conscious assessment of the value of leisure comes from the classic Greek philosophers, and from Aristotle and Plato in particular. The Greek concept was rooted in the ideal of *schole*, a word that originally meant 'to halt or cease', and hence to have peace and quiet. *Schole* was not leisure in the sense in which we would understand it: it was different not only from work but also from those activities and amusements that were seen as necessary because of work, and its qualities lay in contemplation and the cultivation of the mind. In contrast to this ideal, work was *ascholia*, literally, 'the absence of leisure', and was pursued only so that leisure might be achieved. In Aristotle's words, 'we are unleisurely in order to have leisure'.[13] This goal, however, was the privilege of an elite, for Greek society was dependent on slave labour, for whom *ascholia* was an end in itself. The separation between work and leisure was therefore not so much a separation in an individual's uses of time as a separation between 'working' and 'leisured' classes.

Most societies have had, in greater or lesser numbers, a leisured elite, but in understanding contemporary attitudes to leisure it is more important to examine briefly the changing role of leisure in the life of ordinary individuals. In the agricultural communities of pre-industrial (and often pre-literate) societies, work and leisure were closely intertwined. Those communities were mostly small, and both work and leisure were inherently communal and followed a rhythm dictated by the changing seasons. At times the demands of work were all-consuming, but at other times the needs of the land abated and recreational pursuits held sway.

In medieval Britain, holidays were surprisingly numerous. Their roots lay in Christian holy days, but their frequency and timing owed as much to secular as to sacred needs. In the fourteenth-century village they included typically (in addition to Sundays) the twelve days of Christmas, a week at both Easter and Whitsuntide, and several other single days including May Day, Midsummer Day and the parish wakes days. In addition to these recognised holidays, there were breaks from work for fairs and markets, weddings and funerals, sporting events and public occasions.[14]

As the rhythm of the land permitted respite, so the church recognised that men had more than spiritual needs. Prelates might bemoan the profane use of time – Wyclif sorrowed that Christmas was 'gluttony, lechery and all manner of harlotry'[15] – but in practice the church came to terms with reality, and, after church attendance, holidays were given up to recreation. The communities were small and shared in recreation as they shared in work. Food was routinely monotonous and often scarce: feasts and 'ales', with music, songs and dancing, gave welcome pause from harsh reality. Games and pastimes also typically involved the whole community rather than the individual. Some had more than social purpose; from six to sixty, able-bodied men were bound by law to practise with the bow at the village butts on Sundays and holidays.[16] Others were unreservedly for enjoyment, albeit of a vigorous kind. Football has its distant precursors in the numerous local variants of mass-kicking games, where teams ranging upwards in size to whole villages sought to kick or carry a ball or other objects to a predetermined goal.[17] There were also less vigorous and more individual pursuits: medieval people enjoyed such simple pastimes as reading, walking in the fields and picking flowers.[18]

The essence of the medieval attitude was the close integration of leisure with both the experience and the patterns of work. There was no conscious antithesis, no formal segregation: leisure was 'embedded in life, rather than a separate part of it'.[19] In the following centuries, however, two major changes in society brought fundamental changes in attitudes towards leisure whose effects are still plainly evident in practices and attitudes today.

The first stemmed from the changed organisation of work itself. The industrial revolution, and the concomitant growth of towns rather than villages as the usual place of residence for most of the population, meant that the simple organisation and varied rhythms that characterised village life and communal activity were no longer appropriate. The gathering of the workforce into factories of growing size necessitated the imposition of formal hours of working, while the high labour demands of early factory processes dictated long hours of work as a regular feature rather than just at the peak period of the agricultural year. Periodic holidays shrank rapidly in number. In 1761 the Bank of England still closed on 47 holidays in the year in addition to Sundays: by 1834 that number had dwindled to four.[20] By the 1850s the average working week in factories was 70 hours or more. Attitudes to work were coloured not only by long hours with little respite but by the extension of the money economy. As work became paid work, time was more readily perceived to have a literal value, in shop and office as well as factory. In counterpoint, leisure was seen more clearly as a contrast to work rather than an extension of it, a time for personal enjoyment and for the purchase of pleasures with the earnings from work.

Those pleasures grew more varied and more individual in character. As communities increased in size, as urbanism became a way of life, communal enjoyment – a hallmark of village society – could no longer hold sway with its spontaneous involvement of the whole community. Recreations focused more on home and family as well as on a widening range of social institutions. In the Victorian home, rising material standards gave new opportunities. The upright piano brought music to the parlour; the advent of gas lighting and the widening use of spectacles underpinned mass literacy in extending the pleasure of reading. Public and commercial libraries grew in number; weekly papers of varying kinds catered for distinctive tastes. Beyond the home, proliferating churches signified not only religious revival but a new range of social and even sporting institutions. It is no accident that football clubs like Aston Villa, Bolton Wanderers, Everton and Queens Park Rangers have their origins in offshoots of church activities.[21]

The impact of industrialisation on attitudes to leisure and on leisure patterns is common to all developed societies. In Britain, a second parallel influence has been a pervasive puritanism. Its ideology was not new, though it found fresh impetus in the Reformation, but from the mid-seventeenth century it infused both public policy and private practice. It married well with a growing need for new attitudes to work: as early as 1620, Thomas Mun could note that our weak competitive position in international trade was due to 'the general leprosy of our piping, potting, feasting, factions and misspending of our time in idleness and pleasure'.[22] That attitude – equating leisure with idleness, pleasure with misspent time – still dies hard.

Historically, it came to focus on a narrow Sabbatarianism. In 1644 a Puritan parliament banned trading, sports and games on Sundays, and even the Restoration brought little relaxation. In the eighteenth century Sunday trading was restricted in both law and practice, Sunday travel was frowned upon, and plays, public music and dancing were banned. In the nineteenth century the full rigour of the Victorian Sabbath held sway, the product of an ethos that evoked the moral as well as the practical virtue of an industrious life. This conditioned not only attitudes but activities. To some, the denial of any recreation was a worthy end in itself; to others, it was the unhappy but inevitable lot of the labouring classes. For many, Sunday, aside from the formal practice of religion, could offer little but idleness or drink.

But such a situation was too unstable to persist for long. Shorter working hours and growing affluence widened the range of leisure opportunities. New skills and interests gained popular approval. Music flourished, not only in the home, but through such popular outlets as the brass bands of the north and the choral singing of the Welsh valleys. Sport had a remarkable renaissance, approvingly identified with the manliness, courage and physical vitality hymned as virtue by 'muscular Christianity'. The second half of the nineteenth century saw the emergence of a whole new range of sports, complete with rules, governing bodies and competition at both national and international level. Football grew from varied antecedents, not least the highly individual games practised at different public schools earlier in the century. The Football Association was founded in 1863, the Football League in 1888. Soccer rapidly became a professional game, with attractions for spectators as well as players: class as well as code differences were sealed with the formation in 1871 of the Rugby Football Union, a bastion of opposition to professionalism.[23]

On Sunday itself, change was insidious but sure, not least as widening opportunities expanded the range of available recreations and popular opinion saw less reason to discriminate against harmless recreations that were permissible on weekdays and needed no input of labour on the Sabbath. Leafy suburbia offered croquet lawns and tennis; the bicycle opened up the countryside and was the precursor of the car-borne trip of the present century.

Contemporary attitudes to leisure are traced in more detail, implicitly and explicitly, in the remainder of this book, but post-industrial attitudes still echo the values of an earlier era. Victorian society emphasised the work ethic, with leisure in a subordinate, and often morally inferior, role. The element of guilt in leisure dies hard. As the introduction to this chapter showed, the House of Lords Select Committee on Sport and Leisure as late as 1973 found it necessary formally to jettison 'this puritan view' and declare with vigour that leisure had 'an equally important part in man's development and the quality of his life' as work. Even today, the pattern of the British weekend, and of the British Sunday in particular, carries strong Victorian echoes, with legal constraints reducing opportunities for commercialised leisure if not individual enjoyment. But while attitudes linger, leisure itself expands with more time, and more resources, available for it. It is too facile and emotive to speak of a 'leisure explosion', but the leisure component of most people's lives has grown rapidly and there are increasing numbers of people with virtually the whole of their time to dispose of as they will. These changes need a closer look.

OPPORTUNITIES FOR LEISURE

In the lives of most people, the rhythm of leisure opportunity has a fourfold component –by day, week, year and working life. At the height of the industrial revolution, the daily component was the least significant. For those at work the hours were long, without the seasonal respite of earlier, rural, rhythms. For those at home domestic chores were tedious and time-consuming. The major changes, however, had come by the end of the First World War, and advances since that date have been modest. Statistics subsume daily into weekly patterns. For manual workers the 48-hour week, and little in excess of eight hours a day, became normal after 1918. For most, the evening was free from work commitments, with the working day beginning shortly after breakfast and finishing before an early evening meal. Recent changes have been slight (figure 1.2). In 1951 a man in full-time employment worked, on average, 48 hours a week; by 1980, 43 hours.[24] These figures relate to actual hours worked, including overtime: reductions in the 'standard' working week, before the payment

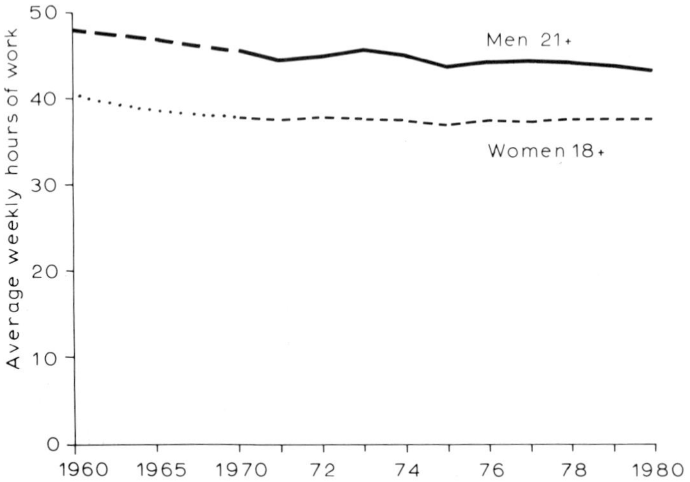

FIGURE 1.2 Average weekly hours of work for persons in full-time manual work in the United Kingdom, 1960-80.
Source: data from Central Statistical Office, *Social Trends 1980* (HMSO, 1981)

of overtime, were often more a device to increase real wages than to reduce working hours. Of that 43 hours, overtime accounted for some 3.9 hours, though fluctuating between 5.5 hours for manual workers and 1.6 hours for non-manual. The overall reduction in hours, slight as it has been, especially in the 1970s, has made little difference to the working day.

The pattern of work in the home, however, has changed dramatically. Its labour requirements have greatly diminished, not only through changing family composition, but also through its design and equipment. Labour-saving durable goods have proliferated, their spread encouraged by rises in real income. In 1956, for example, only 8 per cent of British households had refrigerators, but this had increased to 33 per cent by 1962 and 92 per cent by 1979.[25] Other appliances came into widespread use: 77 per cent of all households now have washing machines, 55 per cent central heating and 47 per cent deep freezers.[26] The time spent on routine household tasks has also diminished, with changes in shopping habits and the advent of such developments as non-iron clothing. The net result has been not only to change the pattern of household activity but to encourage more women to become part of the labour force. The change was at its greatest in the 1960s and the early 1970s: in 1961, 29.7 per cent of married women were in employment and by 1979, 49.6 per cent.[27] If only those aged between 16 and 59 are included, the latter proportion rises to 60 per cent, with about half working part-time. The implications of these changes for leisure patterns within the home will be considered subsequently, but they affect both daily and weekly leisure time.

Although the length of the working week has changed little, most of the change has been in the length of the weekend. Much of the drop in hours worked during the 1960s came with the widespread adoption of the five-day week in industry and in many services such as banking. The trend to a longer continuous weekend is increasing, with working hours curtailed on Friday afternoons. Paradoxically, the growth of commercial involvement in leisure has brought more working of 'unsocial' hours to cater for leisure needs.

While the weekend remains the individual's greatest leisure opportunity, the most startling recent changes have been in the annual cycle. The nadir of holiday entitlement was in the mid-nineteenth century. Sir John Lubbock's Bank Holiday Act of 1871 gave four public holidays a year and fostered the bank holiday as a British institution. Beyond such occasional holidays, progress for most was slow. The idea of an extended annual holiday gradually gained ground, but as it carried no entitlement to pay it could be a dubious benefit: by 1900 a holiday 'was taken for granted as a luxury which could be enjoyed at a certain level of income but which there was no special hardship in going without'.[28] The first half of the present century saw the near-universal extension of holidays with pay, to 80 per cent of all workers by 1945. More recently, the length of that holiday has almost doubled (figure 1.3). In 1960, 97 per cent of manual employees had a basic holiday entitlement of only two weeks a year: by 1980, 74 per cent were entitled to four weeks or more, a rise from 35 per cent only two years before.[29] The length of both the working week and the annual holiday reflect, of course, not only perceived desire but also trade union recognition that changes in hours worked may be at least as beneficial as, and on occasions more readily obtainable than, direct changes in remuneration.

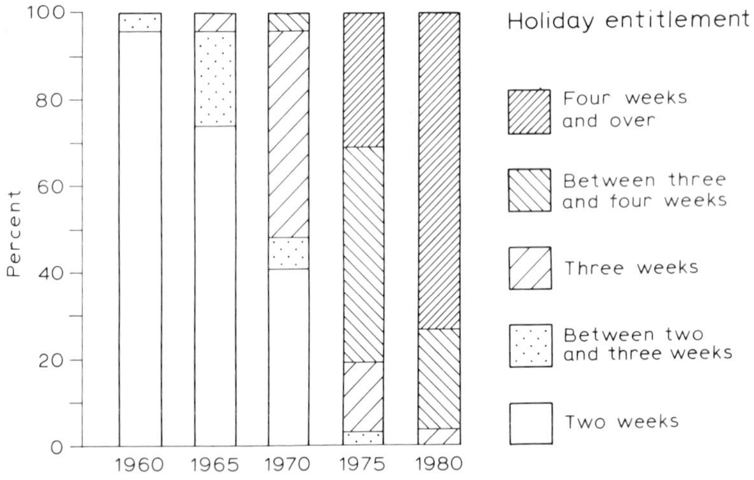

FIGURE 1.3 Basic holiday entitlement, full-time adult male manual workers in the United Kingdom, 1960-80.
Source: data from Central Statistical Office, *Social Trends 9* (HMSO, 1979) and *Employment Gazette* (Department of Employment, April 1981)

The final cycle is that of the working life, and it too has dwindled in recent years. The overall picture is complex, but the general trends are indicated in table 1.1. Entry into work is dependent first on the minimum school-leaving age, last raised, to 16, in the 1972–73 school year. More boys than girls seek work directly on leaving school, but, paradoxically, more go on to advanced forms of further education. In 1966, of school leavers in England and Wales, 8.9 per cent of boys entered degree courses and 4.3 per cent of girls. By 1979 distinction between the sexes had been reduced, but was still substantial, with 8.6 per cent of boys entering such courses and 6.5 per cent of girls.[30] The overall increase therefore is comprised entirely of the larger proportion of girls seeking further qualifications.

At the other end of the cycle, fewer people of pensionable age are now in active employment, and the decline is particularly striking for men, with a

TABLE 1.1 Percentage of age group in labour force,* 1961 and 1979, in Great Britain

	*15**-19 years*		*65+*	*60+*
	Males	*Females*	*Males*	*Females*
	%	%	%	%
1961	74.6	71.1	25.0	10.0
1979	70.7	64.8	10.2	7.4

* 'Labour force' includes all in employment and those identified as unemployed, whether registered or not. Students in full-time education, and the retired, are not included.
** 16-19 in 1979.
Source: data from *Social Trends 12* (HMSO, 1982) table 4.4

drop in less than two decades from a quarter to a tenth of those aged 65 and over. Retirement arrangements differ quite widely between occupations, but the growing trend to earlier retirement has accelerated as jobs overall become scarcer.

THE LEISURED CLASSES

Changes in the recurrent rhythms of the working day, week and year have increased the leisure time available to almost all individuals in work, whereas changes in the rhythm of working life have increased the numbers of those whose whole time is freed from the constraints of work. Such freedom may be far from an unmitigated blessing, for the availability of time is only one of the requirements for satisfaction in leisure: health, financial means and personal mobility are equally important. This is particularly true for the two major groups affected by changing work patterns, the unemployed and the retired.

The unemployed present a special problem. The scale of that problem in numerical terms was set out at the beginning of the chapter, and it is clear that it will remain endemic in society for the foreseeable future.[31] Some of its components are of particular concern in the present context. There are considerable fluctuations in its impact, not only where it is locally acute through specific losses of work opportunity, but at a broader regional level. In November 1981, for example, the UK level of unemployment was 12.2 per cent of the labour force, but those levels fluctuated from 8.9 per cent in the South East to 15.9 per cent in the North.[32] There are growing proportions, as well as growing numbers, of these chronically unemployed, for whom employment is a long-term rather than a short-term phenomenon. In April 1972 one-sixth of the unemployed had been out of work for a year: by April 1981 that proportion had risen to one-fifth, and in that same month half the unemployed had been out of work for over six months.[33] The chronically unemployed tend to be concentrated – though far from exclusively – in two age groups; the young, especially the unskilled and some ethnic minorities, and the older workers, whether formally declared redundant or taking early retirement. Many of these unemployed do not perceive their 'free' time as 'leisure' time in any reasonable sense of the term: indeed, as Vereker has remarked, 'there is a certain irony in the train of events whereby modern technological and scientific advances have provided more leisure time and the health and knowledge to enjoy it for much larger numbers of people than ever before in history only to result in the very idea and experience of not being gainfully and usefully employed being unwelcome and unable to be enjoyed.'[34] Part of that lack of enjoyment obviously stems from a lack of resources: not surprisingly, the unemployed tend to do less of anything that costs money, and they are chary also of free or subsidised schemes where their status, and its perceived stigma, can be identified.

The retired share some of these problems, though the financial impact of retirement has been mitigated by the rise in the real value of state pensions, and by the growing provision of benefit from occupational pension schemes. Indeed, the early years of retirement can be a time of fresh fulfilment, not least as earlier retirement brings a longer period before physical constraints curtail activity unduly.[35] Against that, however, must be set the growing numbers of the 'old' old in society. Current projections of population suggest that the total numbers of those over 65 are unlikely to increase by the end of the century, whereas the numbers of those aged over 75 will increase by 18 per cent.[36]

While those freed wholly from work are a product of economic as much as demographic change, changes in population structure have changed the proportions of those best able to make positive use of leisure time. In earlier years, one major component of growing leisure demands arose not from population structure but from the increasing size of the population as a whole. As late as 1970, it was confidently predicted that the population of the UK would grow to 66.5 million by the end of the century: 'the one statement that can be made today with some confidence is that population growth is the only reasonable basis on which to plan for the future.'[37] However, after a decade when total population grew by only 0.3 per cent (1971–81), much the smallest decennial increase since the census began in 1801, predictions for the century's end are far more cautious and suggest a rise to only 58.4 million from 55.6 million.

Structural changes, however, remain significant, and not least the changing structure of the family. The trend to smaller families substantially compresses the period in the life cycle when parents are tied by the physical as well as the fiscal constraints of a young family (figure 1.4). The period of child-rearing is now typically completed nearly a decade earlier than at the beginning of the century. This has had a double implication for leisure patterns. In the first place, not only are the numbers of children smaller, but the age range of children in the family is much more compressed and recreations involving the whole family unit are more readily undertaken. Second, parents are free of the direct ties of children at an earlier, more active, stage in the life cycle, and can enjoy 25–30 years of unencumbered, active recreation at a time when earning potential is also high.

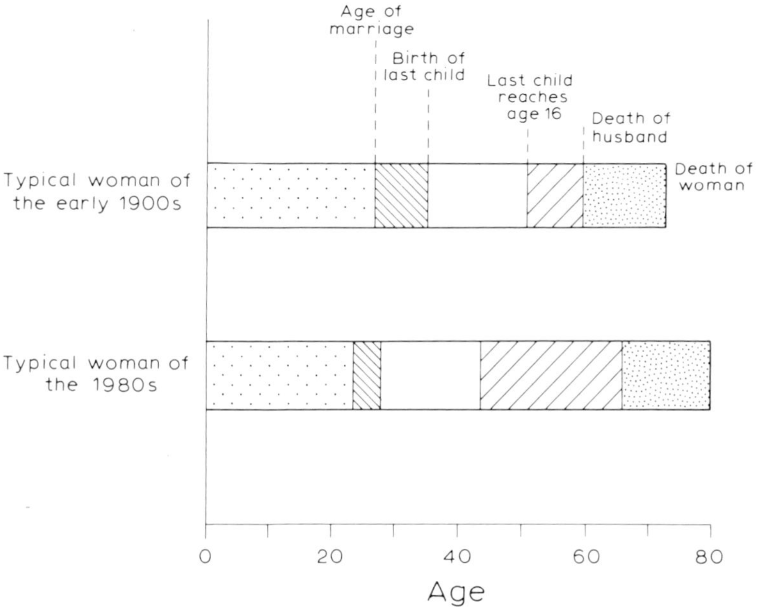

FIGURE 1.4 A diagrammatic representation of the life-cycle of a woman of the early 1900s and of the early 1980s.
Source: based on *Sport in the community: the next ten years* (Sports Council, 1982), figure 6

Other patterns in a changing society are reflected in the number and composition of households. Despite a virtually static population, the number of households has continued to increase. In 1971 there were 18.3 million in Great Britain, in 1981 20.1, and for 1991 a projected 27.1. There has been a sharp increase in one-person households, from 3.3 million in 1971 to 4.7 in 1981, as more young people set up home away from their parents at an early age and as more retired people continue to live on their own even after the death of a partner. Single-parent households are also growing in number, reflecting a deep-rooted change in society's attitude to both marriage and divorce. These, and allied changes, presage a loosening of ties in society, the growth of more varied household structures, and the decline of the extended family as the household nucleus. The growing freedom from direct family ties generates an extended but increasingly varied and complex pattern of leisure demand. Generalisations grow increasingly dangerous in the leisure field, and stereotypes more facile. The archetypal 'two-parent two-child' household, for example, now accounts for only 15 per cent of all households, and is expected to decline still further.[37] While there may be, in a strict context, few whose life-style would place them firmly in the 'leisure classes', far more have new, and more varied, opportunities of unencumbered time to use as they please.

RESOURCES FOR LEISURE

Time is only one component of leisure. Increased leisure time gives increased leisure opportunities, but without increased financial measures, those opportunities may have little value to the individual and may, indeed, be less than welcome. To some extent, increased time has been traded off for increased income. The greater proportion of women now working either full-time or part-time reflects not only their growing freedom from household chores and their changing role in society, but also a conscious attempt to increase household income to enable a higher standard of living, and a more varied use of leisure, to be attained.[38] The same might be said of the growth of spare-time working, especially where the remuneration is undeclared for tax purposes – the so-called 'black' economy, estimated by the Inland Revenue as totalling perhaps as much as 7.5 per cent of the Gross National Product.[39]

Leaving sources of income aside, two generalisations are important concerning financial resources for leisure. The first, simply, is the continued rise in real terms in average earnings and in household incomes. That rise was continuous right through the 1950s and 1960s, with average earnings showing an increase of more than 50 per cent in real terms over the period. In the 1970s and early 1980s increases have been tempered by energy crises, recession, rising inflation and rising unemployment, but despite short-term fluctuations real household disposable income per head increased by 28 per cent between 1970 and 1980.[40] The second trend is the growth in resources devoted by individuals to leisure pursuits, in both relative and absolute terms. The relative increase may be small – one estimate shows a rise from 21.0 per cent of consumer spending in 1971 to 22.1 in 1980 – but this represents an absolute increase of 29 per cent at constant prices.[41] That increase is far from uniformly spread (figure 1.5), nor does the scale of expenditure equate simply with the satisfaction derived: the implications of these figures will be looked at more closely when actual patterns of leisure use are considered.

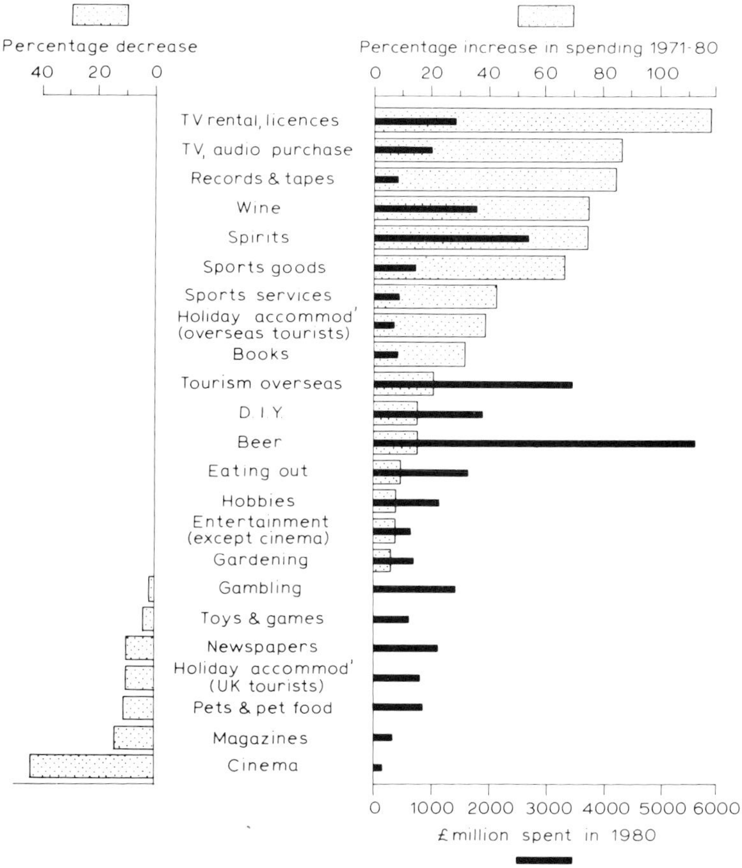

FIGURE 1.5 Trends in leisure spending in the United Kingdom, 1971-80, at constant 1980 prices, and total leisure spending, 1980.
Source: data from *UK leisure market* (Henley Centre for Forecasting, 1981)

Increased financial resources are devoted to leisure not only by individuals but also by public authorities at both national and local level. We have already seen that by the mid-1970s the government could recognise, in the White Paper *Sport and recreation* (Cmnd 6200), that provision for leisure from the public purse is 'part of the general fabric of the social services'. That provision, however, remains curiously sporadic in both scale and direction (figures 1.6 and 1.7), reflecting as much historic accidents of emphasis as an objective and detached view of need.[42]

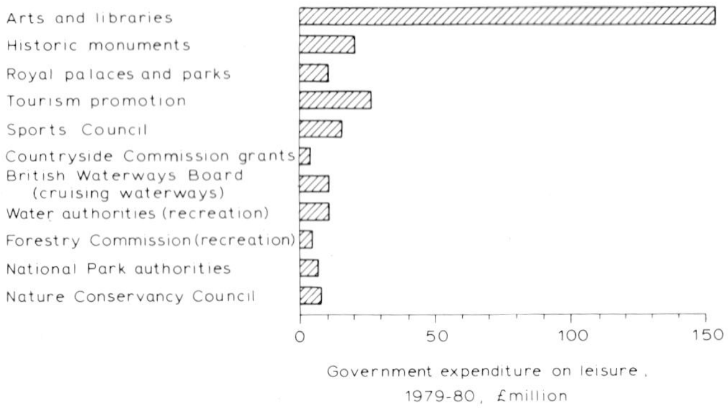

FIGURE 1.6 Government expenditure on leisure, 1979-80.
Source: data from Chairmen's Policy Group, *Leisure policy for the future* (Sports Council, 1981), table 5.3

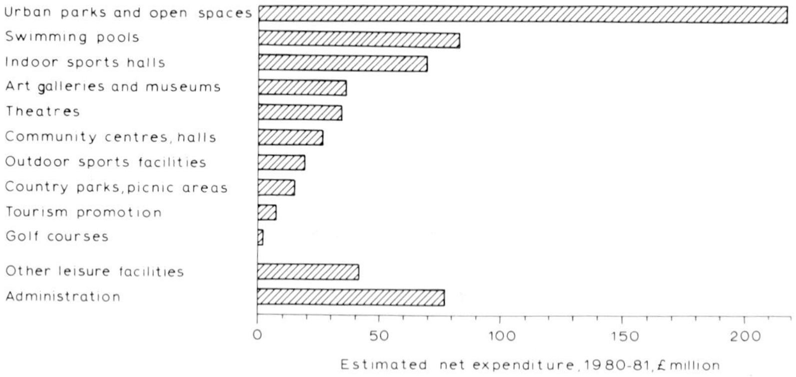

FIGURE 1.7 Estimated net expenditure (current and capital) by local authorities in England and Wales on leisure and recreation, 1980-81.
Source: data from *Leisure and recreation statistics, 1980-81 estimates* (Chartered Institute of Public Finance and Accounting, 1981)

LOCAL LEISURE SERVICES

Some of these emphases deserve brief recall. Local provision sprang from a series of isolated and optional powers granted to local government from the mid-nineteenth century to meet particular social problems and needs. The classic case is the provision of urban parks and open spaces, facilities that still account for the major share of local government leisure expenditure. Parks and spaces were present prior to the Victorian period, but only as commons, as royal parks in London or, on occasion, as private benefactions or speculations.[43] Southampton, for example, has its Common of 100 ha, Newcastle its Town Moor of over 400 ha and Preston its Moor, acquired by its burgesses as a common in 1253 and transformed into a formal park in 1867. In London, the public had long enjoyed access to the royal parks; Hyde Park, for example, was opened to the people by Charles I about 1635. Bath had the first Victoria Park, laid out in 1830 and named after the then heir to the throne when she visited Bath at the age of 11: its origins are clear, for this 'delicious garden' was 'formerly called the Subscription-walk or Bath-Park'.[44]

The urban park movement, however, had its roots in needs more universal and immediate than the accidents of enclosure, of royal beneficence or of aesthetic pleasure. As urban growth mushroomed, so the health of the urban population declined. After 1831 death rates rose alarmingly, from an average of 20.7 per thousand in that year in the major industrial cities of Bristol, Birmingham, Leeds, Liverpool and Manchester to 30.8 in 1841.[45] Such conditions sparked the Health in Towns movement, associated so closely with the work of the indefatigable Sir Edwin Chadwick. Cure was sought by treating symptom rather than cause: typical of the prescriptions was that advocated in the 1833 Report from the Select Committee on Public Walks:

> It cannot be necessary to point out how requisite some Public Walks or Open Spaces in the neighbourhood of large Towns must be; to those who consider the occupations of the Working Classes who dwell there; confined as they are during the weekdays as Mechanics and Manufacturers, and often shut up in heated factories: it must be evident that it is of the first importance to their health on their day of rest to enjoy the fresh air, and to be able (exempt from the dust and dirt of the public thoroughfares) to walk out in decent comfort with their families. . . .

In response, municipal authorities sought to create walks and parks. At first, local Acts of Parliament were necessary, as with the pioneer Birkenhead Park, where powers for the purchase of the necessary land were sought through the Third Improvement Act, sponsored by the town's Improvement Commissioners in 1843. There were no general Acts until the Recreation Grounds Act of 1859; there was a short section on recreation in the Public Health Act of 1875 and Open Spaces Acts in 1887, 1890 and 1906.

Other local powers in the leisure field were equally the product of sporadic and largely unrelated concerns. Concepts of social improvement and the quest for knowledge led to municipal museums, art galleries, libraries and arboreta. Swimming baths stemmed largely from the same concern with public health and cleanliness that underlay the movement for public baths and wash houses.

Nor were these concerns purely a Victorian prerogative. The growing press of townsfolk on the countryside in the 1960s provoked a concern for the damage that such visiting could create: 'the problem is to enable them to enjoy this leisure without harm to those who live and work in the country, and without spoiling what they go to the countryside to seek.'[46] In the Countryside Act of 1968, the prescription was segregation, grant-aided Country Parks to attract the visitor to carefully managed surroundings and so 'reduce the risk of damage to the countryside – aesthetic as well as physical – which often comes about when people simply settle down for an hour or a day where it suits them, somewhere "in the country" – to the inconvenience and indeed expense of the countryman who lives and works there'.[47]

By the early 1970s, other kinds of facility were being added to the local authority repertoire, most notably the major indoor complexes of sports and leisure centres, spurred by the creation of a Sports Council at national level in 1965 'to advise the Government on matters relating to the development of amateur sport and physical recreation services'. The growing range of services had prompted some authorities to think of leisure provision in more corporate terms instead of simply as the prerogative of traditional specialists such as baths or park managers, librarians or museum curators. A spur to such corporate thinking was local government reorganisation in 1974. Powers for recreation were to be exercised concurrently at both county and district level, and many authorities established single-function recreation departments, though the process is far from complete. Indeed, in 1979 less than a third of district authorities operated a single comprehensive leisure services department. In non-metropolitan districts, almost half had these services under a non-leisure department such as 'Technical Services', while 70 per cent of the metropolitan districts retained two or more departments, often separating sport and outdoor recreation on the one hand from libraries and cultural services on the other.[48]

NATIONAL LEISURE INSTITUTIONS

Leisure provision at national level has been equally sporadic and remains even more fragmented in nature. It has again been inherently responsive in character, reflecting the distinctive concerns and aspirations of particular periods and often following in the wake of voluntary action. Countryside conservation and recreation has been one such theme. In Victorian times, only a few perceived the countryside as a threatened resource, and the response came from dedicated individuals rather than government. In 1883, for example, the Lake District Defence Society was created by Canon Rawnsley of Crosthwaite near Keswick and successfully opposed railway penetration into Borrowdale. Rawnsley soon perceived the need for more positive measures, and in 1895, along with Robert Hunter, solicitor to the Commons Preservation Society, and Octavia Hill founded the 'National Trust for Places of Historic Interest and Natural Beauty' with the objective of practical conservation through the acquisition by gift or purchase of land and buildings.[49]

Public action was much longer delayed, and needed time for both attitudes and appropriate powers to evolve. Between the wars, the threat to the best of rural landscapes increased with industrial expansion and formless urban sprawl. Physical planning was in its infancy, however, and only around London was positive action taken, with the idea of establishing a bounding green girdle of open spaces. The London County Council acted under its own powers in 1935 to preserve land, and in 1938 the Green Belt (London and Home Counties) Act was passed by Parliament.

Elsewhere, attitudes were crystallising on conservation issues. The Council for the Preservation of Rural England was formed in 1926 by the amalgamation of many local societies, to become the 'conscience of a nation confronted with the increasing disfigurement of its countryside'.[50] Debate moved more firmly into the public sector with the establishment in 1929 of a Committee of Inquiry to 'consider and report if it is desirable and feasible to establish one or more National Parks in Great Britain with a view to the preservation of natural characteristics including fauna and flora, and to the improvement of recreational facilities for the people . . .'. The Addison Committee reported in 1931, and recommended a number of positive measures to establish a system of national reserves and nature sanctuaries, with national funding and administration by national authorities. The task of such an authority would not be easy, not least in the spending of public funds.

> They will be attacked by those who think that any expenditure on the preservation of the natural beauties of the countryside is unjustifiable; assailed by enthusiasts who wish to press their own fancies or look for action on more heroic lines; importuned by private individuals who see in the proposals an opportunity for private gain; and opposed by others who resent any interference with private interests.[51]

In the event, recession, the clouds of war and the years of conflict gave the nation other priorities and no immediate action was taken, but their advocacy of the use of public resources for this end was an important precedent, and their recognition of the dangers in such a course remarkably prophetic.

In the postwar years public resources were committed, albeit on a relatively modest scale, and countryside conservation and recreation was far from the only leisure field to benefit. Detailed consideration belongs to subsequent chapters, but the main thrusts need brief recount. After the rigours and threats of war, the conservation of the best of British landscapes had high priority. With physical planning firmly enshrined in the 1947 Town and Country Planning Act – though largely concerned in the initial stages with the problems of urban areas – mechanisms were sought through the planning process in the 1949 National Parks and Access to the Countryside Act. The Act's title suggests a dual purpose, and the National Parks Commission that it established had the twin functions of 'the preservation and enhancement of natural beauty' and the provision 'of opportunities for open air recreation and the study of nature by those resorting to National Parks'. Between 1950 and 1955, ten national parks were designated, occupying between them 9 per cent of England and Wales. Nature conservation as such gained further impetus with the formation of the Nature Conservancy in 1949, with its remit to establish a network of national nature reserves.

The governmental view of leisure was perhaps an elitist one at this period, and was further typified by the establishment of the Arts Council in 1946. New pressures for mass recreation, however, disturbed traditional attitudes and made new claims for resources. As early as 1952, the National Parks Commission could note that

> we are living in an age of transition when, for the first time, a preponderantly urban population largely unfamiliar with rural life has acquired a considerable amount of leisure with the opportunity of using that leisure to satisfy the instinctive and wholesome desire to leave the city for the country. We cannot prevent this influx of town into country, nor on a long view of the healthy development of our nation, should we desire to prevent it.[52]

This reluctant recognition gained momentum in the following decade, fuelled by the initial 'Countryside in 1970' conferences in 1963 and 1965 under the presidency of the Duke of Edinburgh. In 1966 the White Paper, *Leisure in the countryside*, foreshadowed the replacement of the National Parks Commission by the Countryside Commission in 1968, with a wider remit covering the whole of the countryside and powers to grant-aid a range of developments, including country parks and picnic sites.

As rural recreation became a fashionable cause, other public bodies developed recreational facilities on their resources. The Forestry Commission had early been involved with forest parks, from 1935 in Scotland and from 1937 south of the border. These parks had little physical provision for recreation beyond camp sites, but from the 1960s the Commission

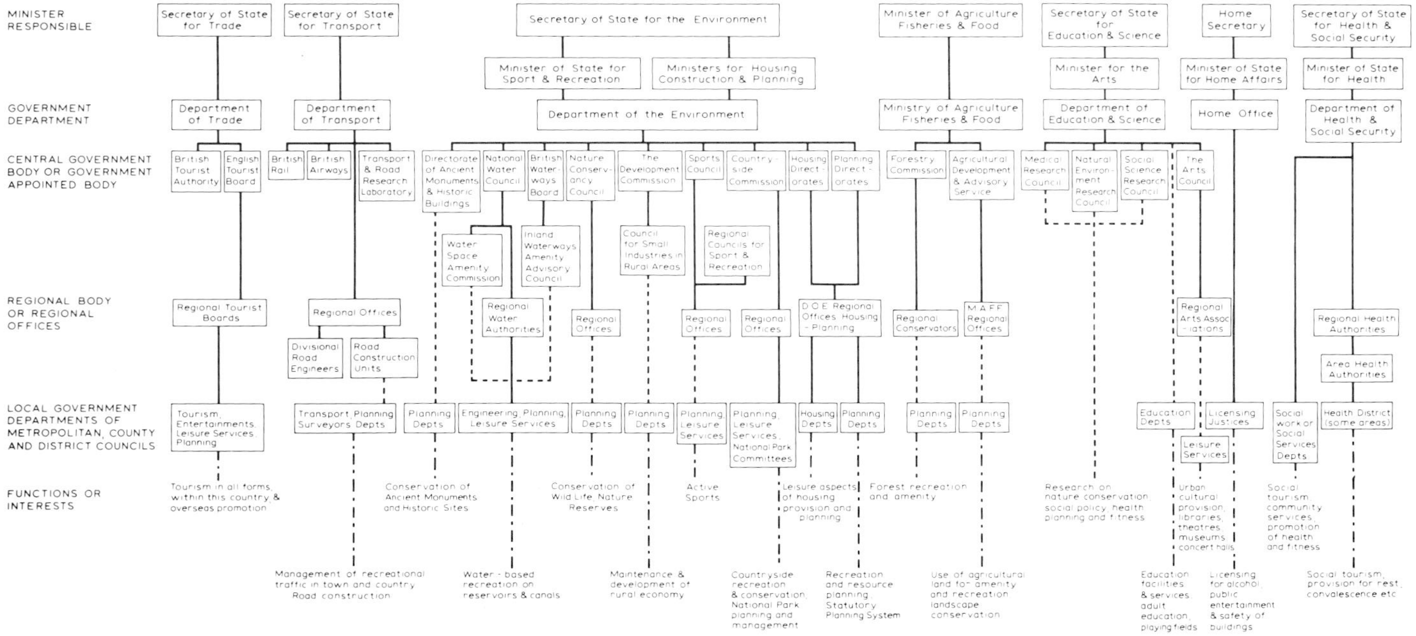

FIGURE 1.8 The structure of public sector leisure services in England, *c.* 1980. As both leisure services and planning are concurrent functions at country and district level in both metropolitan and non-metropolitan areas, no attempt has been made to distinguish between the two tiers of local government in the diagram, or to represent the variety of structures found in differing local authorities. The necessarily simplified diagram also omits many horizontal links, of both a formal and an informal nature.

Source: adapted from a diagram by A. J. Veal in A. S. Travis, *The state and leisure provision* (Sports Council and Social Science Research Council, 1979), figure 1 developed picnic places, forest walks, visitor centres and forest cabins in profusion. Attitudes to water resources also changed. Water authorities had been urged to allow access to reservoirs for recreation in a departmental circular in 1966,[53] foreshadowing the creation of the Water Space Amenity Commission in the Water Act of 1973. The recreational role of canals was emphasised in the White Paper, *British Waterways: recreation and amenity* (Cmnd 3401, 1967) and the British Waterways Board was empowered to maintain a network of cruising waterways and to foster recreation on its waters in the Transport Act of 1968.

Not all the emphases were on rural resources. In 1965 the advisory Sports Council was established and its co-ordinating role in sports development strengthened in 1966 by the formation of Regional Sports Councils. In 1972 the Council became an executive body, with its own royal charter, budget and grant-aiding powers. In a different field, the 1969 Development of Tourism Act created the British Tourist Authority and the English, Scottish and Wales Tourist Boards.

The kaleidoscopic web of institutions and powers at national level that emerged in the late 1960s and early 1970s was a highly fragmented response to evident need. In their review of this situation in 1973, the House of Lords Select Committee on Sport and Recreation urged the need for the government 'to adopt a positive attitude to recreation planning and to promote action within government departments along common and co-ordinated lines'.[54] That need was accepted in the White Paper, *Sport and recreation* (Cmnd 6200), in 1975, but action was modest. In 1974 Denis Howell had become Minister of Sport and Recreation (a decade after his first appointment as Minister of Sport with a narrower remit), but co-ordination was limited to exhortation and regular meetings with the relevant agencies. At regional level, Regional Councils for Sport and Recreation were established in 1976 and enjoined to prepare strategies for recreation in each region; but with no funds at their direct disposal, their role could be only advisory and their impact limited. Since the mid-1970s, economic recession has militated against major initiatives in the public sector of recreation provision.

This historic legacy has resulted in a highly complex pattern of organisation and funding in the public sector. Figure 1.8 attempts to summarise the pattern at the end of the 1970s as it relates to the structure of government. It emphasises the variety of bodies involved at national level, but severely simplifies the links established through local government and omits completely the links, formal and informal, between the bodies themselves.

COMMERCIAL AND VOLUNTARY PROVISION

The development of recreation services in the public sector, the complex legacy of historic thrusts in attitude, concern, fashion and opportunity, has been dealt with at some length, but it gives a very unbalanced picture if the role of commercial and voluntary provision is ignored. In a mixed economy, the margin between public and commercial sector provision not only is blurred, but has tended to shift over time. Some public provision yields little or no financial return, but elsewhere it may cover most or all of its costs (figure 1.9). Such distinctions often owe more to accident and tradition than to logic, and the same might be said of those activities where provision is made in both public and commercial sectors (figure 1.10).

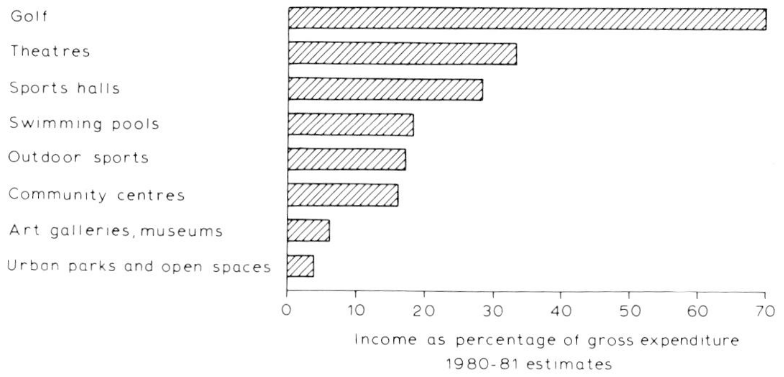

FIGURE 1.9 Local authority leisure facilities: income from fees and charges in relation to gross expenditure (capital and current), 1980-81 estimates.
Source: data from *Leisure and recreation statistics, 1980-1 estimates* (Chartered Institute of Public Finance and Accounting, 1981)

Commercial provision of both services and goods absorbs a high proportion of individual leisure spending, and covers a wide range of leisure activities (figure 1.11).[55] With its underlying profit motive, the commercial sector tends to eschew activities where returns are doubtful and in consequence is wary of innovation. That must not gainsay the role of innovative individuals who have seized particular opportunities and done much to pattern leisure activities in consequence. In their respective generations, Thomas Cook with railway excursions and Freddie Laker with low-cost air travel left a lasting legacy on travel habits, though neither was the originator of cheap travel in their respective spheres of transport.

The commercial sector can be more immediately responsive to demand than the public sector, and conversely is more likely to react speedily to a lessening of demand, or a decrease in profitability. The fluctuations of fashion are thus even more of a determinant in commercial sector leisure

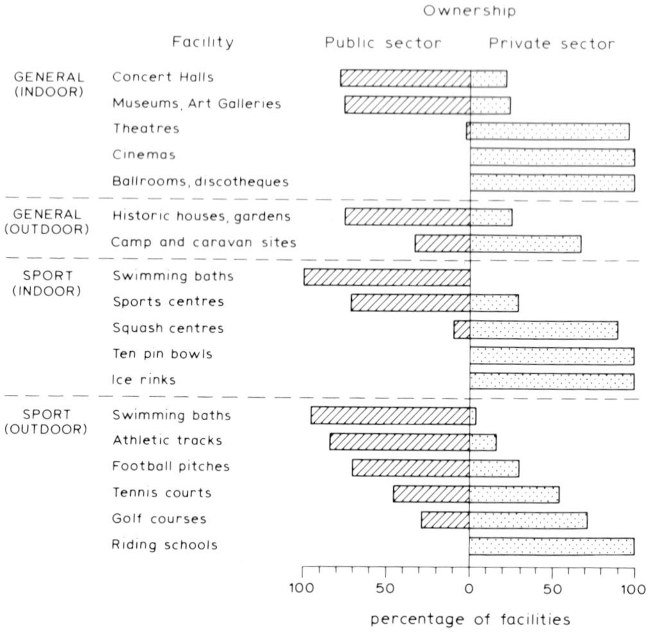

FIGURE 1.10 Public and private ownership of leisure facilities in Greater London, 1976.
Source: data from J. Roberts, *The commercial sector in leisure* (Sports Council and Social Science Research Council, 1979), table 8

provision. The startling rise in bingo is a case in point.[56] In the postwar years the rise of television induced a rapid decline in cinema audiences, and average weekly attendances plummeted from some 27 million in 1951 to less than 9 million by 1961.[57] The passage of the Betting and Gaming Act gave the necessary legal basis for commercial bingo clubs, and redundant cinemas provided the necessary premises. The first commercial bingo hall was opened in 1961 at Maida Vale: in 1974, the peak year, there were 1820 in Great Britain. Since then the number of clubs has declined slightly, but in 1979 there were still 1697. In the late 1970s between five and six million people played bingo with some regularity; over 80 per cent are women, and over 90 per cent more than 30 years old.

A more transient fashion was skateboarding. The origins of the sport go back to the late 1940s in the United States, but its popularity did not increase with any rapidity until the development of urethane cast-moulded wheels in 1968.[58] Skateboards appeared in Britain on a significant scale in 1976; two million were sold in 1977, but by the middle of the following year the pastime had ceased to be of widespread interest despite commercial attempts to promote it further and dispose of surplus stocks.

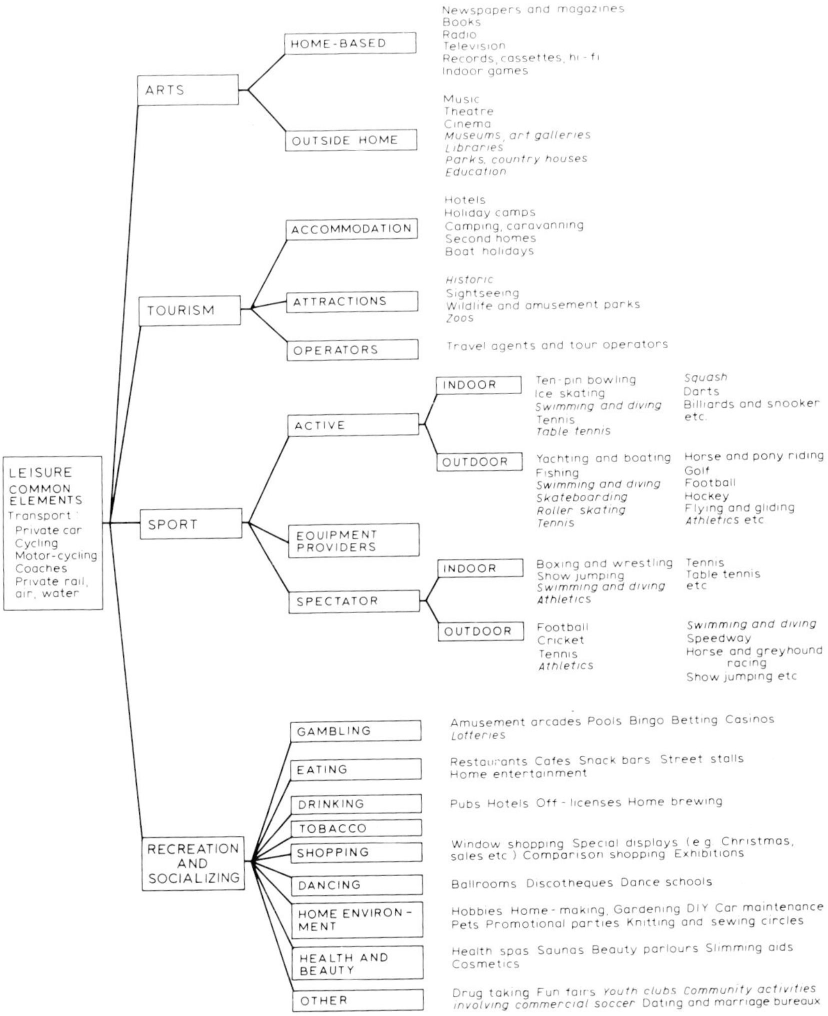

FIGURE 1.11 Roberts' taxonomy of leisure facilities provided wholly or in part by the commercial sector. Items shown in *italics* are marginal to the commercial sector.
Source: after J. Roberts, *The commercial sector in leisure* (Sports Council and Social Science Research Council, 1979), figure 1

In addition to the public and commercial sectors, the private and the voluntary sectors are also significant in leisure provision. The private sector, linked to private and institutional bodies who provide leisure facilities as an adjunct to their operations, has much in common with elements of both commercial and voluntary sectors. The voluntary sector may depend less on money and more on enthusiasm, but its importance in providing stimulus and resources for leisure pursuits must be emphasised, though its mechanisms and links with other sectors are imperfectly understood.[59]

By its very nature, precise statistics of its scale are difficult to obtain. Table 1.2 shows the membership of some 233 national voluntary leisure

TABLE 1.2 Membership of national voluntary leisure groups, 1979

Leisure category	*No. of groups*	*No. of members*
Youth groups	9	2,721,000
Sport	75	2,586,000
Conservation/heritage	56	1,124,000
Touring	5	701,000
Women's groups	2	593,000
Animals	12	562,000
Gardening	17	384,000
Walking	5	73,000
Dancing	2	64,000
Other	50	154,000

Source: data from Chairmen's Policy Group, *Leisure policy for the future* (Sport's Council, 1981), table 5.4

groups, but the list is far from exhaustive and excludes, for example, the numerous local amenity and local history societies. Memberships range to over one million (the National Trust), and at least 100 of these groups have memberships of 5000 or more. Sports organisations are the most numerous and the best documented: figure 1.12 shows the number of members in the ten largest sports bodies in 1980. At local level, clubs and societies are legion. In the 1960s the Government Social Survey, *Planning for leisure*, recorded that 55 per cent of males and 33 per cent of females were members of clubs. In a city like Birmingham there are estimated to be some 8000 active, formally organised voluntary associations, three-quarters of which are in the spheres of culture, sport or social welfare.[60] Hutson identified 59 in two small areas of Swansea alone.[61]

Voluntary clubs reflect not only social identity and patterns of social organisation, but also the changing pattern of leisure activities. Many organisations have had a surprisingly long life (figure 1.13). Of 73 national organisations that have over 5000 members and whose date of origin is known, more than half have been in existence over 50 years while four antedate 1850.[62] Peaks of interest coincide with the halcyon Edwardian years, with the years between the wars once recovery was secure and before the ravaging effects of depression took hold, and with the years of high individual aspiration and participation in the late 1960s. As with leisure institutions in the public and commercial sectors, voluntary organisations cannot be considered in isolation, but must be linked to wider social and economic patterns and attitudes.

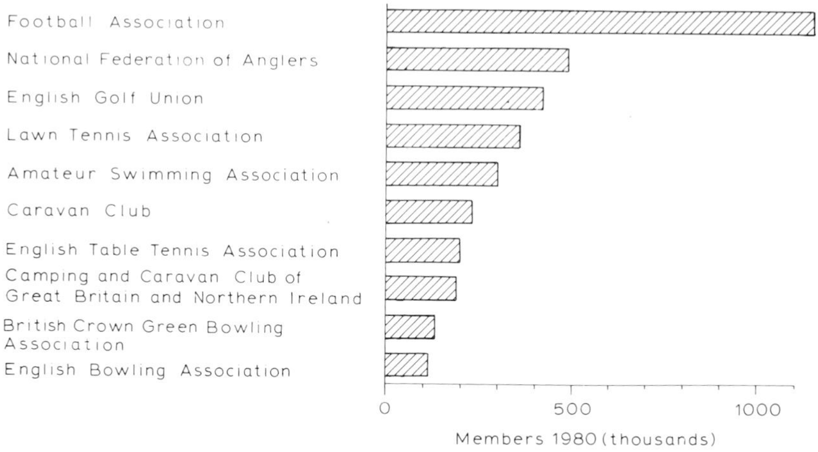

FIGURE 1.12 The ten largest sports bodies, 1980. Membership figures for the FA, the LTA, the ASA and the ETTA are estimates only.
Source: data from B. S. Duffield, J. P. Best and M. F. Collins (eds.), *Digest of sports statistics* (Sports Council, 1983), table 2

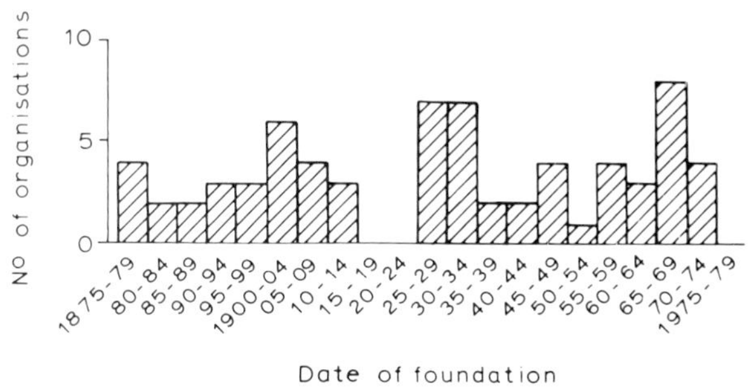

FIGURE 1.13 The data of foundation of leisure groups with over 5000 members in 1980. Five groups were founded prior to 1875, the oldest being the Royal Horticultural Society in 1804. Local societies are excluded.
Source: data from *Aspects of leisure and holiday tourism* (English Tourist Board, 1981), table 4

2 Leisure Patterns and Places

LAND FOR LEISURE

> Three great waves have broken across the face of Britain since 1800. First, the sudden growth of dark industrial towns. Second, the thrusting movement along far-flung railways. Third, the sprawl of car-based suburbs. Now we see, under the guise of a modest word, the surge of a fourth wave which could be more powerful than all the others. The modest word is *leisure*.[1]

Michael Dower's graphic portrayal in *The fourth wave*, his seminal study of 1965, highlights the impact of leisure as a spatial phenomenon. In breaking, that wave released creative and destructive forces whose reverberations are still felt, but its surge has marked the landscape less dramatically than was first envisaged. In the perspective of time, indeed, there has been not one wave but many, each adding distinctive marks to the landscape, each reflecting the kaleidoscope of attitudes and opportunities, resources and institutions outlined in chapter 1.

In its direct claims on space, leisure is remarkably modest. Just how modest is difficult to assess, for two reasons. In the first place, leisure as a unique land use is not a category separately recognised in most inventories.[2] In rural areas, with an agricultural provenance and focus, it is largely subsumed in a miscellaneous 'other' category, while in urban areas it is usually aggregated with all open space, whether it is in direct leisure use or not. Second, comparatively little of the land used for leisure, especially in rural areas, is devoted exclusively to that purpose. The needs of leisure are highly concentrated in time, and much leisure use is compatible with other uses, most notably those of agriculture and forestry. In such multiple-use situations, leisure is usually the minor component, and it is the primary use that is registered for data-gathering purposes.

Any general statistics must therefore be hedged about with qualifications and viewed with great caution. One estimate has suggested that some 1·2 million hectares of England and Wales are 'rural land available for public recreation' – about 8 per cent of the total area.[3] Even the limited categories used for this estimate, however, permit varied interpretation and give an overall range between 0.55 and 1.65 million hectares. In urban areas, which in 1971 covered 11 per cent of England and Wales, open space is, after housing, the second most extensive use of land in individual settlements, ranging from 11 to 19 per cent in different settlement types. Primary sports areas, in both urban and rural settings, cover perhaps 1 per cent of Britain as a whole.[4]

While such figures indicate the general scale of recreation's direct impact on the land, they cannot indicate the intensity of that impact or its variations through time. Leisure is unusual among the uses of land in that, outside the immediate confines of house and garden, all leisure use involves a journey for the user, often of substantial length. A review of the changing impact of leisure on the land may therefore conveniently have two distinct facets: the links between transport patterns and leisure patterns, and the resulting changes in the location as well as the scale of land in leisure use. The one is linear, the other nodal in impact, a distinction to which we shall have occasion frequently to return.

LITTLE AND LOCAL

Prior to 1750, when the population of England and Wales was largely rural in habit and habitat, most recreations were confined to the immediate area of the villages and towns themselves. Even in the largest cities the countryside was within easy walking distance – and the less appreciated for its ubiquity. There is evidence that the simple pleasures of strolling in the countryside were enjoyed. As John Stow wrote in 1598 in his *Survey of London*,

> On May Day in the morning, every man, except impediment, could walk into the sweet meadows and green woods, there to rejoice their spirits with the beauty and savour of sweet flowers, and with the harmony of birds, praising God in their kind.

May Day was a special case – when not all pleasures were so bucolic – but the land around the village, especially the commons of pre-enclosure days, had a very real recreational role. Nor were the village bounds the limit: village 'wakes' and feasts brought friends and relations from other nearby settlements, and fairs also were 'a sort of carnival to all the neighbouring villages'.[5]

None the less, conditions of travel inhibited substantial movement for recreation for all except the few with money and time for self-indulgence: as Henry Fielding observed in 1751, 'in Diversion, as in many other Particulars, the upper Part of Life is distinguished from the Lower.'[6] The leisured classes indeed sought diversion further afield. London was their first resort, and as roads and road transport improved in the seventeenth and eighteenth centuries, so they ranged further afield to the spas and nascent coastal resorts. This was also the period of the Grand Tour; part education, part diversion for the young aristocrat. Horace Walpole recorded that an estimated 40,000 English travellers passed through Calais in the two years after the Peace of Paris in 1763,[7] and even if the exact total must be treated with some reserve, the numbers were undoubtedly substantial.

RAILWAYS AND RESORTS

Mass movement for recreation had perforce to await the emergence of other means of travel. The first real opportunity came with river transport on the Thames. Ramsgate and Margate were early beneficiaries; the number of visitors brought in by boat rose from 17,000 in 1812-13 to 106,000 in 1835-36.[8] The Thames, however, was a unique situation with the navigable river linking a major concentration of people to the coast: the growing towns of the industrial revolution had to await the development of other means of transport before ready recreation movement became commonplace.

With the advent of the railway, this was not long delayed. Leisure travel was not, of course, a prime stimulus for railway development and even by the 'parliamentary' trains, rail travel was initially too expensive to become part of most people's leisure experience. As the network grew, however, railway companies were keen to generate traffic from every possible source, and early provided excursion trains, at cheaper fares than normal, to match – and generate – recreation demand. Indeed, excursion trains were provided less than three weeks after the opening of the pioneer Liverpool & Manchester Railway in September 1830. On 1 October, the 'Duke's train of carriages' used at the opening was run from Liverpool to a specially laid siding at Sankey Viaduct and back, though with a fare of 5*s.* (25p) the occasion must have been fairly exclusive.[9] A more general portent was an excursion in May 1831 for the Bennett Street Sunday School in Manchester to visit Liverpool – during the Manchester Races!

Early excursions paid less regard to safety than to capacity. Many were great caravans of locomotives and coaches – one teetotallers' excursion from Redruth and Camborne to Hayle on the West Cornwall Railway in

1852 had three engines and no less than 76 carriages.[10] But with the low fares made possible by such numbers, many could acquire a taste for travel that had hitherto been wholly beyond their means.

Destinations were varied. The coast, and coastal resorts, soon took pride of place as the Victorians aped their aristocratic betters and joined the rush to the sea. The excursion trains were cheerful if primitive:

> For bustle and breeze
>   And a sniff of salt seas,
> Oh Brighton's the place! not a doubt of it; –
>   But instead of post-chaise
>   Or padded coupés,
> If you had to get there a l'excursionnaise –
> I think you'd be glad to keep out of it![11]

But 'Brighton and back, All the way for a shilling' was a powerful incentive. The resort had recorded as many as 117,000 visitors to the town in 1835 in the heyday of the coaching trade, but in 1850 the railway carried 73,000 in a single week and on Easter Monday 1862, 132,000 in a single day.[12]

While the coastal resorts showed the most dramatic effects, the excursion train and the railway network opened up other destinations as well. The lure of the city, and of London in particular, was early evident. The Great Exhibition of 1851 was perhaps the first truly national occasion of its kind, as excursion fares from the West Riding dropped as low as 5*s.* (25p).[13] The railway companies used their running powers over other lines to full effect for excursion traffic. On August Bank Holiday 1878 the tiny North Staffordshire Railway took 1000 people to Liverpool, 700 from Leek to Derby and Nottingham, and 900 from the Churnet Valley to Manchester, though a train to the same destination from the Potteries was 'only a train of 10 coaches carrying 400 people'. Other places served by the company's excursions that day were London (two trains), Birkenhead, Birmingham, Matlock and Buxton.[14]

As the network became more nearly ubiquitous, so the townsman gained access to the countryside as well as to other towns. Such intrusions were not always welcomed by the residents. At Ambleside, wrote James Payne,

> our inns are filled to bursting, our private houses broken into by parties desperate for lodgings . . . A great steam monster ploughs up our lake and disgorges multitudes upon the pier; the excursion trains bring thousands of curious, vulgar people . . . our hills are darkened by swarms of tourists; our lawns are picnicked upon twenty at a time, and our trees branded with initial letters. . . .[15]

Intrusion or not, leisure traffic came to be a mainstay of several rural lines, and some, like the Leek & Manifold Valley Light Railway of 1904, were built primarily to promote it.[16]

Despite its ubiquity, the railway was not the only leisure transport out of the Victorian City. Tramways gave access to the urban fringe: it was no accident that Britain's first street tramway, opened in Birkenhead in 1860, should run from the ferry terminal opposite Liverpool to the gates of Birkenhead Park.[17] Of greater importance in the later years of the century was the bicycle. Its heyday came in the 1880s. The Cyclists Touring Club was founded in 1878, and reached a peak membership of 60,449 in 1899, though its subsequent decline was not so much an indication of waning popularity as a recognition that a craze had become an institution. The role of the bicycle in renewing urban acquaintance with the countryside must not be underestimated, though like mountaineering, golf and tennis, cycling at this period was a relatively elite, middle-class recreation.[18]

MASS MOBILITY

During the twentieth century, the internal combustion engine has completely transformed personal mobility. The impact of the motor car was far from instantaneous, however (figure 2.1). Prior to 1914 motoring was the prerogative of a rich minority, with only 132,000 cars on the road at the outbreak of the First World War. Even between the wars numbers grew comparatively slowly, with just over 2 million registered in 1939. Indeed, it is important to remember that it was the advent of the bus as much as the car that revolutionised transport opportunities at this period. By 1926 there were already 40,000 buses on the roads: the peak was reached in 1964 with 82,100. Few bus routes were operated purely for recreational purposes, but the extensive rural network, particularly in the years immediately before and after the Second World War, did much to open up the countryside for recreational use with a density and flexibility of service that the railway, with its far more restricted network, could not hope to match.

Since the mid-1950s, the growing ubiquity of the car for personal transport has been the underlying theme of the majority of recreational patterns (figure 2.2). Access to a car is still, of course, far from universal, but the proportion of households owning one (or more) rose from 31 per cent in 1961 to 58 per cent in 1980, the change being particularly marked in the 1960s, with a rise from 31 to 51 per cent between 1961 and 1969 (figure 2.3). From the recreational point of view, these changes have had a tremendous impact. Unlike public transport, with fixed routes and fixed schedules, the car offers flexibility of both destination and time. At local

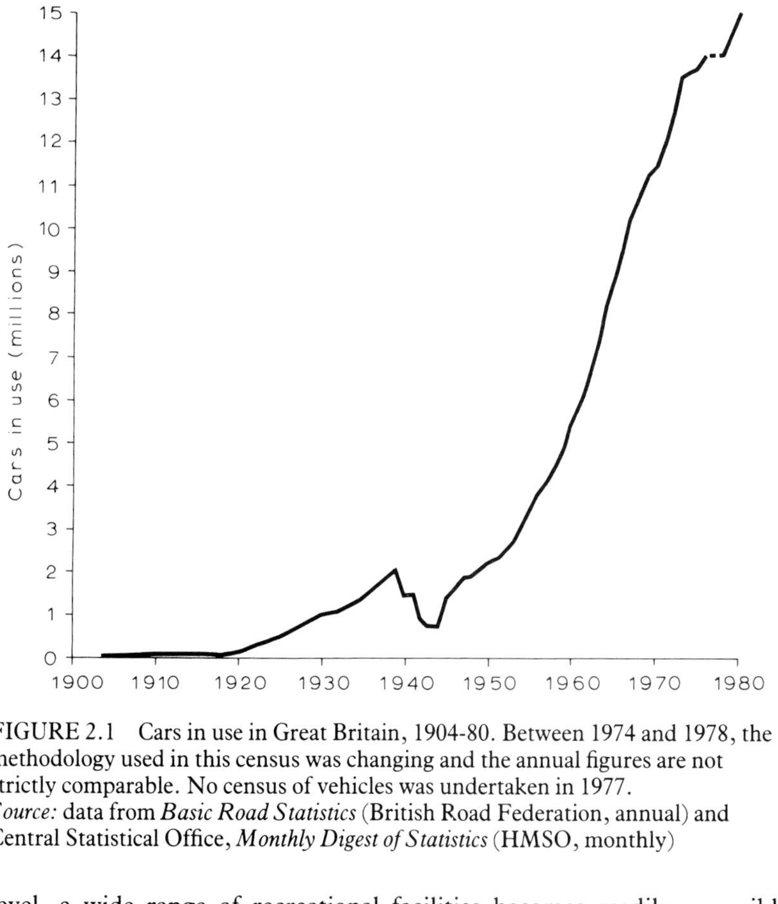

FIGURE 2.1 Cars in use in Great Britain, 1904-80. Between 1974 and 1978, the methodology used in this census was changing and the annual figures are not strictly comparable. No census of vehicles was undertaken in 1977.
Source: data from *Basic Road Statistics* (British Road Federation, annual) and Central Statistical Office, *Monthly Digest of Statistics* (HMSO, monthly)

level, a wide range of recreational facilities becomes readily accessible within an urban context. There had already been some foreshadowing of this in the 1930s with the advent of the roadhouses on the arterial roads of the period,[19] but it has been of vital importance to the success of the new generation of facilities, such as indoor sports centres, which are often ill-served by public transport but are accessible within minutes by car at distances of up to five miles.

Perhaps the greatest impact of the car in spatial terms has been on recreation in the countryside. Destinations are no longer constrained by the narrow corridors of rail and bus routes, but can extend to the most remote rural areas, conditioned only by the extent of the actual road network. In practice, recreational pressure is very far from uniformly spread, and the breaking of Dower's Fourth Wave has left much of the countryside unscathed. A greater problem remains the growing disparity of opportunity between car owners and those who have no access to a car.

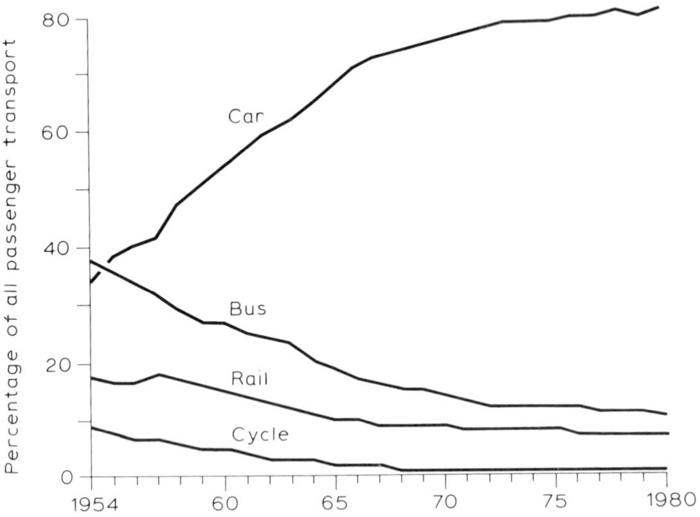

FIGURE 2.2 Passenger transport in Great Britain by mode, 1954-80, as a proportion of the total distance travelled. 'Car' includes all forms of private vehicles except cycles. Over the period, overall distance travelled increased by 246 per cent.
Source: data from Department of Transport, *Transport statistics Great Britain, 1970-80* (HMSO, 1981), table 1.1

For more than two decades, the emphasis has been on changing patterns of recreation as car-borne opportunities were seized by growing numbers. By the beginning of the 1980s, the indications are that a plateau of activity has been reached in this regard (figure 2.4). The extension of car owner-

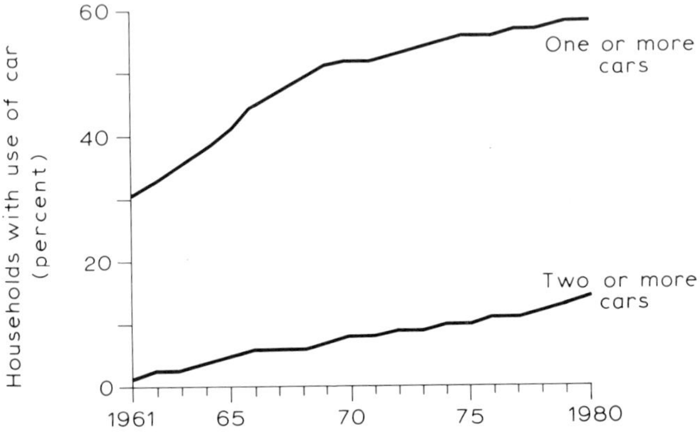

FIGURE 2.3 Households in Great Britain with regular use of a car, 1961-80.
Source: data from Department of Transport, *Transport statistics Great Britain, 1970-80* (HMSO, 1981), table 2.28

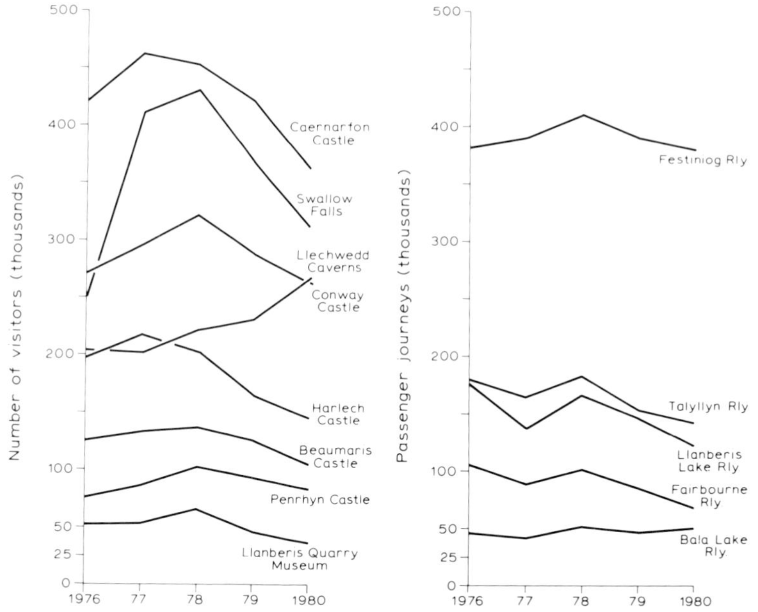

FIGURE 2.4 Visitors to tourist attractions and narrow gauge railways in Gwynedd, 1976-80.
Source: data from Wales Tourist Board

ship by household is now proceeding extremely slowly, and patterns of car use have been affected by periodic fuel shortages and the wider economic impact of recession. The car, however, is still relatively cheap to acquire and run: compared with costs in general, running costs of cars have remained remarkably steady, while public transport fares have climbed sharply (table 2.1).

TABLE 2.1 The relative cost to the consumer of passenger transport, 1961–80

	Price index: 1975=100				
	1961	*1966*	*1971*	*1975*	*1980*
Retail price index	38	45	59	100	196
Rail fares	31	40	57	100	225
Bus fares	30	40	61	100	237
Car purchase (new and second-hand)	56	48	61	100	209
Car running cost	35	41	53	100	193

Source: Social Trends 12, 1982, table 9.1

The car is not the only form of transport to have revolutionised recreation patterns. The advent of cheap air transport and the package tour has been a major influence on holiday habits. The first fare-paying scheduled trip between London and Paris took place in August 1919, but high costs (at first six times more expensive than by rail) and low comfort militated against significant growth. The major changes came in the postwar period, not least with the coming of jet aircraft. Foreign currency restrictions taxed the ingenuity of tour operators, and the resulting package holidays paradoxically brought overseas holidays within the financial range of far greater numbers. In 1980 UK residents made 17.5 million trips abroad, with 61 per cent of these by air: the comparable figures for 1966 were 6.9 million trips, 51 per cent by air.[20] Of the 1980 trips, 75 per cent were purely holidays and a further 6 per cent combined a holiday with visits to friends and relatives.[21] Moreover, foreign holidays are not only a summer prerogative: the rise of winter package holidays seeking snow and sun has been startling. In 1963-64 only 6900 such holidays were sold, but by 1971-72 this had risen to 600,000.[22] In the first three months of 1981 there were 844,000 trips abroad on inclusive holidays – 31 per cent of all overseas travel in the period.[23]

Successive transport innovations have left earlier networks abandoned or under-utilised for their prime (commercial) purpose. These linear resources may have a potential for recreational use, as seen by the growth of cruising as opposed to commercial traffic on inland waterways: in 1980, 25,728 pleasure craft were licensed or registered by British Waterways Board, compared with 10,566 licensed in 1967, a figure that had remained little changed through the 1960s.[24] In other cases the recreational potential is less readily realised. There were 32,300 km of railway route open to traffic in Great Britain in 1923, and 29,400 km still in 1960. By 1980 that had dropped dramatically to 17,600 km. In England and Wales, it is estimated that 60 per cent of the closed length remains derelict and unused, 4 per cent is used for private railways and some 9 per cent has been made available for walking, cycling and horse-riding. Recreational conversion involves many problems, not only of cost but also of form and location.[25]

PARKS AND PLAYGROUNDS

Changing patterns of recreational transport have profoundly influenced not only forms of recreation but also their location. Indeed, while the home remains the prime focus of leisure time, many leisure pursuits have involved lengthening journeys for their satisfaction. The impact of transport changes on the use of land for leisure must now be traced.

Prior to the nineteenth century, little public land had recreational use. The major playgrounds, in a spatial context, were the private prerogative of the monarch and the great landowners. The Norman kings created great tracts of 'forest' land – land reserved for the king's hunting and subject to forest rather than common law. The term was essentially a legal one, for much forest in this context was neither wooded nor waste. Such land reached its maximum extent about the middle of the twelfth century, when estimates suggest it may have covered as much as one-third of England.[26]

Reserved more specifically for pleasure were the immediate grounds of the great houses. From the early sixteenth century onwards, as internal and local conflicts lessened, fortified dwellings were replaced by great country houses surrounded by parks, at first enclosed for game but increasingly landscaped for visual pleasure. In the eighteenth and early nineteenth centuries, landscape gardeners like William Kent (1685-1748), Lancelot ('Capability') Brown (1715-83) and Humphry Repton (1752-1818) brought order and formality on a grand scale. The major parks covered large areas – Blenheim some 1100 ha and Knowsley over 1000 ha, for example. Social change in the present century saw the end of such creation: Castle Drogo in Devon (1911-30) is usually accounted the last to be built. However, private legacy has now become in large measure public attraction as properties are opened to the public.

Little land was devoted primarily to public recreation in pre-urban England. The public house was the prime everyday meeting place for social gatherings away from work, and where they existed village greens had a recreational role. In pre-enclosure days, access to the surrounding countryside for informal recreation was easy enough, though the recreational role of commons and wastelands was relatively minor.

The rapid growth of towns, and the rapid urbanisation of the people, in the early nineteenth century ended that. Even in rural England, enclosure removed recreational opportunities. In 1824 Robert Slaney wrote that in rural areas, 'owing to the inclosure of open lands and commons, the poor have no place in which they may amuse themselves in summer evenings, when the labour of the day is over, or when a holiday occurs.'[27] More formal recreations suffered too: after enclosure at Hornsea in 1809, for example, 'the sport of foot-ball, which was much practiced up to that time, has necessarily been disused . . . '[28] This was mass football, 'the play being from village to village, two or three miles apart'.

For the towns the problem was even more acute. As towns grew, the enclosure of commons removed much-needed open space, and by the middle of the nineteenth century any kind of open space for recreation was very much at a premium. Concern over lack of space was accentuated by a wider concern for the health of the urban population. From 1840, therefore there was a growing provision of public parks within the towns themselves: parks that were seen not only as places of recreation but quite literally as the lungs of the city, providing ventilation for the overcrowded streets.[29]

Victorian parks were not always placed in the best location to serve the majority of the local populace, however. The extent of the existing built-up area suggested peripheral sites. Many were also private benefactions, and while such gifts were often genuine philanthropic gestures, others were concerned to create a buffer between working- and middle-class areas of towns. Individual or corporate desire for a fitting memorial frequently made schemes grandiose beyond real need. A Middlesex magistrate of the 1850s

> regretted that these large parks should be formed at the public expense, in preference to squares of four or five acre pieces, in particular districts. . . . The parks are too far off from the poor districts for them to avail themselves of them to the extent which they might otherwise do.[30]

In the details of their layout, the parks of the period were a clear reflection of their origins and followed the tenets of the landscape gardeners of the country estates with an ordered rural air of trees and turf. The prime activity was 'promenading', continuing the tradition of earlier public walks. Variation came later in the century, when flower beds and bedding plants swept into fashion. Activities widened, too, as formal sports developed, and cricket and football pitches and bowling greens came to be incorporated in the layout.

While the Victorian park was the classic response to the need to bring something of the countryside back to the burgeoning towns, park development was not, of course, confined to that period. Later development owed less to individual philanthropy and more to direct municipal provision. In Birmingham, for example, the corporation bought only 8 per cent of the land now used for parks between 1856 and 1890, but 85 per cent between 1890 and 1910.[31] After 1918 there was a shift in emphasis from parks to recreation grounds, often smaller in area and providing a wider range of sports facilities. The movement was accelerated by the creation of the National Playing Fields Association in 1925 and by the 1937 Physical Training and Recreation Act, which gave legislative support for local authorities to acquire and establish playing fields. A parallel development, and of immense importance in terms of land use, was the growing provision of playing fields alongside schools, a development formalised by the provisions of the 1944 Education Act which imposed on local authorities the duty to secure adequate facilities for recreation and physical training for all educational establishments under their control. In areal terms, local education authorities became the key providers: in the mid-1960s, Lancashire had 3220 ha of sports grounds in the county, but an additional 3098 ha of school playing fields.[32]

WATERING PLACES

Transport improvements extended the range of recreation, and created a new type of settlement – the 'parasite towns' of Demangeon's apt phrase.[33] The spas and coastal resorts have been well chronicled,[34] but their continuing importance in contemporary recreation merits more than passing mention. Both have their roots in medical practice and the desire for diversion.

Apart from London, the spas were the first true resorts. Their origins date from the late sixteenth century, when the medical profession began to place trust in the therapeutic value of mineral waters and to publicise the virtue of the cure in their writings. There was no shortage of suitable springs: in the early eighteenth century Short noted 228 'spaws', 'besides several others of less note'.[35] Far more than medical approval was needed, however, for spas to flourish. Until the Restoration they remained primarily medical in purpose, with little accommodation and few formal facilities for taking the waters: as such they survived the Puritan régime relatively unscathed. After 1660, however, they changed rapidly in character: they came to fill a particular need for the wealthy and leisured upper classes seeking new diversions away from London. As Defoe observed in 1724, 'the coming to the Wells to drink the Waters was a mere Matter of Custom, some drink, more do not, and few drink physically. But Company and Diversion is, in short, the Main business of the Place.'[36]

The rise of individual spas was a matter of fashion or of conscious promotion, but in a more general context reflects changes in transport facilities. While roads were primitive and coach traffic was in its infancy, the emphasis was on proximity to London, typified by the importance of Epsom and Tunbridge Wells in the seventeenth century. As road traffic developed it became easier to range further afield, with the rise in turn of Bath, Cheltenham and Leamington. The clientele, however, remained small in number and socially exclusive. Beau Nash could welcome each visitor to Bath in person, and at this, by far the largest spa in the eighteenth century, the annual total of visitors did not exceed 12,000. Their landscapes were elegant and distinctive, as befitted places of high fashion. Apart from baths and hotels, there were other places of formal assembly – assembly rooms and promenades, where not only could exercise be taken but social intercourse could easily ensue.

The earliest seaside resorts had identical roots, but with the curative

1 Scarborough South Bay in 1735. This engraving shows the spa on the left, and sea bathing without benefit of costumes, but with an early bathing machine (courtesy David Gray).

value of seawater extolled in place of that of the spa springs. Indeed, Scarborough, the first coastal resort of consequence, owed its importance not to the sea but to the mineral springs whose waters happened to rise at the foot of the cliffs (illustration 1). By 1700 Scarborough was a spa of wide reputation, but the proximity of other waters was not long neglected. In the early 1730s a visitor wrote 'It is the Custom for not only the gentlemen, but the ladies also, to bath in the Sea: the gentlemen go out a little way to Sea in Boats . . . and jump in naked directly. . . . The ladies have the Conveniency of Gowns and Guides.'[37] The use of seawater was greatly encouraged by the publication in 1752 of Richard Russell's *A dissertation on the use of sea water in the diseases of the glands*, which set the seal on the seawater cure in general and on the reputation of Brighton in particular, for Russell went to live there in 1754.

Seawater drinking had an understandably brief vogue. The belief in sea-bathing as an aid to health remained, but the seaside resorts, like the spas before them, rose rapidly through social rather than simply medical esteem. The sea itself in all its moods became an object of admiration as the inspiration of nature became more valued in the nineteenth century. The real change came, however, with the advent of the railway. With growing means, urban denizens could ape their social superiors: from the 1840s, excursion trains brought them in their crowds, 'some with a month's range, others tethered to a six hours limit, but all rushing with one impulse to the water's edge'.[38]

Funnelled by the railway, the movement to the seaside was urban in origin and urban in expression. Seaside resorts developed a distinctive landscape, with a linear emphasis on beach and bounding promenade, backed by a line of boarding houses, whose narrow frontage and several stories made the most of the seafront location. The beach was adaptable to a wide range of activities, its use emphasising the family nature of the Victorian seaside holiday. The bathing machine, as a concession to modesty in the earliest days, survived until the revolution of morals and manners in the first two decades of the present century. The piers were perhaps the greatest symbol of resort maturity; they survive in surprising numbers (54 in 1973[39]), though their spindly elegance has succumbed alarmingly to storm, fire and economic vicissitudes.

Habits as well as landscapes were distinctive, and no more so than in the ready acceptance of crowding on the beaches. Richard Jefferies distilled the Victorian experience of the seaside when he wrote in 1885 (in *The Open Air*) of

> a squealing, squalling, screaming, shouting, singing, bawling, howling, whistling, tin-trumpeting, and every luxury of noise. It is a sort of triangular plot of beach crammed with everything that ordinarily annoys the ears and offends the sight.
>
> Yet you hear nothing and see nothing; it is perfectly comfortable, perfectly jolly and exhilarating, a preferable spot to any other. The way in which people lie about on the beach, their legs this way and their arms that, their hats over their eyes, their utter give-themselves-up expression of attitude, is enough in itself to make a reasonable being contented. Nobody cares for anybody; they drowned Mrs Grundy long ago.

Little has changed in the succeeding century (illustrations 2 and 3). Styles of dress – and undress – may differ, bingo and gambling machines may oust other promenade entertainment, but the resorts and their beaches remain deep-rooted in British recreation habits. They are the major single destination for day trips and still attract over 70 per cent of British holidaymakers on their main holiday.[40] Their ability to attract, and absorb, large numbers does much to lessen pressures on more sensitive environments.

If promenade and beach change little in landscape and less in spirit, the same cannot be said for the whole of their hinterland. Since 1945, holidaymakers have increasingly sought more informal, self-catering accommodation (figure 2.5). This overall trend is clearly reflected at the coast. All but the biggest resorts show concentric circles of accommodation sweeping out from the sea front. At the core, 'some sea front hotels gave up trying and changed to rented apartments, to be followed by several smaller hotels and guesthouses, with a change to that most awful of

2 Scarborough South Bay in the 1890s (courtesy Peter W. Dove).

3 Scarborough South Bay in 1979. The viewpoint is virtually identical to that of illustration 2.

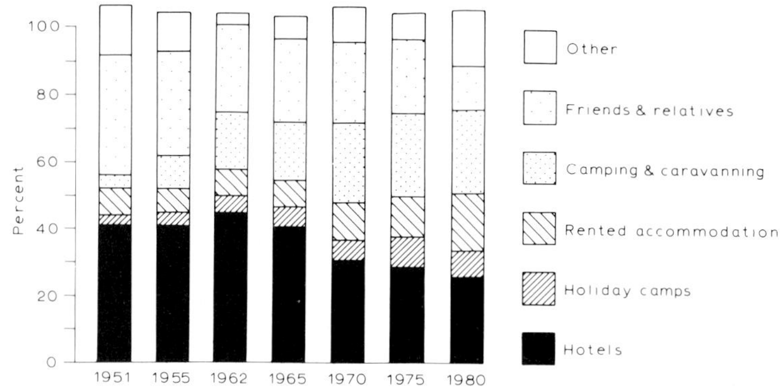

FIGURE 2.5 Type of accommodation used on main holidays in Great Britain, 1951-80. Totals exceed 100 per cent as some holidaymakers use more than one type of accommodation. In 1951, caravanning was excluded and youth hostels included in the total shown as camping and caravanning.
Source: data from British Tourist Authority, *British National Travel Survey*

tourist terminology, "flatlets".'[41] At the rim came new types – caravan parks, camping sites and holiday camps, many of the last almost self-contained resorts.

These trends reflect changes in mobility as well as in social habit. The Victorian family's attachment was to two towns, the one where they lived and the one where they went each year. The confining link was the railway. For individual resorts, the railway provided more than transport: it delineated the hinterland. For many smaller resorts the links were local and obvious, like Withernsea and Hornsea to neighbouring Hull.[42] For others they were more complex, rooted in the nuances of railway company history. Morecambe's affinity with the West Riding, and with Bradford in particular, came with the building of the Midland line to that west coast resort.[43] At the other extremity of its network, the Midland's part-ownership of the Somerset & Dorset Joint Railway across the Mendips from Bath towards Bournemouth, and the running of through services like the Pines Express, led to a surprisingly high proportion of Midlands visitors at that south coast resort.[44]

RURAL RENDEZVOUS

Even in the railways' Edwardian heyday, resort visitors were not confined to the resorts themselves, but explored the immediate surroundings in growing numbers. The advent of the charabanc accelerated this, a trend actively fostered by some railway companies: the North Eastern Railway was running ten bus trips a day from Scarborough in the summer of 1914, ranging as far afield as Whitby, Bridlington and Rievaulx Abbey.[45] As the private car supplanted public transport, the importance of the region surrounding the resort increased and pressure was dispersed away from the resort itself.

In a wider context, the advent of the car brought a growing impact of recreation on the countryside in general. That impact is highly dispersed, but still concentrates very largely on known 'beauty spots' and 'attractions'. The initial reaction to the impact was twofold. A wider concern to preserve the crucial quality of the rural scene found its outlet through special designations under statutory planning procedures. The 1949 National Parks and Access to the Countryside Act produced both national parks and Areas of Outstanding Natural Beauty, between them to cover 18.6 per cent of England and Wales. Very little of this land, of course, is devoted directly to recreation, and even in the national parks only 1.3 per cent of their total area is owned by the park authorities. The 1947 Town and Country Planning Act included powers for local authorities to define and propose for the Minister's approval Areas of Great Landscape, Historic or Scientific Value, though in practice the degree of additional protection afforded such areas was flimsy. By the mid-1960s, when the fashion for designation had run its course, designated areas of one kind or another covered some 40 per cent of England and Wales. To some extent, such blanket designation almost defeated its own ends by covering too great an area to have real effect, though it remained a salutary reminder of the quality of the rural landscape heritage. Figure 2.6 is based

4 Mass trespass on Bamford Moor in the Peak District, 28 March 1982, to protest against restrictions on public access to the countryside, 50 years after the mass trespass on Kinder Scout in April 1932 (courtesy *The Guardian*).

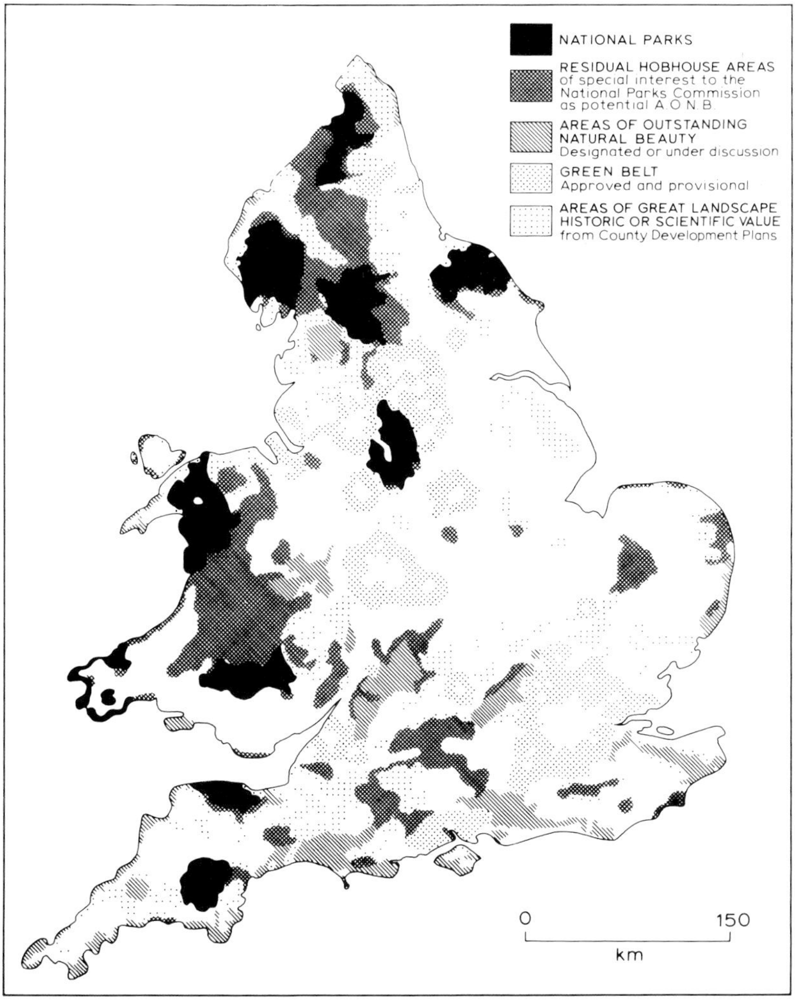

FIGURE 2.6 Protected land, 1965.
Source: based on a map in *Power and the countryside* (Central Electricity Generating Board, 1965)

on a map produced by the Central Electricity Generating Board in 1965 to illustrate the difficulties that designation could cause in siting transmission lines if the Board were 'to reconcile efficiency with the preservation of amenity'.

The second thrust, embodied in the title of the 1949 Act, sought to improve actual access into the countryside. Many upland areas, especially the grouse moors of the north, were sealed off from casual recreation use:

in the Peak District, for example, some 550 km^2 of moorland had only 12 footpaths exceeding 3.7 km (two miles) in length, and none of the principal heights were accessible except by trespass.[46] Ramblers had adopted the tactics of mass trespass in the 1930s to secure access, and the 1949 Act gave powers to local authorities to negotiate access agreements, and also required them to prepare definitive maps of public rights of way on bridle paths and footpaths. Countryside access gained a further fillip under the Act with the creation of Long Distance Footpaths, hopefully to develop a national network of walking routes through the most striking upland and coastal scenery, though their completion was to be long delayed.

Both thrusts – conservation through designation and the securing of access to open land and footpaths – were rooted in an elitist view of rural landscapes, satisfying primarily the country lover with high aesthetic ideals and the desire to savour the countryside through physical endeavour at first hand. The growing waves of car-borne visitors in the 1950s and 1960s imposed problems and pressures scarcely dreamed of in 1949. Recreation could no longer simply be absorbed into the rural scene, requiring only security of access: rather, the need was perceived to accommodate the new generation of countryside visitors in publicly owned, purpose-designed reception areas, largely reserved for recreation use. From this need came the new generation of country parks and picnic sites, created by local authorities under the grant-aid provision of the 1968

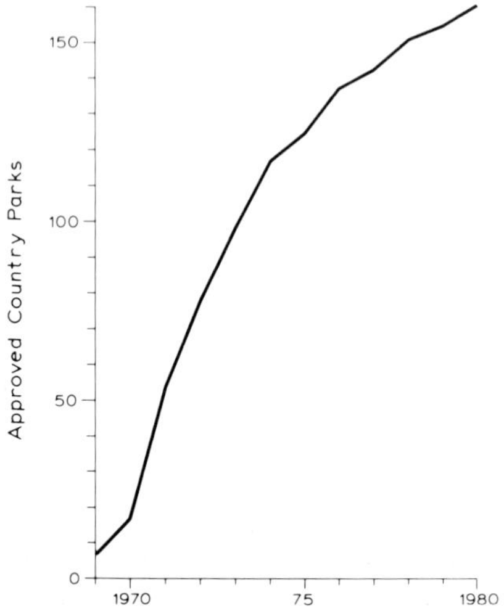

FIGURE 2.7 Country parks in England and Wales approved by the Countryside Commission, 1969-80.
Source: data from annual *Reports* of the Countryside Commission (HMSO)

Countryside Act. Their growth was amazingly rapid (figure 2.7), though they were but one example of a wide range of recreational attractions developed in this period throughout the whole of the countryside – not only to control and contain, but also to tap the commercial potential of the growing numbers, and more varied tastes, of countryside visitors.

Some of these new attractions were simply additions to an existing stock (figure 2.8). For example, the growing numbers of stately homes opening

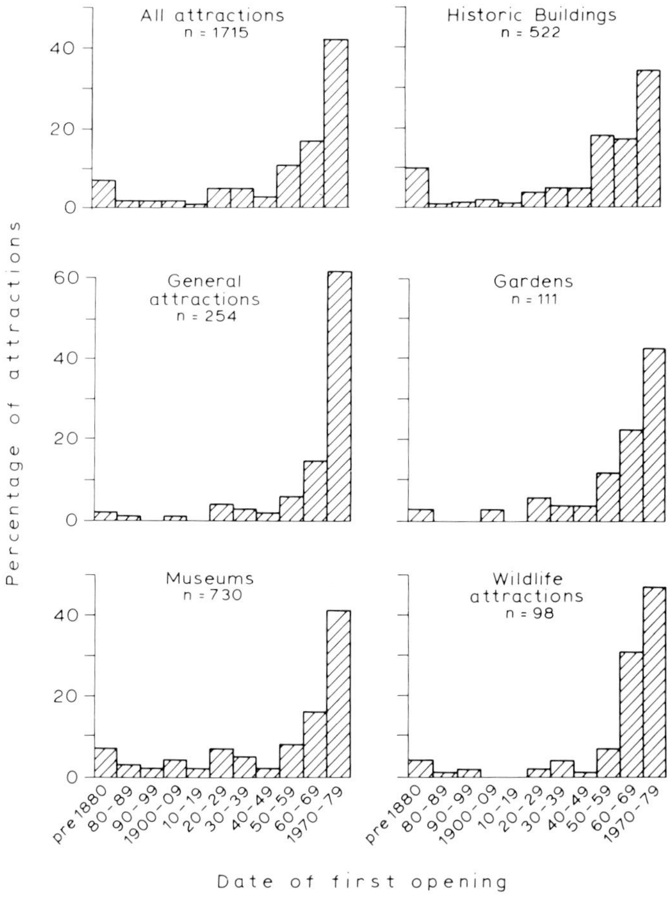

FIGURE 2.8 Date of first opening to the public of visitor attractions in England in 1980. Historic buildings include cathedrals and churches; general attractions include such facilities as country parks, model villages, steam railways, leisure parks, vineyards, caves, workplaces, brass rubbing centres and heritage centres; museums include art galleries; and wildlife attractions include zoos, safari parks, farms and nature reserves.
Source: data from *Sightseeing in 1980* (English Tourist Board, 1981), table 5

their gates to visitors intensified a long-established trend. Others, however, were largely new in type, reflecting new fashions in diversion or the availability of new resources, and where the rural setting was almost incidental to the entertainment offered. Safari parks, using the spacious

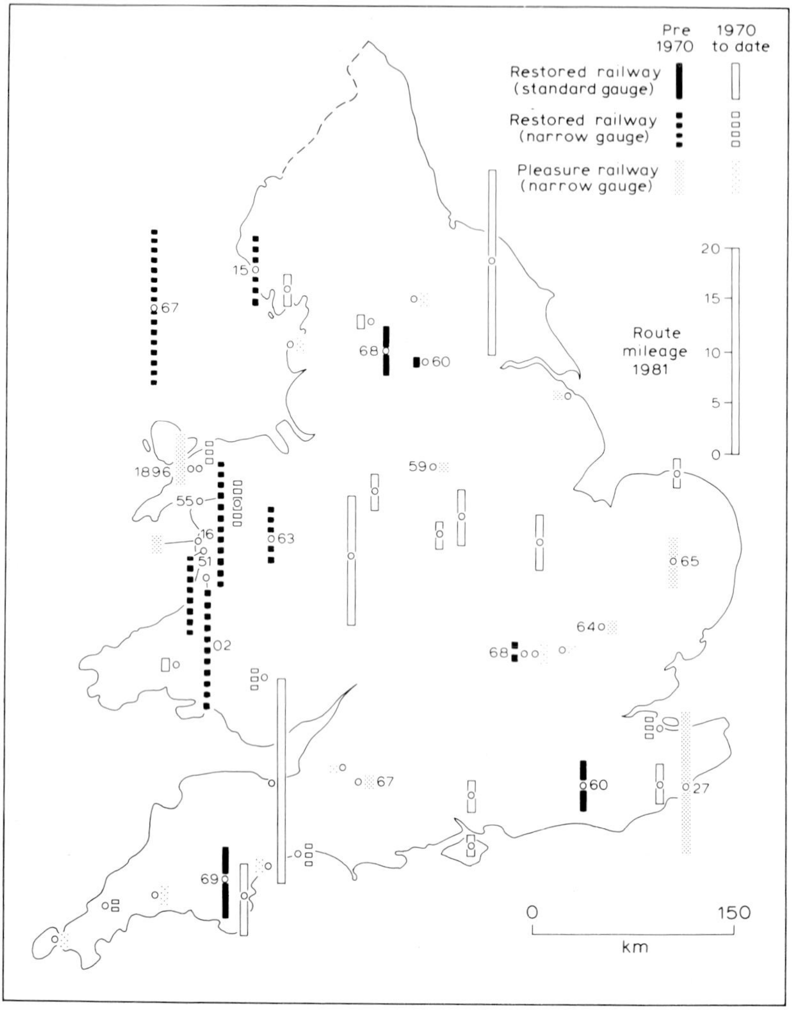

FIGURE 2.9 Restored and pleasure railways, 1981. Only railways more than one mile in length, and open for public travel on 30 or more days per year, are shown. 'Restored' railways utilise the trackbed of a previous general service railway; 'pleasure' railways are built on a new formation.
Source: data from *Railways Restored,* Association of Railway Preservation Societies' Official 1981 Year Book (Ian Allan, 1981); and R. Crombleholme and T. Kirtland, *Steam '81* (George Allen & Unwin, 1981).

grounds of country houses, were one such fashion. Steam railways capitalised on a love of nostalgia, and the volunteer labour of enthusiasts, to reopen closed lines as tourist attractions (figure 2.9). A scenic setting in a recognised tourist area helped receipts, but was far from essential. The earliest examples, apart from a handful of purpose-built pleasure railways, were the narrow-gauge lines of upland Wales, the doyen being the Talyllyn Railway, run by enthusiasts since 1951. Railway closures, accelerated after the Beeching Report of 1963,[47] and the final withdrawal of steam traction in 1968, gave both stimulus and opportunity for the extension of the idea to standard-gauge lines. Four schemes antedate 1970,[48] and a veritable rash ensued in the following decade.

The widely scattered rural recreation sites of the last two decades reflect, then, not only the massive rise in volume of car-borne countryside visits, but, in their variety, the desire of many countryside visitors for more than the simple visual delights of the countryside scene, for entertainment and diversion as much as aesthetic pleasure. A parallel trend, imposing more varied demands on the countryside and again fostered by enhanced personal mobility, has been the startling growth of many active sports with a countryside setting. Figure 2.10 gives one indication of this: of the ten sports growing most rapidly in membership between 1970 and 1980, six are open-air countryside or water-based activities. Other rural and water-based pursuits have also seen substantial growth – most notably hang gliding, orienteering, caving and climbing, canoeing, sub-aqua and sailing. Most have very specific site needs and add further to the widespread, if sporadic, pressures on rural areas for recreation.

In spatial terms, the growth in leisure activity, and in active rather than passive pursuits, has had its greatest impact outside the towns, but is far from being purely a rural-based phenomenon. The 1970s were marked by an upsurge in the provision of indoor sports facilities, particularly local authority sports centres and sports halls. Between 1973 and 1977, the provision of indoor dry sports areas trebled and provision for swimming increased by 70 per cent. In 1973-74 alone, the remarkable number of 137 sports centres and 190 swimming pools were opened.[49] This upsurge in provision was matched by an upsurge in participation: data from the General Household Survey suggest that participation in indoor sports almost doubled between 1973 and 1977 and continued to increase until the end of the decade. Most of these new facilities were urban in location, their use frequent and their users local. They occupied little land, but with their often suburban location depended much on car use for their effective functioning.

Leisure patterns have rarely been static for long. Wealth, time and technology have an enabling role, while changing fashion and the

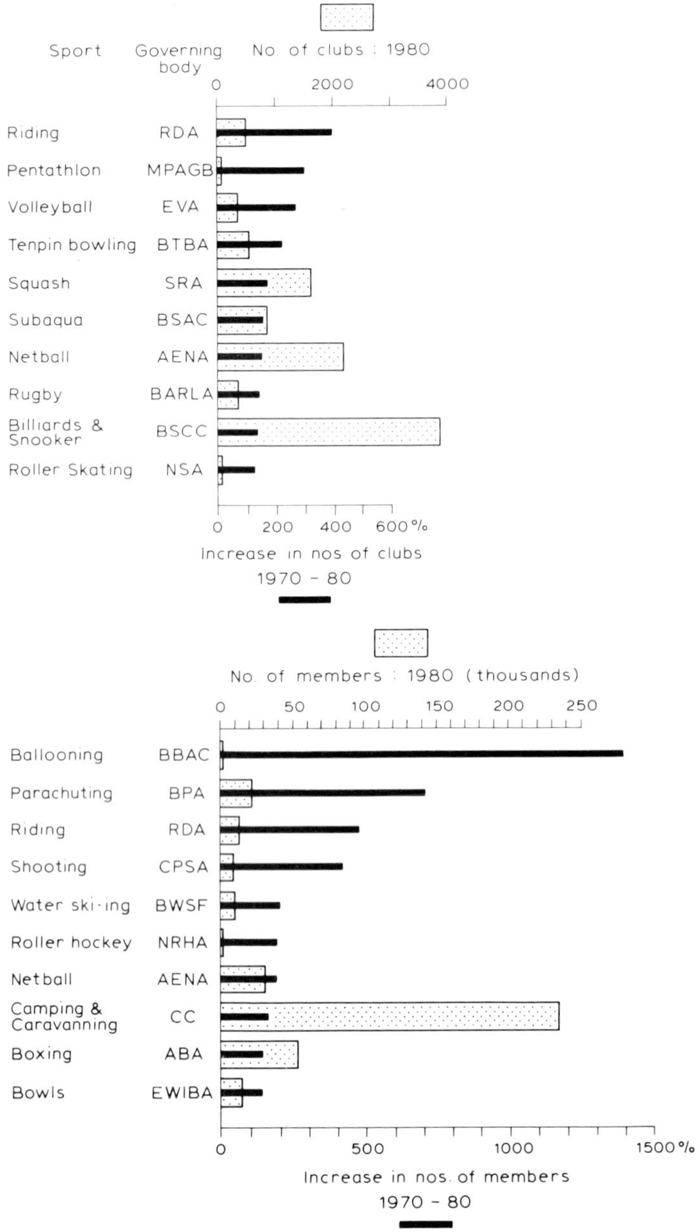

FIGURE 2.10 The ten fastest-growing sports bodies, by number of affiliated clubs and by number of members, 1970-80. The governing body indicated is not necessarily the only one for the particular activity. In 1980, the BBAC had 1190 members and the NRHA, 644.

Source: data from B. S. Duffield, J. P. Best and M. F. Collins (eds.), *Digest of Sports Statistics* (Sports Council, 1983), table 4. The abbreviations used for governing bodies are as follows:

ABA	Amateur Boxing Association
AENA	All-England Netball Association
*BARLA	British Amateur Rugby League Association
BBAC	British Balloon and Airship Club
*BPA	British Parachute Association
BSAC	British Sub-Aqua Club
BSCC	Billiards and Snooker Control Council
BTBA	British Tenpin Bowling Association
BWSF	British Water Ski Federation
*CC	Caravan Club
*CPSA	Clay Pigeon Shooting Association
EVA	English Volleyball Association
*EWIBA	English Women's Indoor Bowling Association
MPAGB	Modern Pentathlon Association of Great Britain
NRHA	National Roller Hockey Association of Great Britain
NSA	National Skating Association of Great Britain
*RDA	Riding for the Disabled Association
*SRA	Squash Rackets Association

* Other governing bodies exist for the sport.

unceasing quest for novelty lend a restless edge to the activities of each generation. Few activities are wholly superseded, and the very range of leisure pursuits makes their study both fascinating and frustrating. Remaining chapters are concerned with the spatial context of contemporary leisure patterns, but it must never be forgotten how much they have been moulded by the legacy of time as well as the opportunity of place.

3 The Use of Leisure

THE ANALYSIS OF DEMAND

> Precisely separating leisure from the rest of life, from work and other activities where individuals have little choice, becomes difficult when we move from abstract concepts to real cases. Hence the impossibility of giving *exact* answers to the question of how much leisure people have, and by how much it has grown. These difficulties, however, pale into insignificance when we try to look inside leisure and distinguish among its many uses.[1]

Roberts neatly encapsulates a basic problem in leisure studies. Leisure is far more easily recognised than objectively analysed, not least when the actual use of leisure by individuals is concerned. The difficulties are only in part conceptual: equally important are the nature and limitations of available data.

At the heart of any discussion of the use of leisure is the concept of recreation demand. Demand in this context has several meanings.[2] The most common, and the most important in the interpretation of data, is that of *expressed demand*: the current level or structure of demand as expressed by present patterns of participation. The alternative term, *effective demand*, is sometimes used, but both refer to the actual situation as measured by a survey of people's existing use of leisure.

This chapter of necessity concentrates on expressed demand, for here the problems of data, formidable though they may be, are at their least. Other concepts, however, may be of at least equal importance to recreation providers. Expressed demand directly reflects the constraints on patterns of recreation imposed by the existing scale and location of recreation resources. New resources, or better accessibility, may lead to marked changes in patterns. These changes are a measure of *latent demand*: that element of demand frustrated by an existing lack of opportunity. By its very nature, latent demand cannot be readily measured, for it refers to a projected rather than an actual situation.

'Before and after' surveys of demand patterns related to the opening of a specific facility may give important insights, but any assessment in anticipation is of necessity speculative. Some surveys have included questions on people's recreation aspirations, but answers are misleading on two counts. First, answers can be valid only if respondents have a full knowledge of all likely recreation opportunities. Second, and even more significant, aspiration may remain precisely that, and may never be translated into participation, even with the removal of all constraints.

Despite these inherent practical problems, the concept of latent demand remains important to the recreation provider. The provider's ultimate concern is with *potential demand*, the demand that should occur at a given time in the future, and compounded of existing expressed demand, of changes in expressed demand arising from structural changes in the population and its demographic characteristics, and of latent demand released by changes in the range and nature of facilities. At the heart of any assessment of potential demand is the problem of prediction, and we shall briefly return to this problem when the present pattern of expressed demand has been considered.

Knowledge of leisure patterns is severely inhibited by a continuing lack of adequate data. The nature and limitations of that data will be discussed in greater detail in subsequent sections, but the overall problem needs early emphasis. Prior to the 1960s sources were scattered and fragmentary, and lacked any coherent basis. The studies undertaken for the American Outdoor Recreation Resources Review Commission and published in 1962[3] gave the impetus for work in Britain. Two wide-ranging national surveys were carried out in the latter part of that decade: the *Pilot National Recreation Survey* (fieldwork 1965, and published by the British Travel Association and the University of Keele as Report Number 1 in 1967 and Report Number 2, *Regional analysis*, in 1969), and the Government Social Survey's *Planning for leisure* (fieldwork in 1965-66, and published by HMSO in 1969). These surveys remain unique at national level. They were, however, followed by a number of valuable studies at regional level, with growing degrees of sophistication but an unhappy lack of comparability. First in the field was the Northern Region (fieldwork 1967, report 1969), followed by the North West (fieldwork 1969, reports 1972 and 1977), Greater London (fieldwork 1972, official reports 1975-76) and the South East (fieldwork 1972-73, reports 1977).[4]

Useful though these surveys were, their 'one-off' nature and the often considerable delay between fieldwork and the publication of results, as well as their overall lack of comparability, greatly restricted their value beyond the immediate planning purposes for which they were devised. No general surveys of recreation demand have been undertaken since 1972, but a major advance was the inclusion of leisure questions in the

General Household Survey (GHS) in 1973, 1977 and 1980. As part of a wider survey, the number of questions on leisure that could be included was severely limited (four only in 1977),[5] but this major disadvantage in scope was balanced by the size of the overall sample (23,000 over the age of 15)[6] and by the ability to discern trends through time. The last-named will become of growing importance, though initial comparisons were made more difficult by changes in 1977 in the way the leisure questions were presented. The overall aim was to improve the accuracy of the survey, but a simple comparison between 1973 and 1977 suggests increases in participation levels that owe more to this technical point than to changes in leisure habits.

Of necessity, this chapter draws heavily on the results of the 1977 GHS leisure questions, for the detailed 1980 results were not available at the time of writing. This one source alone, however, leaves far too much scope for misinterpretation and far too many questions unanswered. It must be used not only in the light of the results of the earlier general surveys but with the additional perspectives provided by several more specific surveys. The latter are characterised by restrictions either of activity covered or of the area from which the sample is drawn: they range from the Countryside Commission's National Surveys of Countryside Recreation (fieldwork in 1977 and 1980, but no full results yet published) to the numerous surveys of the users of individual recreation sites.

PROBLEMS OF DEMAND MEASUREMENT

The problems of describing recreation demand stem not only from the relative paucity of survey data but from the very nature of leisure activities themselves. The practical difficulties of measuring demand must therefore be explored further before patterns of demand can be discussed.

Even when limited to activities that currently take place – to expressed demand – participation in recreation is no simple concept. To take a simple instance, the question 'Do you play tennis?' is meaningless in itself. It must be related first of all to a specific period of time – 'Have you played tennis in the last four weeks?', for example. The period chosen is obviously critical: the longer the period for recall, the more likely is the activity to have taken place and the higher the apparent rate of participation. A shorter period may be more realistic for many activities, but problems then arise over inherently seasonal activities. If a question on tennis participation related to the previous four weeks was posed in January, it would give a totally different answer to one posed in July.

The simple distinction between participation and non-participation is rarely sufficient in itself, and some measure of the frequency of participation is needed. This is usually achieved by supplementary questions probing beyond the straightforward fact of participation. The General Household Survey, for example, asks first for a simple record of 'What . . . things have you done in your leisure time . . . in the 4 weeks ending last Sunday . . . ?' and assists individuals' recall with a second similar question but based on activities listed on a prompt card. It then probes further for frequency by asking for each activity 'On about how many days did you . . . [activity] in the 4 weeks ending last Sunday?' Such questions enable a crude measure of 'participation/days' to be established, though this still begs the question of the overall duration of the activity. A person may play tennis on eight days in a month and visit the countryside on only one day in the same month, but though the frequency of participation obviously differs, the overall time spent on the activity – say, some eight hours – may be approximately the same.

These distinctions are not mere semantics, but are necessary for accurate description. Most survey data rarely yield the whole truth and may further suffer from a particular emphasis in interpretation. A simple example must suffice. The Sports Council and the Countryside Commission both have an obvious interest in persuading the public (and their funding agency) of the importance of the recreational activities for which they are responsible. Both have published 'popular' accounts for a general audience of surveys undertaken in 1977, the General Household Survey and the National Survey of Countryside Recreation respectively.[7] Both surveys were concerned with participation in the four weeks prior to interview, and both had results for interviews in the summer period. Even at the straightforward level of the proportion of the population participating, there are major discrepancies (figure 3.1). In commenting on the GHS graph, the Sports Council simply notes: 'In the summer quarter almost 40 per cent of the adult population take part in an outdoor sport or physical activity; 20 per cent take part in indoor sport. . . . Almost 30 per cent go on open air outings (to parks, countryside and seaside) . . . ' The Countryside Commission has a different view from its own survey: 'next to gardening, the countryside is the most attractive form of outdoor recreation, with over half the population visiting it at least once . . . countryside recreation proves to be much more attractive than outdoor sport.'

The problem is very much one of definition, a problem to which we shall return later in the chapter. Here it is sufficient to note that the GHS definition of an 'open-air outing' includes only passive countryside activities and excludes several important activities that are an inherent part of the NSCR definition of 'countryside recreation', most notably all countryside sports and visits to stately homes. The biggest anomaly comes from the inclusion of all walks over two miles as an outdoor sport in the

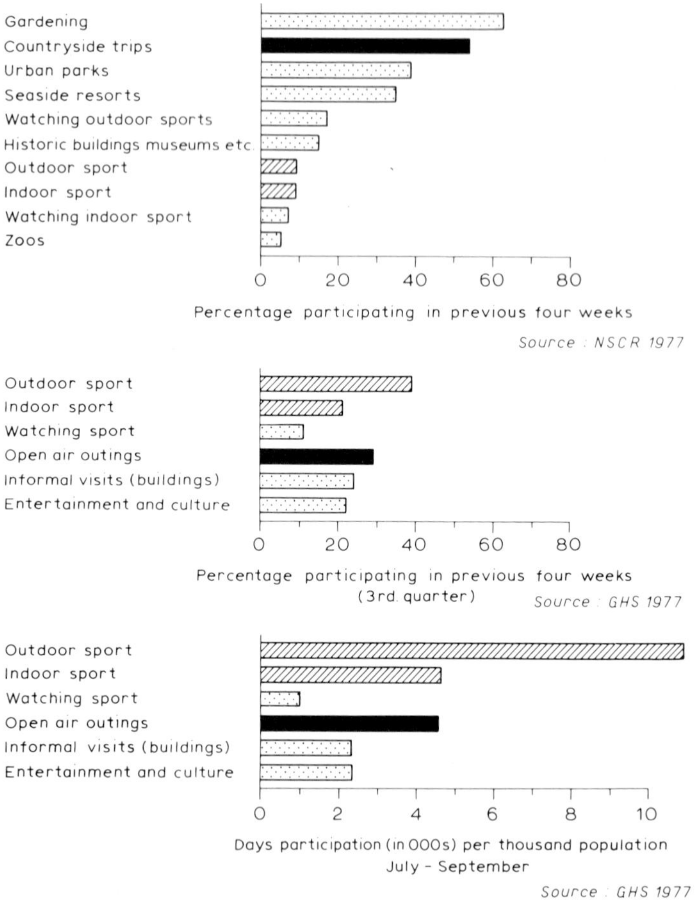

FIGURE 3.1 Contrasting views of participation in sport and countryside recreation, 1977.
Source: data from the National Survey of Countryside Recreation, as published in *Leisure and the countryside* (Countryside Commission, CCP 124, 1979), and from General Household Survey as published in *People and sport* (Sports Council, 1979)

GHS: in contrast, 'long walks, hikes or rambles' account for 20 per cent of 'countryside activities' in the NSCR results and are subsumed in countryside trips.

Frequency measures obviously favour sport. The NSCR report includes no direct measure of frequency of participation on countryside trips: it provides instead a graph of annual participation and notes comfortingly that 'taken over the year as a whole the countryside beats even gardening, with over three-quarters of the population – 37 million people – having a day out at least once.' The graph is headed, a little misleadingly, 'relative popularity over the year', and the scale, which is simply marked 'percentage', shows a healthy 75 per cent for countryside trips and only 9 per cent for both indoor and outdoor sports. The Sports Council, using the GHS data, provides a tally of 'activity days' for each quarter of the year (shown for the summer quarter on figure 3.1). By this measure, outdoor sport alone has well over double the number of days' participation for open-air outings, and the report can note that 'almost four times as many days are spent in playing sport as in informal outings.' The same measure can be used to provide an aggregate total of 'days participation spent by the whole adult population on various types of activity in England and Wales in the course of a year' – a satisfying total of 1900 million for active sport compared with 350 million for open-air outings. If, however, the actual time spent were known rather than simply the number of days when some participation took place, the difference between the totals would be much less.

The problems of interpreting even the simplest measures of expressed demand pale into insignificance if measures of satisfaction rather than participation are sought. Yet at least a subjective assessment of relative satisfaction may be necessary when alternative strategies for the investment of resources in recreation facilities are considered, not least in the public sector, where the disciplines and directions of commercial returns may be inappropriate. To extend the example of the previous paragraphs, a choice may be necessary between the provision of an indoor sports centre and a country park in the urban fringe. Expressed demand, measured where such facilities already exist, can clearly show a 'need' for both and may give an indication of the latent demand that will be released when the new facility is built, and thus can provide forecasts of probable use. It cannot, however, give any indication of the enhanced levels of personal satisfaction each would provide: techniques in this field remain virtually unexplored.

TECHNIQUES OF DEMAND MEASUREMENT

In seeking to measure the demand for recreation, three broad approaches have been adopted. The first is concerned to establish a continuous record of activities over a given period of time by the sample population, and involves keeping a diary of activities by each participant. The principal limitations of this 'time budget' approach concern the length of time over which a diary might reasonably be kept and the fineness of the time gradations used in recording. Diary entries are tedious to make, and both accuracy and completeness suffer if an extended period of recording is required, or if activities are timed with undue precision. The biggest exercise of this kind in Britain is that carried out by the BBC Audience Research Department, most recently in 1961 and 1974/5:[8] on both occasions, the diary record was asked for over a full week with entries covering each half hour.[9] Even over this relatively brief span, 'the willingness of diarists to keep a careful record of their daily activities declined in both surveys towards the end of the diary-week.'[10]

These limitations mean that the diary technique is excellent for recording basic patterns of time use on a diurnal scale, but much less effective in obtaining information on activities carried out relatively infrequently. For that, some kind of questionnaire survey is necessary with questions seeking a record of activities over a longer period of recall but without the same precision in the time frame. The two techniques have occasionally been combined with advantage. The best example, perhaps, is that of Young and Willmott's study of work and leisure in the London region, *The symmetrical family*.[11] Their main survey, carried out in 1970, covered 1928 respondents: from these, those married and aged 30-49 were asked to complete a diary covering a full weekday, four additional weekday evenings and a full Saturday and Sunday. Of the eligible sub-sample of 699, 411 completed diaries, though only 285 provided adequate details of the weekday evenings.

Questionnaire surveys themselves have been the principal instrument used for recording leisure patterns and leisure demand. Two distinct types may be recognised. The first has been primarily a sociologist's tool and is associated particularly in the leisure field with the work of the Rapoports and the Institute of Family and Environmental Research.[12] The approach is essentially that of the individual case study, with a probing, in-depth interview seeking to establish more than a simple statistical pattern, being concerned rather with the linking of activities into distinctive leisure life-styles and the motivations and satisfactions inherent in activities. Such studies have yielded valuable insights at the micro-scale, though samples are of necessity small, much of the evidence anecdotal, and wider generalisations more difficult to achieve.

The second, more frequently used, type of questionnaire survey characterises the third broad approach to demand measurement. Here a much larger sample is employed, sufficient in size for the varied sub-samples to be statistically significant in themselves and using for the most part straightforward questions inviting a simple factual response and readily capable of statistical analysis. Such surveys have been reasonably numerous, but two general categories may be usefully distinguished.

The first focuses on a specific recreation activity. Where that activity is one in which a large proportion of the population participates, sample selection poses few unusual problems: the Countryside Commission's National Surveys of Countryside Recreation in 1977 and 1980, already discussed, are obvious cases in point. Far greater problems arise when minority activities are considered, and some kind of filter is usually necessary to derive an adequate sample. Most sports fall into this category. In 1970 the National Angling Survey, for example, first used a postal survey of 30,000 questionnaires to isolate households with anglers: this yielded 3429 such addresses, from which the eventual sample of 2044 anglers was drawn.[13] In the follow-up survey in 1980, a sample of 1963 anglers was derived from contacts identified through NOP Market Research Ltd's Random Omnibus Survey.[14] Another approach identifies participants at the place of activity: numerous surveys have used this technique, but while it yields good data about the actual participants, it fails to set them in the wider context of the population as a whole.

The second category of large-sample questionnaire survey is concerned with the whole spectrum of leisure activities and aims to describe overall patterns of participation. Such surveys, with a lengthy questionnaire and an extensive sample, are expensive to mount and remain relatively few in number. The major examples were noted earlier in the chapter, with two at national level undertaken in 1965 and four at regional level between 1967 and 1972 (table 3.1). More recent evidence is confined to the limited number of leisure questions included in the General Household Survey in 1973, 1977 and 1980.

TABLE 3.1 Major household questionnaire leisure surveys

Survey	*Date of fieldwork*	*Age range*	*Sample size*	*Response rate (%)*
Pilot National Recreation Survey	1963	12+	3167	—
Planning for leisure:				
(i) urban areas England and Wales	1965	15+	2682	80
(ii) inner London	1965	15+	1321	82
(iii) new towns	1965	15+	1732	67
Outdoor leisure activities in the Northern Region	1967	12+	3416	80
Leisure in the North West	1969	12+	5055	83
Greater London Recreation Study	1972	15-69	3858	78
Study of informal recreation in South East England	1972	15-69	3462	76
General Household Survey	1977	15+	20,880*	—

* Successive quarterly samples were 5350, 5200, 5150, 5180. Samples for the GHS surveys in 1973 and 1980 were of comparable size.

Important though these general surveys have been in creating a basic knowledge of leisure patterns, they also suffer from serious limitations. The first stems from the size of sample employed. As table 3.1 shows, the samples are relatively large, but even so sub-samples for the analysis of particular activities or of regional and sub-regional characteristics soon become unacceptably small. This limitation is of little significance for activities undertaken by the majority of people – watching television or countryside visiting, for example – but means that the evidence for minority activities is far more restricted in value. This applies particularly to individual sports. The Northern Region survey, for example, gives numbers of participants for 34 activities on an average Sunday, but notes that for 18 the estimate involves considerable sampling error and 'should be treated with reserve'. All the 18 are sports of one kind or another: indeed, among sports only swimming, fishing, cricket, golf and cycling yield a sufficient sample for confident analysis. The usual solution is to group activities, most often by the type of facility used. The North West survey, noting that 'many sports are too feebly supported by the sample for any data beyond general participation levels to be derived', uses five groups for further analysis: turf sports; indoor and small room sports; outdoor water sports; rural area sports; and indoor water sports. Such a grouping has obvious disadvantages. It links sports as dissimilar as rugby league and lacrosse, or folk dancing and karate, and it may attempt a general analysis of a group that is unduly dominated by a single sport – outdoor water sports by angling, for example, which made up 80 per cent of the total group.

Similar limitations apply in a spatial sense. The Pilot National Recreation Survey sample was deliberately derived to give equal representation from each of the Registrar General's nine 'standard regions' in England, with Wales and Scotland in addition: even so, the second report ruefully notes that 'at the "standard region" level the absolute sample is too low for confident use', and proceeds to regroup the standard regions into only four areas for England as a whole. The broader grouping itself still poses problems, for 'it would be very hazardous, from our figures, to try to calculate regional levels of demand . . . ' and the results should be seen 'merely as a set of signposts to the general directions in which regional recreation patterns differ from the national norm', with 'actual percentage values . . . quickly abandoned in favour of a ranking process'.

Sample size is not the only problem, for sample derivation may give rise to equal hazards. The North West survey used a stratified sample to give a better representation of a wider range of settlement sizes. The sampling procedure gave selected wards from Blackpool, Burnley, Preston, Southport, Wigan and Crewe as representative of the 'towns over 50,000' category, for example, with a resultant emphasis on Lancashire in particular. Such a randomly-generated emphasis does not, of course, invalidate the work, but it does increase the caution necessary in any close interpretation of results.

To these technical problems must be added limitations inherent in the organisation of the surveys themselves. First and foremost, all the surveys of the 1960s and early 1970s were, as already noted, 'one-off' exercises, lacking any repeat work to enable trends through time to be established with any confidence. This limitation does not apply to the leisure questions of the General Household Survey, though detailed comparisons between years have been made difficult by slight changes in procedure. In the 1973 survey it was concluded that a number of activities were being under-represented in the results because of the way in which the question on participation was asked. To improve accuracy, therefore, changes were introduced in 1977, not least by extending the range of activities mentioned on the prompt card shown to respondents to indicate the type and range of activities counted as leisure. More specifically, the following activities were mentioned on the prompt card in 1977 but not in 1973: racing; walking (plus probing on the length of walk); swimming; darts; billiards; bowls; table tennis; fishing; and 'other outdoor activities'. The

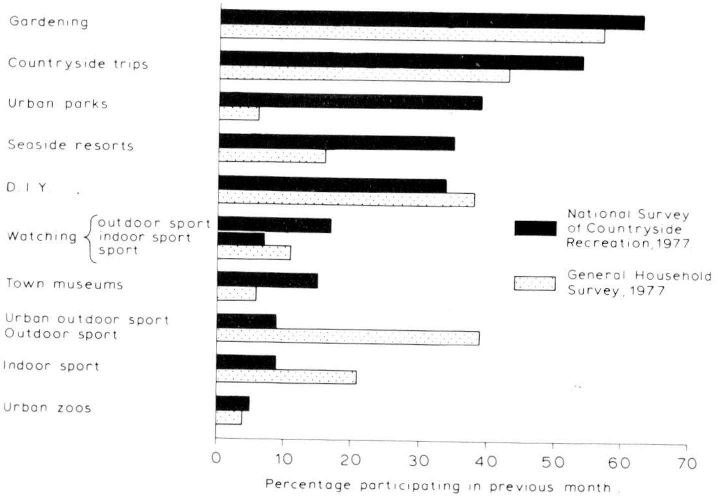

FIGURE 3.2 Participation in selected recreations in England and Wales, 1977, according to the National Survey of Countryside Recreation and the General Household Survey.
Source: NSCR data from A. M. H. Fitton, 'The reality – for whom are we actually providing?' in *Countryside for all?* (Countryside Commission, CCP 117, 1978), table 1; GHS data for this and subsequent figures from A. J. Veal, *Sport and recreation in England and Wales: an analysis of adult participation patterns in 1977* (Centre for Urban and Regional Studies, Research Memorandum 74, 1979), table 2

more detailed prompt card may have stimulated respondents in any case to search across a wider range of activities, but it must certainly be in part responsible for an apparent increase between 1973 and 1977 of 165 per cent in walking, 272 per cent in darts, 293 per cent in billiards and snooker and 187 per cent in table tennis.[15]

Comparisons between surveys are made more difficult by the widely varying definitions adopted at both questionnaire design and analysis stages, as well as by the widely differing types of information collected.[16] Comparison was made earlier between published comments on the results of the National Survey of Countryside Recreation and the General Household Survey (figure 3.1), and the misleading implications that could arise if the data were accepted without critical examination were emphasised. Figure 3.2 represents a further stage in the comparison between the two surveys. In this instance, the more obvious discrepancies have been removed by a regrouping of some of the GHS categories, particularly in terms of 'countryside trips'. The activities now included for each survey in this category are listed in table 3.2. The definitions still differ considerably

TABLE 3.2 Activities included in the definition of 'countryside trips' in Figure 3.2

National Survey of Countryside Recreation	*General Household Survey*
Active sport in countryside	Camping and caravanning
Horse riding, pony trekking	Cycling
Long walks, hikes or rambles	Field sports
Fishing in the countryside	Field studies
Visiting sea coast, cliff tops	Horse riding
Drives, outings, picnics	Mountaineering
Visiting historic buildings and stately homes	Walking
Visiting safari parks	Fishing
	Sailing
	Swimming in sea, rivers, lakes
	Visits to countryside
	Visits to historic buildings
	Visits to safari parks

in detail, and the categories reported permit no further 'fine-tuning' of consequence, but the discrepancy is now much less than earlier seemed apparent. The initial published result gave, over the previous four weeks in summer, 29 per cent participation in 'open-air outings' (GHS) and 54 per cent in 'countryside activities' (NSCR): the revised GHS grouping lifts participation in a wider category of countryside recreation to 43 per cent.

The problem of definition, however, remains paramount in the interpretation of all available data. Too few definitions are directly comparable between different surveys, though where straightforward activities permit relatively simple definitions, as with gardening and do-it-yourself in the present example, the results can be comfortingly close.

LEISURE PATTERNS

Data availability and data problems have been discussed at some length, but it is important fully to understand the limitations of much existing data before considering actual patterns of leisure use. In examining these patterns, two distinct approaches will be followed, the one time-based, the other activity-based.

The best evidence for a time-based approach comes from time-budget surveys, the most recent available of national significance being the BBC study of 1974-75 (figure 3.3). In this study, diaries were actually kept over a full week from 5 am to 3 am the following day, but analysis is here restricted to the period 6.30 am to midnight to permit ready comparison with the 1961 BBC data, which were gathered only over the more limited time span.[17]

The eight categories are virtually self-explanatory. 'Passive leisure' includes watching television and listening to the radio and music. 'Hobbies' subsumes reading and other leisure in the home. 'Civic' activities covers a variety of religious, political and civic activities; 'personal care', sleeping, eating and washing; 'domestic work', child care, cooking, cleaning and repairs; and 'paid work', travel to work, meals and rest breaks at work as well as actual work time itself.

The diagram averages time spent over the week as a whole. It emphasises the large proportion of time spent in the sheer business of living – in work, sleep (remembering the missing 390 minutes in the record of each day), domestic chores and personal care. On average, in terms of these definitions, some 348 minutes per day are spent at leisure and of that virtually 70 per cent (69.2 per cent) is spent at home. This dominance of home-based leisure in time terms is frequently forgotten in leisure studies but is of fundamental importance.

Gershuny and Thomas's work in matching the 1974-75 data to the earlier 1961 results enables broad patterns of change in the use of time to be discerned. Several important facets may be noted. 'Personal care' remains virtually the same, but if the two categories of work – 'paid' and 'domestic' – are combined, the time devoted to this has declined by more than 10 per cent. Conversely, total leisure shows a considerable increase over less than a decade and a half, of nearly 18 per cent. Within leisure,

FIGURE 3.3 Changing patterns of time allocation in the United Kingdom, 1961-1974/5. The data were derived from the time budget surveys of the BBC Audience Research Department and relate to time per day averaged over the whole week. *Source:* data from J. I. Gershuny and G. S. Thomas *Changing patterns of time use: Data preparation and some preliminary results, UK 1961-1974/5*, (SPRU Occasional paper series no. 13, University of Sussex, 1980), table 3.1

there has been a substantial growth of constructive pursuits. Passive leisure at home has changed but little, whereas the time spent on active hobbies has increased by 17 per cent. Activities outside the home have grown quite dramatically, by no less than 64 per cent overall to a mean of 107 minutes a day, and by 75 per cent in the case of indoor activities away from home – activities such as eating out with friends or at a restaurant, or visiting pubs and clubs.

Simple averages, of course, mask wide variations between different groups of the population, between different seasons and different days. Some of these variations will be looked at in more detail subsequently, but the biggest time distinction comes between weekends and weekdays. The

North West survey, for example, reported that the average sample member had about seven hours of leisure each weekday and a little more than ten on both Saturday and Sunday.[18]

If the analysis is moved from a time basis to an activity basis, the overwhelming importance of home-centred leisure activities remains the striking feature (figures 3.4 and 3.5). The measure now is no longer the time spent on an activity, but the proportion of the population who participate in it. Figure 3.4 aggregates all the 1977 GHS participation data, while figure 3.5 shows in more detail those activities in which over 10 per cent of the population participate.

Some activities are virtually ubiquitous – watching television for 97 per cent of the sample, and social visiting for 91 per cent. Other activities are still common, but with a substantial minority of non-participants – reading and gardening at home, going for a meal outside the home. The clearest distinction, however, is between the broad categories of home-based and social activities, which are common to most people's recreation life-style, and other kinds of activity (such as visits to recreation facilities and sports participation), which, even when specific activities are aggregated into broader groups, still appeal to only limited sections of the population. Yet it is these latter activities that absorb a very large share of expenditure on leisure facilities, especially in the public sector.

Figures 3.6 and 3.7 examine the GHS data for sports participation in more detail. In 1977 outdoor sport attracted 39 per cent of the population as a whole in the most popular quarter, indoor sport 22 per cent. These figures on their own, however, are misleading. They not only aggregate a

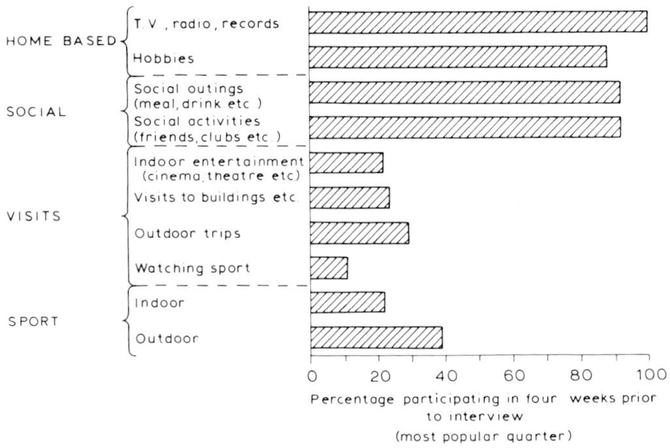

FIGURE 3.4 Participation in major types of leisure activity, 1977, in the four weeks prior to interview.
Source: data from General Household Survey

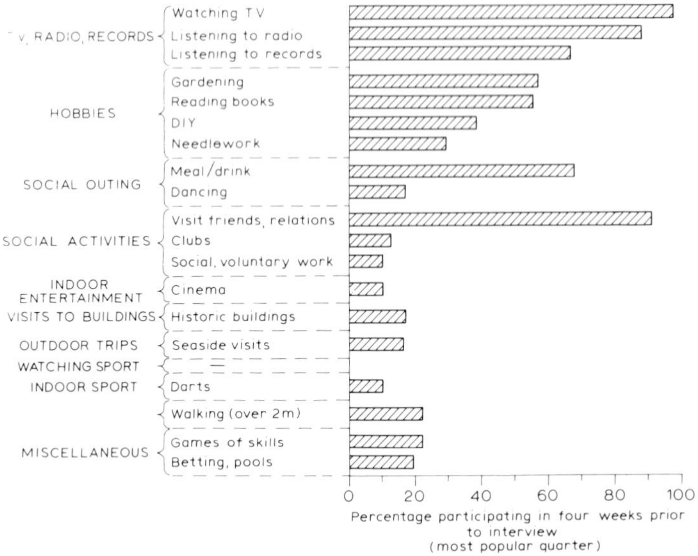

FIGURE 3.5 Leisure activities in which more than 10 per cent of the population participated in the four weeks prior to interview in 1977.
Source: data from General Household Survey

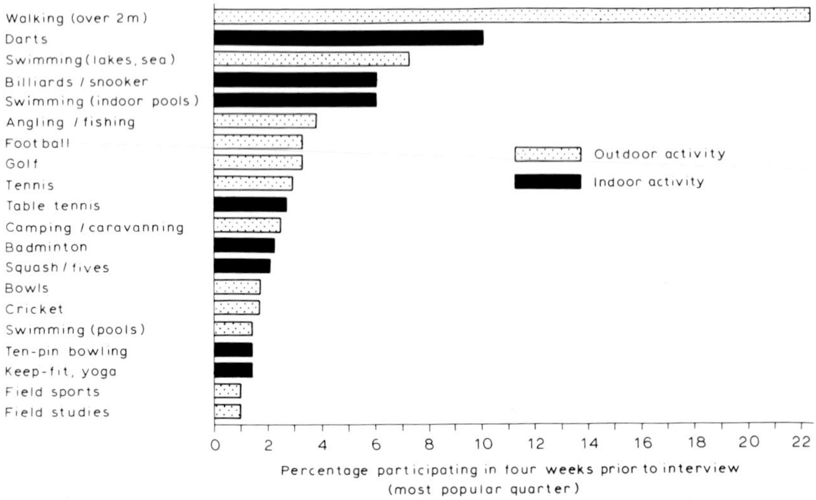

FIGURE 3.6 Sporting activities in which more than 1 per cent of the population participated in the four weeks prior to interview in 1977.
Source: data from General Household Survey

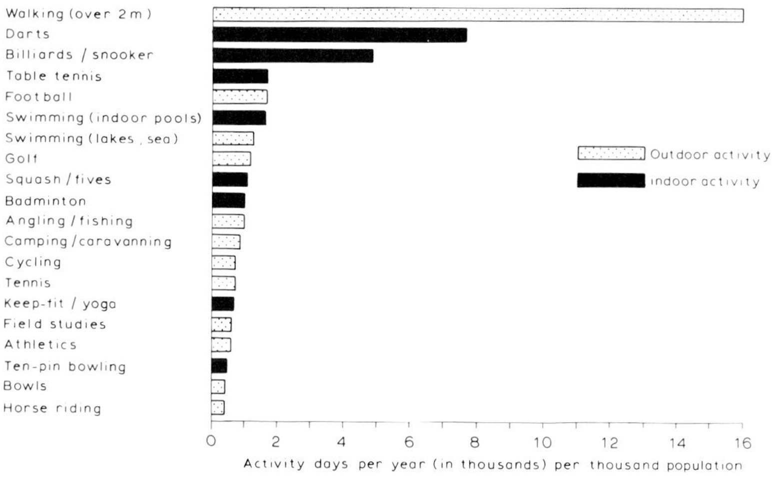

FIGURE 3.7 The twenty sporting activities with the highest total of activity days in 1977.
Source: data from General Household Survey

large number of individual activities, but are dominated by two informal pursuits – walking and darts – which alone account for a very substantial part of participation in the two categories.

Figure 3.6 includes those 20 activities in which at least 1 per cent of the total population recorded participation in the four weeks prior to survey in the most popular quarter. Two points are worth emphasising in this context. In the first place, very few activities reach even the 5 per cent mark, with only such informal activities as swimming and billiards and snooker to add to walking and darts. Second, a large number of sporting activities do not qualify even at the 1 per cent level. Cycling and climbing are near misses, but notable omissions are horse-riding, rugby, and all forms of athletics and water-based activities except swimming. In part, of course, the sheer variety of opportunities prevents significant concentrations on individual activities: to give but one measure of their number, the Sports Council currently grant-aids some 64 separate sports, not including the variety within individual activities such as the martial arts.[19]

Figure 3.7 emphasises intensity of participation by considering 'activity days' rather than proportion participating as the measure. Again, the 20 sports recording the highest rates of activity are included. There are some changes in both the activities included in the list and in the internal ranking. Cycling, athletics and horse-riding appeal to relatively small numbers, but their devotees tend to be frequent participants and they are thus included in the list when 'activity days' are the basis for calculation. Highly seasonal activities, like outdoor swimming at the seaside or in rivers and lakes, fare relatively badly by this measure, and thus fall in the ranking. Informal, casual pursuits, however, assert their dominance to an even greater extent: walking appeals not only to a very high proportion of the total population, but is also frequently enjoyed.

PHYSICAL CONSTRAINTS ON DEMAND

The simple description of leisure patterns emphasises their variety both through time and between individuals. The evidence for changes through time is tantalisingly meagre in the sense of data for precise description, though more circumstantial evidence is clear enough. Some trends have already been examined, and we shall return to look at the causes of these changes and their relationship to resources for recreation in subsequent chapters.

The *extent* of distinctions between differing activities and between differing individuals has also been clearly evident, but those distinctions themselves need further examination. They represent a response to a variety of constraints: constraints that may be inherent in the very nature of the activity and the participants, or constraints that may themselves be susceptible to change through time.

One of the most unyielding of constraints is that imposed by climate,

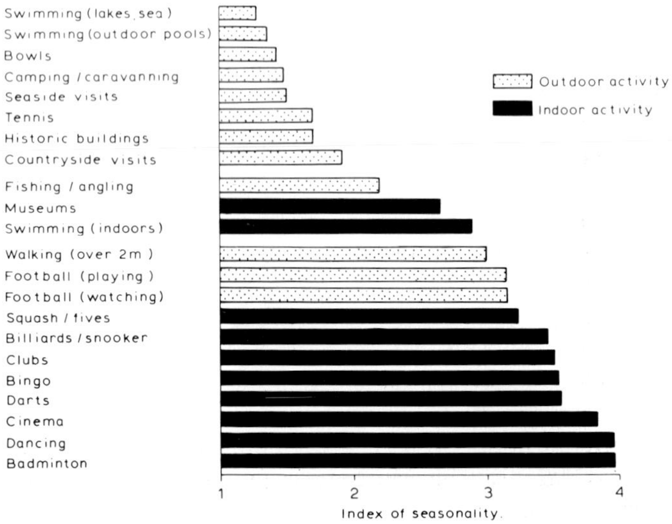

FIGURE 3.8 An index of seasonality for sporting activities, 1977. The derivation of the index is discussed in the text.
Source: data from General Household Survey

most obviously where outdoor activities are concerned. The rhythm of the seasons affects both the hours of daylight available and the extent to which temperatures are conducive to participant comfort outdoors. Figure 3.8 gives some measure of the seasonality of specific recreations. The General Household Survey data, being collected on a quarterly basis, enables an index of seasonality to be derived for individual activities. The index represents the ratio between the 'activity days' generated in the most popular quarter for that activity and over the year as a whole. Thus, for visits to the seaside, the ratio is approximately 1:1.5 (index=1.51), indicating that two-thirds of such visits take place in the most popular quarter: in contrast, that for badminton is almost 1:4 (index=3·96), showing virtually identical rates of activity throughout the year. Some quarterly samples from this source are too small for confident comparisons: these activities are omitted from this analysis.

The range for activities on figure 3.8 represents a continuum from 'highly seasonal' to 'little seasonal variation', but three distinct groups may be distinguished for convenience with indices respectively of 1-1.9, 2.0-2.9 and 3.0-4.0. The first represents the most seasonal. These are outdoor activities, often of an informal nature and relying on warm weather as well as long days for full enjoyment. They may also be particularly associated with an annual holiday, again enhancing their seasonality. The archetype is outdoor swimming, especially in the sea or rivers. In Britain's uncertain climate there are relatively few days on which this can be undertaken with any real degree of pleasure. Indeed, the climatic constraint on most outdoor activities in Britain greatly increases their seasonality, and by accentuating the peaks of participation further exacerbates the problems of provision.

The second, intermediate, group is in every sense transitional. It includes outdoor activities either less dependent on temperature for full enjoyment or whose devotees are ardent enough to discount some measure of personal discomfort. Walking and both playing and watching football record indices marginally in excess of 3.0, but belong essentially to this group. The indoor activities are those either linked to more general outings (visits to museums) or those where even indoors seasonal chill can induce a shiver of disinclination (swimming).

It is no surprise that the third group, with the exceptions already mentioned, comprises indoor pursuits, whether formal sports or informal social activities. Indeed, the only major lessening of the overall seasonal constraint has come from increased indoor provision for some pursuits (in tennis, for example) or from improved clothing and equipment (in climbing, for example) enhancing personal comfort.

To these broad seasonal constraints may be added the more specific constraints of climate and weather on individual activities. In this context

Thornes distinguishes three particular categories of sport.[20] *Specialised weather sports* need certain weather conditions to take place at all. Examples include sailing, gliding and skiing, with their requirements for wind velocity, thermals and snow. The participant is competing against nature as well as with other participants, and nature may indeed be sufficiently challenging to provide the only competition. *Weather interference sports* need freedom from adverse weather, and ideally take place in warm, dry, bright but overcast conditions, with little or no wind, excellent visibility, not too humid and with a firm ground surface – in fact, as Thornes remarks, 'in conditions in which most of the sports in the first category could not take place'. In practice, conditions are rarely so ideal, but in team games such as soccer and hockey all participants suffer the same degree of general interference and more specific factors such as wind direction are compensated for by playing two halves in opposing directions. The third category comprises the *weather advantage sports* where weather changes may bring unequal conditions for participants. In competitive golf, weather variations through the day may affect scores depending on when players tee off: again, in first-class cricket, with matches extending over three and five days, weather conditions rarely remain constant over the whole period of play and may give a distinct advantage to one side.[21]

Physical conditions may also directly affect the resources used for a specific activity. Grass pitches are readily susceptible to wear through intensive use. The Sports Council suggests that on grounds with suitable soil, 'well laid, drained and maintained pitches can be used three or four times each week, provided they are not used more than once on each of two consecutive days.'[22] This suggests a pitch availability of at most some six hours a week: the alternative is an artificial turf surface capable of some 35 games a week. The addition of artificial lighting may further extend playing opportunities.

The physical constraints of season, climate and weather inhibit demand by curtailing the periods of time over which a particular resource can be used for the activity concerned. For some activities, human intervention, through the reseeding and drainage of turf pitches, for example, may extend the period or increase the intensity of use of a resource, but such changes are relatively marginal. The constraints may be relaxed further by subsituting a different kind of resource, less subject to the vagaries of physical conditions. In most cases the subsitute is of a man-made nature, like an artificial ski slope, or brings the activity indoors, where light and temperature are more readily controlled. For the aficionado, however, the extension of opportunity may have been made at the expense of the quality of experience: the indoor climbing wall is poor compensation for a Lake District crag.

BIOLOGICAL AND SOCIAL CONSTRAINTS

Most other constraints bear less equally on potential participants, and relate to their biological, social or economic circumstances. The scale of these distinctions is broadly indicated in figure 3.9, where the proportion

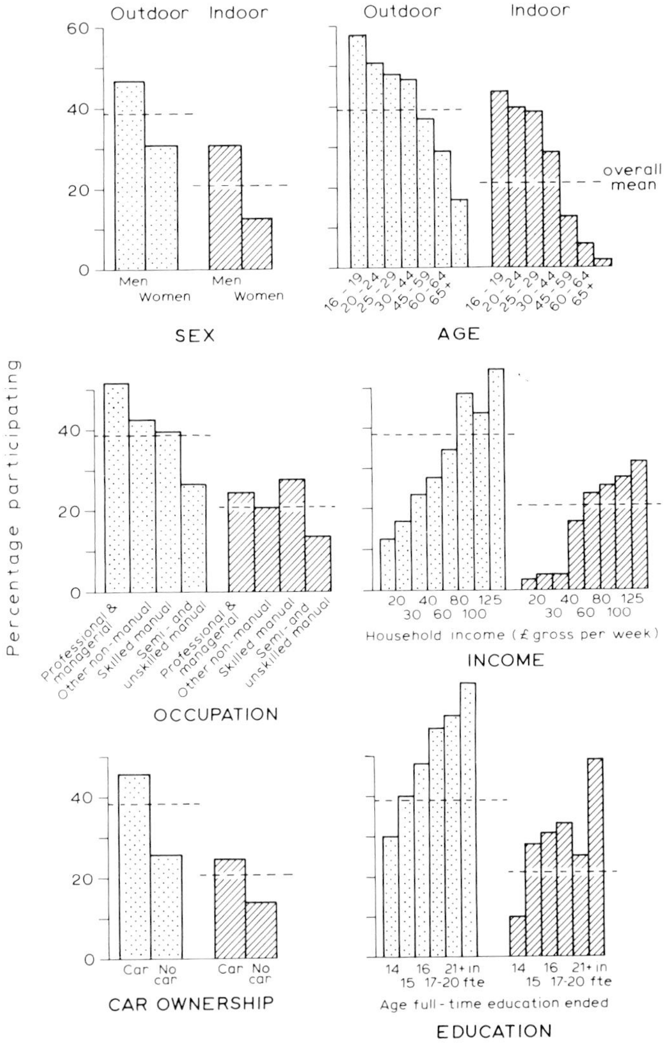

FIGURE 3.9 The effect of social and economic factors on participation in outdoor and indoor sport, 1977.
Source: data from General Household Survey

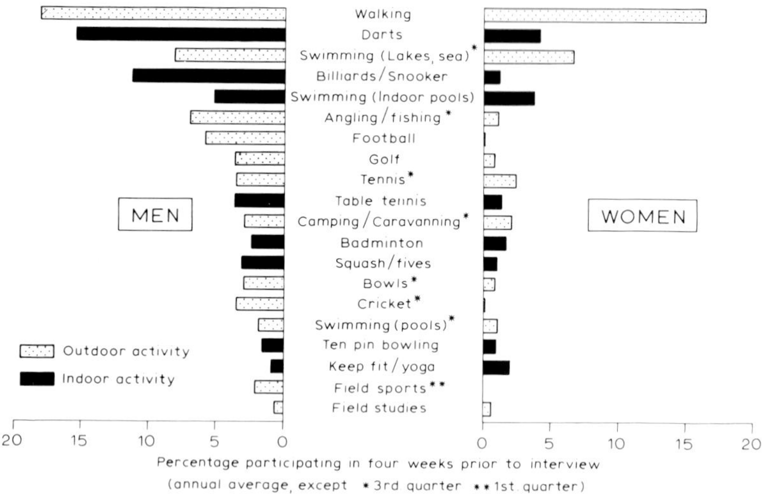

FIGURE 3.10 Contrasts in sports participation by men and women, 1977.
Source: data from General Household Survey

participating in outdoor and indoor sports is examined for a number of basic personal parameters.

The influence of gender remains paramount. The distinction is greatest in those activities involving considerable physical exertion. Amongst the major physical activities represented in figure 3.10, only walking, swimming, tennis and badminton have a female participation rate comparable to that of men, and only in keep fit and yoga does it exceed it.[23] The distinction is much less marked, or non-existent, for more passive, informal activities. Countryside visiting is an obvious case in point: the National Survey of Countryside Recreation recorded participation rates of 55 per cent for men and 52 per cent for women in the four weeks prior to survey.

How far these distinctions are rooted in biological characteristics and how far in gender stereotyping remains a matter of debate.[24] For sport, certainly, the evidence suggests that the existing pattern is capable of considerable change. In a wider European context Rodgers has shown that the discrepancy between male and female participation is much greater in Britain than in other countries, though direct comparisons must be viewed with some caution because of the widely differing nature, definitions and date of the surveys involved. In Britain (in the North West survey) there were 188 male participants in sport for every 100 females, in Spain 176, France 159, Belgian Flanders 127, Norway 127, Holland 116 and West Germany 111.[25] Recent trend data for England and Wales suggest the gap is narrowing quite markedly, though considerable discrepancies remain.

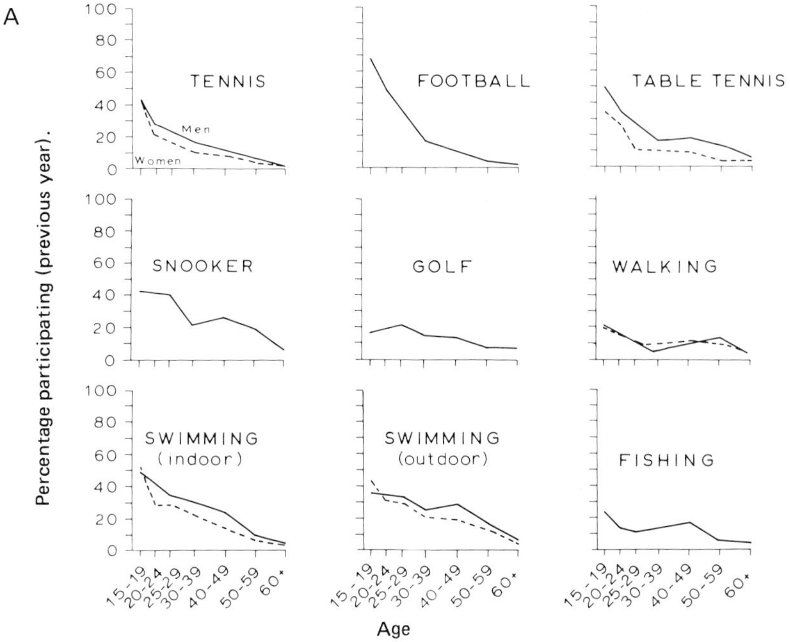

FIGURE 3.11A Participation of different age groups in London in selected sporting activities, 1972. These graphs show male participants only, except for tennis, table tennis, walking and swimming.

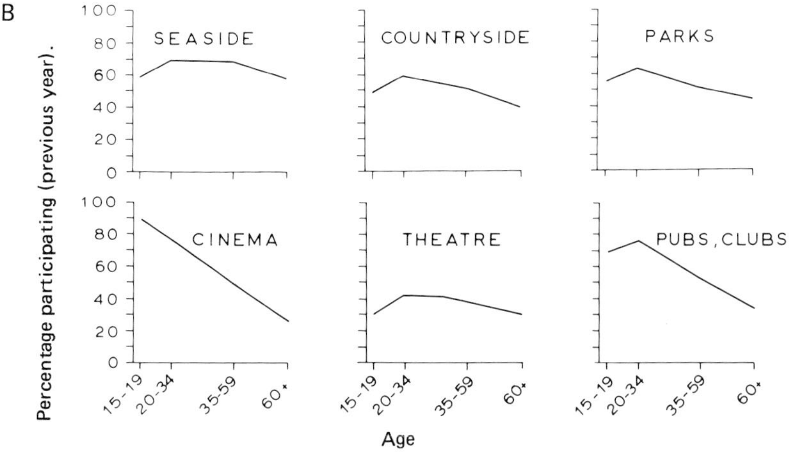

FIGURE 3.11B Participation of different age groups in London in informal leisure activities, 1972. Male and female participants are not separately distinguished.
Source: data from *Greater London Recreation Study. Part 2, Participant profiles* (Greater London Council, Research Report 19, 1976), tables 1.3, 1.7, 1.9, 1.10, 3.1, 3.2, 3.3, 4.1, 4.2, and 4.6

For outdoor sports there were 183 male participants for every 100 females in 1973, 152 in 1977 and 139 in 1980. For indoor sports the ratios for the three years were 225, 238 and 189 respectively.[26]

For many activities, the constraints of age are also innately physical. Most recent surveys give inadequate data for detailed age profiles to be constructed for a range of individual activities, and figure 3.11 is therefore based on the Greater London Recreation Survey of 1972. The general trends, however, are of wider application. Three broad types of activity may be discerned: those with a marked falling off in participation with advancing years; those with sustained participation through the life-cycle, and those where participation increases as a person gets older.

Most physical activity falls into the first type (figure 3.11a), though there are wide variations. Some highly energetic sports show a rapid decline with age (football, for example), while others are sustained for much longer (tennis, indoor swimming). Some activities show a resurgence in middle age, perhaps marking participation by the family as a whole (table tennis, outdoor swimming). On occasion, the decline in participation with age is related more to life-style than the physical demands of an activity: visits to the cinema or to pubs and clubs are cases in point (figure 3.11b).

Activities sustained through life are less physically taxing and, particularly at the higher participation levels, fit readily into the pattern of family life. Golf and walking typify the former, and visits to seaside, countryside and parks the latter. Most passive indoor activities – watching television, reading – and hobbies also fall into the category for which age has little effect. A few activities predominate in the later phases of life, and not merely those associated with increased passivity. In the present graphs, fishing and walking give some hint of this, but the evidence is insufficient for the full impact to be seen.

Gender and age need consideration not only on their own, but as part of the whole pattern of family circumstance. Changes in recreation habits occur not only gradually with age, but in quite dramatic form at points of change in life-style – leaving school, marriage, the birth of children, change of occupation and retirement, for example. The impact of these changes, and the 'triggers' that instigate their detailed nature, need much further research. In the major surveys, they were best described in *Planning for leisure*, and figure 3.12 is based on this source. While as evidence this is now dated, the basic patterns still hold good for comparison. The graphs relate to time spent on an activity rather than the proportion who participate. They reinforce the effects of gender and age already discussed, but their most striking feature is the distinction in patterns of time use between single and married persons. This is most marked for the 23-30 age group, where data are available for both

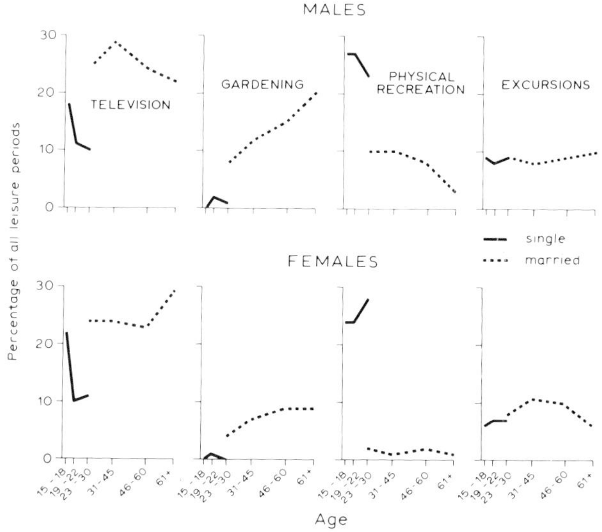

FIGURE 3.12 Age, sex, marital circumstance and participation in leisure activities, 1965-66. Married respondents in the 23-30 and 31-45 age groups had children, those in the 46-60 group no children. Those aged over 60 were in full-time employment.
Source: data from K. K. Sillitoe, *Planning for leisure* (HMSO, 1969), tables 9 and 10

categories. The graphs refer to married couples with children, but even where there are no children the distinction is almost as clear. Unmarried women between 23 and 30, for example, spent 28 per cent of their leisure time in physical recreation: after marriage that dropped to 10 per cent, and after the birth of children to 2 per cent.[27]

MONEY AND MOBILITY

The impact of gender, age and family circumstance on leisure activities is clear and predictable, and though there have been changes, these are of degree rather than of kind, for the fundamental biological and physical constraints remain. Other elements of social and economic circumstance, however, have a much more wide-ranging impact, and an impact that has varied as circumstances have changed for the population as a whole. These circumstances may be considered under several heads. They relate to income, occupation, the possession of a car and the extent of formal education, but though they are often considered in isolation they are so interlinked that such distinctions have little meaning. Indeed, many surveys use one measure as a surrogate for others – occupation for income or social class, for example.

The basic effect is clear. Those with more skilled and responsible occupations, with higher incomes, with ready access to private transport and with a longer period spent in full-time education tend to lead a much more active and varied leisure life, with less emphasis on passive recreations both within and beyond the home. Figure 3.13 illustrates this in terms of time spent on broad categories of recreation. In this BBC study, the three social grades were not related solely to occupation or income, but were an assessment of the respondent's social characteristics based at least in part on subjective observation. At home, the emphasis for class A was far more on constructive leisure, on active hobbies and pursuits, and far less on passive television watching or 'just relaxing'. Away from home, class A was more concerned with active sport, walking, visits to the countryside and other places of interest than with visits to friends, clubs or pubs. For class C in both cases the converse is true, with class B occupying an intermediate position.

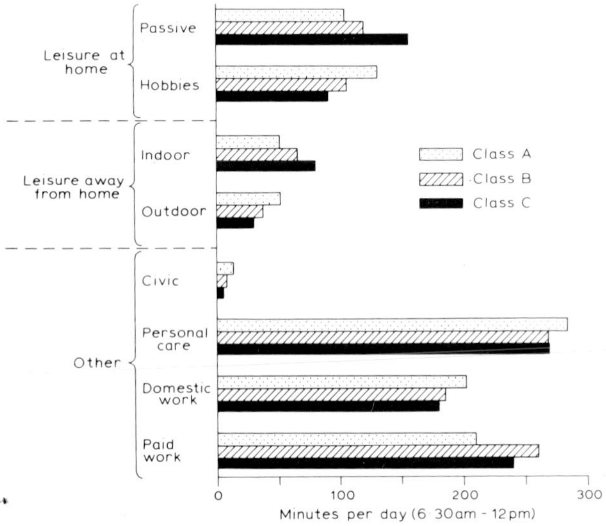

FIGURE 3.13 Patterns of time allocation by social class in the United Kingdom, 1974-75. The data were derived from the time budget surveys of the BBC Audience Research Department and relate to time per day averaged over the whole week. The social categorisation used was as follows:
Class A: professional, managerial, highly skilled;
Class B: moderately skilled, clerical;
Class C: semi- and unskilled.

Source: data from J. I. Gershuny and G. S. Thomas, *Changing patterns of time use: Data preparation and some preliminary results, UK 1961-1974/5* (SPRU Occasional paper series no. 13, University of Sussex, 1980), table 3.1

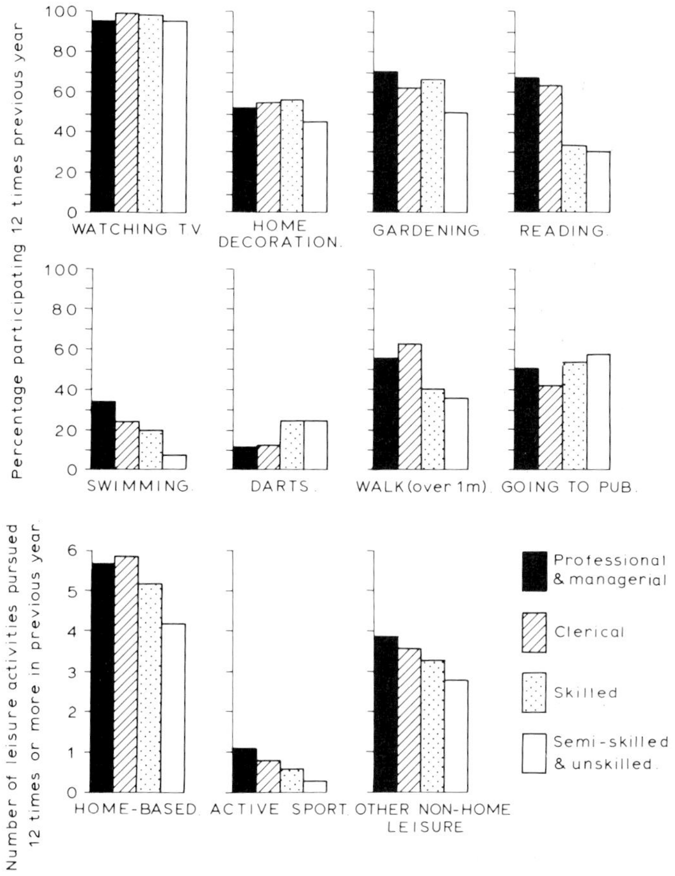

FIGURE 3.14 Occupation and participation in leisure activities among married men in London working full time, 1970.
Source: data from M. Young and P. Willmott, *The symmetrical family* (Penguin, 1975), tables 35, 37, 38 and 39

A variety of evidence points to the same general conclusion, and a few illustrations must suffice (see also figure 3.9). Willmott and Young, in their survey of the London region, showed that not only does the level of participation in specific leisure activities differ markedly between occupational groups, but the number and range of activities also varied considerably both within and beyond the home (figure 3.14). Thus, while television viewing was virtually ubiquitous when measured in simple terms of participation, actual hours of viewing varied markedly. For men, they ranged from 10.0 hours a week for those in the managerial and professional group to 13·3 for the semi-skilled and unskilled: for women the hours were 9·9 and 13·4 respectively.[28]

These distinctions may be as characteristic of an area as of a specific social group. This theme was explored by Boothby, Tungatt, Townsend and Collins in their study of two adjacent areas of Teesside.[29] Hardwick comprised predominantly council property, while the majority of Fairfield homes were owner-occupied. In terms of sports participation the two areas were clearly distinct, with 49 per cent of Hardwick respondents currently active and 70 per cent of Fairfield. Fairfield generated more than two-thirds of all the sports recorded in the survey, and both men and women there (despite the overall differences between the sexes) had a far more varied sporting experience. Fairfield men had played an average of 7·8 sports per person, Hardwick men 5.1. For women, the rates were 4.5 and 2.5 respectively.

In geographical terms, both these areas of Teesside had equal access to a wide range of sports facilities. There were wide distinctions between them, however, in terms of many social indicators, and in none more so than car ownership. At the time of the survey (1978), 90 per cent of households in Fairfield had a car, but only 40 per cent in Hardwick. In this survey, as in so many others, car ownership is vital not only in providing a ready means of access to a wide range of leisure facilities, but in being associated with a much more active and varied leisure life.

The growth of car ownership was traced in the previous chapter: the impact of high personal mobility that it brought remains the most important single feature of the changing recreation habits of the 1960s and 1970s. All surveys show, with remarkable consistency, that participation rates in most forms of sport and in outdoor recreation are roughly twice as high in car-owning households as in those without a car (table 3.3). Nor is it participation rates alone that are affected; the patterns and the very nature of participation tend to differ also, as subsequent chapters will show.

The distinctions, of course, are far from absolute:

> the fact that non-car-owners do take part [in sport and informal recreation] suggests that, though low mobility can act as a deterrent, higher mobility is not necessarily a pre-requisite of greater participation; rather it can reduce some of the inconvenience associated with travel.[30]

That inconvenience is obviously greatest for activities taking place in areas away from the immediate surroundings of home, and where time is at a premium. It affects especially those informal recreations that make the greatest demand on land resources and with which this book is predominantly concerned. For longer periods and greater distances away from home, the pattern is more complex. The obvious convenience of the car attracts the non-car-owner: in a 1974 study of the leisure patterns of non-

TABLE 3.3 The influence of car ownership on sport and recreation

Survey and year	*Households without car*	*Households with car*	*Measure*
Active recreation (Sillitoe, 1969)	30	57	% participating
Informal recreation (National Travel Survey 1972–73)	6·2	10	% adults making trips any one date
Open-air outings (General Household Survey, 1973)	13	27	% adults participating previous four weeks, summe quarter
Countryside recreation (National Survey of Countryside Recreation, 1977)	33	64	% adults participating previous four weeks
Countryside recreation (National Survey of Countryside Recreation, 1980)	29	50	% adults participating previous four weeks

car-owning households in Hull, Tungatt recorded that 23 per cent of those in his sample going on holiday obtained the temporary use of a car for the purpose, the great majority by sharing with other members of their family or with friends.[31] For journeys abroad, however, the convenience of the car is much less marked. In 1980, cars were used for 71 per cent of all tourist trips within Britain, but for only 14 per cent of such trips overseas.[32]

RESOURCES AND FASHIONS

The biological, social and economic constraints considered in the previous sections greatly influence patterns of recreation demand. They have provided the core of several attempts to develop models of participation. In the Teesside study, for example, it was shown that a consideration of age, sex, marital status and four related social variables (social class, housing tenure, income and car ownership) could accurately predict the likelihood of an individual taking part in sport in 76 per cent of all cases, though the extent to which these variables duplicate each other is shown by the fact that 72 per cent of individuals could be correctly classified as participants or non-participants by considering age and sex alone.[33] These correlations are much less strong, of course, when individual activities are concerned – when sport, for example, is disaggregated into its numerous components. Choice then becomes much more a matter of individual preference within a range of options, though that choice may itself be constrained by further factors.

Of these, the most significant in a geographical context is the range of resources that is available to match demand and the ease of access to them. The relationship is far from simple, and still awaits much more research in detail. One measure is the propensity of people to engage in activities that require specific resources for their satisfaction and where those resources show considerable variation in their occurrence. Rodgers attempted such an analysis at broad regional level in the second report of the Pilot National Recreation Survey, though sample limitations inhibited anything beyond generalised, qualitative statements. Some of the differences bear an obvious relationship to resources – the propensity for hill-walking and climbing in the North, sea sailing in the South and West and golf in Scotland, for example. Other variations, however, permit no such simplistic explanations. In Wales, almost every activity showed a lower rate of participation than the national average, even coastal, countryside and water-based pursuits, the resources for which are abundantly and freely available. Such results in part may reflect the inadequacies of a small sub-sample, but as Rodgers notes, 'there is no very strong environmental influence in the Welsh recreational profile: social influences are apparently much the stronger.'[34]

Other surveys have yielded tantalising glimpses of these relationships. The North West survey gave data for the relative importance of different trip destinations from the two major conurbations of Merseyside and Greater Manchester (table 3.4). In this context, the major distinction between the two is their location in relation to the coast, with Merseyside having the beaches of south Lancashire, Wirral and North Wales in close proximity whereas Manchester lies some 55 km away inland. For full-day

TABLE 3.4 Trip destinations, Merseyside and Greater Manchester conurbations, 1969

	Percentage of full-day trips (over 5 hours)		*Percentage of half-day trips (2-5 hours)*	
Destination	*Manchester*	*Merseyside*	*Manchester*	*Merseyside*
Coast	53	58	11	72
Countryside	29	27	36	10
Town parks	4	2	37	11
Other towns	9	9	14	6
Outside region	9	6	3	—

Source: data from *Leisure in the North West* (1972), figures 6.8-6.11

trips, where time is not a major constraint, the two areas compare closely in destinations chosen, though the table masks the fact that the Merseysiders show both a higher rate of participation in trip-making and a frequency rate almost twice as high. The contrast in destination is clearly evident for half-day trips of more limited duration. More than 70 per cent of Merseyside trips are to the adjacent coast, compared with 11 per cent for Manchester, and participation and frequency rates are also again much higher. Habits therefore vary widely with accessibility to resources.

Demand surveys yield clear evidence of variation in demand and permit some explanation of why that variation occurs. But such 'explanations' are inevitably locked into the time frame of the particular survey and make demand forecasting based on simple extrapolation hazardous in the extreme. As Rodgers has commented, 'trend-based prediction in general has its dangers unless it can be assumed with fair confidence that the recent past is truly the key to the near future.'[35] In practice, this is rarely the case. Higher real incomes and expanding car ownership do not mean that the majority today follow the habits of the minority of an earlier generation: recreation behaviour is far too complex and too mercurial for such simplistic assumptions. 'Taste and fashion affect it; the media mould it; obscure psychological factors motivate it at the level of the individual, and cultural influences shape patterns of participation at the sub-group level (e.g. among teenagers or immigrants).'[36]

Even more, the technological, as well as the social, economic and geographical, framework of resources is subject to rapid and far-reaching change. As a prime illustration, the most widespread and time-consuming of all recreations – watching television – is of comparatively recent origin. The first public transmissions in Britain date only from 1936, two channels from 1955, three from 1964, four from 1982, and colour from 1969. Other innovations have had a far less universal impact, but have revolutionised the enjoyment of, and greatly encouraged participation in, particular activities. Sailing has benefited enormously from glassfibre hulls, nylon cordage and terylene sails; music listening of all kinds from solid state electronics, stereophonic reproduction and cassette tape recorders. Superimposed upon these deep-rooted changes are more fickle fashions sparked by devices as varied as the hula hoop and the skateboard, the Rubik cube and the video game.

LEISURE LIFE-STYLES

Rapid changes in these leisure contexts do indeed make predictions hazardous when confined to individual activities, but a more promising, if as yet little researched, approach looks at aggregations of leisure activities into leisure life-styles. This views the use of leisure by individuals as not so much the sum of specific activities but rather as being characterised by particular leisure approaches. Such characterisations might be 'sports-centred', 'home-centred', or hobby-centred', for example. Groupings of individuals on this basis may cut across the social and economic distinctions – and 'explanations' – that other parameters suggest, with leisure life-styles being less directly associated with variations in age, income and social status. As Roberts has commented, 'individuals do not so much engage in *ad hoc* miscellanies of activities as develop broader systems of leisure behaviour consisting of a number of interdependent elements.'[37]

These 'systems' are as yet little understood. They relate to the meaning the individual ascribes (albeit subconsciously) to leisure, the perceptual context and its relationship to the experience of work as well as leisure; they relate to the human networks that provide the social context of leisure, whether in solitary pursuits or with family and friends; and they relate to the venues where leisure activities are undertaken – the locational context in which home figures to a greater or lesser extent. In all of these, the specific activity may be symbol rather than focus. Sailing, for example, may offer physical challenge, the company of valued friends and the lure of open water. In each context, alternative activities may bring comparable satisfactions, but may not combine in a system wholly satisfying to the individual concerned. It is this very feature that has made simple studies of the 'substitutability' of activities liable to misleading results, because of their necessary concentration on the activity itself rather than the wider satisfactions to which it gives rise.[38]

While the contexts may offer useful conceptual insights, they remain difficult to approach in terms of practical understanding. Paradoxically, despite the caveats of the previous paragraph, an activity-based approach can be helpful when activity groups are carefully used to characterise leisure life-styles. The methodology is still at an early stage, but the work of Glyptis has given some fascinating glimpses of what might be achieved.[39] Her study was concerned with a sample of countryside visitors, and to that extent all her subjects had an activity (and a limited locational context) in common. Their wider leisure life-styles were approached through a diary record of their activities over a span of three days and five evenings, reporting the dominant pursuit in each half-hour period. Her 595 respondents recorded as many as 129 activities, but significantly each individual cited only 11 on average. Cluster analysis revealed a very high degree of life-style specialisation. The specific groups had widely differing foci, with hobbies, home, pub and social visits and more wide-ranging outings providing particular contexts and emphases (figure 3.15). The groups cannot be simply characterised, for many

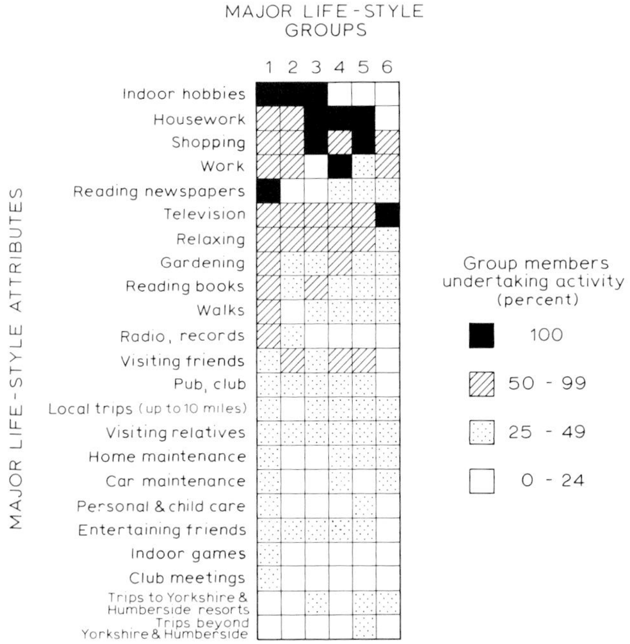

FIGURE 3.15 The major life-style groups and activity characteristics of a sample of visitors to two countryside sites in North Humberside, 1975.
Source: based on S. A. Glyptis, 'Leisure life-styles', *Regional Studies*, 15 (1981), figure 2

activities were common to several groups, but distinctive and varied leisure life-styles clearly emerged. Even more intriguing, these life-styles were remarkably independent of traditional parameters: people of different social class engaged in similar clusters of activities while others from the same social class showed contrasting life-styles.

This work, focusing on a limited sector of the population – the countryside visitor – can at best be only indicative, but it offers the stimulating, if still distant, prospect of a much fuller understanding of leisure life-styles and their expression in patterns of leisure activity. Above all, it emphasises the limitations of an approach to leisure demand that concentrates on the biological, social and economic parameters of participants in particular activities, rather than on the contexts in which these activities are pursued and their wider significance in leisure life-styles. The methodological problems remain formidable, but the whole approach is an apt reminder of the limitations of existing data on the use of leisure: while we may, with some hesitations, describe that use, we still remain well removed from a real understanding.

4 Recreation and the City

In acerbic mood, D. H. Lawrence wrote that 'the English are town-birds through and through. . . . Yet they don't know how to build a city, how to think of one, or how to live in one.'[1] Town-birds they certainly remain. In simple numerical terms, the 1981 Census recorded 77 per cent of the population of England and Wales as living in towns,[2] and of this 46 per cent was in Greater London and the towns and cities of the six metropolitan counties.

The pattern, however, is changing. Between 1971 and 1981 the actual number of urban dwellers declined slightly, from 38.4 to 37.7 million (a loss of 1.9 per cent, compared with a gain of 0.5 per cent for the population as a whole). More significant has been the concentration of population losses in the large cities, and in their inner areas in particular, and the spread of gains over smaller towns. Greater London lost 10 per cent overall in the decade (with 18 per cent from the inner London boroughs) and the major conurbations more than 8 per cent (with 25 per cent in Salford, 21 per cent in Gateshead, 17 per cent in Manchester and 16 per cent in Liverpool and Bootle). Outside the conurbations, the population of towns grew by some 559,000, but those with over 100,000 population actually lost a total of 110,000, leaving a gain of 670,000 for towns with less than 100,000 population. Increases characterised not only outer suburban communities, new towns and areas of planned overspill but many small, free-standing towns. Notable examples included Leighton Linslade and Witham (increase 46 per cent), Guisborough and Royston (43 per cent) and St Neots, Minehead and Ashby de la Zouch (39 per cent).

In the same decade, the population in rural areas increased by almost exactly one million, a gain of virtually 10 per cent. Here, however, the limitations of Census data are clearly evident: as the Census report acknowledges, 'it seems likely that growth has been concentrated around small towns and large villages and in the more accessible parts, while other parts have experienced depopulation.'[3] The overall picture remains, therefore, of population loss at the two extremities of the settlement spectrum – the inner cities and the remote rural areas – and of high growth in leafy suburbs and small towns. Town-birds we continue to be, albeit tied in lesser numbers to the crowded fabric of our Victorian forebears.

In recreation terms, therefore, the vast majority of leisure time is spent in an urban setting. This is not only because the majority of homes lie within towns, and because 70 per cent of leisure is spent at home, but because many other leisure activities are typically pursued in a local – and therefore urban – setting. The constraints are not only of time, in the short periods of leisure available in the working day, but also of resources, for the facilities needed for most social, cultural and sporting recreations outside the home are typically found within the built-up area, close to the major sources of demand.

This evident truism needs early emphasis. In the past, geographers, with their inherently spatial interests, have tended to concentrate on outdoor recreation in rural areas, where spatial demands, and spatial conflicts, have been greatest.[4] The concentration, while having some justification in disciplinary terms, has tended to perpetuate a false dichotomy between urban and rural recreation. For many recreation seekers, the distinction lies not so much between town and countryside settings as between local and distant pursuits. This chapter concentrates on patterns of recreation and recreation resources found typically in an urban context, but many are distinct for their local setting rather than for a peculiarly urban quality.

RECREATION AND THE HOME

Paradoxically, the greatest changes in recreation habits in the last fifty years have taken place in two opposing directions. High personal mobility has extended opportunities away from home and brought a growing complexity to the scale and direction of leisure patterns. Conversely, the home has come to provide a far greater range of leisure opportunities, and home-centred leisure has acquired a still greater significance. That significance is rooted in three complementary trends. The family has become socially more self-sufficient, its links with the immediate community and with its own extended kinship network weaker. Social independence has been underpinned by the greater physical independence of homes in the expanding suburban communities; by the weakening need for communal space that comes with lower housing densities and the command of greater private space. Social and physical independence has been compounded by the growing range and sophistication of entertainment within the home. Despite its self-evident importance, however, home-centred leisure is still but little researched and there remain major gaps in our understanding of it. Most existing work concentrates on the use of time and on individual activities; patterns of recreation within and around the home, and their relationship to its physical characteristics, remain largely uncharted territory.[5]

The dominance of home-based leisure in time terms has already been stressed, and that dominance shows no sign of slackening. On the contrary, as figure 3.3 made clear, the time devoted to active hobbies in the home increased by 17 per cent between 1964 and 1974-75 even if the time spent in more passive recreations remained largely the same. Overall averages, however, mask wide variations, variations typically through the life-cycle as well as between individuals and differing sections of society.

For the life-cycle, the variations are clearly evident in the BBC time budget survey data of the mid-1970s (figure 4.1). Adolescents are the least home-centred sector of the population. Independence is signified by activity outside the home, and peer-groups rather than parents are the stronger influence. Contemporary youth is not only independent, but relatively affluent: much commercial leisure is aimed at the substantial spending power of this group, with pubs, clubs, discos and cafes vying to provide a venue for its activities.

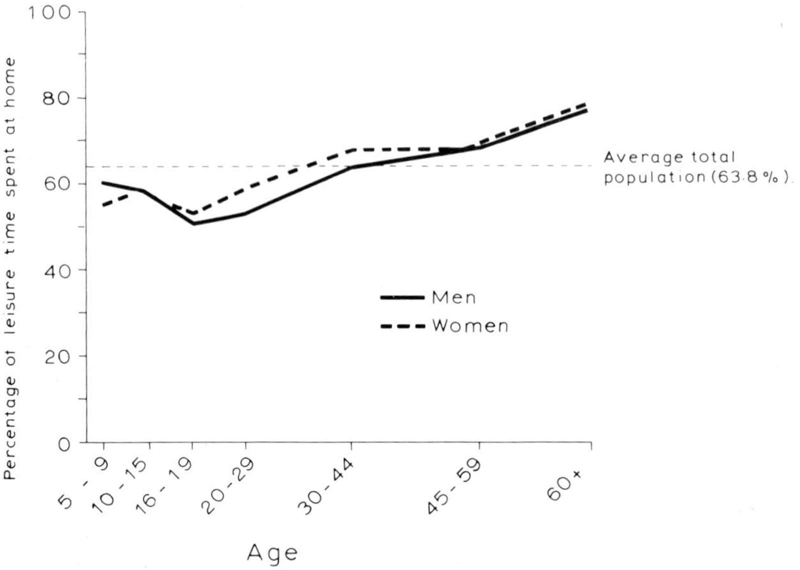

FIGURE 4.1 Leisure time spent at home as a percentage of all leisure time, 1974-75.
Source: data from *The people's activities and use of time* (British Broadcasting Corporation, 1978)

With marriage and a family, the significance of home, and of home-focused leisure, rapidly increases, along with the chores that house and children bring. It is scarcely surprising that this trend is more marked for women than men, for men typically give up fewer out-of-home leisure pursuits after marriage. As the children grow the disparity becomes less marked, but there is no lessening in the importance of the home as the venue for the majority of leisure time. For the over-60s, life becomes even more home-centred. At first there is a growth of home-based hobbies and gardening, but the ties of home are often enforced later by declining finances, health and mobility.

While these broad trends are clear enough, variations between different groups in society have received little attention. It is evident that, far beyond the life-cycle distinctions already outlined, the variations are considerable. For one group of countryside visitors, diary studies showed that an average 56 per cent of their time was spent at home, but for as many as one in four that figure rose to 70 per cent.[6] Much more needs to be known of the scale of these differences and of their relationship to the physical and social environment of the home and to the number and nature of home leisure resources possessed.

Domestic leisure resources have become both more numerous and more ubiquitous. The simple pleasures of the Victorian home – book or embroidery by gaslight, or music shared round the upright piano – pale before the typical leisure inventory of a century later. The lengthening list includes radio and television, record players and video recorders, micro-computers, musical instruments in profusion harnessing a range of skills, and books and magazines for every conceivable interest and taste. Hobby equipment underpins more individual tastes; saunas, sun-ray lamps and exercise machines blend health and pleasure for a growing minority. The home itself becomes not only setting but focus. The home-making ethic has raised DIY activities from a chore to a creative and pleasurable endeavour for many. Commercial pressures have spurred technical innovation: non-drip paints, ready-pasted wallpapers and tools designed specifically for easy use by the hobbyist have helped to bring satisfying results for the average handyman. In 1980 almost £2 billion was spent on DIY products:[7] in 1978 householders in Britain pasted nearly 1 million kilometres of wallpaper to their walls and used about 100 million litres of paint.[8]

The scale of home-based activity, at least in a commercial context, is relatively well documented, but the actual use of space within the home for carrying out these activities has received little attention. Such space must be considered in terms of extent, equipment and management. The changing nature of the housing stock is shown in table 4.1. The bulk of change came prior to 1970. Semi-detached and detached houses now

TABLE 4.1 Housing types in Great Britain, 1947–80

Housing type	1947	*Percentage of total* 1971	1977	1980
Flats and tenements	12	21	22	21
Terrace	45	30	28	30
Semi-detached	30	33	32	32
Detached	13	16	17	17

Source: Social Trends 10 (1980), p. 27 and *Social Trends 12* (1982), table 8.3

account for virtually half the total. The major change has been the decline in the proportion of terrace housing and the increase in flats. Much of this stems from the postwar clearance of Victorian (and earlier) close-packed terraces and their replacement by other forms. A substantial part of this replacement in the 1960s, especially in local authority housing, was in high-rise flats – until, with the accumulation of social and structural problems, this form fell rapidly out of favour: by 1978 only 2 per cent of all housing completions were of this type. Low-rise, compact forms returned in greater abundance: the honest terrace or the euphemistic town house once more makes up a growing share of the housing stock.

Types of housing tenure have changed as markedly as types of dwelling (table 4.2). Tenancies in the private sector have dropped from over half to only one-eighth of the total, while owner-occupied houses have increased from less than a third to well over half. Local authority tenancies now account for almost one-third overall.

These figures are of interest not only in themselves but in their implications for the availability of space for the individual and for the level and standard of equipment within that space. The increase in the overall stock of housing by 55 per cent between 1950 and 1980 reflects the

TABLE 4.2 Housing tenure in Great Britain, 1950–80

Type of tenure	*1950*	*Percentage of total* *1960*	*1970*	*1980*
Owner-occupied	29	42	50	55
Rented from local authorities	18	27	30	32
Rented from private and other owners	53	31	20	13
Total housing stock (thousands)	13,900	16,215	19,180	21,540

Source: Social Trends 1 (1970), table 90 and *Social Trends 12* (1982), table 8.2

growing number of households and the consequent decrease in average household size, from 3.37 to 2.68 over the same period. An even better measure of changing space standards for the individual is seen in the number of people per room. For larger households, the changes have been dramatic. In 1951, 24 per cent of households with five or more people were living at densities of more than 1.5 people to each room in the dwelling, but by 1977 the figure was only 2 per cent. In 1977 only 3 per cent of all households lived at a density of more than one person per room.[9]

The increase in available space has been matched by an increase in amenities in the home. The widespread adoption of central heating has made the usage of space much more flexible; in the 1970s alone the number of centrally heated homes increased from 34 to 57 per cent of all households. Of course, the trend has been far from uniform over all tenures. Not surprisingly, the proportion is highest among owner-occupied dwellings – 68 per cent in 1980 – but even here there are interesting distinctions: in those dwellings owned outright the level is 58 per cent, but it is 75 per cent in those where a mortgage or loan is still being paid off, suggesting higher standards among the younger age groups who have more recently acquired a home. In local authority housing the level doubled, from less than a quarter to almost half the total stock, between 1971 and 1980: there was a similar rate of increase in the privately rented sector, but even now central heating is available to only about one-third of such tenants.[10]

The extent of space available to the individual in the home, and the character of the equipment in it, can be readily established from existing data, at least in general outline. The real problem, from the point of view of leisure studies, is the paucity of information about the management and use of this space and equipment. Official concern and design guidance has concentrated almost exclusively on standards for space and equipment. An honourable exception was the Report of the Parker-Morris Committee, published in 1961,[11] where the functional needs for leisure were not neglected. The paradoxes of family life were clearly recognised: 'the design must be such as to provide reasonable individual and group privacy as well as facilities for family life as part of a community of friends and relations.' The overall management problem in a leisure context was succinctly stated:

> At every stage in the life of the family the home has to provide for an extremely wide range of activities; and even when bedrooms come to be put to wider daytime and evening use, living areas in the family home will still be in use for children's play, homework, watching television, sewing and mending, hobbies, entertaining friends, and dealing with casual callers, often with two or more of these activities going on at once.

In subsequent years, Parker-Morris standards became a measure of attainment rather than departure, as space standards, and aspirations, were eroded by inflation in land prices and in labour and building costs. Above all, there has been virtually no development of specialised recreation space – the 'family room' or the games basement, typical of much North American suburban housing.

The actual use of space for leisure in the home remains largely uncharted research territory, and the effects of the opportunities and constraints posed by its physical characteristics are little known. Not only is simple descriptive evidence of expressed demand required, but also a much clearer understanding of motives, satisfactions and frustrations. Hitherto, all concepts of recreational abundance and disadvantage have been rooted in assessments of the recreational environment beyond the home, but that of the home itself may be of equal importance to both the family group and the individual within the family.

For many, the home environment is not contained by the walls of the dwelling alone, but also includes a measure of private external space: the garden. Here again, evidence of scale, equipment, role and use is sadly limited, and the time is overdue for a study comparable to that of Halkett in Adelaide.[12] The 'garden city' movement of the late nineteenth century spurred the provision of gardens much further down the social scale of dwellings, a movement stimulated still more by the rapid suburban sprawl of the interwar years. By 1944, 66 per cent of dwellings in England and Wales had gardens, a figure that has now risen to some 80 per cent.[13] The most recent general study of garden size and use dates back to 1964: at that time, only 1 garden in 25 exceeded 0.2 ha in extent, three-quarters were less than 0.1 ha and more than half (including the space taken up by house, garage and outbuildings) were less than 0.025 ha, or a plot measuring some 15 m×15 m.

In a leisure context, gardens have a threefold function. They serve, firstly, as an extension to the house itself, giving additional space for ancillary household activities such as keeping pets, storing equipment or car maintenance. Second, they provide space for outdoor recreation, whether passive pursuits like sunbathing or active games. Third, the garden itself may be the focus of recreation (if gardening is perceived as such), both in its maintenance and in the aesthetic satisfaction that its appearance provides. There are few data available on the extent and detailed nature of these activities. The role of the garden changes not only between households with differing interests and aspirations, but for the same household as its composition changes (figure 4.2) Its significance as a safe place for children's play is particularly important, and it is scarcely unexpected that interest in gardening is in inverse proportion to the number of young children in the household.

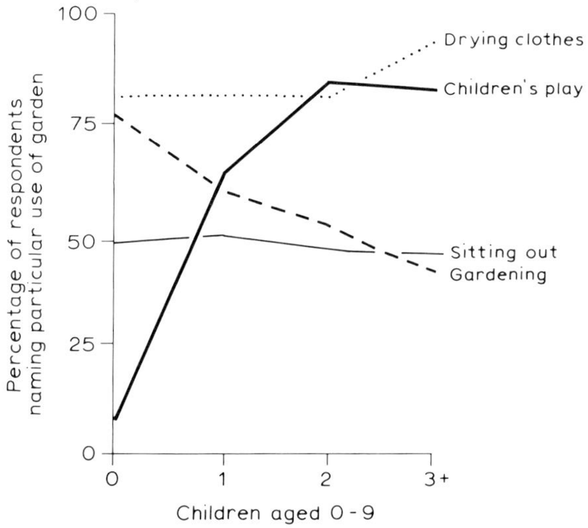

FIGURE 4.2 The effect of young children in the houshold on the use of the garden.
Source: based on J. A. Cook, 'Gardens on housing estates', *Town Planning Review*, 39 (1969), pp. 217-34, figure 12

More needs to be known about the effect of garden size on garden use, and whether there are significant thresholds below which a particular function is less appropriate. One study of gardens on housing estates in widely varying areas showed that the number of young children in a family strongly influenced attitudes to garden size, but only when the garden is relatively small.[14] For households with gardens of up to 75 m^2, 85 per cent of those with three or more children of nine and under thought their garden was too small, compared with 47 per cent of those with one or two children. At around 85 m^2, the larger families were not markedly more critical of lack of space, though over 100 m^2 was needed before the general level of dissatisfaction fell below 25 per cent. The proportion regarding their gardens as too big was negligible until sizes exceeded 130 m^2.

Gardening as a recreation is less dependent on size for satisfaction, for approaches can be adjusted to match the space available. If food production rather than visual appearance is the prime requirement, however, space needs are more rigorous. In 1964 almost half of all gardens (48 per cent) had vegetable plots: in larger gardens (*c.* 1000 m^2) they were found in two out of three of the sample. In this context, the role of allotments must not be overlooked. In areal terms, they reached a peak of 57,900 ha in England and Wales during the Second World War, but by 1965 they had declined to some 28,000 ha: in number of plots, the decline was from 1,450,000 to 635,000 over the same period.[15] They still represent, however, a major resource for those with gardening interests that cannot, for space or other reasons, be satisfied by a garden adjacent to their dwelling.

In the last two decades, garden use has changed a great deal, though detailed evidence is not available. One indication of new approaches has been the rise of the garden centre. The first of these in a contemporary context date only from the late 1960s, but there are now an estimated 600 such centres in Britain. In one sense, these have become recreation attractions in their own right, with up to 200,000 visits being made to each in the course of a year.[16]

URBAN RECREATION HIERARCHIES

The household's private space in home and garden is only the first stage in a whole hierarchy of space for leisure use within the urban fabric. When homes were more cramped and communities more closely knit, the boundary between private and public space was less rigorously drawn, for the street was a prime place for play, contemplation and social intercourse. For children, at least

> the street is no further than their front door, and they are within call when tea is ready. Indeed the street in front of their home is seemingly theirs, more theirs sometimes than the family living room, and of more significance to them, very often, than any amenity provided by the local council.[17]

The intimacy and informality of such space still exercise a powerful attraction. A study of children's play in the early 1970s emphasised both the relatively high proportion of children playing unsupervised outdoors and the importance of informal rather than formal play space.

> The healthy, unrepressed child has tremendous physical energy which cannot find sufficient outlet indoors . . . The child needs outdoor space to develop basic physical skills, such as running, jumping, balancing; and also to meet his friends . . . In an ideal world mothers would have the time and inclination to see that these demands were met irrespective of their physical surroundings.[18]

In practice, on the recently built local authority estates studied, no more than 30 per cent of the under-fives playing outdoors were seen with adults, and it was less than 10 per cent on more than half the estates. Half, however, were with children from older age groups. Of all children aged 0–10 living on the estates, an average of 25 per cent were playing outdoors at any one time during the school holidays: the average rose to 30 per cent when low-rise estates alone were considered.[19]

TABLE 4.3 Observed location of children's play (percentage of all children 0–15 playing outdoors)

	Type of estate Low-rise	Medium-rise	Mixed-rise
Roads and Pavements	39	11	9
Paved areas	24	41	23
Internal access areas	—	23	40
Grassed open space	10	7	8
Gardens	18	2	1
Play areas	4	11	13
Other areas	10	10	20

Source: Department of the Environment, *Children at play* (HMSO, 1973), figure 28

It is the place as much as the fact of play that is important in the present context. Location is more important than form (table 4.3). On the estates with houses, two-fifths of the children were playing on the adjacent roads and pavements: in a parallel study of an area of older terraced housing in Oldham, 54 per cent of all play was on the roads and pavements. In the more complex mixed-rise estates, the access areas immediately outside the dwellings were the most important single area; in the medium-rise estates, it was the paved areas threading through the dwellings. The importance for play of the areas immediately adjacent to the home, seen by the child as a simple extension of domestic living space, is emphasised by the relatively low popularity of spaces formally designed for play; while their exact location, their size and the nature of their equipment markedly affects their use, their overall role was surprisingly small. Even the short journey to them from the immediate domestic environment appeared to act as a strong deterrent. Conversely, the relatively low use of gardens when they were available seemed to relate to the details of both design and location: the space might not be suitable for unfettered play, and it could too easily separate the child from other friends.

Patterns of children's play emphasise the importance of location in any consideration of urban recreation outside the home. Once away from the immediate domestic environment, a 'journey to play' becomes a necessity, and the willingness to make the journey is balanced against the attraction of a particular facility. The obvious result is the creation of a hierarchy of facilities, comparable with hierarchies of retailing and other services, with each facility having a distinctive catchment area relating to the users' willingness and ability to travel to it.

For some facilities, the catchment is local by necessity, with users unable, or unwilling, to travel far to use them. Constraints may be of time or of distance. An informal open space in the city centre may have particular value for a lunch-time stroll, when the time available between periods of work is insufficient to reach a larger park. Young children and old people may have time in plenty, but their inability to travel far independently limits the extent of their movement. Even with children, however, the constraints may not be purely physical: in the words of the Design Bulletin,

> apart from parental concern about letting children stray too far, during school term at least, with all the competing activities which take place inside the home, the children have little time to travel far to play spaces. A child's play environment is extremely circumscribed and neighbourhood provision, however near, is no realistic substitute for play areas which children can use casually at any time without relying on adults or older brothers and sisters to take them there.[20]

For other facilities, the scale of demand is such that there is a high level of provision, and in consequence, location is local by tradition rather than necessity. This is true for many of the most popular sports (figure 4.3), where the requirement is for pitches and courts of relatively modest extent, rather than the more specialised or space-absorbing needs of such activities as angling or golf. The devotee of football or tennis rarely has to travel far to satisfy the wish for a game, though many may choose to travel

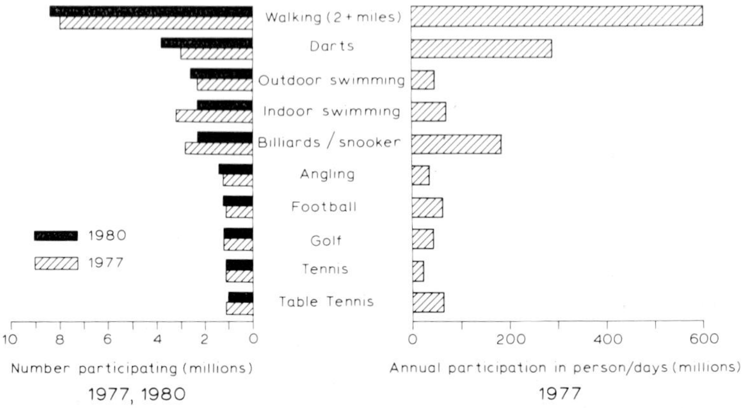

FIGURE 4.3 The ten most popular sports by numbers participating, 1977 and 1980. The data are derived from the General Household Survey and cover people aged 16 and over. 'Participation' is defined as participation within one month of the interview during the most popular quarter of the year for the sport.
Source: data from B. S. Duffield, J. P. Best and M. F. Collins (eds.), *Digest of sports statistics* (Sports Council, 1983), table 1

further than they need in order to play with a particular club of their choice. For example, Liverpool's public parks and playgrounds provide a close network of sports facilities, but many participants travel twice as far as the distance to their nearest ground to play, and in the case of football more than four times as far[21] (figure 4.4).

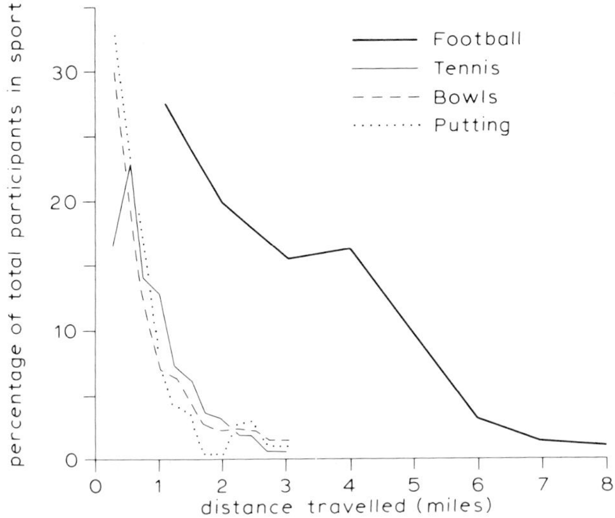

FIGURE 4.4 The distance travelled to sports facilities in Liverpool parks. *Source:* data from K. R. Balmer, *Open space in Liverpool* (Liverpool Corporation, 1973)

Some facilities are much less numerous and of necessity serve a far wider catchment. A single facility, such as a theatre or a large indoor sports centre, may be enough to satisfy the needs of a medium-sized town. Other facilities may need an extensive area or a more specialised kind of space – a golf course or an area of water for sailing – and their location may be related more closely to the nature of supply than to the intensity of demand. In the latter case, provision is increasingly in a rural setting beyond the limits of the built-up urban area, though the demand is for adequate space at reasonable cost rather than a rural setting as such.

These examples of locational constraints emphasise the hierarchical nature of the arrangement of recreation facilities with, in an urban context, specific facilities serving neighbourhood, local or city-wide populations. Most facilities operate typically at one level in the hierarchy – playground, tennis club or art gallery, for example, at neighbourhood, local or city-wide levels respectively. A few, more varied in scope or form, are less easily characterised: urban parks range from simple grassed areas with no more than neighbourhood appeal to large expanses with a wide range of specialised facilities serving the whole of the city.

LOCATION AND ACCESS

Patterns of facility use are not related to location alone: effective access is not synonymous with convenience of location. Barriers to access are numerous, but may be categorised under four heads.

Physical barriers preclude access through the infirmities of age or the lack of independence of children. The barrier is not simply that of distance but the nature of the intervening space. A main road, with no ready provision for pedestrians crossing, may effectively seal off an open space from use even though it is readily visible from the other side.

Financial barriers impose a direct economic constraint to access, either because of the high level of equipment costs or because of the high level of admission charges. The latter in particular raise social and political as well as economic issues, especially where public sector provision is concerned. As chapter 1 emphasised, public sector provision is often as much a matter of historic legacy as of conscious policy: charging policies owe equally as much to accident and tradition as to logic (figure 1.9). Some facilities, such as town parks, have traditionally been provided free of charge; some, such as swimming baths, have recouped through admission charges only a small proportion of the cost of provision; and some, such as municipal golf courses, have sought to recover from users most, if not all, of the costs involved. Attempts to change policies meet fierce opposition, as the Conservative government of the early 1970s found when it attempted to impose admission charges for national museums and art galleries.

The problem has been seen in particularly stark form in the new generation of local authority indoor sports centres. Pricing policies vary widely, reflecting not only different styles of centre management but the different financial philosophies of the authorities concerned. Table 4.4, though dated, gives some indication of the range of charges, and indicates the wide differential between centres and between the sports provided at the centres. For some, even the most modest charge represents a major barrier: as a Department of the Environment report commented, 'the policy to provide sport and recreation facilities for the "whole community" has not benefited the disadvantaged, who make proportionally less use of them, more particularly the sports centres which are mainly catering for the "better off".'[22]

Financial barriers are often reinforced by *social barriers*. As the same report continues, 'various experiments have been tried to attract those from the lower socio-economic groups into sports centres but they have not generally been successful. By emphasising the need to keep prices low, insufficient attention has been given to institutional barriers.' The social

TABLE 4.4 Variations in charges at 50 indoor sports centres, 1973*

Sport	*Average cost (p)*	*Highest cost (p)*	*Lowest cost (p)*
Badminton	23	46	10
Tennis	64	107	25
Five-a-side Football	24	41	8
Volleyball	18	29	4
Netball	18	29	5
Basketball	23	40	8
Weight training	23	46	9
Table tennis	18	38	8
Cricket net	21	42	6
Squash	42	93	17

* All costs relate to the cost per person for one hour's play, at peak periods and to adult non-members.
Source: data from L.C. Thomasson, *Admission charges to indoor sports centres* (Sports Council, undated), table 4

context of many recreational activities is an important part of their enjoyment, but if an individual feels uncomfortable in that social context, enjoyment will be seriously impaired. Many activities have an image that inhibits participation by the uninitiated, opera-going and golf being cases in point. Changes in image are most often associated with activities with low financial barriers. This has been particularly the case with many active countryside pursuits, with climbing perhaps the most noted example.

The fourth barrier – *transport* – is in many ways the most powerful, and the most selective. Car ownership is as important in the local, urban context as in the wider context of countryside activities.[23] The possession of a car not only increases the likelihood of participation,[24] but enables a greater range of facilities to be reached with ease. The perceived cost to the car-owner of a short recreational journey in the car is extremely low, and is rarely a deterrent factor in itself. Time is more often an important constraint. For most local recreational activities, a journey time of some 20 minutes is often regarded as a reasonable limit: for the traveller on foot, this limits the range to 1.6 km, but by car it is extended to some 6-8 km (table 4.5). The car user, in consequence, has a much wider range of facilities he views as 'local', and this frequently means that he can choose between alternative facilities of the same kind. A premium is then placed on better-quality facilities as patterns of use become more selective.

One glimpse of this was given in a 'before and after' study of the effect of the replacement in Ashton-under-Lyne of an obsolete Victorian swimming pool with a modern pool in 1975.[25] Within a five-mile radius of

TABLE 4.5 Travel mode, journey time and journey distance, as percentage of all users of Harlow Sportcentre, 1968 and 1973

	1968	*1973*
Travel by car	66	77
Travel on foot	17	15
Journey time less than 22 min.	85	83
Journey distance less than 1·6 km (users aged over 20)	34	30
Journey distance less than 1·6 km (users aged under 20)	54	41

Source: data from Built Environment Research Group, *The changing indoor sports centre: users and usage at Harlow, 1968 and 1973* (Sports Council Study 13, 1977), tables 26 and 27, and p. 53

Ashton, there were 16 other pools of various sizes, amenities and ages, and six of these were included in the study. At Ashton, the new pool not only increased usage by 100 per cent or more, but also attracted a higher proportion of users from greater distances. Only 12 per cent of the users of the old pool had travelled more than 3.2 km, but that proportion rose to 24 per cent in 1975. In the surrounding pools, the mean proportion travelling more than that distance dropped from 15 to 10 per cent over the same period.

RESOURCE INVENTORIES AND PATTERNS

Any consideration of recreation within towns is concerned not only with the idea of hierarchies in the location of facilities and with the factors that inhibit the individual's access to particular facilities, but also with the highly varied pattern of actual facility provision. An immediate problem is the frequent lack of sufficient evidence to establish that pattern in any precise and comprehensive manner. The evidence has been gathered in some areas,[26] but rarely in a form that permits ready comparisons at national level.

Several opportunities have been squandered. In the mid-1960s, the government suggested that local authorities should review their areas to determine what provision existed for sport and recreation and what future requirements should be.[27] Close on the heels of this suggestion came the creation of the advisory Sports Council in 1965, and the consequent Regional Sports Councils were used to co-ordinate surveys of facilities within their respective areas. Unfortunately, the surveys were neither uniform in their treatment nor wide-ranging in their topics: they were of limited use for compiling national inventories or for ready comparisons between regions.[28]

A decade later, the same mistake was repeated. Department of the Environment Circular 47/76, *Regional Councils for Sport and Recreation* (1976), not only established these councils as successors to the Regional Sports Councils and with a wider remit, but laid on them the requirement 'to promote the preparation of broad, long-term proposals for the planned provision of sport and recreation facilities on a region-wide basis (a "regional recreation strategy")'. Unfortunately, the guidelines for preparing the strategies gave little direct guidance on approaches and methods, and in consequence not only do the strategies themselves differ widely in scope and scale, but the detailed studies on which they are based are again an inadequate basis for national inventories or interregional comparisons.[29]

The problems are the result of more than a simple lack of detailed direction. Surveys are made at different dates. Sports are not only numerous, but have widely varying facility requirements, many of an informal and inherently unrecorded nature. Facility provision ranges across public, commercial, voluntary and private sectors: should an inventory record all facilities or only those available to the public at large? If the former, problems of data acquisition are almost insuperable in many sports: if the latter, a substantial share of local provision is ignored. There are basic problems of definition: when, for example, does an indoor hall with a wide variety of community uses become an indoor sports hall, and what size has a sports hall to reach for recognition as a sports centre?

Figure 4.5 illustrates both the opportunities and the limitations of such data: it could be repeated, though not in directly comparable form, for the area of each regional council. In any interpretation, several caveats about the form and provenance of the data must be made. They relate to different years, and have been compiled as aggregate data for local authority districts: individual sports halls and squash courts are identified, but not individual golf courses. Data for sports halls are derived from returns from local authorities: they exclude community halls such as school gymnasia, village halls and church halls, for which there is no formal record but which make a substantial contribution to the available facilities for some indoor sports. Data for golf courses and squash courts are derived from governing body information and questionnaires circulated to clubs. Questionnaire returns are not complete, and while there is no reason to doubt the simple tally of facilities, a more detailed analysis of, for example, the extent of membership and of waiting lists is not possible.

Despite these reservations, maps of this kind bear important lessons for facility planning. Disparities between districts clearly emerge when facility provision is expressed in terms of population per facility: for

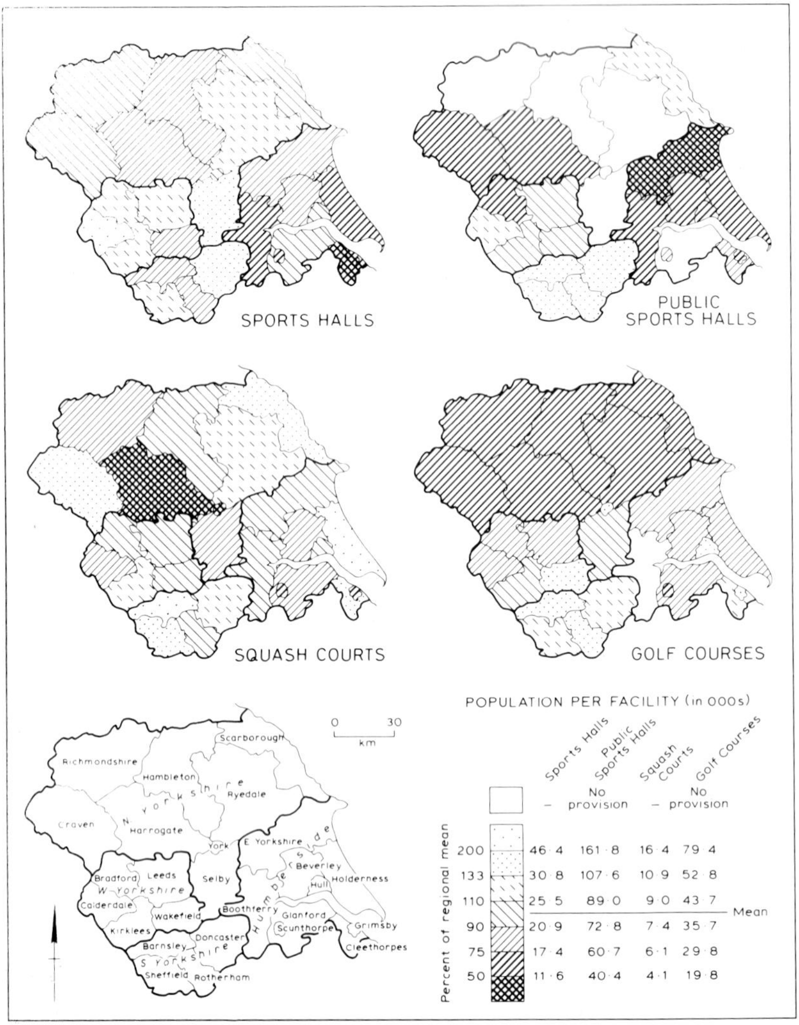

FIGURE 4.5 Sports facilities, Yorkshire and Humberside. Sports halls include those exceeding 350 m^2 in area. 'Public' sports halls are those operated by the local authority for public use, including joint provision schemes with local education authorities, and by voluntary bodies. Halls operated by education authorities and private bodies are included on the general map of sports halls irrespective of the degree of wider public use. Data relate to 1980 (squash courts and golf courses) and 1981 (sports halls).
Source: data from *Facility provision – golf courses* (Yorkshire and Humberside Council for Sport and Recreation, 1980); *Facility provision – squash courts* (Yorkshire and Humberside Council for Sport and Recreation, 1980); *Facility provision – sports halls* (Yorkshire and Humberside Council for Sport and Recreation, 1981); and Office of Population Censuses and Surveys Census 1981, *Preliminary Report, England and Wales* (HMSO, 1981)

squash, for example, the range is from 3640 people per court in the Harrogate district to 22,350 people per court in Holderness. The recommended level of provision, based on current demand, is one court per 7000 population in urban areas and one court per 5000 population in rural areas. On this basis, 23 of the 26 districts in Yorkshire and Humberside were underprovided, with the deficiency particularly serious (and provision less than half the regional mean) in the Holderness, Barnsley, Scarborough, Craven, Cleethorpes and Sheffield districts.

Some patterns reflect the particular character of a sport. Golf provision is much above average in all the districts of North Yorkshire, except for York and Selby: this not only reflects the high demand of a relatively prosperous, rural-based population, but the comparatively few courses needed for an adequate level of provision when actual population is low. In the county, only the Harrogate district has as many as five courses. Ryedale and Richmondshire have two each, but in both cases, the population of the district is less than 50,000. In contrast, South Yorkshire has virtually the same number of courses as North Yorkshire, but they must serve more than double the number of population.

The complexities of assessing the adequacy of provision are well illustrated by the maps of sports halls. These halls vary widely in size, and in the range of sports they can offer:[30] of the 209 in the region, 145 are small halls of less than 550 m^2. Even more important is the variation in access: only 60 of the 209 are open in some measure for use by the general public. The map of public sports halls shows many areas of North Yorkshire, for example, devoid of provision, though some provision is available for those who may be at school, or members of a private club or working for a particular firm. Again, in other areas where provision seems adequate, restriction on the size of hall may limit both the number of sports that can be played and the intensity with which the hall can be used.

Much of the evidence, therefore, even when it is available, must be interpreted with caution. In the bigger cities and conurbations, it is not only provision as such that is significant, but also the location of that provision within the urban fabric if there is to be ready accessibility. The case of London may be unique in scale, but is an apt illustration of the different kinds of pattern that emerge. In this instance, inventory data are remarkably complete, being gathered in 1972 for the Greater London Recreation Study. While there have been changes in absolute provision since the inventory was compiled, the relative patterns remain relevant.

In figure 4.6, three quite distinct kinds of pattern emerge. Theatres, museums, exhibition halls, concert halls and art galleries cluster largely at the centre of the conurbation. Their function is city-wide: many, indeed, serve a national and international catchment, and are firmly at the top of the recreation hierarchy. Swimming pools, in contrast, are far more

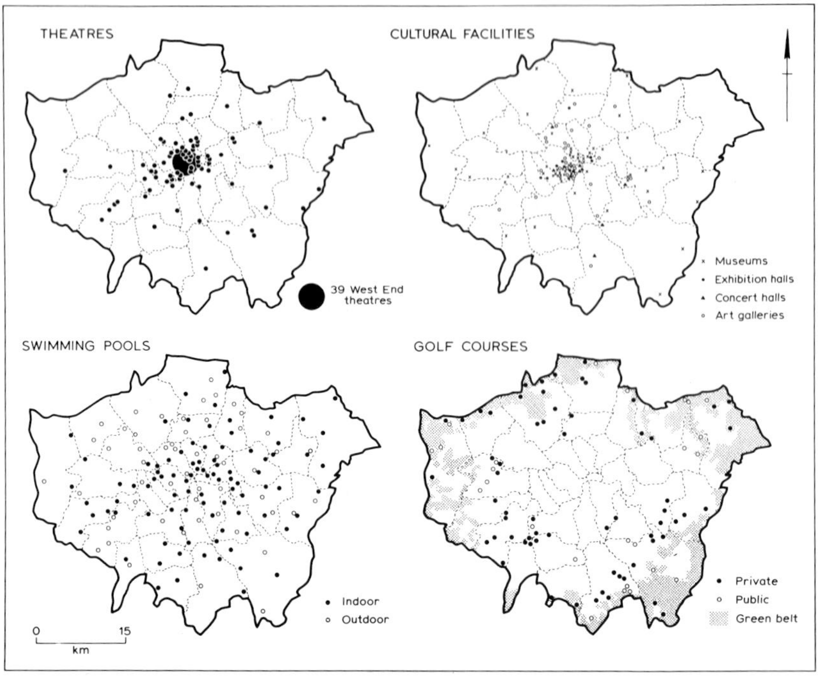

FIGURE 4.6 The distribution of theatres, other cultural facilities, swimming pools and golf courses in Greater London, 1972.
Source: data from *Greater London Recreation Study, Part 3, Supply Study* (Greater London Council, Research Report 19, 1976), pp. 95-6, 102-3

widespread: their function is essentially local, their requirements for space comparatively modest. Golf courses show a characteristically peripheral distribution. Their catchment is relatively local, though to nothing like the same extent as swimming pools, but their space requirements (of some 40 ha as a minimum for an 18 hole course) dictate a peripheral location with lower land costs.

Similar contrasts emerge in figure 4.7, where distributions are related to population. Even in London, with its major central parks, open space provision is well below the mean in almost the whole of the inner London area, with the most notable deficiencies in the inner areas of east and south London. The opposite is characteristic of the outer boroughs, with far more generous provision in the less densely developed areas towards the periphery. For public houses, almost the reverse is true. Throughout most of the outer boroughs, provision is at a remarkably constant level, suggesting supply carefully matched commercially to the little changing demand of the largely residential areas. Towards the centre, however, public houses serve a wider clientele, with the lunch-time needs of city workers and the demands of visitors justifying a far greater provision.

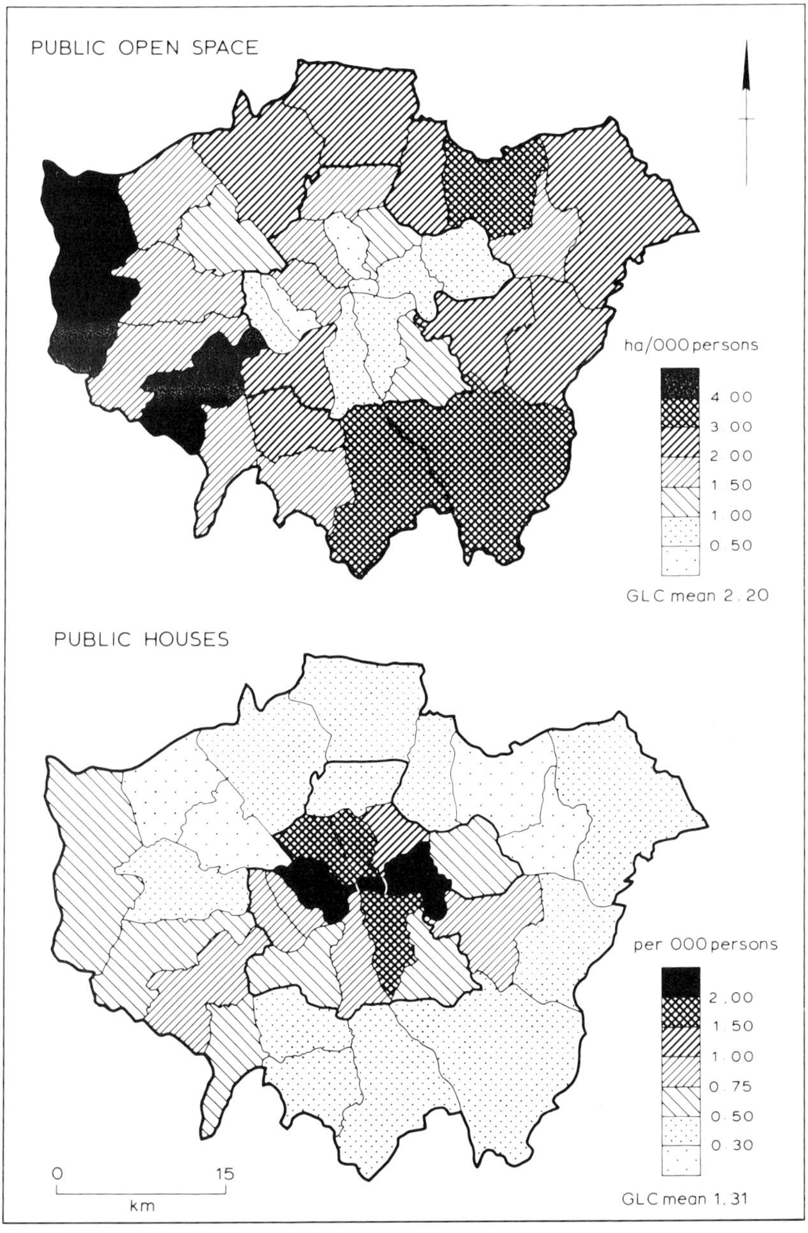

FIGURE 4.7 The density of provision of public open space and public houses in the Greater London boroughs, 1972. The inner London area is delineated by the heavier boundary line.

Source: data from *Greater London Recreation Study, Part 3, Supply Study* (Greater London Council, Research Report 19, 1976), table 5.6 and p. 100

CAPITAL-INTENSIVE FACILITIES

The location of facilities within the urban fabric deserves a closer look, though space forbids more than a selective review. Facilities may be divided into two broad groups: those with relatively modest land requirements but a high capital cost, and those where the land requirement is far more extensive. Swimming pools and sports centres are characteristic of the first group, parks and golf courses of the second.

Swimming pools are the earliest example of large-scale, indoor sports facilities. As noted in chapter 1, they sprang initially not so much from a concern to provide for sport as such as from a recognition of their potential in improving public health and cleanliness. By 1870, for example, Liverpool had nine indoor and four outdoor public baths, and 14 indoor school baths.[31] Growth in numbers has been continuous for over a century, with 964 in use in England by 1981.[32] Particular bursts of activity were evident between 1881 and 1914, with 322 completed, and between 1971 and 1981, with 524 added.[33]

This relatively generous provision has helped to make swimming by far the most popular of active indoor sports. Even so, the use of swimming pools shows marked disparities in age and sex.[34] The great majority of users are under 20: 71 per cent for all pools, and 73 per cent for pre-1939 pools. Male swimmers outnumber female by 3:2, a proportion that rises as high as 7.6:2 amongst single people in the 20-24 age group. There is little change in these characteristics in the most recent free-form leisure pools: one study at Bletchley found that 76 per cent of users were under 16, though among adult users, at least, the proportion of men to women was 1.6:2, perhaps a reflection of the need to supervise young children.[35]

With such a high proportion of juvenile users, it is no surprise that catchment areas are restricted: 54 per cent of all users travel from within 3 km. For older pools, the concentration is even more marked: 71 per cent of the users of pre-1939 pools travelled from within 3 km, 42 per cent from within 1 km. When the measure is time rather than distance, the concentration is equally marked: 81 per cent of all users had travel times of 22 minutes or less, 50 per cent, 12 minute or less. For pre-1939 pools, the figures were 89 and 64 per cent, respectively. Again, with the age profile of users in mind, the relatively subordinate role played by the car in transport to the pool is unsurprising – 40 per cent for all pools, 21 per cent for the pre-1939 pools. Conversely, 26 per cent used buses, and 31 per cent walked or cycled: at the older pools, these figures were 32 and 46 per cent respectively.

The swimming pool, therefore, functions as an essentially local facility with a comparatively restricted catchment, and with a particular appeal for younger age groups. This poses obvious problems for provision, as swimming pools are expensive both to provide and to maintain, with revenue providing on average less than one-fifth of their costs. None the less, the overall popularity of swimming has continued to justify the building of new pools and the refurbishment of austere Victorian examples: in this context it is comforting to recognise the attraction of new pools, and the extent to which their users will pay higher admission charges and travel further to benefit from the higher-quality facilities they provide.[36]

Indoor sports centres afford some interesting contrasts, though many incorporate swimming pools in the facilities they offer. The concept of the large, multi-sport indoor centre is comparatively recent. Prior to 1970, they were highly sporadic in occurrence, with only Teesside offering anything approaching widespread provision (figure 4.8). As noted in chapter 2, this pattern changed completely in the 1970s: in England, totals rose from 27 centres in 1972 to 490 major and a further 280 lesser centres by 1981.[37] While to some extent sports centre provision was a local authority fashion of the period, it certainly satisfied an evident need and contributed to the dramatic rise in participation in indoor sports in the same decade.

Provision is still far from universal. Best served are the outer suburbs of cities and the free-standing towns of medium and large size. Conversely, three types of area have well below the average provision of one centre for 75,000 people. First, many inner cities have a substantial deficit. Wandsworth, with a population of 255,000, has none, Liverpool (510,000) and Oldham (220,000) but one each. Second, the more remote rural areas are often ill-provided, for few settlements rise to an effective population threshold. At county level (figure 4.9), both Norfolk and North Yorkshire have less than one centre per 300,000 population and Cornwall less than one per 200,000. In some cases, as figure 4.5 made clear for North Yorkshire, the deficit may be alleviated partially by smaller sports halls, albeit often with access restricted to specific groups. Third, some resort towns are also notably deficient: there are no centres, for example, in Brighton, Blackpool or Eastbourne.

As new, expensive facilities, individual sports centres have attracted considerable research, and data on patterns of use exist for some 70 of them.[38] It is not easy to make simple generalisations, for user profiles and catchment areas tend to vary with individual activities, and one of the prime characteristics of the centre is the wide range of activities available at each. In general, centres cater for some 35 different activities, but only five consistently attract more than 2 or 3 per cent of users. In order of popularity these five are swimming, squash, badminton, football and table tennis.

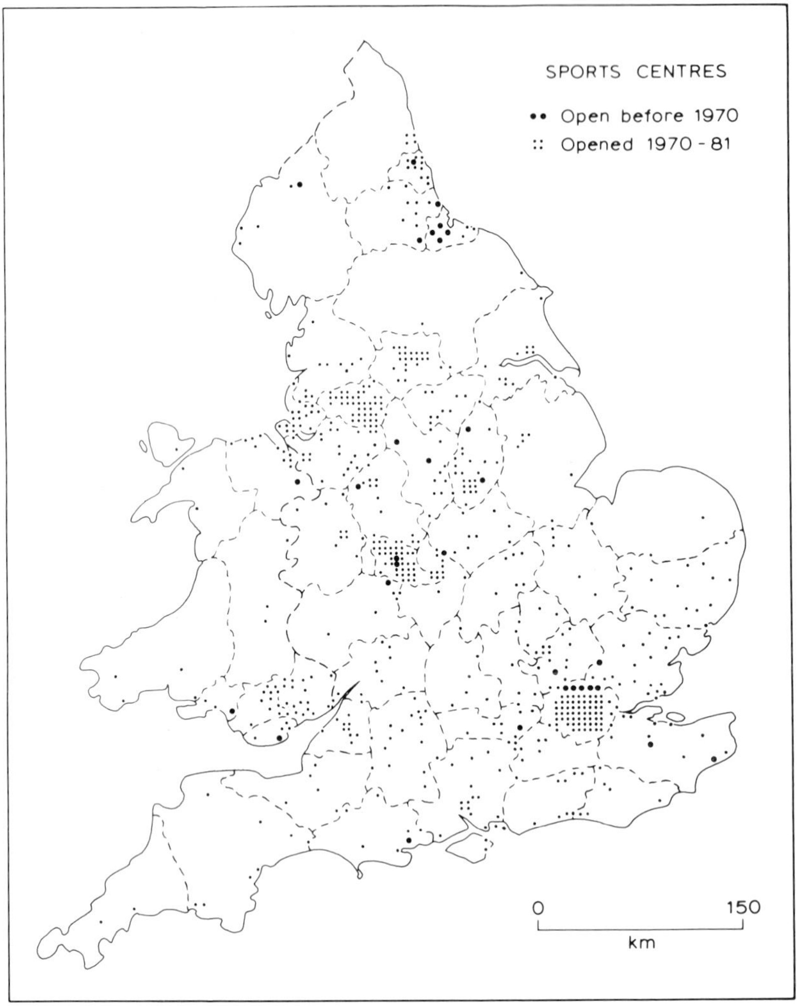

FIGURE 4.8 Sports Centres, October 1981. Because of the limitations of scale, distribution within Greater London and within other major conurbations is shown conventionally and is not related to the detailed location of each centre.
Source: data from Sports Council

Users tend to be dominated by young adults. At the Michael Sobell Centre in Islington, 43 per cent of members were aged between 20 and 29, and 32 per cent between 10 and 19. At the Meadway Sports Centre, Reading, these two age groups constituted 34 and 26 per cent, respectively. Usage tends to drop off rapidly after the mid-30s; while the over-60s represent only 2 per cent of users. The proportion of female participants has gradually increased: early studies showed a ratio of 2:1 in

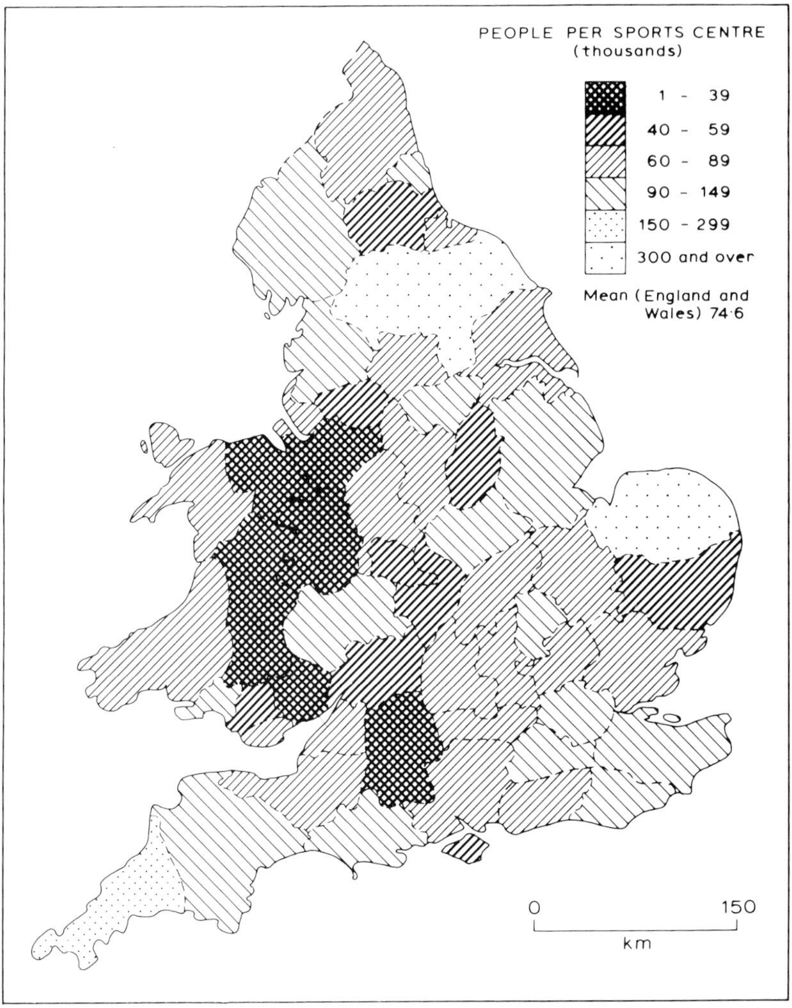

FIGURE 4.9 Sports centres: density of provision by county, 1981.
Source: data from Sports Council

favour of males, but a more typical ratio in the early 1980s is 1.5:1. Centre users are predominantly professional, managerial and other non-manual workers and their families, but only the *un*skilled manual worker is seriously under-represented.

Catchment areas remain comparatively compact. The car plays a dominant part in access: typically, at least two-thirds of users travel by car, and in many medium and large centres the proportion exceeds 80 per cent. Public transport plays a significant part for a few, well-sited centres

(34 per cent of users at the Sobell Centre in 1974-75, 15 per cent at Billingham Forum in 1976, and 14 per cent at Pontypool in 1974), but in general it accounts for less than 10 per cent of journeys, and frequently for only 2 or 3 per cent. Typically, between 10 and 20 per cent of users walk: only in small, local centres is that proportion substantially exceeded. Journeys are short: half of users travel for 10 minutes or less, 80 per cent for less than 20 minutes. Distances are also short: three-quarters of users travel from within five miles. Where data have been gathered on visit rates – the number of visits per 1000 population per week – they indicate a marked falling off beyond a radius of one mile from the centre.

In the hierarchy of urban recreation facilities, sports centres may be compared with suburban shopping centres, largely car-dependent, generating new loyalties and providing new experiences. Individual centres are surprisingly resistant to competition from subsequent centres, for each tends to create its own coterie of local users; at Atherton in Lancashire, for example, 2000 new users were generated in five years, despite there being seven other sports centres and 12 swimming pools within six miles.

On the basis of early experience, the Sports Council recommended provision at the rate of one centre for 40,000 people, with a further centre for each additional 50,000 people. The simple application of these criteria may be inappropriate in particular circumstances. In a conurbation of, say, 300,000 population, a hierarchical approach suggests several possible solutions. Three or four similar centres might be provided, scattered evenly through the built-up area. Again, the same number of centres might be provided, but with a concentration of specialist interests in one centre: thus, one might concentrate on fencing and another on rifle shooting, while both continued to provide the full range of more popular activities such as swimming and squash. A third model might create one large centre capable of catering for all the major sporting activities of the conurbation and the full range of minority sports but supplemented by a number of smaller district centres catering purely for the local demand for the most popular activities.[39]

The study of catchments is a clear prerequisite for the effective location and adequate provision of facilities such as sports centres. The rigid application of national 'norms' may, however, stifle much latent demand. The suggested sports centre 'standard' of one per 50,000 population suggests considerable unsatisfied need when compared with current national provision of one per 75,000, and enables deficient areas to be identified readily (figures 4.8 and 4.9). Where the standard is exceeded, continuing demand suggests that the standard itself may be unduly cautious. The case of Atherton has already been quoted; another instance is the district of Torfaen in Gwent, with more than double the national level of provision, but with at least four times the average level of participation: 83 per cent of the district's population live within two miles of a centre, and almost twice as many users walk as to the average sports centre. A vigorous, consumer-oriented management has helped to attract a much higher proportion than average of manual workers.[40]

Such results raise questions that are more political than geographical. How far should sports provision of this kind attempt to match expressed demand, or should it rather seek to generate new demand? How far is such provision a social service and how far should pricing policies seek to cover realistically both capital and running costs? Current thinking takes a cautious, commercially oriented view, but even after a decade of unprecedented building, sports centre provision in England and Wales is still only one-third of that found in parts of West Germany and most of the Netherlands. In the Netherlands, indeed, there is one sports hall (of 924 m^2 or larger) for every 27,300 people, yet the country is still looking to more than double present provision.[41] In 1982 the Sports Council saw as one of its priorities for the ensuing decade the provision of an additional 800 sports halls, the majority either of low-cost design or conversions and adaptations of existing premises. Current provision has been 'a signal achievement, but numbers are only part of the story. The pattern of provision is equally important if all who wish are to have access.'[42]

PARKS AND OPEN SPACES

The land requirements of indoor sports centres are comparatively modest, though many of them have associated outdoor pitches, but even these modest requirements have tended to make suburban location typical. Other types of urban recreation resource are far more voracious consumers of land, with a growing presumption to a peripheral location.

Open space represents a major land use within towns: as noted in chapter 2, open space is second only to housing in its consumption of urban land, ranging from 11 to 19 per cent in different settlement types. Open space and land in recreation use are not, of course, synonymous, for open space has an aesthetic as well as a recreation function. The former adds, visually and psychologically, to the whole quality of the urban environment; the latter fulfils the needs of the urban dweller for both active and passive, formal and informal outdoor recreation. These functions are far from mutually exclusive. The landscaped setting of an office tower may also provide a space to relax in the sun during the lunch break, while houses ringing an urban golf course may command a premium price for the open setting they enjoy.

To fulfil its recreation role, open space takes many forms. Playing fields, sports and recreation grounds cater for active sport. Parks of varied design, whether informal open spaces, formal gardens, or areas of woodland and heath, fulfil more passive needs. Specific demands are served by children's playgrounds, allotments and golf courses, while areas of water, both natural and artificial, enhance amenity and add further opportunities for recreation.

The kaleidoscope of supply varies widely in both form and distribution in individual towns, reflecting the opportunities and accidents of individual history and the complexities of ownership in both public and private sectors. Space permits a closer look at only limited examples of open space provision, and parks and golf courses must suffice.

Most towns and cities retain an extensive and varied network of public parks, though studies of their use, as opposed to their provenance, are surprisingly few.[43] The legacy of history remains strong not only in the details of distribution, but in form and function, for 'not only has the Victorian resource been inherited, but also the nineteenth-century rationales for urban open space provision still prevail.'[44] In practical terms, it is difficult, and expensive, to alter radically the structure as well as the philosophy of the original design.

Leicester affords a typical example of the historical constraints and opportunism inherent in the evolution of a park system.[45] In 1850, Leicester had a population exceeding 60,000, but with one small exception, its only public recreation space was the New Walk, laid out in 1785 and now the only surviving urban pedestrian way of its period in England. In the second half of the nineteenth century, however, Leicester typically acquired a number of large parks in the Victorian fashion, the first being Victoria Park itself, 27.6 ha opened in 1882 (figure 4.10). Nearer the centre of the city, Abbey Meadows, a marshy area unsuitable for building, was purchased by the city council in 1877, and developed as a park. Spinney Hill and the first section of Western Park followed in 1885 and 1899, respectively. These were all parks in the high Victorian fashion, with fountains, bandstands and gardens, as well as open grass. Abbey Park had an even wider range of attractions, with boating and river views. All these parks continue to serve at least a district function, and Abbey Park remains of city-wide significance.

At the end of the period, two smaller recreation grounds were built, and in the period up to 1920 they were complemented by a number of small playgrounds and ornamental gardens, though only Aylestone Playing Fields in the south covered any substantial area. In the interwar period the pace of development again quickened. A conscious programme by the city council matched the rapid expansion of the built-up area with a major park close to each emerging suburb. Six multi-purpose parks were created, ranging in size from 18 to 67 ha: they were supplemented by smaller

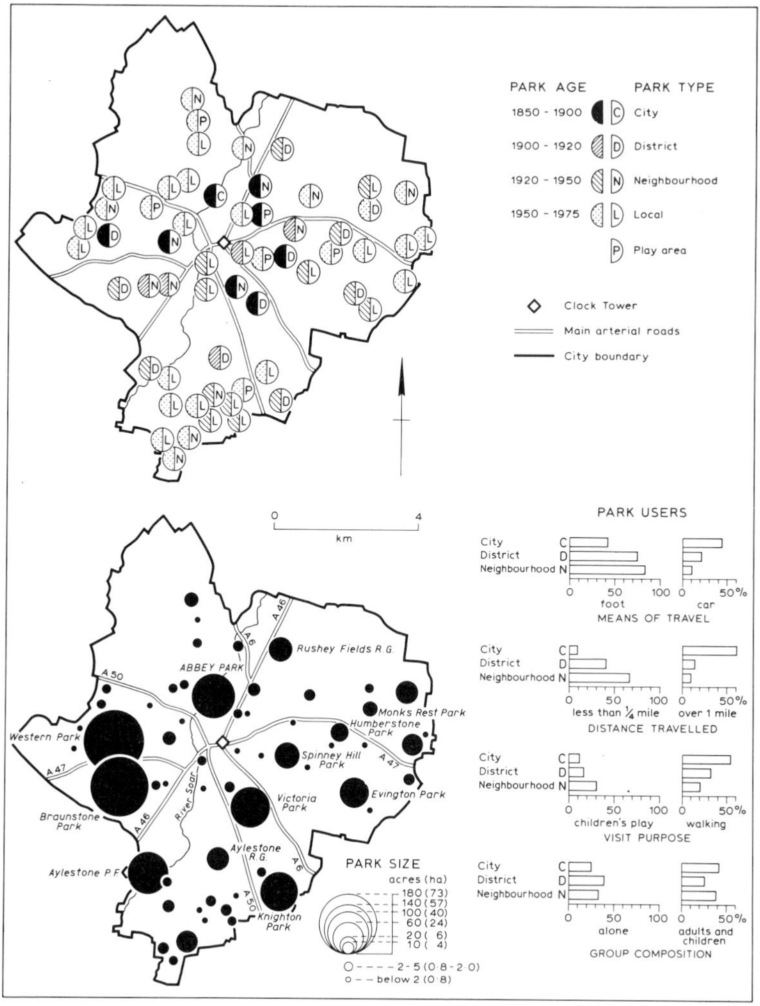

FIGURE 4.10 Parks in Leicester, 1975.
Source: data from I. R. Bowler and A. J. Strachan, *Parks and gardens in Leicester* (Leicester City Council, 1976), figure 3, tables 2.5, 3.3.1, 4.1 and 4.5.1

neighbourhood parks and open spaces scattered through the major council estates.

The existence of this outer ring of large, interwar parks has greatly affected park development policies since 1950. Attention has been concentrated almost exclusively on small neighbourhood and local facilities as integral elements in the design of new council estates, and on small parks and play areas in the old villages which formed the foci of expanding private residential districts. This close integration of open space with housing contrasts with the larger set-piece development of earlier years, often peripheral to the contemporary built-up area but now engulfed by urban expansion.

The functional hierarchy reflects size, provenance, location and facilities. The hierarchical distinctions have been recognised in all the studies of park use, and most distinguish three levels above that of the purely local play area. On the basis of observed demand in Liverpool, Balmer suggested the need for 'neighbourhood' parks of 0.8-2.0 ha, with an effective catchment area extending 0.4 km; 'local' parks of 14.2-18.2 ha and a catchment area extending 0.8 km; and city parks of over 40 ha and with a city-wide catchment area.[46]

Park use remains essentially local and informal. In Liverpool, 53 per cent of all park users travelled less than 0.4 km and almost 80 per cent less than 1.2 km. In Leicester the comparable figures for all parks were 41 and 70 per cent respectively; for neighbourhood parks, 66 and 90 per cent. Park activities, apart from ancillary sports facilities, are dominated by walking (whether alone or with a dog) or just sitting: in Leicester these three categories accounted for 70 per cent of users in city parks, 64 per cent in district parks and 52 per cent in neighbourhood parks. Much of the remaining use was associated with children's play: highest, not surprisingly, in neighbourhood parks, with 30 per cent visiting the playground or associated with children's games; lowest in the city park, with 11 per cent so occupied. Park users also tend to be frequent users: in Leicester again, 77 per cent of visitors to neighbourhood parks and 80 per cent of those to district parks made at least one visit a week, and 35 and 40 per cent respectively made daily visits.

Evidence relating park users to the urban population as a whole is limited. It is sometimes asserted that urban parks have outlived their usefulness, supplanted by more sophisticated entertainment at home and by a more accessible countryside. This was certainly not the case in the London study. Of the population aged 15 and over, 70 per cent had visited at least one open space in the month prior to interview, 39 per cent the previous week. The highest visit rates were associated with dog ownership, with the 15-19 age group, and with those who lived in areas exceptionally well supplied with open spaces.

The continuing need for space for informal recreation within the urban fabric is clearly evident. It satisfies a widespread need for short-distance, short-duration recreation, a need that cannot adequately be fulfilled by more distant rural scenes. That need is not just for outdoor sports facilities, or for space for children's play: the ability to walk or stroll in a pleasant setting close to home ranks high in perceived priorities. The setting need not always be a conventional park: too little attention has been given in recent British urban design to linear recreation areas, pleasing ribbons of pedestrian ways threading through the built-up area but effectively screened from it. The Georgian town walk was perhaps a better precursor than the Victorian park promenade in cost-effective provision.

GOLF

Urban parks are used and enjoyed by so many that they fully justify the space devoted to them; the scale of provision for that voracious consumer of land, the golf course, is more open to question.

Golf remains a minority sport, albeit with vocal, and powerful, adherents. The 1980 General Household Survey suggests that 3.1 per cent of the adult population (about 1.2 million) play golf on a regular basis in England and Wales during the most popular season. The English Golf Union recorded its highest number of members, 460,000, in 1978, compared with only 179,000 in 1963: by 1980 membership had dropped slightly, to 425,000.[47] Of golfers, four out of five are men, and nearly four out of ten are from the professional and managerial group compared with only one out of ten in that group in the population as a whole. This proportion is higher than for any other sport. Again, in contrast, golf is pursued right through the age ranges: three out of five adult golfers are aged between 30 and 59, one in eight is aged over 60.

As a sport, golf has many advantages. It requires little organisation to participate, it can be played through all seasons and be enjoyed by players with a wide range of skill and age. Golfers also tend to be frequent participants. In 1974 a sample national survey suggested that 81 per cent of golfers played at least once a week in summer and 67 per cent at least once a week in winter.[48] Characteristically, golf courses are well used throughout available daylight hours: while there is some seasonal variation, both daily and weekly fluctuations of demand are by no means as marked as for most other sporting activities (figure 4.11).

The sport, however, has two prime disadvantages. First, access is often restricted. The access problem is rarely of a physical nature. Nine out of ten golfers are car owners, and few parts of the country are more than 16 km from a course. In this context, the Northern Region is not untypical (figure 4.12). The main concentration of courses is around the immediate periphery of the Tyneside and Teesside conurbations, with a marked linear extension along both east and west coasts, where stretches of sandy soils and sand dunes give an opportunity for course development on true 'links'. There is, however, a considerable scatter through the more sparsely populated inland areas, and a few parts of the region lie beyond a 16 km limit.

Problems of economic and social access are more serious. Apart from

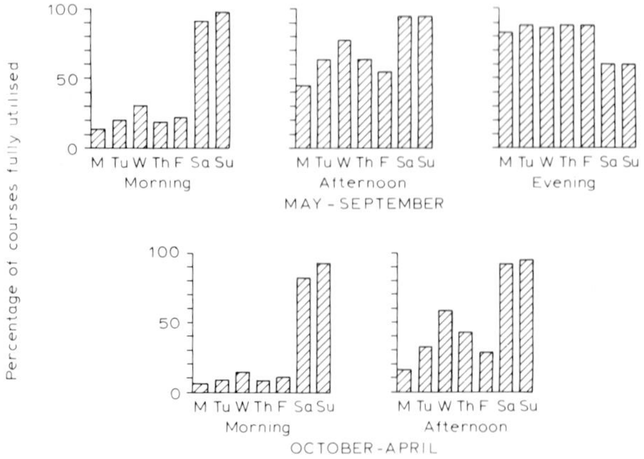

FIGURE 4.11 Daily utilisation of golf courses in the Northern Region, 1975. *Source:* data from *Golf in the Northern Region* (Northern Council for Sport and Recreation, 1978), table 27

equipment costs, the membership subscriptions of private clubs are a financial disincentive. In 1978 they averaged £33 for 18-hole courses in the Northern Region, and were notably high in the clubs adjacent to the two conurbations. The growth of municipal courses, where payment is normally made per round played, has alleviated the problem to some extent, though publicly owned courses are still very much in the minority. It is significant that a much greater proportion of the players on these courses are in the younger age groups: in the 1974 study, 54 per cent of golfers using public courses were under 35 years old, compared with 24 per cent on private courses.[49] There is, however, little incentive to reduce membership costs while membership remains buoyant, and many clubs, especially near major population concentrations, have considerable waiting lists. Economic barriers are often reinforced by social barriers, by the perceived view of golf as a sport 'for the upper classes': such images are, unfortunately, self-perpetuating.

The second disadvantage of golf is, in the present context, more serious: its large demands on land. A minimum of 40 ha is needed for an 18-hole course. In 1981 there were an estimated 2242 'nine-hole units' in England and (in 1980) a further 174 in Wales.[50] This suggests a minimum of 48,000 ha devoted to the sport, though 55,000 ha is a more reasonable estimate. While this is only 0.36 per cent of the area of the country, it still represents a very substantial share of the total land surface for a single sport. The impact of that share is increased by its concentration near major centres of population, and while courses are readily constructed on inferior, sandy soils (the archetypal 'links'), such land is not always readily available and better-quality land is of necessity used. Nor is golf readily

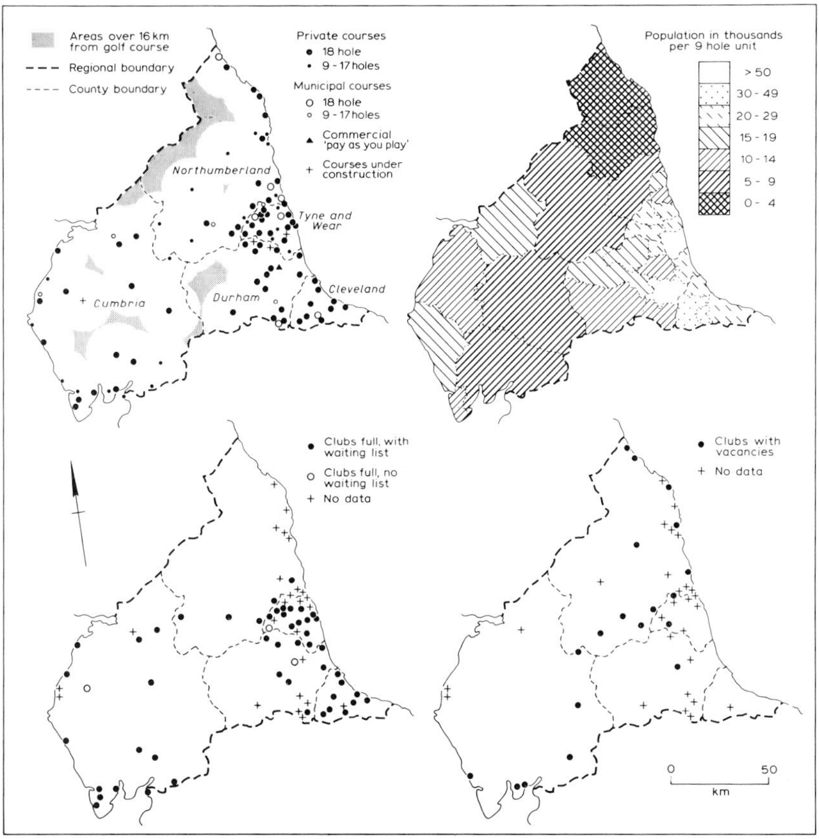

FIGURE 4.12 Golf provision in the Northern Region, 1975.
Source: data from *Golf in the Northern Region* (Northern Council for Sport and Recreation, 1978), figures 3 and 5 and table 24

compatible with other sports, though footpaths and even spaces for informal recreation can be incorporated in course design with little real loss of golfing amenity. It remains, however, an exclusive sport in more senses than one, for 1 ha is needed to satisfy the needs of every 15 golfers.

PLANNING STANDARDS AND PLANNING APPROACHES

Even these few examples highlight both the opportunities and the problems of providing for recreation in an urban context, problems of which the spatial aspect is only one component, albeit a fundamental one. It may be possible to view provision in a rational, hierarchical frame, to develop models for that provision that equate access and opportunity in a spatial pattern with mathematical precision, but reality rarely gives an empty canvas where such a model can be developed in unfettered form. Rather, reality is conditioned by the accident of historic legacy, by the fashions of spending from the public purse and by the commercial dictates of the private sector.

In spatial terms, the need for more conscious, rational provision of recreation facilities grew as towns expanded in size and land costs escalated; the dictates of fashion and habit alone were no longer adequate. As in many other aspects of physical planning guidelines were sought: guidelines that were simple to apply and were readily comprehended by decision-makers. One of the oldest, and one of the most enduring, was that devised in 1925 by the National Playing Fields Association for 'permanently-preserved playing space'. The Association's calculations, though based on a number of arbitrarily devised assumptions on sports participation and population structure, had a valuable simplicity: they gave a recommendation of 2.4 ha (6 acres) of such space per thousand population, expressly excluding school playing fields except where available for general use, woodlands and commons, ornamental gardens, full-length golf courses and 'open spaces where the playing of games by the general public is either discouraged or not permitted'. This standard was commended by successive governments as a general guide, to which should be added one acre of ornamental public open space. In 1956 the Ministry of Housing and Local Government asserted that 'no better assessment of need has so far been put forward.' The Association last reviewed the standard in 1971 and saw 'no present basis for a departure from this general recommendation.'[51]

The prime virtue of the standard was its simplicity; not least, in post-1947 development plans, it gave a yardstick against which existing provision could be measured. It had, however, many limitations apart from those related to the basic assumptions from which it was derived. It related only to *playing* space, not to total recreation space, and was often misunderstood, and misapplied, in consequence. Indeed, the need for informal space was often as great as that for playing space, though it was emphasised that 'space for organised games is only one aspect of space for play.'[52]

The virtue of simplicity, however, disguised the complexity of reality. Three further considerations are fundamental to the planning of effective provision, and not just for play alone. First, in the public sector the full use of all facilities is inhibited by competing systems of provision. The problem is most acute between the educational and recreational sectors of local authority provision. Until the 1970s, education authorities controlled more playing space than other municipal providers, and while that is no longer the case, school playing space, both outdoor and indoor, remains a resource with great potential for wider community use beyond school hours. Two distinct concepts are involved. *Dual use* is the shared use of facilities by members of the public for whom the facilities were not primarily intended, *Dual provision* takes the process a stage further and involves the active co-operation of two (or more) authorities in the joint planning and provision of facilities: it relates normally to the creation of new or additional facilities.

The basic idea that the secondary school should, in a much wider context, be the hub of its community antedates 1939 with the development of community colleges in Cambridgeshire and Leicestershire.[53] Shared use was advocated by the Department of Education and Science: circular 2/70, *The chance to share*, asked all local education authorities to review existing arrangements to ensure that every opportunity for dual provision was fully explored. Local authority associations urged the advantages: 'the cardinal principle surely applies . . . that joint provision and dual use, sensitively implemented, stretch further the resources available to help improve the quality of life in local communities.'[54] The economic and social benefits of schemes have been demonstrated by research.[55]

In reality, however, practical schemes have been slow to evolve. In the words of one commentator,

> the field of dual use produces the greatest degree of hypocrisy. There is formal recognition, frequently publicly and widely stated, of a need for dual use of many facilities for physical recreation, but in practice the self-protective element successfully inhibits the implementation of the publicly declared policy.[56]

By the end of the 1970s, just over one in six secondary schools had sports facilities for community use: even of these, 10 per cent remained closed during the evenings and weekends and a surprising 40 per cent during school holidays. Of the remaining five-sixths with sports facilities at the school, a quarter were unused in term time and 78 per cent in school holidays. For primary schools the situation was much worse: some 38 per cent of primary schools had sports facilities, but of these only a quarter were used in term time and a bare 8 per cent in school holidays.[57] Some authorities, like Cheshire and Walsall, have shown what can be achieved, but overall school facilities remain a grossly under-utilised resource for recreation.

Beyond the fullest possible use of all facilities, the second consideration in planning is the range of facilities that shall, or can, be offered. The judgements here remain essentially political. They are conditioned by the historical legacies discussed both in this and in previous chapters, but there are no simple, academic solutions to the inherent problems. Which activities should be the prerogative of the public sector and which of the voluntary and commercial sectors? What level of charges are appropriate in the public sector? Should golf provision, for example, be left in the private and commercial sectors, or should the expansion of municipal courses be encouraged? On municipal courses, should charges be levied in accordance with strictly commercial principles, or should they be so low (or non-existent) as to ensure no financial barrier to access to the sport?

In a leisure context, concepts of deprivation owe more to considerations such as these than to overall deficiencies of facility provision.[58] It is ironic that in many cities deprived inner areas are actually closer, in a purely spatial sense, to a wide range of leisure facilities than more affluent suburban areas. The centre of the city still houses the widest range of cultural and entertainment facilities: Victorian parks are often close at hand, together with a range of sports facilities. The problem remains that of social and economic barriers, though even the quite short distances involved may be a powerful disincentive.

Facility planning remains more than ensuring full use of facilities and providing an adequate range of them: the third consideration, implicit in so much of this chapter, is their proper location. The problem has been recognised in setting guidelines for standards, but generally as a matter for local resolution rather than general principle. The Sports Council, for example, in setting targets for major sports facilities in the early 1970s, was concerned to relate facilities more to population totals than to location. For indoor sports centres, for example, it was noted that 'the mean journey time for all users was approximately 15 minutes . . . this factor emphasises the local nature of each facility and affects the total number required if a desirable level of provision is to be achieved.' That locational guidance was not refined more fully.

> The scale of provision adopted for use . . . first establishes spheres of influence related to the crucial factor of travel time. . . . The requirement within each sphere of influence allows a first indoor sports centre for a population of between 40,000 and 90,000 and an additional centre for every 50,000 population above 90,000.[59]

These 'spheres of influence' were little more than a recognition of the size of population concentrations, and gave little guidance on the location of facilities within them.

In practice, the opportunist availability of sites has been more important than theoretically derived locations: the scale of demand has been such that the penalties of poor location have rarely been severe. There has been a growing tendency for peripheral as opposed to core location for new developments, and even suggestions that facilities traditionally associated with city centres might be more effectively relocated towards the edges. Bale has advocated the need 'to suburbanise British football' and argues that 'given the prime central sites of many football grounds, clubs would probably benefit financially by moving to a suburban site as part of a modern sports complex'[60] as well as reduce the impact of the nuisance of spectator behaviour.

The hierarchical concept of facility location has obvious merit. In practice, many facilities already adhere to such a pattern, as previous sections have shown. The great danger remains that a pattern of facility provision related to ease of physical access alone may further disadvantage groups whose existing social and economic disadvantages seriously inhibit both their mobility and their leisure opportunities. Within the city, at least, social and economic considerations must weigh as heavily as spatial in assessing the adequacy of recreational provision, and in suggesting patterns for its enhancement.

5 Recreation Patterns in Countryside and Coast

THE RURAL-URBAN DICHOTOMY

> . . . the countryside [is] now used for leisure on a massive scale . . . But there is a close interrelationship here with the towns and cities. Over 80 per cent of recreational demand in the countryside originates from towns, and we need to think in terms of dealing with this partly at source. Certainly the concept of total community provision, town and country seen as an integral recreational resource, needs to be kept firmly in the forefront.[1]

The integrated approach to recreational provision, urged by the Countryside Review Committee, has been too often neglected by both researchers and providers.[2] There is no sharp discontinuity between urban and rural resources for recreation, but rather a complete continuum from local park to remote mountain peak. To the user, the distinction is as much one of distance as locale: as the previous chapter emphasised, much urban recreation is essentially 'local' rather than 'urban' in the participant's perception. This is nowhere more true than for informal activities: town walk and country walk differ in degree rather than in kind. Most areas afford a range of recreational opportunities, and the distinctions in the pattern of their use change but gently with distance from the place of residence.

Figure 5.1 illustrates a case in point. Wirral offers a variety of informal recreation venues, from town centre parks like Birkenhead Park, urban fringe and green belt open spaces and parks like Bidston Hill, Arrowe Park, Royden Park, Thurstaston Hill and Wirral Country Park, the estuary frontage of small resorts like West Kirby and Parkgate, and specialised rural attractions like the University of Liverpool's Botanic Gardens at Ness. Use patterns differ not only according to the character of the resource, but also with its position in relation to the major built-up areas and its accessibility to transport routes. At one extreme, the majority of users of the downtown Birkenhead Park live in Birkenhead, visit the

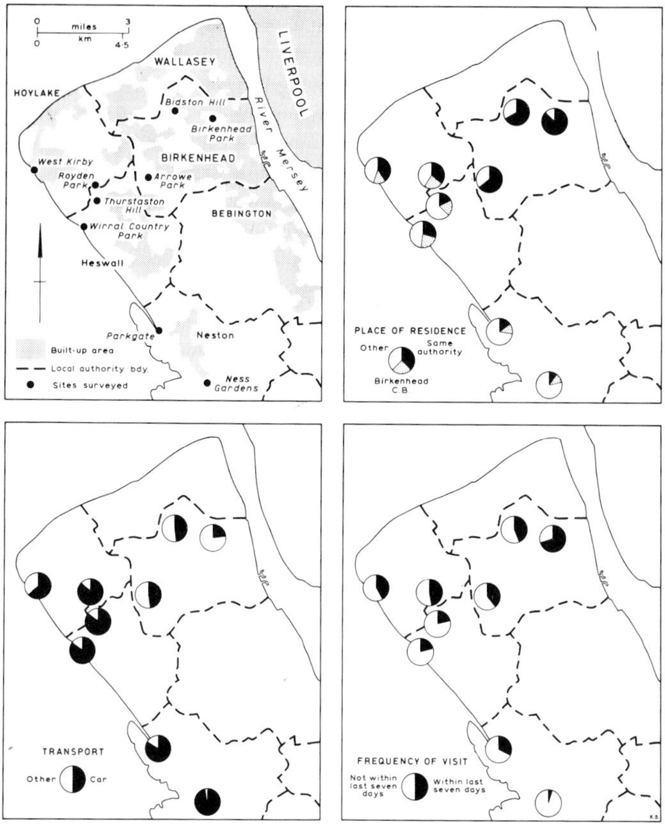

FIGURE 5.1 Visitor characteristics at informal recreation sites on Wirral, March 1973. A total of 1925 interviews were analysed, covering both weekday and weekend visitors. Totals for individual sites ranged from 161 (Royden Park) to 317 (West Kirby front).
Source: data from student survey, Department of Geography, University of Liverpool

park frequently and come largely on foot. At the other extreme, Ness Gardens, with an entirely rural setting, has few visitors from the relatively sparse population of the immediate locality: most visitors come only occasionally and travel by car. Between these extremes, patterns show gentle gradations, though intermediate categories of 'immediate urban fringe', 'remote urban fringe', and 'free-standing small settlements' may be discerned.

Nevertheless, while the continuity must be emphasised, outdoor recreation in rural areas rapidly achieves a distinctive character of its own and needs separate consideration for more than mere convention. Not only is the setting obviously different, with opportunities and satisfactions that the urban environment cannot provide,[3] but the problems of recreation provision assume a new dimension. In the countryside, unlike the town, few areas are devoted exclusively to recreation: recreation use must compete with agriculture, forestry, water abstraction, mineral extraction and military training. This chapter is concerned with patterns of countryside recreation: subsequent chapters will look more closely at the resources it uses and the conflicts that arise in that use.

THE FOURTH WAVE

Countryside recreation is no new phenomenon, but in the last two decades its increase in scale, and in the consequent pressure on fragile rural environments, has fully justified Dower's vision of a great surge of townspeople breaking across the countryside, the 'fourth wave'.[4] By any measure, the phenomenon is of immense significance. The Countryside Commission estimates that, on a typical summer Sunday, 14 million people visit the countryside, and that during a typical summer month, 82 million such visits are made.[5]

From the early 1950s, the volume of countryside visiting has shown almost continuous increase. In the absence of adequate survey data, the precise scale of that growth cannot be known, but admission figures at 45 National Trust properties open throughout the period 1955-78 suggest

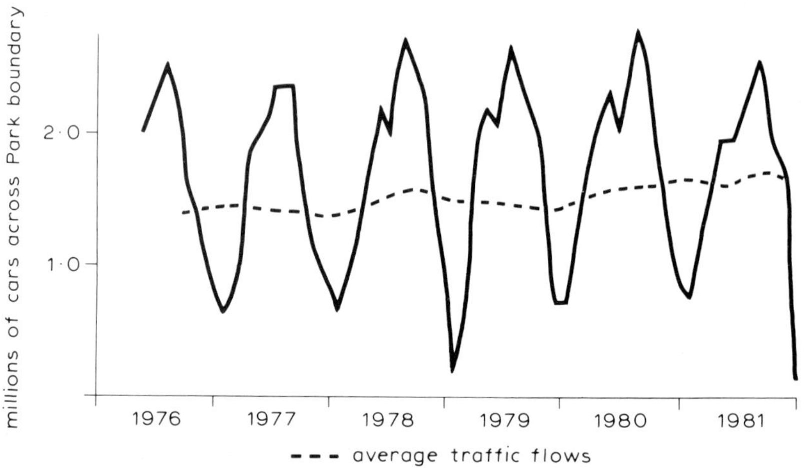

FIGURE 5.2 Monthly and annual variations in recreational traffic crossing the boundary of the Peak District National Park.
Source: based on a graph in Peak Park Joint Planning Board, *Annual Report* (1981-2), Appendix 8

that 7 per cent per annum was a realistic overall figure, with relatively minor fluctuations until the mid-1970s.[6] More recently, however, the increase has been much more uncertain. The 1973-74 oil crisis saw the first significant steadying of the rate of growth, though by 1978 visitor numbers had recovered to such an extent that it appeared that the crisis produced no more than a hiccup in the general pattern of expansion. In 1979, the Countryside Commission could confidently assert that 'the main messages are that . . . recreation travel has proved very resilient to significant increases in the price of petrol.'[7]

Subsequent experience strongly suggests that the major phase of growth is over. The Commission's National Survey of Countryside Recreation recorded that in 1977 64 per cent of adults in households with access to a car had made a visit to the countryside in the previous month, but in the 1980 Survey the figure had dropped to 50 per cent. For households without a car, the proportions were 33 and 29 per cent respectively.[8] The North York Moors National Park received an estimated 11.30 million visits in 1973 and 11.14 million in 1979.[9] The Peak District National Park estimates 'there has been only slight growth in visitor traffic, averaging about 3 per cent per annum,' since 1976 (figure 5.2).[10] Growth, at best, is now only modest.

Increases in fuel costs are only one reason for this, and probably an insignificant one: indeed, there seems little reason to dissent from the earlier view that recreational travel by individuals is surprisingly resilient to relative changes in petrol prices. More general recession undoubtedly has had a part to play, with leisure spending as a whole an early target for economy by individuals. More important, perhaps, has been the drastic slowing down of the rate of car acquisition. Car ownership and countryside visiting are almost synonymous: 73 per cent of all trips to the

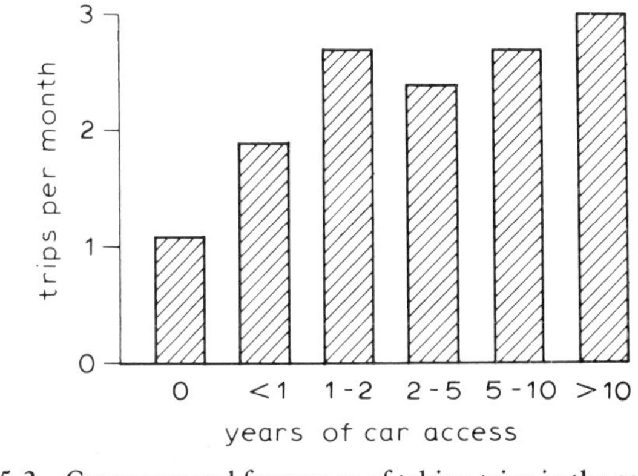

FIGURE 5.3 Car access and frequency of taking trips in the countryside.
Source: data from National Survey of Countryside Recreation (1977)

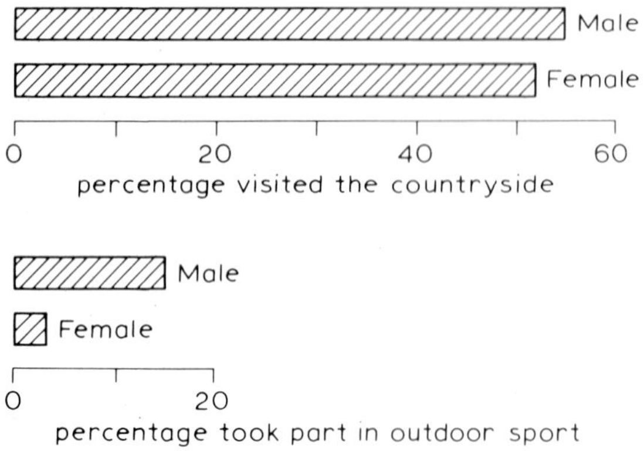

FIGURE 5.4 Male and female participation in previous four weeks in countryside visiting and outdoor sport.
Source: data from National Survey of Countryside Recreation (1977)

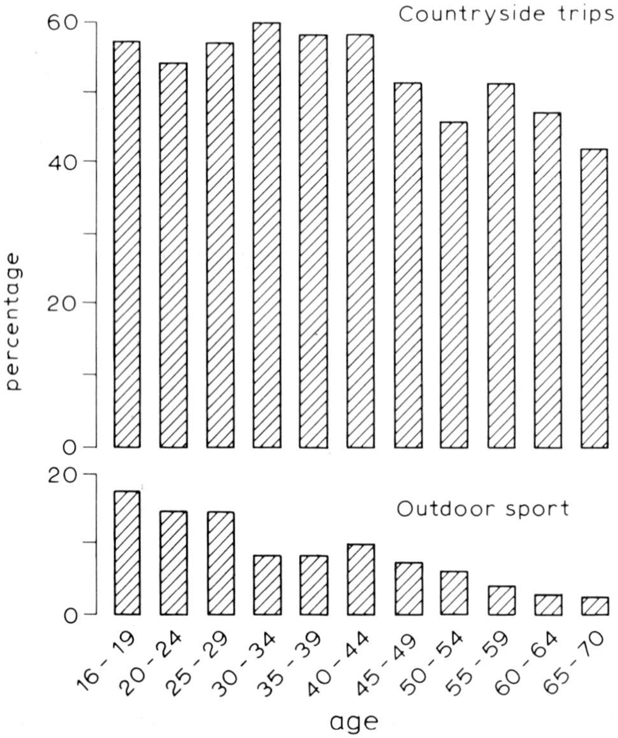

FIGURE 5.5 Participation by age groups in previous four weeks in countryside visiting and outdoor sport.
Source: data from National Survey of Countryside Recreation (1977)

countryside were made by car in 1977 and 76 per cent in 1980. The acquisition of a car rapidly changes the participation rate of a household in countryside recreation, but the new pattern of higher participation quickly reaches stability (figure 5.3). Overall growth in countryside recreation must therefore be closely linked with car acquisition by the population as a whole. Between 1961 and 1970, the proportion of households with a car rose from 31 to 52 per cent; between 1971 and 1975, from 52 to 56 per cent; and between 1976 and 1980, from 56 to 58 per cent.[11]

All the evidence, therefore, suggests that the slowing of growth in countryside visiting is likely to be more than temporary. While that growth may not yet have reached a complete plateau, the period of explosive growth is undoubtedly over. The Countryside Commission is unduly optimistic to suggest that the 'fall-off in countryside trips . . . is likely to be temporary. We can expect resumed growth, especially in short

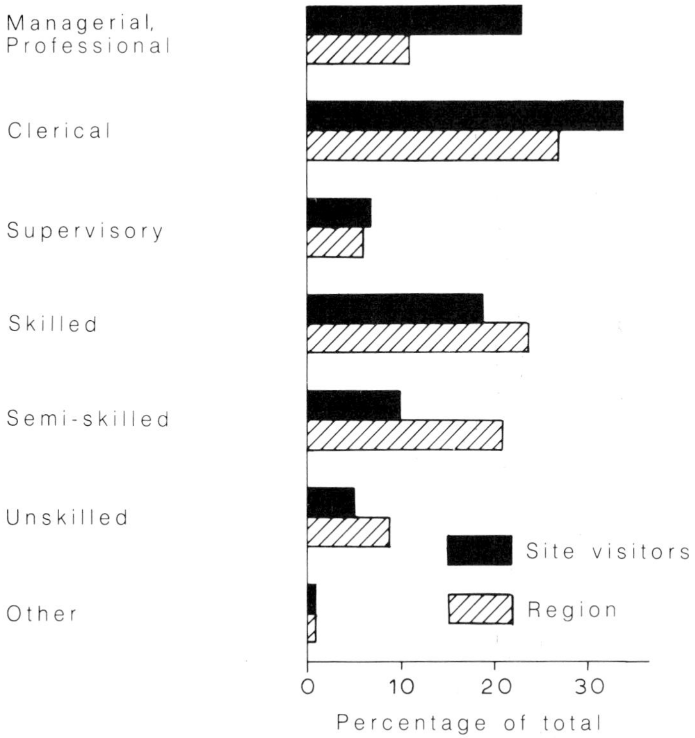

FIGURE 5.6 The occupational grouping of visitors to recreation sites in South East England, 1973, compared with that of the total population of the South East region.
Source: data from M. Elson, *A review and evaluation of countryside recreation site surveys* (Countryside Commission, 1977), table 19

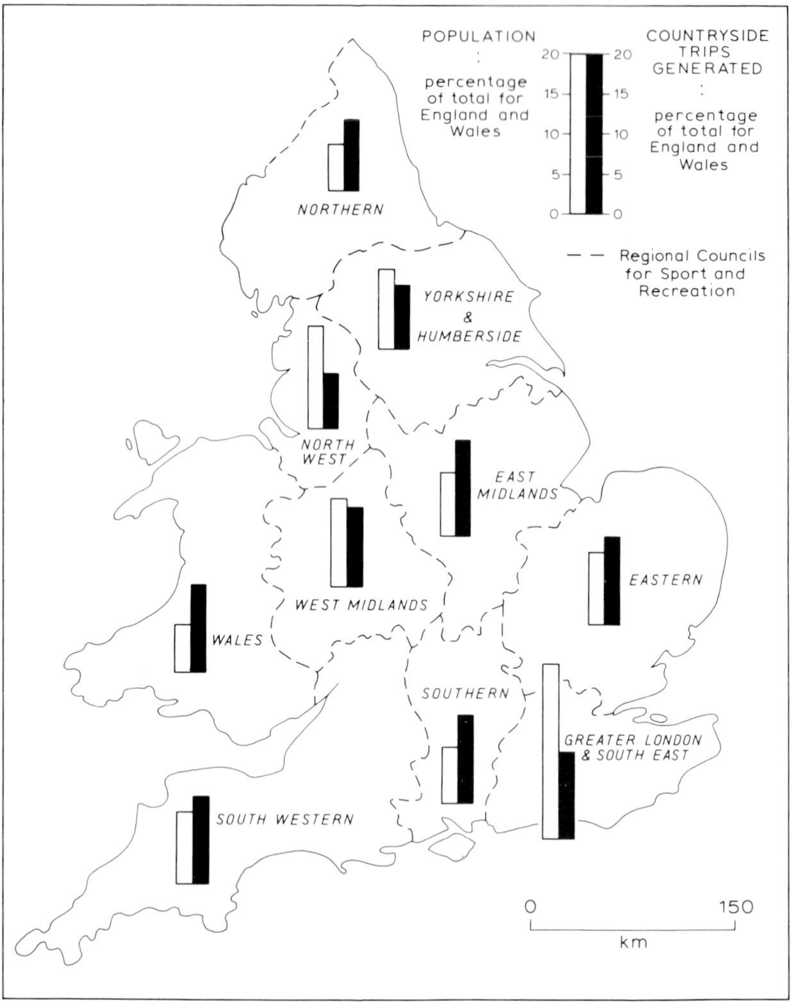

FIGURE 5.7 Day trips to the countryside from home generated in the region in relation to the population of the region. Total sample size for trips: 11,353.
Source: data from National Survey of Countryside Recreation (1977)

trips from towns to nearby countryside. In the longer term, all the signs point to a resumed growth in countryside recreation.'[12]

Even if the major phase of growth is largely complete, however, countryside visiting remains a large-scale phenomenon by any standards. It is enjoyed almost equally by men and women (figure 5.4), and interest is sustained with little diminution right through the life-cycle (figure 5.5). In occupational terms, only semi-skilled and unskilled manual workers are seriously under-represented (figure 5.6), and it is in these groups that car ownership is often well below average. The practice is widespread throughout the country as a whole: where there are variations, they tend to relate either to the advantages enjoyed by an area with a plenitude of accessible opportunities on the one hand, or to the presence of major conurbations with countryside effectively inaccessible to many inner-area inhabitants on the other (figure 5.7).

The term 'countryside visiting' encompasses a tremendous variety of activities that can be enjoyed in rural surroundings (figure 5.8). Not only are the activities themselves numerous, but they make use of the countryside in a variety of ways. As the Countryside Review Committee remarked,

> countryside recreation is a convenient term for a wide range of leisure activities whose only common factor is that they take place in the open air on land or water in the countryside. For many people the activity is likely to be the primary attraction and the countryside location incidental. But probably, for most townspeople visiting the country, it is the countryside experience which is the main consideration, the particular activities they engage in depending very much on chance opportunities, and impulses, in the course of an outing with no clearly pre-defined objective.[13]

The very variety inhibits ready generalisation, but with the dominance of informal activities whose main characteristic is the enjoyment of a rural setting, the broader trends may be discerned. The following sections

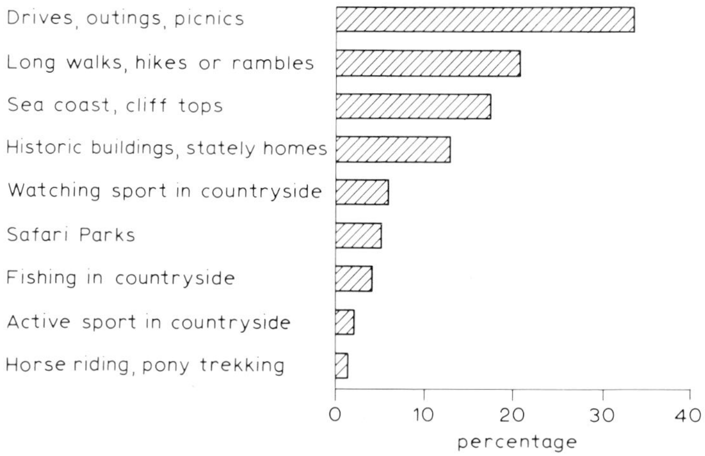

FIGURE 5.8 The proportion of visitors participating in different recreational activities in the countryside.
Source: data from National Survey of Countryside Recreation (1977)

deliberately concentrate on the visitor who seeks access to the countryside for the enjoyment inherent in the setting rather than the visitor who simply seeks space for an activity.

DESTINATIONS

That setting is itself complex and offers a variety of opportunities. An initial distinction must be drawn between coast and countryside. The coast of England and Wales remains a major recreational magnet. It is both extensive and accessible. It is some 4400 km long,[14] and no part of the country is more than 120 km from it. It offers a wide variety of resources and opportunities, of hinterland, beach and open water, of lonely cove and developed resort.

The longer the time available for recreation, the more likely is the coast to be chosen as a venue. In 1971, 72 per cent of all main holidays in Britain of four or more nights included a stay at the seaside compared with a total of 38 per cent for all other kinds of destination, both rural and urban.[15] For day visits related to holiday periods, the proportion remains high, with seaside resorts the single most important destination, followed by the open coast (table 5.1). When there is a more serious time restriction the coast loses in relative popularity, though a visit to a seaside resort is still the second most frequent destination. As time becomes a more crucial factor, so the location of the starting point becomes more significant. In an earlier comparison between trips from Merseyside and Manchester (table

TABLE 5.1 Journey purpose on holiday-related and non-holiday trips in England and Wales

	*Percentage of those making trips in previous 3 months**	
Journey purpose	*Holiday-related trips*	*Non-holiday trips*
Seaside resort	75	44
Sea coast	38	19
Historic building	19	22
Zoos	8	8
Drives, outings	30	71
Long walks	23	41
Fishing	4	8
Horse-riding	—	3
Other sports	4	8
Watching sport	8	14

* Totals exceed 100 per cent as all journey purposes are included.
Source: data from National Survey of Countryside Recreation, 1977

3.3), the coast was shown to be almost equally popular as a destination for full day excursions, but, when excursions were of less than five hours duration, more than six times as many people from Merseyside as from Manchester went there. The case of Hull is a further illustration. The city is sited only 20 km from the coast and has no major inland attractions close at hand. In 1969, of pleasure trips by car from Hull, 59 per cent were to coastal locations, and 43 per cent to the four resorts of Scarborough, Bridlington, Hornsea and Withernsea alone.[16]

Despite such exceptions, the coast is too far away for most people to reach easily on trips unrelated to holidays, and here the countryside comes into its own (table 5.2). More than three out of four non-holiday trips include the countryside as a destination, and almost half are to the countryside alone. It is important to emphasise that the countryside may be not necessarily the preferred destination, but simply the most readily accessible in the time available.

TABLE 5.2 Destinations of holiday-related and non-holiday trips in England and Wales as a percentage of trips taken in the previous three months

Destination	*Holiday-related trips*	*Non-holiday trips*
Undeveloped coast		
Coast only	8	4
Coast and seaside resort	18	4
Coast and countryside	5	6
Coast, resort and countryside	13	8
Total coast	44	22
Seaside resort		
Resort only	36	15
Resort and undeveloped coast	18	4
Resort and countryside	8	17
Resort, coast and countryside	13	8
Total resort	75	44
Countryside		
Countryside only	13	47
Countryside and undeveloped coast	5	6
Countryside and seaside resort	8	17
Countryside, coast and resort	13	8
Total countryside	39	78

Source: data from B.S. Duffield and S.E. Walker, 'People and the coast – current demands and future aspirations for coastal recreation', in Countryside Recreation Research Advisory Group, *Recreation and the Coast* (Countryside Commission, CCP 127, 1979), figures 1 and 2, and derived from National Survey of Countryside Recreation, 1977

ROUTES AND RANGE

The impact of the trip, however, is not just on the destination. Recreational travel is unique in that the actual journey itself is frequently a part of the total recreation experience, rather than just a means to an end. Table 5.2 emphasises that many trips have more than a single destination, and this is particularly the case when the private car, with the freedom of individual movement it conveys, is the means of transport. It has already been noted that three out of four trips to countryside and coast are made by car, and it is these that will be examined more closely.

Data on detailed patterns of movement are comparatively scarce. They derive generally from questions asked on studies at individual sites or from cordon surveys in major recreation areas. It is clear from such work that the direct route to a destination is not necessarily the most preferred route, nor do outward and return journeys, even to a single destination, necessarily coincide. In the Lake District on an August Sunday in 1974, for example, a cordon survey showed that one journey in three was neither a direct journey across the area nor a simple return journey, but was part of a loop or U-route or an even more complex pattern.[17] In the same survey, questions were asked as to the reasons for the choice of route. While 52 per cent of those on day trips gave the reason as 'the only route' or 'the quickest route', 29 per cent had chosen it for 'good views', 18 per cent because it was 'interesting driving' and 6 per cent because it 'avoided busy roads'. A surprising 13 per cent noted that it was 'the signposted route'.[18]

A further distinction may be made between travel to an area and travel within it, since the motorist's objectives may vary for different parts of the journey. Outside the national park or other popular countryside or coastal area, the main purpose may be to cover the distance between home and the general destination as quickly as possible, but once within the chosen area other factors, such as the simple enjoyment of the scenery, may well predominate. Colenutt, in his study of the Forest of Dean, found that the majority of visitors (over 60 per cent) tended to select the shortest journey to or from the *edge* of the Forest area, at least for one direction of their journey. Paradoxically, however, there was also a conflicting desire to minimise the distance duplicated on any trip: only 26 per cent of visitors travelled home by exactly the same route as the outward journey, and on average only 45 per cent of the total trip distance was duplicated.[19]

The complexities of both patterns and motives have inhibited the effective mathematical modelling of recreation traffic flows, for the normal assumptions in traffic models of minimising time or distance do not necessarily apply. A full discussion of approaches is beyond the present purpose, but in a recent review, Elson had to conclude that 'conceptual and data deficiencies appear to leave many observed variations in behaviour unexplained.'[20] In the context of transport as a means rather than an end, as a focus of enjoyment rather than utility, 'attempts to incorporate what is known about the nature of recreational trips into models of them may ultimately lead to models of greater reliability for the purposes of predicting future use, evaluating the benefits of site provision and the other purposes to which they have been put,'[21] but existing work has proved of limited practical application.

The actual distance travelled on recreational trips to the countryside varies widely. Generalisations at aggregate level may be seriously misleading in individual cases. The National Survey of Countryside Recreation recorded an average *return* distance of 86 km for non-holiday trips in 1977, falling slightly to 80 km in 1980. Most data on distance travelled have been derived from individual site studies, and are concerned largely with the direct distance from the point of origin to the site and not with the whole of the journey undertaken on that day. Even with this limitation there are wide variations – variations with the nature of the site and the type of demand it satisfies, with the range of comparable opportunities from the point of origin, and with the time available for the trip.

Figure 5.9 illustrates something of that variation from a site point of view, in relation to a variety of sites in the South East. A clear hierarchy emerges, with sites exerting a local, sub-regional and regional influence, though the differences are of degree rather than of kind. At the local end of the scale are the 'attractive villages' and 'urban fringe' sites, both of which draw more than 75 per cent of their visitors from within 20 km, the former over 60 per cent from within 10 km. The distinction between them is emphasised by the difference in length of stay: the villages function as archetypal short-stay sites, with more than half the visitors departing within half an hour, while the 'fringe' sites have more than half the visitors staying between 30 minutes and two hours. The 'large informal sites' and the 'small picnic sites in open country' have a sub-regional, intermediate function. While half their visitors come from within 20 km, they have larger numbers from further away, particularly from the 20-50 km zone. As places for simple, informal recreation, they are also dominated by medium-stay visitors, with seven out of ten remaining between 30 minutes and two hours. The final group of 'coastal sites' and 'historic houses' are of regional significance. They draw visitors over considerable distances, and having made the journey, more than half stay over two hours.

The range of available sites, and their relative accessibility, strongly influence distances travelled when point of origin rather than destination is considered (figure 5.10). The sheer scale of London makes it a unique case in one sense, but it serves to emphasise inherent variations. The outer London boroughs exhibit a pattern typical of most cities of any size. A

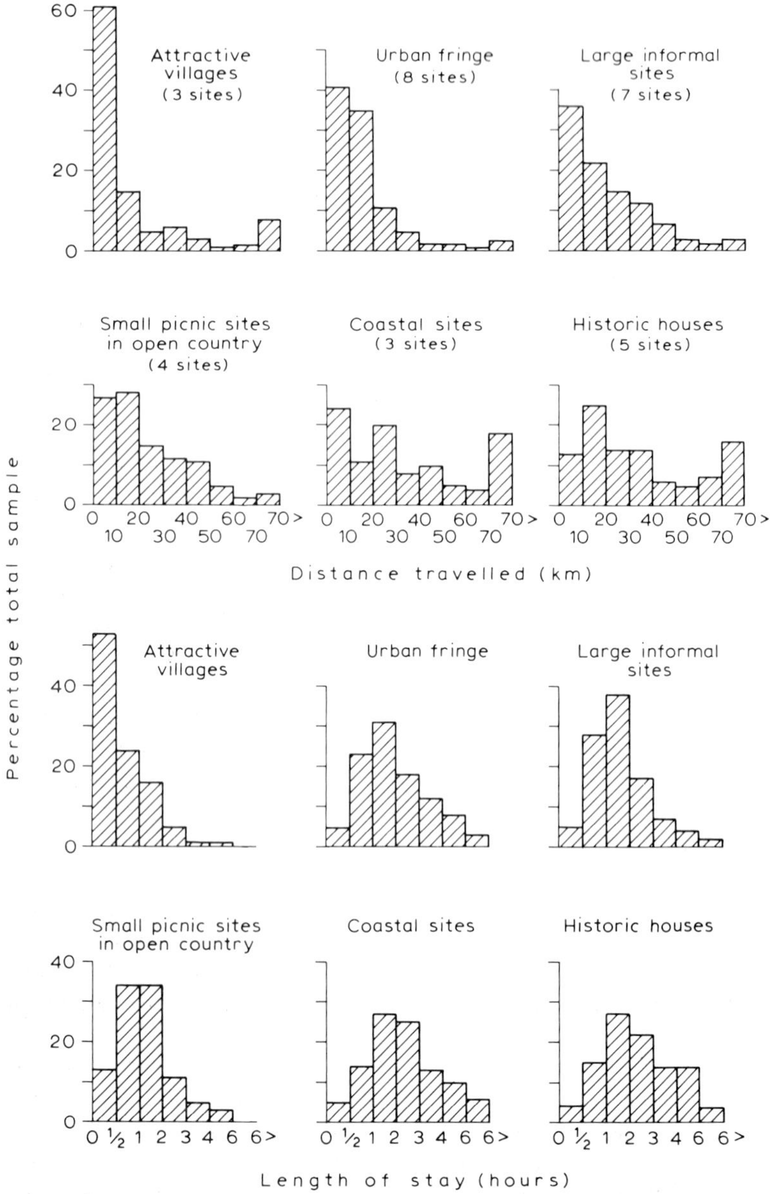

FIGURE 5.9 Informal recreation in South East England, 1973: distance travelled to sites, and length of stay at sites. 'Historic houses' include Woburn Zoo Park and Broxbourne Zoo.
Source: data from M. Elson, *A review and evaluation of countryside recreation site surveys*, (Countryside Commission, 1977), tables 4 and 5 and para. 3.28

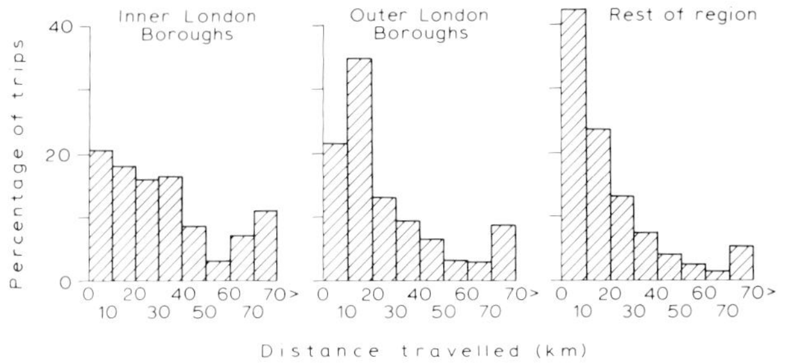

FIGURE 5.10 Distance travelled to recreation sites in South East England, by location of residence, 1973.
Source: data from M. Elson, *A review and evaluation of countryside recreation site surveys* (Countryside Commission, 1977), figure 8

journey of more than 10 km is generally needed, both to reach the countryside as such and to give the psychological feeling of having travelled far enough to be able to relax in different surroundings away from the immediate vicinity of home. Nevertheless, when opportunities locally are available, most journeys are not extended unduly: one in three of all journeys are between 10 and 20 km. Beyond that, there is a steady decline in the proportion of journeys in each distance band, though one in twelve still travels more than 70 km.

The impact of opportunity is emphasised by the other graphs. For inner London, there is a remarkably even distribution of trips throughout the full range of distance bands. For most, even the countryside of the urban fringe is some 20 km away, but the friction of travel is sufficient for a substantial proportion to seek some satisfaction nearer home. However, having made the effort to get out of the city, there is a tendency to maximise the opportunity and travel to the more outstanding (and frequently more distant) attractions of coast and countryside. The reverse is true for those who live outside the conurbation. With striking countryside often close at hand, journeys are makedly shorter, with more than two in five travelling no more than 10 km.

The case of the South East emphasises one highly important facet of countryside recreation. While some attractions remain unique at national level, and draw visitors, even on day trips, from very substantial distances, most people on most occasions are content to seek satisfaction close at hand. Even 'national' attractions are dominated by local visitors. In the late 1960s 34 per cent of all visitors to Dartmoor on a July Sunday were residents of Plymouth, and a further 31 per cent residents of the rest of Devon. Visitors on holiday accounted for 28 per cent, but only 3 per cent were day visitors from outside Devon.[22] A more recent study shows the same pattern for the North York Moors National Park (table 5.3).

Virtually four out of five visitors had travelled from within the park or the immediately adjacent local authority areas – almost a third from Teesside alone. Even the traditional source areas of the conurbations of West and South Yorkshire contributed less than one in ten of visitors. As many as one in five visitors came from Whitby and Scarborough, modest but immediately adjacent resorts with populations of some 13,000 and 53,000 respectively: even more surprising is the high proportion of these who were residents rather than holidaymakers.

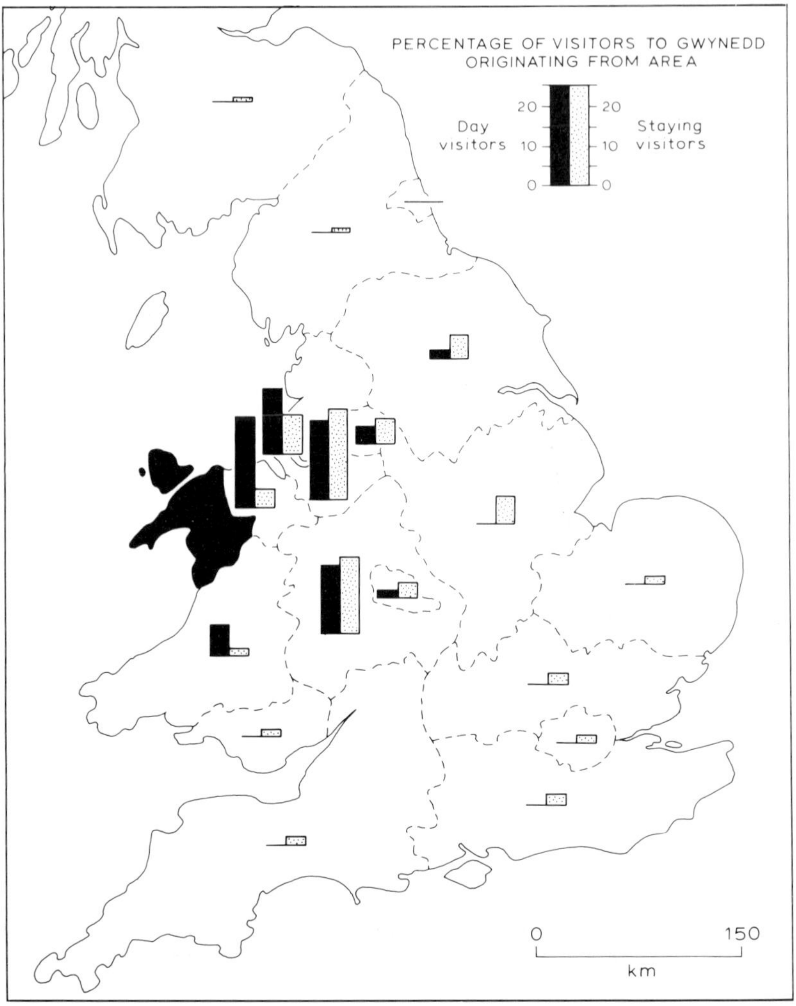

FIGURE 5.11 Origins of day and staying visitors to Gwynedd, 1980.
Source: data from *Gwynedd 1980 Tourism Survey* (Gwynedd County Planning Department, 1981), figure 4.1A and 4.1B

TABLE 5.3 Trip origin of visitors to the North York Moors National Park, Sundays, 22 and 29 July 1979

	Percentage of all visitors originating in area	*Percentage of visitors originating in area on holiday*
National Park	10	28
Scarborough	15	26
Whitby	6	38
Remainder N. Yorkshire	18	19
Remainder Cleveland	30	5
W. and S. Yorkshire, Humberside	9	13
Remainder of Great Britain	12	19
Total	100	18

Source: data from *Patterns of informal recreation in the North York Moors National Park* (North York Moors National Park, 1981), tables 5 and 6

Figure 5.11 reiterates the friction of distance for holidaymakers as well as day visitors to Gwynedd. The predominance of Merseyside, Manchester, the North West, the West Midlands and Birmingham was to be expected among day visitors. Some 61 per cent came from these five areas, though relatively sparsely peopled but neighbouring Clwyd contributed no less than 26 per cent of the total. That same predominance is repeated for staying visitors, with 63 per cent of the total: Clwyd's share, at 5 per cent, is now more representative of population than distance.

TIMES AND SEASONS

Recreational traffic is short in range and brief in time. Daily, weekly and annual rhythms confine its impact to remarkably limited periods, and create in consequence substantial planning dilemmas.

At the daily level, widely varying sites give substantially similar patterns (figure 5.12, A and C), with a slow build-up during the morning, a rapid climb after 2 pm to a clearly defined maximum between 4 pm and 5 pm, and a rapid decline thereafter. The weekly rhythm, where holiday traffic does not add complications, is equally marked (figure 5.12 D). The Sunday peak is clear, and absolute. It is typically at least three times as great as a normal weekday and may reach five times or more, though it will vary according to the character and the location of individual sites.[23]

Daily and weekly rhythms are sustained in proportion throughout the year, but not in volume. The seasonal swing is a little less marked than for

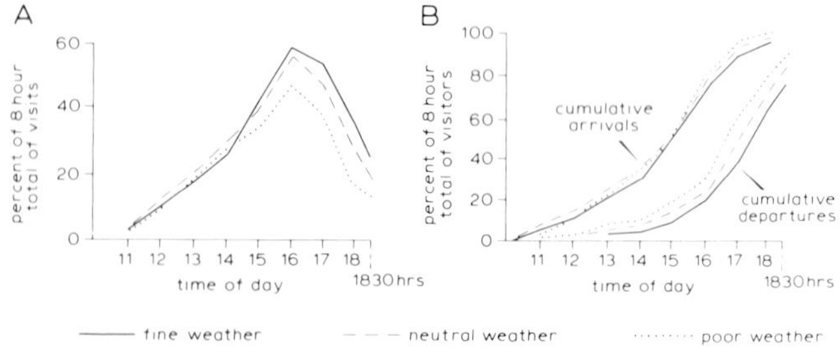

FIGURE 5.12 A The accumulation of pleasure traffic in the Goyt Valley, summer Sundays, 1971.
B Arrival and departure patterns of pleasure traffic in the Goyt Valley, summer Sundays, 1971.
Source: based on W. Houghton-Evans and J. C. Miles, 'Pleasure traffic in the countryside', *The Surveyor* (17 November 1972), figures 2 and 3

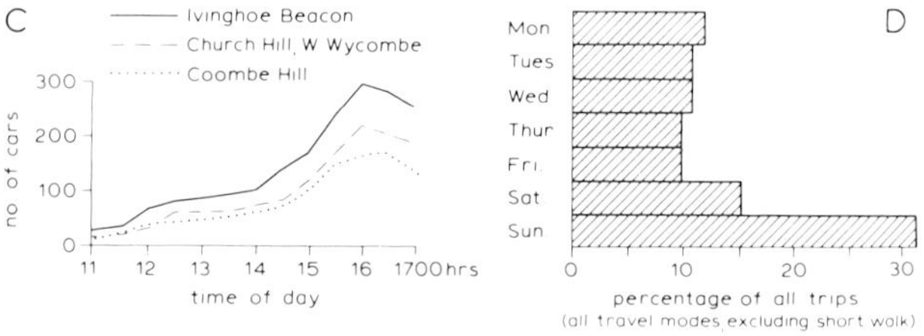

Figure 5.12 C Cars parked at recreation sites in the Chilterns, June Sundays, 1968.
Source: data from *Public gathering points survey, 1968/1969* Buckinghamshire County Council, 1970), table III
D Day trip distribution by day of week.
Source: data from National Travel Survey (1975-76)

holiday traffic, but remains strong none the less, with more than one in three of all trips taking place at the height of summer in July and August (figure 5.13). The other variable affecting volume on any given day is weather. Surprisingly little work has been done on the effect of different weather conditions on traffic volumes at specific sites, for few surveys have been mounted continuously over a long enough period. One exception was the monitoring of the Goyt Valley traffic experiment in the Peak District in the summer of 1971 (figure 5.14). Data were collected over 18 weekends from the end of May to the end of September. During that period, parking volumes varied from 66 to 174 vehicles on a Saturday, a range of 1:2.5, and from 95 to 493 vehicles on a Sunday, a range of 1:5. Most of these variations are weather-induced, though the precise relationships merit fuller investigation. Indeed, understanding has advanced little since Wager, in the mid-1960s, suggested the following adjustment factors to

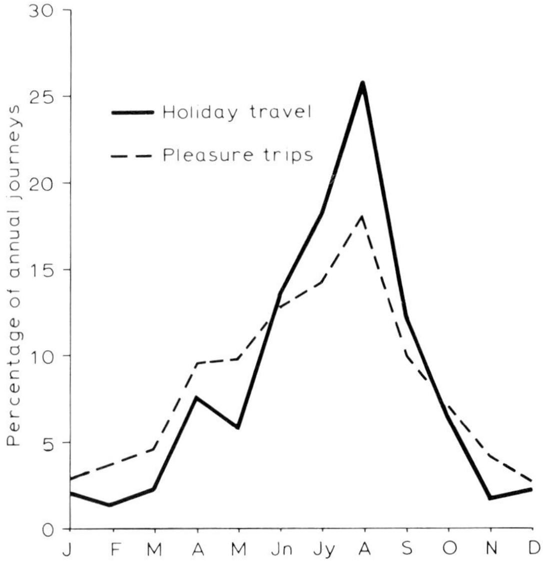

FIGURE 5.13 Monthly incidence of holiday journeys and pleasure trips of more than 25 miles in length, 1975-79.
Source: data from Department of Transport, *Transport Statistics Great Britain, 1969-79* (HMSO, 1980), table 1.10

compare attendances at open spaces under differing weather conditions: constant sun, 1; intermittent sun, 0.8; overcast, 0.5; showers, 0.6; continuous rain, 0.2.[24]

Weather affects not only the volume of traffic, but also the length of visit to the site. The Goyt Valley data (figure 5.12 B) show this clearly. There is little tendency for the arrival time of visitors to vary with the weather, but in fine weather stays are more prolonged and departures delayed.

When peaking in time, through the day, the week and the season, is coupled with peaking due to the weather, the limited periods of maximum demand are strikingly evident (figure 5.15). For only some ten hours in the whole year did the number of vehicles parked in the Goyt Valley exceed 200: by the twentieth highest hour, the volume had dropped to only 53 per cent of the highest peak. Such figures pose the prime dilemma of recreation traffic: with acute peaks of demand, but peaks sustained for a very short time, what level of demand can the planner reasonably expect to accommodate? In the Goyt Valley, the top 20 hours occurred over only seven days: outside these, the peaks did not exceed more than half the absolute maximum, and the obvious temptation is to consider some such lower level in developing a management strategy.

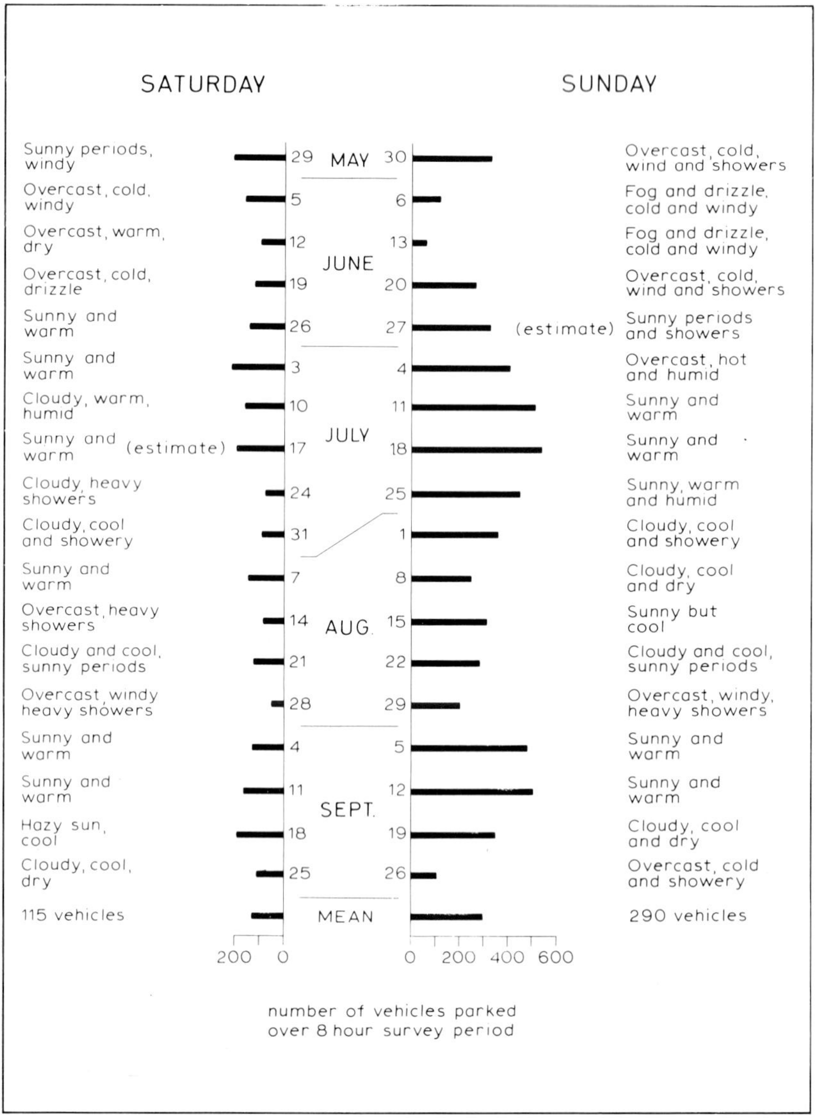

FIGURE 5.14 Total number of vehicles parked in the Goyt Valley on Saturdays and Sundays, summer 1971.
Source: based on W. Houghton-Evans and J. C. Miles, 'Pleasure traffic in the countryside', *The Surveyor* (17 November 1972), figure 1

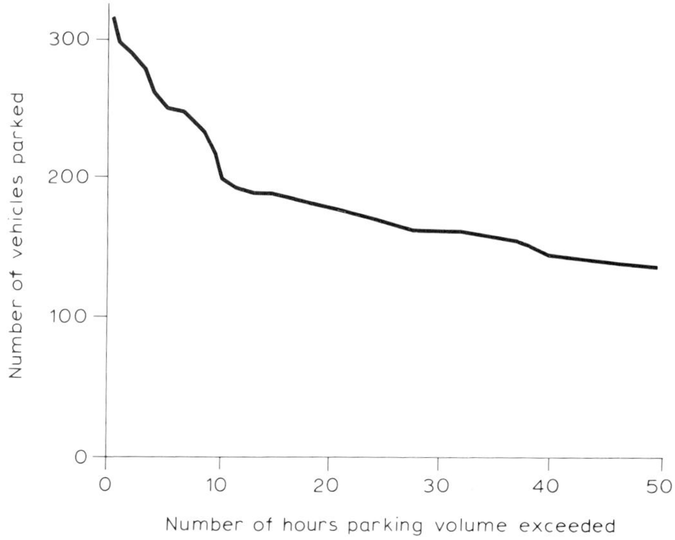

FIGURE 5.15 Goyt Valley car parks, parking volume during the 50 busiest hours, summer 1971.
Source: modified from M. Elson, *A review and evaluation of countryside recreation site surveys* (Countryside Commission, 1977), figure 2

COUNTRYSIDE IMPACT

Countryside recreation is concentrated not only in time but also in space. Few countryside activities range over the land as a whole: the vast majority are confined to a pattern of lines and nodes. The lines are the corridors of movement – roads, footpaths and waterways. The nodes are the sites of specific activities, whether active sports or more passive forms of enjoyment. Many nodes may not be in exclusive recreation use: those that are comprise a very tiny proportion of the total rural space – 1 per cent or less.[25]

The degree of concentration is evident in a variety of studies, most notably in surveys made of recreational patterns in many of the national parks.[26] The patterns differ widely in detail as the character of the resource differs, but all belie the idea of a widespread 'wave' of recreation users, ubiquitous in their impact. Two examples must suffice. The major source of day visitors to the Yorkshire Dales is the West Yorkshire conurbation: 35 per cent of such visitors come from the Leeds and Bradford areas alone.[27] This traffic tends to enter the national park in the south east, at Bolton Abbey, and many visitors are content to go no further (figure 5.16). This one site accounts for over 21 per cent of all stops in the

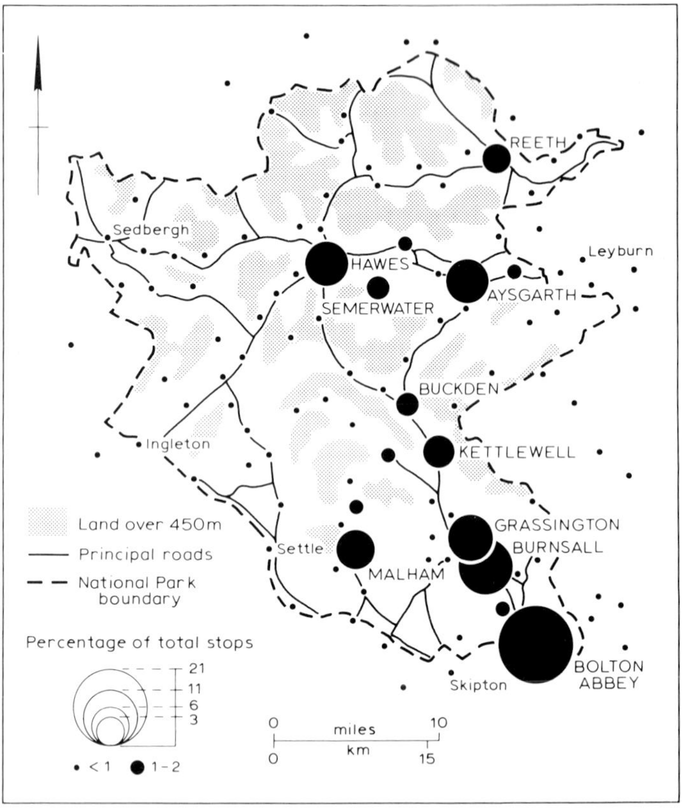

FIGURE 5.16 The distribution of stops made by visitors to the Yorkshire Dales National Park on Sundays, 17 July and 3 August, 1975. Individual totals for sites with less than 2 per cent of stops are unavailable, and these are therefore shown schematically in two size groups. The ten most popular sites (named in capitals) account for 70 per cent of the total estimated number of stops.
Source: data from P. A. K. Greening, and P. G. Smith, *A survey of recreational traffic in the Yorkshire Dales* (Transport and Road Research Laboratory Supplementary Report 539, 1980), table 1 and figure 4

Park. Its two large car parks give access to riverside walks, picnic places, fishing and safe bathing as well as to the abbey ruins themselves, but though the area is pleasant enough, it is scarcely the most beautiful site in the Dales. When Burnsall and Grassington are added, 41 per cent of all stops have been accounted for. This concentration in the south east is related far more to the origin of visitors than to the quality of the resource. While the filter effect may be accidental, however, it does much to protect the more sensitive environments of the higher areas from greater pressure. Aysgarth and Reeth act in a similar way for traffic from the east.

The Lake District (figure 5.17) shows a similar pattern of traffic focusing on a few major centres, not least the three urban resorts of Windermere, Ambleside and Keswick. More informal parking also shows heavy concentrations in a few areas, not least the environs of Keswick and Derwentwater, the Grasmere-Windermere corridor, Coniston, Ullswater and Wastwater. Elsewhere pressures are lower, though they may still be severe in their impact on narrow, winding roads.

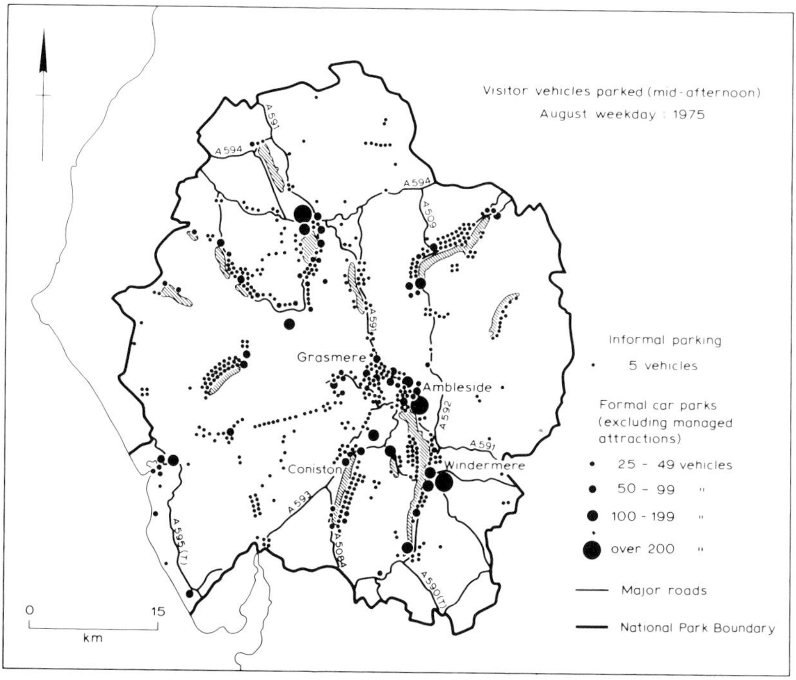

FIGURE 5.17 Cars parked in the Lake District National Park on an August weekday afternoon, 1975.
Source: based on *Lake District National Park: National Park Plan* (Lake District Special Planning Board, 1978), figure 6.3

This variation in pressure and in use reflects not only variation in facilities but also important variations in the nature of people's perception and enjoyment. Indeed, pressures may be best contained by enhancing this variation rather than lessening it. As the Lake District National Park Plan noted,

> Many people in the past have thought that the answer to the problems of the 'busy areas' is to spread the load – to direct people to those areas of the Lake District still relatively untouched by the countryside recreation explosion.

> Yet the visitors to Bowness are presumably quite content to mix with the crowds, and to attempt to direct them to other areas may enhance few people's enjoyment. At the same time, the National Park cannot be wholly reserved for those who seek some kind of 'wilderness experience' . . . A policy which encouraged a more even spread of recreation activity would not cater for the wide range of aspirations, and in particular would pose a threat to the enjoyment of those people who seek solitude or quiet and unspoiled countryside.[28]

This theme will be examined again when the concept of capacity is discussed, but it is fundamental to any understanding of both the nature and the management of recreation in the countryside.

The two examples mapped have used cars as surrogates for people, for obvious reasons of practical survey techniques at regional level. Beyond their cars, people fan out through a variety of informal sites and on to the footpath network. Site activities and patterns are considered in the following sections, but the footpath network is remarkably effective itself in containing pressures. Where an evident route exists, few people stray from it. On open heather moorland in the Peak District, only 5 per cent of visitors were observed to stray from paths during a 1969 survey of six areas of moor, even though the only impediment to free access was the coarse heather itself.[29]

The footpath network shows concentrations of use every bit as marked, in both time and space, as that on the roads. In 1979 some 40,000 people walked to the summit of Snowdon in July and August: on the busiest days,

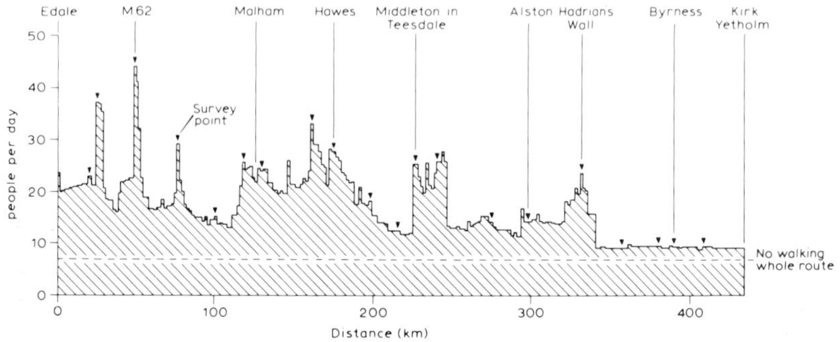

FIGURE 5.18 Variations in use of the Pennine Way Long Distance Footpath, summer 1971. The diagram is based on a questionnaire survey conducted on four days. As there were only 20 survey points, those walking only a few kilometres were estimated efficiently only at or near the sample points, and similar peaks might have been expected at intermediate access points. Of those questioned, 48 per cent walked less than 8 km.
Source: based on *Pennine Way Survey* (Countryside Commission, CCP 63, undated), figure 1

some 1500 people reach the top on foot, compared with 1000 by rail. On the six major footpaths on the massif, use varied in those two months from 20,344 on the Miner's Track to 8220 on the Snowdon Ranger Path: this represented 30 and 51 per cent of annual use respectively.[30] Many footpaths record no use at all. In a rural area of north Lancashire, a sample count of eleven paths on a sunny August Sunday afternoon showed two with 87 and 21 users respectively, but of the remainder, only one had more than six users and three, none at all.[31]

Fluctuations are not only between paths but along paths. Major routes like the Pennine Way show heavy use by short-distance walkers near major access points, but long stretches of a more remote nature have far lower levels of use (figure 5.18).

SITE PATTERNS AND ACTIVITIES

The regional pattern of concentration is repeated at local level. Studies of individual sites, particularly publicly owned sites, proliferated in the late 1960s and early 1970s, but most concentrated on questionnaire surveys of users, and were concerned with trip characteristics, social and demographic profiles of users, and the timing and range of activities rather than the spatial patterning of site use.[32] Some notable exceptions use simple observation techniques to study visitor behaviour, though their scope for analytical as well as descriptive purposes has scarcely been tapped.[33]

Informal recreation sites typically show wide internal variations in

5 Informal recreation on Beverley Westwood. Most people remain in or near their cars – and the ice cream van – leaving the open areas of the common largely unoccupied.

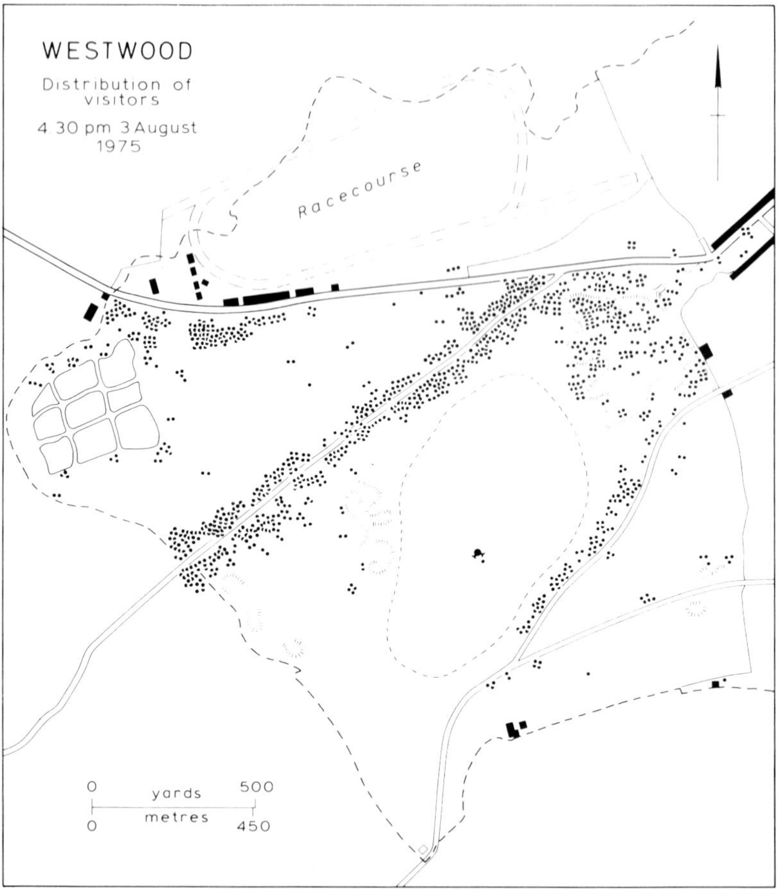

FIGURE 5.19 Beverley Westwood, North Humberside: distribution of visitors to the site on a peak Sunday afternoon. Free pedestrian access is available to all parts of the 242 ha of common pasture: car parking is permitted within 15 m of the roads.
Source: based on S. A. Glyptis, 'Countryside visitors: site use and leisure life-styles' (unpublished PhD Thesis, University of Hull, 1979), figure 16d

density of use. Some of the concentrations relate to site features such as access points and parking areas, landscape features, the location of facilities and specific activities; but even where there is freedom, and incentive, to roam, the pattern remains one of striking concentration (figure 5.19). The open common of Beverley Westwood is a popular venue for informal recreation 13 km north of Hull: it consists largely of undulating grassland, but is threaded by several roads. Vehicles can park up to 15 m from the road. Even at times of peak pressure, however, with over 1000 people present, visitors remained strongly tied to the roadside: at the time depicted on the map, the 15 m fringe along the roadsides accounted for 70 per cent of the total, with particular concentrations where good views and refreshment vans coincide (illustration 5). Indeed, the continuing importance of the car as part of the recreational experience needs strong emphasis: not only does it provide transport to and from the chosen site, but even at the site, Wager's 1967 assertion remains true that 'the majority of trippers can satisfy their recreational needs within a few yards of a parked car or by remaining inside it.'[34] It represents modest comfort – a travelling lounge, with windscreen replacing TV – and familiar, defensible space.

Paradoxically, the degree of concentration increases as pressures intensify, even when there is freedom to spread more widely. At Beverley Westwood, Glyptis measured the degree of voluntary clustering by comparing the actual distances visitors were spaced apart with the distances that would be possible if visitor groups were to maximise the space available to them. The results were striking (table 5.4). On no occasion did visitors occupy more than 21 per cent of the space that was theoretically 'theirs', and even more surprisingly, that figure decreased rather than increased as the site grew more busy.

TABLE 5.4 Mean nearest neighbour distances at Beverley Westwood, 3 August 1975

Time of count	*No. of visitors*	*No. of visitor groups*	*Actual mean neighbour distance (m)*	*Theoretical mean neighbour distance (m)*	*Actual as percentage of theoretical*
11.30 am	346	148	35.2	164.6	21.4
1.35 pm	771	302	19.9	115.2	17.3
3.00 pm	1059	305	16.8	99.5	16.9
4.30 pm	1094	397	15.7	100.5	15.6

Source: data from S.A. Glyptis, 'People at play in the countryside', *Geography*, 66 (1981), table 1

It is clear, then, that on a site of this character, it is the density of visitors, and not their distribution, that changes throughout the day. These results, confirmed elsewhere, suggest a simple diagrammatic model of the typical sequence of site occupation (figure 5.20).

> The first arrivals at a site tend towards a few favoured locations, tied principally to parking areas, sheltered locations or focal landmarks. Rapid

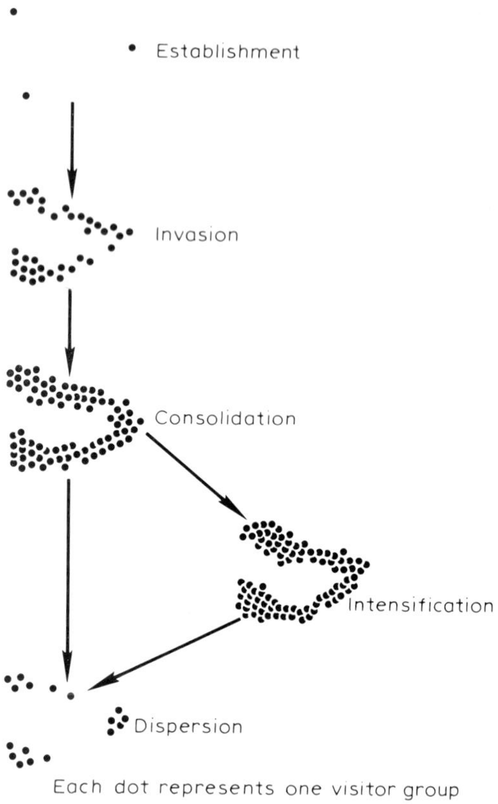

FIGURE 5.20 Glyptis's model of visitor dispersion on an informal recreation site.
Source: based on S. A. Glyptis, 'Room to relax in the countryside', *The Planner*, 67.5 (1981), figure 4

> inflow of visitors during an early afternoon 'invasion' phase extends these primary clusters. Further infilling and 'consolidation' occur as the pace of arrivals slackens. At the end of the day 'dispersion' takes place, the distribution once again reverting to an irregular scatter. Before this happens, however, there may be a phase of 'intensification', as at Westwood, with new arrivals continuing later into the afternoon and clustering even more tightly at favoured locations.[35]

For most visitors, countryside recreation is an informal, passive activity, with the emphasis on sitting in or near the car, or walking a short distance (figure 5.21). Activities vary both between and within sites, according to the characteristics of site and visitors. The examples in the diagram have been chosen because they relate either to a number of sites

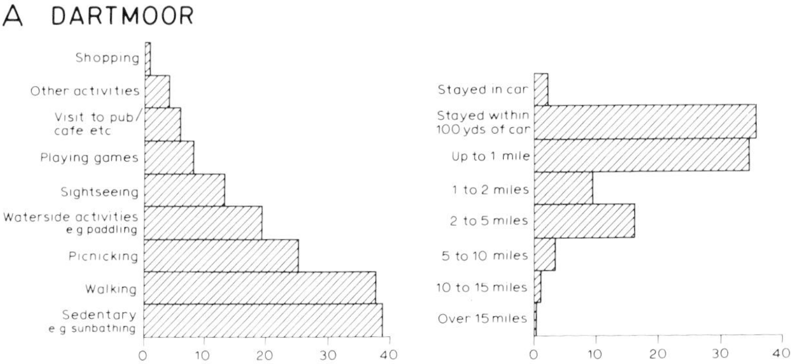

FIGURE 5.21A Visitor pursuits and distance travelled from the car in the Dartmoor National Park, summer Sunday 1975, based on visitor questionnaire survey.
Source: data from *Dartmoor National Park Plan* (Dartmoor National Park Authority, 1977), figures b and c, p. 8

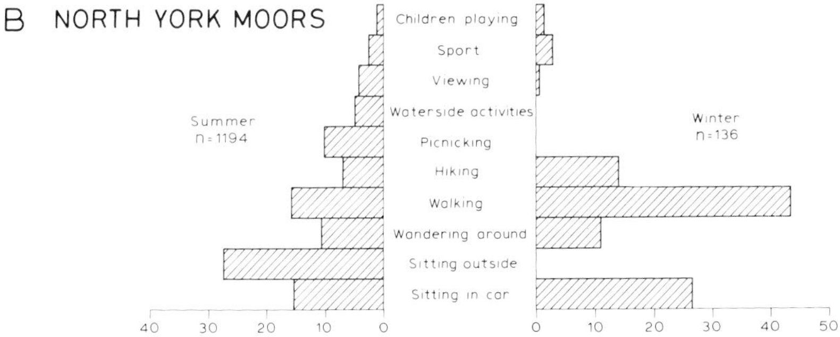

FIGURE 5.21B Visitor pursuits observed over 42 km^2 of the North York Moors National Park in summer and winter, 1976-77.
Source: data from D. Haffey, 'Recreational activity patterns on the uplands of an English National Park', *Environmental Conservation*, 6.3 (1979), table II, p. 239

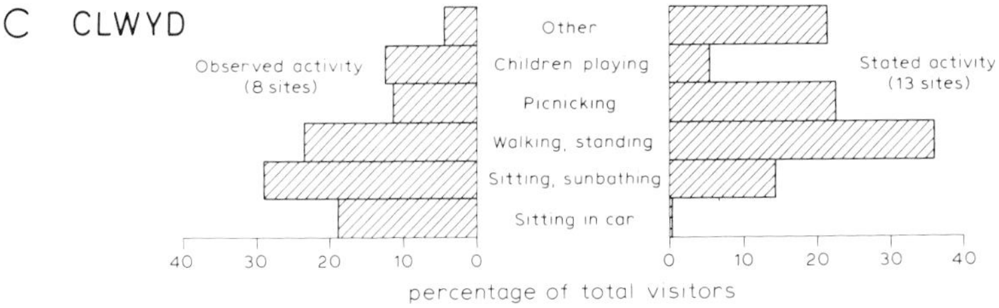

FIGURE 5.21C Visitor activities at recreational sites in Clwyd, as recorded by observers and as stated by visitors in response to questionnaires, July and August, 1973. While the form of the surveys precludes exact comparisons, the broad distinctions are valid.
Source: data from C. A. J. Jacobs, *Countryside Recreation Site Survey*, vol. 1 (Clwyd County Council, 1976), tables 22 and 23

or to a substantial tract of countryside, and are thus less susceptible in their results to the vagaries of a single site. Inter-site variations may indeed be great: in Clwyd, for example, picnicking varied from 2 to 36 per cent of observed activities between sites, sitting in vehicles from 14 to 44 per cent, and children playing from 1 to 24 per cent. There are also variations in time, both through the day[36] and between seasons (figure 5.21B).

The British public, however, appears to have a serious conscience about its inert image in countryside pursuits. Many surveys, the Dartmoor one included (figure 5.21 A), rely on information provided by the visitor to determine the characteristic activities. Observations suggest that visitor recall and perceived reality may differ substantially. The Clwyd survey (figure 5.21 C) combined both techniques, and while the results from each are not directly comparable, they highlight some broad variations. In particular, only 0.4 per cent of visitors admitted to simply sitting in cars: as the report dryly remarks, 'visitors either underestimated the time spent on this activity or possibly did not consider it a valid activity at all, despite the fact that it was included in the questionnaire'.[37] Sitting and sunbathing also appeared to arouse feelings of guilt, albeit in a less acute form!

SECOND HOMES

While some day trips range over considerable distances, these are the exceptions, as earlier sections have shown. Constrained by time and cost, the mean one-way distance travelled is only 40 km, even if occasional individual journeys range up to 300 km or more. The sheer variety and quality of Britain's coast and countryside means that there are few urban areas where seaside and rural enjoyment cannot be found relatively closely at hand.

Nevertheless, when the constraint of time is removed, there is a far greater opportunity to range further afield, to seek a more sustained recreation experience and to enjoy a higher quality of coastal and countryside resources. For most people such an opportunity is confined to holiday periods, but some have sought to extend their range through the purchase of a second home, giving them a residential base in a favoured area.

In the early 1970s it was estimated that there were some 300,000 to 350,000 second homes in England and Wales, with the number divided roughly equally between built homes – houses, cottages, bungalows, chalets and flats – and caravans.[38] At the time, the growth rate was thought to be about 25,000 a year, with built second homes growing more rapidly in number than caravans. In the event, that growth has not been sustained. The evidence is sparse, but for built second homes, Sarre suggests that a peak of 150,000-175,000 was reached in 1972, followed by a decline to 100,000-125,000 in 1975 and a slow recovery since that date, though perhaps not yet reaching the 1972 level.[39] The growth of static caravans has been curtailed by the reluctance of planning authorities to give planning permission for additional sites, especially in coastal areas where the demand is greatest. The extreme case is seen in Devon (figure 5.22). Static caravans, and static caravans owned by individuals as second homes, are not of course synonymous, but in that county the number of static caravans had declined by more than 7 per cent in a decade.[40] Nationally, numbers of static caravans are growing at perhaps one or two per cent per annum.[41]

By the standards of many Western European countries, second home ownership in Britain is on a very modest scale. If the numbers have changed but little in the last decade, only one household in 50 possesses a

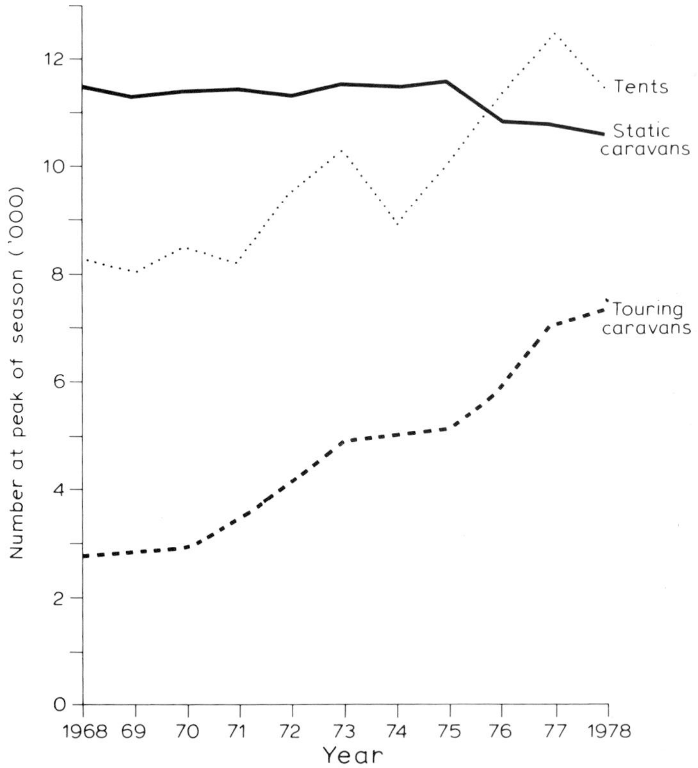

FIGURE 5.22 Caravans, tents and chalets used for holiday accommodation in Devon at the peak of the holiday season, 1968-78.
Source: data from *Annual survey of holiday development* (Devon County Council, 1979), table 7

second home, compared with one in five in Sweden, one in six in France and one in ten in Denmark.

There are marked regional concentrations, though the pattern is difficult to establish with any accuracy. The major concentrations of holiday homes are in the South East, the South West and Wales: these three regions between them have perhaps 60 per cent of the second homes in England and Wales, compared with 39 per cent of the total housing stock. The proportion of second homes in Wales is particularly high – 2.7 times its proportion of houses as a whole, or 2.4 times if caravans are excluded.[42]

Even more important are local concentrations within these regions. In several areas, second homes form more than a third of the total housing stock (figure 5.23). In the Lleyn peninsula in North Wales, the coastal parish of Llanengan had 39 per cent of its dwellings in second-home use in 1972: if the coastal resort of Abersoch alone is considered, the total rose to 55 per cent.[43] Nor are the concentrations along the coast alone: the parish of Betws Garmon on the west side of the Snowdon massif recorded a total

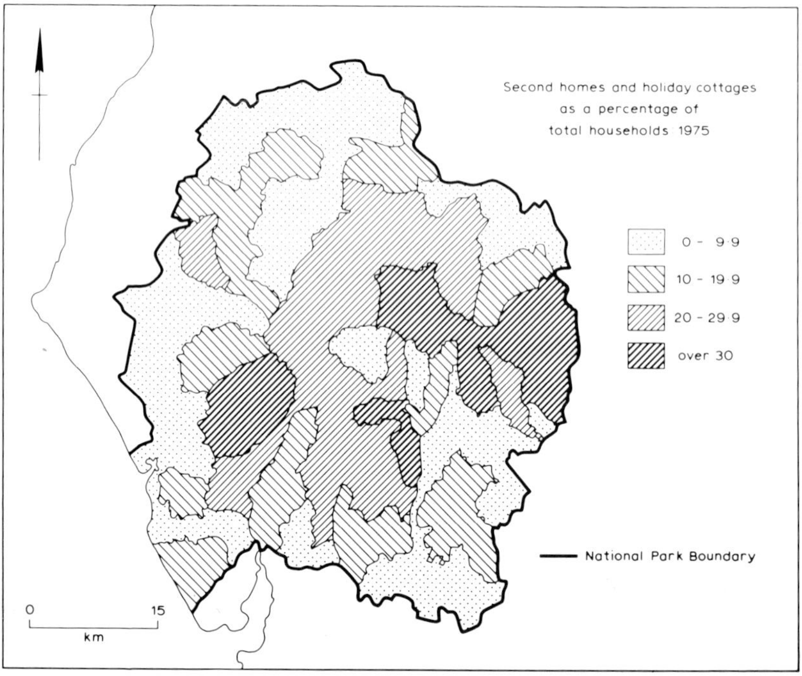

FIGURE 5.23 Second homes in the Lake District, 1975.
Source: based on *Lake District National Park: National Park Plan* (Lake District Special Planning Board, 1978), figure 10.3

of 35 per cent. Such concentrations reflect an intimate blend of opportunities of supply and demand. On the supply side, depopulation and declining job opportunities tend to concentrate the remaining indigenous population in the towns of a region, leaving a surplus of property suitable for built second homes in the more remote rural areas. On the demand side, would-be owners place a premium on the presence of an attractive coastline or mountain scenery, with facilities such as good beaches, harbours and walking country close at hand. Accessibility to the area of origin is also important.

This interplay of factors has led to issues of second home ownership becoming of much more than recreational significance, and to growing problems of an economic, social and political nature. These problems have been most acute through two sources of conflict. First, in some attractive areas, would-be purchasers of second homes are prepared to pay comparatively large sums for properties and thereby to price local people out of the market, which accelerates depopulation still further. In the Lake District, the Planning Board has not been content to leave the issue to market forces alone: 'It will be the Board's policy to pursue every possibility to ensure that in the future any new houses anywhere in the National Park will be for local use.' The only mechanism at its disposal is that of development control. Despite the difficulties,

> 'the Board is not content to play a passive role in exercising its development control powers; it believes that there is a need for more positive planning and that discrimination between the needs of local people and wishes of retirement or second-home owners is justified. Such a policy need not deter people coming to the Lake District from other parts of the country . . . if they wish to . . . have a holiday home there, then there is the existing housing stock to choose from . . .'[44]

In Wales the issues have touched an even sharper emotive chord; for, in addition to their more general economic and social impact, they are seen by some as a serious assault on indigenous culture and values. Reaction has been not only vociferous comment, but a continuing campaign of occupation and arson. The problem is exacerbated in Wales not only by the element of nationalism invoked, but by the high proportion of non-Welsh owners involved, estimated as high as 91 per cent in the Wye study.[45] How really representative the reaction remains is a matter for some doubt, however. In the area around Aberystwyth surveyed for the Wye study in 1969, only 15 per cent of local residents thought second home development was 'a bad trend', compared with 51 per cent in the southern Lake District.

The wider issues of second home ownership have perhaps attracted more than their fair share of attention. As a purely recreational phenomenon, their patterns of distribution and use occasion little surprise. They are predominantly coastal in location, with some 70 per cent of second homes having ready access to the sea.[46] They tend to be located at no great distance from the primary home: the Wye sample showed 36 per cent of second homes located in the same British Travel Association region as the primary home and a further 48 per cent in an immediately adjacent region. Much depended on local opportunities. Local movement was most strongly marked in the north of England, with coast and countryside close at hand. It was least evident in Wales, with a relatively small local population but a ready market in the conurbations of the North West and the West Midlands: in Gwynedd, 63 per cent of owners came from those two areas. Cornwall and Devon not only have a small local ownership potential, but are remote from major centres of population. With distance as a deterrent, and with ample intervening opportunities, it is not surprising that only 8 per cent of all second homes are situated there, despite these counties' role as the most popular holiday area in England and Wales.[47]

HOLIDAY HORDES

While second homes remain the cherished possession of a tiny minority, holidays away from home are the annual pinnacle of recreation experience for the great majority, saved for, longed for in prospect and savoured in retrospect. In total leisure spending, they are second only to alcohol (figure 1.5). In 1980, holiday spending by British residents in Britain was estimated as totalling £2420 million: holidays abroad added a further £3510 million.[48]

Expenditure on this scale emphasises the importance of holidays and tourism as an economic as well as a social and spatial phenomenon. In a wider context, nearly 6 per cent of all Britain's export earnings and almost 17 per cent of all her invisible export earnings come from tourism. Tourism is also a major source of employment: it has been estimated that about 1.5 million people in Britain owe their livelihood directly or indirectly to tourism.[49]

In the present context, however, it is the spatial rather than the economic aspects of holidays that are of concern.[50] It matters little whether the visitor to coast and countryside is out for the day from home or on holiday in terms of his use of the resource, but holiday visitors increase the pressures on many areas in both time and space. The proportions of holiday visitors obviously vary widely both within and between recreation areas (table 5.5). Even in a relatively remote area, increasingly popular for

TABLE 5.5 Day visitors and holidaymakers in the Northumberland National Park, summer 1980, as percentage of total visitors

	Sunday		*Weekday*	
	Day	*Holiday*	*Day*	*Holiday*
Cheviot area	68	32	55	45
Hadrian's Wall	35	65	19	81

Source: data from *The 1980 visitor surveys* (Northumberland National Park, Occasional Paper 4, 1981), tables 70 and 73

holidays, the importance of the day visitor remains surprisingly strong. On Dartmoor, for example, in the mid-1970s, 52 per cent of all visitors were home-based; on a summer Sunday that proportion rose to 60 per cent, but varied at individual sites from 84 per cent at Huccaby Bridge to 23 per cent at Buckfast. On a weekday, on the other hand, only 39 per cent were home-based.[51]

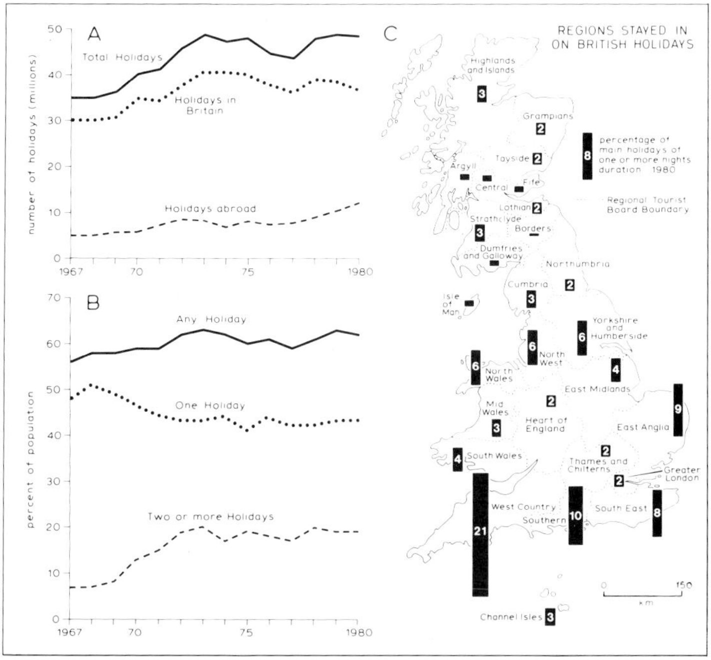

FIGURE 5.24 Holidays, holiday-taking and holiday destinations.
Source: data from *Digest of Tourist Statistics*, no. 9 (British Tourist Authority, 1981), tables 50, 52 and 56

Since the late 1960s, holidays have increased appreciably in number, from 35 million in 1965 to over 48 million by 1980 (figure 5.24 A).[52] In relative terms there has been a modest increase in holidays spent in Britain, though for these, a peak was reached in the mid-1970s. Much more striking has been the startling rise in holidays taken abroad, from one in seven of all holidays in 1965 to one in four in 1980. The gain continued in the difficult economic circumstances of the late 1970s: between 1975 and 1980, holidays in Britain decreased by 9 per cent while holidays abroad increased by 50 per cent.

Holidays and holidaymakers are not, of course, synonymous. For more than two decades the proportion of people taking any holiday in the course of the year has remained remarkably constant at around 60 per cent (figure 5.24 B). This is not to say that 40 per cent do not go on holiday: earlier work suggests that, over a period of three years, 75 per cent of the total population would take one or more holidays. Nevertheless one in four rarely, if ever, take a holiday – a lack, not surprisingly, most prevalent among the elderly and the lowest-income groups. In 1980, 24 per cent of all adults who took no holiday were aged 65 and over, though this age group comprises only 18 per cent of the adult population. Again, 43 per cent of social classes D and E had no holiday, though they form only 30 per cent of the adult population.

The most striking change has been the growing practice of taking more than one holiday away from home. Increased affluence and increased holiday entitlement (figure 1.3) brought a quick response in the early 1970s. Since 1973, up to one in five of the population has enjoyed two holidays of four or more nights away from home each year.

HOLIDAY HAUNTS

The two prime factors in the choice of holiday destination are the friction of distance and the lure of the sun, factors that are equally applicable abroad and at home.

Distance is a matter not only of actual cost but also of perceived convenience. This is particularly the case for holidays abroad. Cost is obviously significant: while social classes A and B form 15 per cent of the adult population as a whole, they comprised 31 per cent of those who took a holiday abroad in 1980. Convenience has been fostered by the twin stimuli of the package holiday, with its remarkable value for money in a highly competitive market, and the ease and speed of transport brought by jet aircraft. Package holidays accounted for 61 per cent of all holidays abroad in 1980, and air travel for 68 per cent. Perceived journey times are brief, with Corfu seemingly more accessible than Cornwall.

Destinations have a strong Mediterranean emphasis. The top five European countries visited in 1980 were all, in part at least, Mediterranean: Spain (including Majorca) had 23 per cent, France 14 per cent, Italy 8 per cent, Greece 7 per cent and Malta 5 per cent of the total market. The only country outside Europe with comparable drawing power was the USA with 7 per cent of the total. Cheap Atlantic fares, a favourable exchange rate with the dollar, and package holidays to Florida sun more than trebled the United States' share of visitors in less than a decade.

The same basic factors hold good for destinations at home (figure 5.24 C). The lure of the coast was emphasised earlier in the chapter, and the continuing role of the traditional seaside resorts must also be stressed. Of Devon's estimated 269,100 holidaymakers at the height of the season, for example, 95 per cent stayed in the coastal districts, 35 per cent in Torbay alone.[53] But overlying the move to the coastal periphery is the overall drift to the south and west. More than one in five of all holidays in Britain is spent in the West Country: if the remaining south coast counties and the Channel Islands are added, the proportion rises to more than two in five. The pull is not so much sand and scenery but sun; the differences slight but significant. In August, for example, Brighton, Bournemouth and Torquay have a mean temperature 1 degC higher than Scarborough and Blackpool – 17°C against 16°C. Hours of sunshine show a stronger contrast: Brighton, Bournemouth and Torquay have a daily August average of 6.8, 6.6 and 6.7 hours respectively, compared with 5.2 hours for Scarborough and 5.5 hours for Blackpool.

None the less, the friction of distance remains surprisingly strong. The British Tourist Authority now unfortunately uses Tourist Board regions to distinguish visitor destinations, but Economic Planning Regions to record their origins for the annual British Home Tourism Survey. It is thus no longer possible to determine readily for the country as a whole the proportion of visitors to a region resident in that region or in adjacent regions,[54] though where Tourist and Planning regions coincide this can still be done (table 5.6). Exact proportions reflect both boundary location and the particular characteristics of the region, but in all three cases, some seven out of ten visitors are resident either in the same region or in one adjacent. Other evidence underlines the pattern of relatively short distance movement, as the Gwynedd study showed (figure 5.11). Elsewhere, in 1980 75 per cent of holiday visitors to Surrey, Kent and East and West Sussex came from London and the South East, and 67 per cent of holiday visitors to Cumbria (including the Lake District) from the North, North West and Yorkshire and Humberside regions.[55]

The impact of holidays is confined not only in space but also in time (figure 5.13). The acute seasonal peak, much more sharply pronounced than for outdoor recreation in general, shows few signs of abating, ruled

TABLE 5.6 Origins of British holiday visitors to selected English tourist regions, 1980

	From same region (% of total)	*From adjacent regions (% of total)*	*From other regions (% of total)*
Yorkshire & Humberside	38	31	32
North West	28	43	30
West Country	21*	57	23

* The South West Economic Planning Region includes Gloucestershire and a part of Dorset, which are not included in the West Country Tourist Board region.
Source: data from English Tourist Board, *Tourism regional fact sheets 1980* (ETB, 1981)

not so much by the vagaries of the fickle British summer as the dictates of education authorities in fixing school holidays. In 1951, 64 per cent of main holidays began in July or August; in 1980, 58 per cent: for much of the intervening period, it has hovered close to 60 per cent.

The peak is even more accentuated for particular groups of visitors. The trend to the use of more informal accommodation was noted in an earlier chapter (figure 2.5). Such informal accommodation is particularly characteristic of holidays by families with children, where the relative freedom it offers, as well as its economy, is an obvious attraction (figure 5.25). Its use, however, is markedly more peaked than for accommodation as a whole. In contrast, hotels have had some modest success in spreading the peak, for more of their characteristic customers are free to take holidays away from the height of summer (figure 5.26).

On a day-to-day basis, holidaymakers' patterns of activities within the holiday area differ but little from those of day visitors, and in that respect have been discussed earlier in the chapter. Little attention, however, has been given to the *sequence* of those activities as the holiday progresses. For how long does the holidaymaker stay in the chosen resort, and how far does he range in seeking other venues? How are these other sites discovered, when in the course of the holiday are they visited, and is there a greater propensity to search for variety as the holiday progresses?

The answers to such questions will vary radically according to weather and season as well as with the character of the resort and the nature of its hinterland, but some interesting insights emerged in Cooper's study of holidaymakers' behaviour patterns on Jersey (figure 5.27).[56] As an island, Jersey has particular advantages for such work, affording in effect a closed system, but the basic approach is worth pursuing for other resorts.

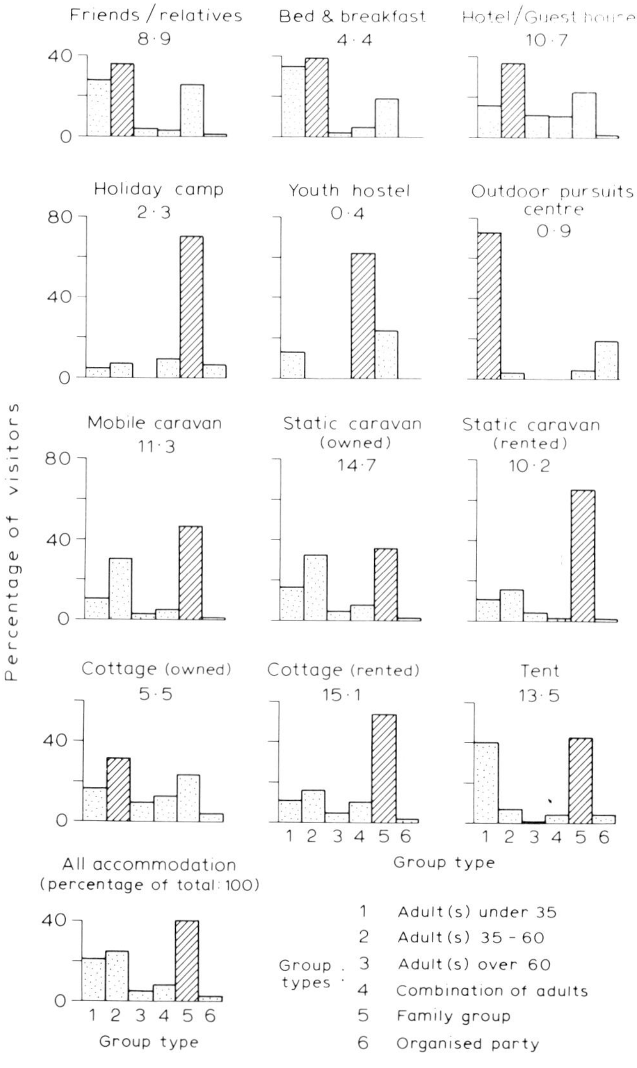

FIGURE 5.25 The types of group using the major kinds of holiday accommodation in Gwynedd, 1980.
Source: data from *Gwynedd 1980 Tourism Survey* (Gwynedd County Planning Department, 1981), tables 14.1 and 14.3

Visitors are, of course, far from homogeneous, and different groups show considerable variety in the number of sites visited in the course of the holiday (figure 5.27A). Overlying this variety, however, was a clear sequence in the ordering of the visits (figure 5.27B).

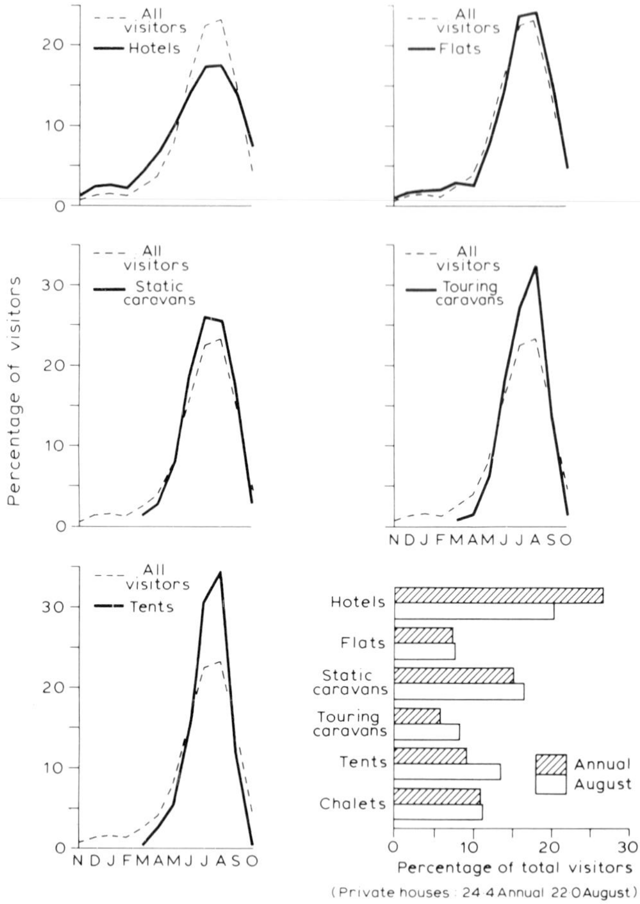

FIGURE 5.26 The seasonal use of different types of holiday accommodation in Devon, 1977-78.
Source: data from *Annual survey of holiday development, 1978* (Devon County Council, 1979), table 6

At each stage, the tourist seeks to maximise enjoyment by reducing the uncertainty inherent in visiting an unknown site. Typically, the holiday begins at either the resort where the visitor is staying or at the best known centre. In Jersey, St Helier fulfils this role. It contains 62 per cent of the holiday accommodation, and 75 per cent of the tourists sampled were there on the first day. The next targets are the best-known beaches: on Jersey, the two largest, St Brelade's Bay and Gorey, received most visits (from 35 per cent of the sample) on the second and third days. This is also the peak period for touring the island, an effective way to gather

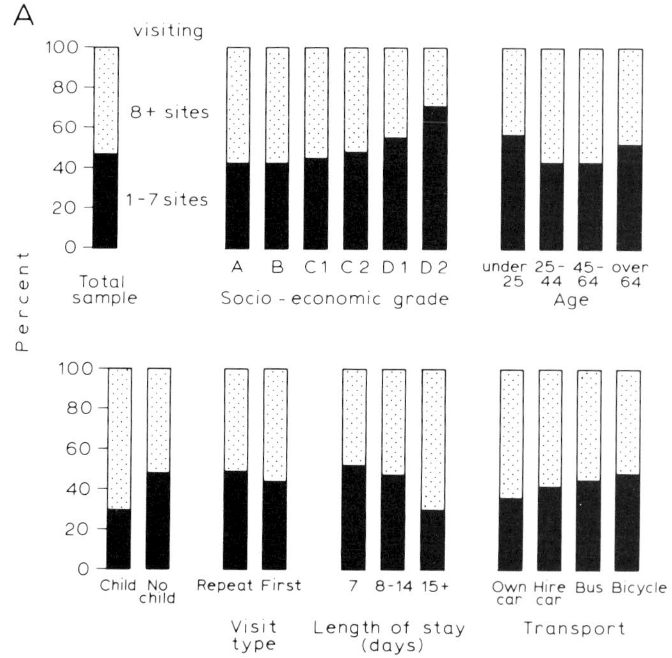

FIGURE 5.27A The number of different sites visited by holidaymakers in Jersey, 1974. The data relate to the first five days of the holiday, with each day broken into five time periods.

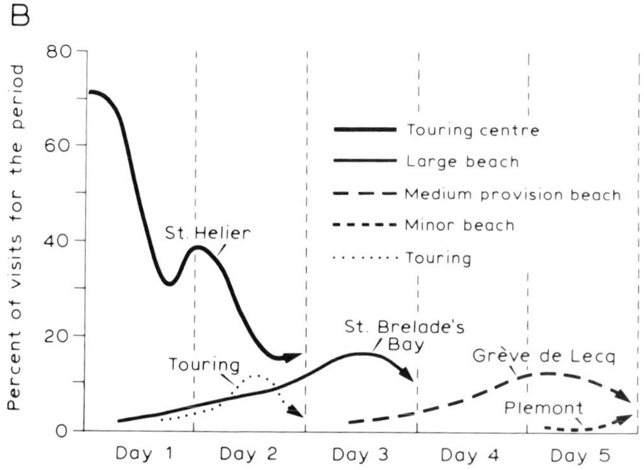

FIGURE 5.27B Idealised sequence of visits by holidaymakers to sites in Jersey, 1974.
Source: data from C. P. Cooper, 'Spatial and temporal patterns of tourist behaviour', *Regional Studies*, 15 (1981), table 3 and figure 3

information by those unfamiliar with its opportunities. Indeed, general touring without a long stop at any one place is confined almost entirely to the first two days, reaching a peak (of 18 per cent of the sample) on the second day. As knowledge increases, and time progresses, so smaller sites lower in the hierarchy are visited, but their visiting peaks are not only later in the week but of smaller amplitude. Greve de Lecq, for example, a medium-provision beach on the north coast, has a visiting peak (of 14 per cent of the sample) on the fourth day, while the tiny cove of Plemont reaches its peak (a mere 1 per cent) on day 5.

Overall, a clear pattern emerges of 'a wave of visits which spreads down the hierarchy, decreasing in amplitude as it dissipates among increasing numbers of sites'.[57] Not only do such patterns of diffusion have an intrinsic interest in themselves, but, if they are shown to be equally characteristic of other, less homogeneous, areas, they can influence the design of management schemes to manipulate visitor information levels and help channel visitor movement away from sensitive areas towards those where enjoyment is heightened and conflict lessened.

6 Countryside Resources

THE RURAL PARADISE

> The German sociologist, Erwin Scheuch, once asked people what sort of environment they would like to live in: a substantial number wanted a detached house by a lake, in its own extensive grounds, five minutes from an office job in a city centre. The job of the planner is to recognize the impracticality of that solution, and then to do his best to get as near to it as possible.[1]

As with living, so with playing: Peter Hall's view of the planner's dilemma is as true of recreation as of planning as a whole. Limpid lake, lush meadow, lone mountain just beyond the garden fence may be the ideal: reality for most is far more prosaic.

But as a nation of towndwellers, we retain at heart a vision of a rural paradise. As Marion Shoard put it so evocatively,

> England's countryside is not only one of the great treasures of the earth, it is also a vital part of our national identity. All of us – even those who rarely step outside our towns – cherish somewhere in our souls the same vision of our real homeland: a rural vision . . . England's patchwork quilt of fields, downs and woods, separated by thick hedgerows, mossy banks, sunken lanes and sparkling streams. For hundreds of years, our English countryside has given us such ideas as we have had of what paradise might be like.[2]

For all the hyperbole, recreation for many is still a search for that paradise – the movement of the eight out of ten who are urban dwellers from the eighth of the land that their towns occupy to the seven-eighths of rural hinterland.

Paradise regained, however, is not a simple matter of movement enabled, for that hinterland is not a common resource of common quality and common opportunity. The pattern and periodicity of movement has been traced: it remains to consider the resource itself in all its variety and utility. In the confines of the present book, that consideration must be brief and selective, for both the character of the resource and its wider problems have generated a full and recent literature,[3] but it would be equally unbalanced not to reiterate and emphasise some of the themes that have emerged.

In recreation terms, three themes are important. First, there is the visual character of the resource itself, the very quality that gives stimulus and satisfaction. So much of that quality is intertwined with the theme of conservation and the composition of the rural landscape as a whole: for all its importance, however, that aspect is marginal to our purpose and will receive comparatively scant attention. The second theme is recreational opportunity, the direct use of the rural environment for recreational pursuits, both on sites with a uniquely recreational purpose and on those where recreation must compete directly and indirectly with other uses. The third theme is recreational variety, the variety of rural landscapes and the variety of recreational opportunity that each affords. It is that variety that is the geographer's concern; the frequent imbalance of recreational demand with resource supply, and the consequent compromises and patterns that such imbalance engenders.

Conceptually, this imbalance was at the root of one of the earliest of recreation analyses. Clawson and Knetsch, in their seminal work on outdoor recreation in the USA, conceived in the 1950s and published in the 1960s, used the economist's classic demand and supply approach. Of the supply aspects of the equation, they wrote

> Public and private [recreation] areas each have their own special problems. But they also share problems, for although areas may differ in ownership and in name they may be similar in nature and use.
>
> Because there are so many physically different kinds of outdoor recreation areas, some classification into fewer groups is helpful for understanding and analysis. Our classification is a threefold one . . . At one extreme . . . are the *user-oriented areas* . . . Their most important characteristic is their ready accessibility to users . . . *Resource-based areas* are at the other extreme. Their dominant characteristic is their outstanding physical resources . . . *Intermediate areas* lie between these extremes, both geographically and in terms of use.[4]

The simplicity of the concept remains its strength. Where the resource is the focus, its character and conservation are the dominant issues; where the user is the focus, the creation and design of adequate opportunity predominate. Strictly, Clawson and Knetsch thought of user-oriented areas as being developed largely within the urban fabric: more conventionally, they have now come to mean all those where location rather than resource quality is of prime importance. The shorter distances involved overall in Britain have lessened the significance of the transitional, intermediate category.

In this chapter, the basic Clawson approach will be followed, with resource-based areas first considered and then some user-oriented areas reviewed. For convenience, a further distinction will be drawn between land-based and water-based resources, with the latter accorded separate and subsequent treatment.

PARADISE LOST?

Fashion has played almost as large a part in countryside concerns as in countryside appreciation. Two hundred years ago, William Gilpin could write, of the view over Derwent Water, 'Nothing conveys an idea of *beauty* more strongly, than the lake; nor of *horrour* than the mountains.'[5] Of that same scene, Vaughan Cornish, a century and a half later, could exult that 'Each morning as the sun climbed I watched that pageantry of far-flung shadows which passes so quickly in the plain, but among the mountains is a long-drawn delight.'[6]

For many, physical challenge and physical exhilaration outweigh aesthetic pleasure, in lowland as in upland countryside, but whatever the preference and whatever the roots of the experience, the visual character of the rural scene is the essential setting of its recreational value. Current concern has concentrated anew on changes in that character. In part, concern springs from deep-rooted reaction to any change: 'love of the past complements English devotion to the open air.'[7] But the pace, the scale and the direction of change has quickened to a degree that has linked the protest of the enthusiast to a far wider swell of public opinion. Above all, it has combined the twin threads of landscape conservation and nature conservation, threads parted in the 1949 National Parks and Access to the Countryside Act with the separated powers of the National Parks Commission and the Nature Conservancy.[8]

Hugh Prince avers that 'the English like landscapes compartmented into small scenes furnished with belfried church towers, half-timbered thatched cottages, rutted lanes, rookeried elms, lich gates, and stiles – in short, "the intimate and appealing beauty which our forebears impressed upon it".'[9] While some might cavil at this judgement, it is this very intimacy of scene, rooted in the landscape of enclosure, that has suffered most in the changed agricultural practices of the postwar years.

In the arable areas, mechanisation, with more and bigger machines, has led to the wholesale amalgamation of fields to give unencumbered spaces within which the machines can work most efficiently. Hedgerows and other field boundaries, clumps of trees and woods have been rooted out on an alarming scale. Between 1946 and 1974, a quarter of all the hedgerows of England and Wales were removed – about 190,000 km in all, or 7250 km a year – and there is every sign that the process is continuing.[10] The toll has been particularly high in the arable eastern counties: for example, 45 per cent of Norfolk's hedgerows, some 13,000 km, were removed between 1946 and 1970.

The direct impact on the landscape is immediate and obvious: equally serious, and even more insidious, has been the concomitant reduction of habitats for both flora and fauna. To hedgerow removal must be added other contemporary practices – the draining of wetlands, the ploughing of roughland and the clearance of broadleaved woodland – and the destructive impact of the widespread use of herbicides and pesticides.

Marion Shoard's polemic, *The theft of the countryside*, published in 1980, encapsulated the new mood of concern. Her message was simple and direct:

> Speedily, but almost imperceptibly, the English countryside is being turned into a vast, featureless expanse of prairie . . . This new English landscape can offer little delight to the human eye or ear. It cannot sustain our traditional wild flowers, birds and animals. But each year it takes over hundreds more square miles of England . . . And unless something is done to curb agricultural intensification, virtually the whole of the countryside will be no more than a food factory by the early part of the next century.[11]

The problem, of course, is far from new. Indeed, the original enclosures, creating the now treasured intimacy, brought their own riposte. Muriel Ashby records that at Tysoe in Warwickshire:

> Land had formerly been like the falling rain, free alike in some measure to the just and the unjust. On foot or on your pony you could thread your way by balk and headland over to any village in the neighbourhood, but some of these were set miles further away by the new private fields. Now the very Red Horse itself had been penned up within hedges, without even a footpath past it. The Whitsun Games were never held again. The enclosure of the open fields was a visible sign and symbol that rampant family and individual power had gained a complete victory over the civic community.[12]

Change, however, is far from exclusively a lowland phenomenon. At times more insidious, but equally severe, changes in the uplands bid fair to etch unwanted traits in the most dramatic and valued scenery. The problems are rooted in social, economic and environmental decline, in 'failure to integrate effectively the various policies and incentives devised by government in both Whitehall and Brussels.'[13] These issues, and the wider debate on conservation and the countryside, are beyond the scope of this book, but their impact on the recreation setting needs constant emphasis.

One instance of the scale of upland change must suffice. The North York Moors owe their characteristic beauty, and their designation as a national park, to the open sweeps of heather-dominated moor. This moorland extends over 511 km^2, the largest tract of heather-covered upland in England.[14] Throughout history, there have been wide fluctuations in its extent,[15] but much of this has resulted from changes in the position of the moorland edge. Between 1904 and 1950, for example, 65 km^2 of moorland were reclaimed but 70 km^2 of cultivated land reverted. Now a more serious contraction has occurred: since the national park was designated in 1952, virtually 25 per cent of the moorland has been converted to forest or to improved agricultural land (figure 6.1 and illustrations 6 and 7). While much of the change took place in the years immediately after designation, between 1975 and 1980 conversion was still occurring at an annual rate of 2.8 km^2.

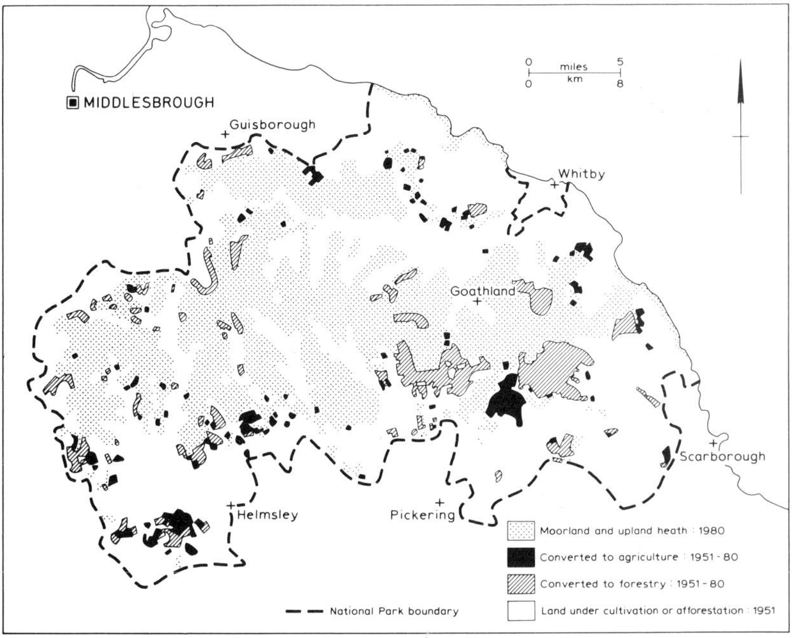

FIGURE 6.1 Moorland loss in the North York Moors National Park, 1951-80. *Source:* data from *The future of the moorland* (North York Moors National Park Committee, 1981), map 4

6 The Cleveland scarp from Hasty Bank, North York Moors, 1955.

Even more disturbing is the fact that 88 per cent of all remaining moorland is suitable on technical grounds for afforestation or agricultural improvement: of the other 12 per cent, 7.5 per cent is susceptible to erosion or degradation. Indeed, the remaining constraints are largely economic and legal, not technical: it is ironic that the biggest single measure of protection is afforded not by national park status and

7 The same scene as illustration 6 in 1979: most of the scarp face is now covered with conifers.

designation but by registration as common land. In 1980, 53 per cent of moorland was registered common, and cannot in this context be legally enclosed or afforested without ministerial permission.

Cereals or conifers represent the extreme of moorland change, but moorland degradation insidiously saps the visual experience. Traditional management practice, with controlled burning of the heather over a 10- to 15-year cycle to maintain young growth for sheep to graze, is labour-intensive. The withdrawal of sheep from the moors, and a general decrease in active management, has led to large areas of very old heather carrying a high fire risk. The resulting indiscriminate burning, at the wrong time of the year, has led to serious encroachment by bracken, an encroachment hastened by the lack of bracken-cutting for bedding and the overall reduction in the intensity of grazing. Bracken is currently spreading at the rate of some 120 ha a year (figure 6.2).

Recreation cannot be divorced from wider issues of landscape management, and of landscape and wildlife conservation. While the area available for recreation may be little affected, the quality and the continuity of the recreation experience most certainly is. It is no accident that landscape conservation and rural recreation have been inextricably, if confusingly, linked in legislation and the development of institutions.

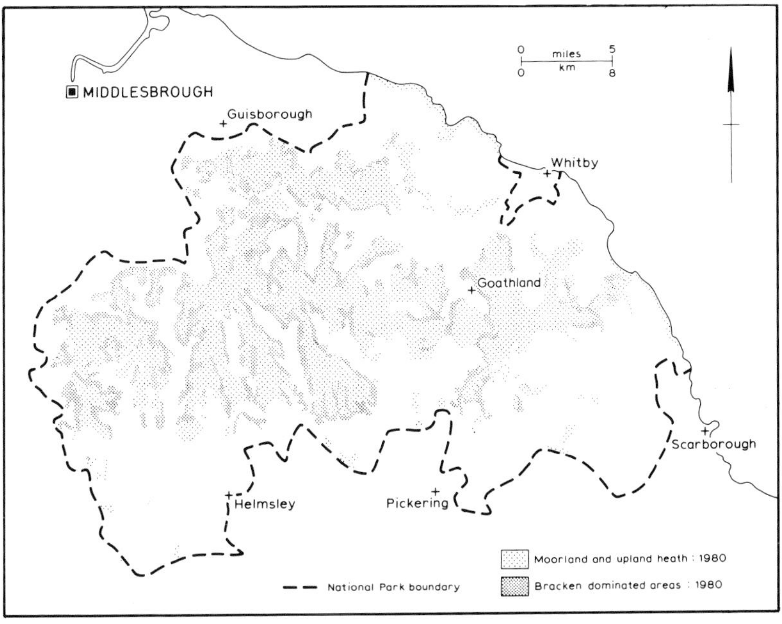

FIGURE 6.2 Bracken infestation in the North York Moors National Park, 1980.
Source: data from *The future of the moorland* (North York Moors National Park Committee, 1982), map 6

PARADISE PRESERVED

These links are seen at their most compelling in the emergence of national parks, and in the changing emphases and concerns of their management. The ten national parks of England and Wales cover 13,600 km^2, 9 per cent of the total area (figure 6.3). Their scale, and the quality of the scenery they encompass, have meant that, both as landscapes and as institutions, they have been the subject of close and critical review.[16] To add to those reviews would be tedious and presumptuous, but some themes need reiteration.

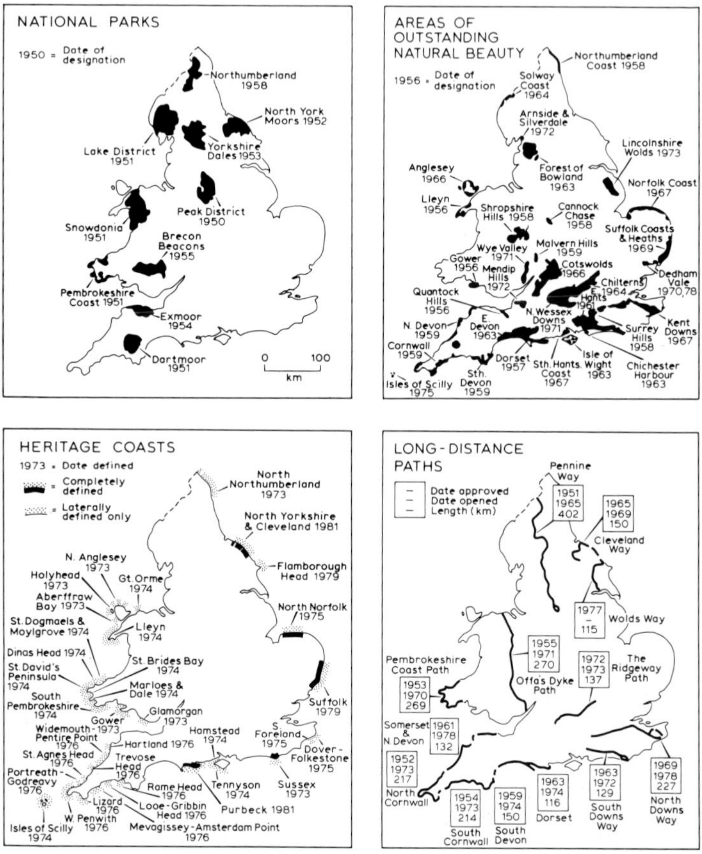

FIGURE 6.3 National parks, Areas of Outstanding Natural Beauty, Heritage Coasts and Long Distance Paths at 30 September 1981. The Wolds Way was opened in October 1982.
Source: data from *Fourteenth report of the Countryside Commission for the year ended 30 September 1981* (HMSO, 1982)

In an international context, Britain's national parks came late and were of a very different character to their precursors overseas. In the United States, an Act of Congress in 1864 during the Civil War ceded the Yosemite Valley to the state of California as a public park on the condition that it would be 'inalienable for all time'. In 1872 the first national park was established at Yellowstone: its scale was truly heroic, covering an area almost half the size of Wales. A parallel concern was shown in other developing areas of European settlement. By 1900 there were three national parks in Canada, six in Australia and two in New Zealand. All these, however, were concerned to preserve, in public ownership, truly outstanding areas of *natural* scenery: the parks were separated areas, dedicated to landscape conservation.

This philosophy is explicit in the International Union for the Conservation of Nature and Natural Resources (IUCN) 1969 definition of a national park as:

> a relatively large area
> [a] where one or several ecosystems are not materially altered by human exploitation and occupation, where plant and animal species, geomorphological sites and habitats are of special scientific, educative and recreative interest or which contain a natural landscape of great beauty and
> [b] where the highest competent authority of the country has taken steps to prevent or eliminate as soon as possible exploitation or occupation in the whole area and to enforce effectively the respect of ecological, geomorphological or aesthetic features which have led to its establishment and
> [c] where visitors are allowed to enter, under special conditions, for inspirational, cultural and recreative purposes.[17]

The whole ethos is of separated areas, publicly owned, where the visitor has no inherent right of entry and is subordinate to the needs and values of conservation.

By the end of the Second World War, such an approach was clearly impossible in a British context.[18] The whole landscape had long been 'materially altered by human exploitation and occupation' and the vast majority was in long-established, fragmented private ownership. An alternative concept was needed: 'the British experiment may be seen as an imaginative step that extended the idea of preservation from wilderness reserves to the countryside at large, in areas where the land remained in diverse ownerships and sustained a population through a diversity of uses.'[19]

Of crucial importance was the type of landscape to be so conserved. John Dower, in his seminal report prepared during the Second World War and published in 1945, wrote of 'an extensive area of beautiful and relatively wild country',[20] words that came to enshrine the national park ideal. His own list of areas 'suitable, and desirable for establishment as national parks during the first period of operations' covered ten such areas. They coincided save in one respect with the eventual designations: he included the Cornish coast but omitted from the first list the North York Moors. In many cases, however, he envisaged smaller, more narrowly defined areas than those ultimately created. His listed areas covered some 9300 km^2 compared with the 13,600 km^2 of the ten parks now existing. Dower's ideas were refined by the Hobhouse Committee, whose Report was published in 1947.[21] They broadly accepted Dower's view of the nature of national parks, but were concerned not only that sheer quality of landscape was important, but also that proximity to centres of population should be considered, and that, if possible, at least one should be readily accessible from London. They recommended twelve in all, covering some 14,700 km^2. In addition to rejecting the Cornish coast and including the North York Moors, they also added the Broads (despite Dower's insistence that they did not fit in with his definition of a national park) and the South Downs, overtly selected because of 'the importance of including at least one . . . within easy reach of London' (para. 39).

In the event, neither the Broads nor the South Downs was designated, but the boundaries of the others were drawn wide enough to include much 'beautiful', but not always 'relatively wild' country. In the uplands, the essential interdigitation of hill and valley, of rough grazing and cultivated land, precludes a narrow definition, but in the North York Moors, for example, enclosed and improved agricultural land covers 48 per cent of the national park,[22] and in the Brecon Beacons, 49 per cent.[23]

There is, indeed, an argument that a crucial weakness of the existing national parks is their very size, precluding effective conservation. The debate was waged with vigour in the *Report of the National Park Policies Review Committee* in 1974. Some members of the committee wanted to create 'national heritage areas', believing 'that there are areas of our national parks, most of which will be relatively small, which have such unsullied rural beauty and character that they should be sustained for future generations as jealously as we sustain our cathedrals, castles and ancient monuments' (para. 20.4). Others felt that such recognition would be at the expense of the parks as a whole, for 'the introduction of an additional superior category of protected area would inevitably depreciate the status of the remaining areas in the minds of the public and of decision takers . . . In practice it is the settings, rather than the gems, which are at risk' (para. 21.3).

The system has,.in fact, remained virtually unchanged in size since the designation of the final park in 1955. It remains predominantly a privately owned preserve (figure 6.4). Overall, only 27 per cent of the land in the

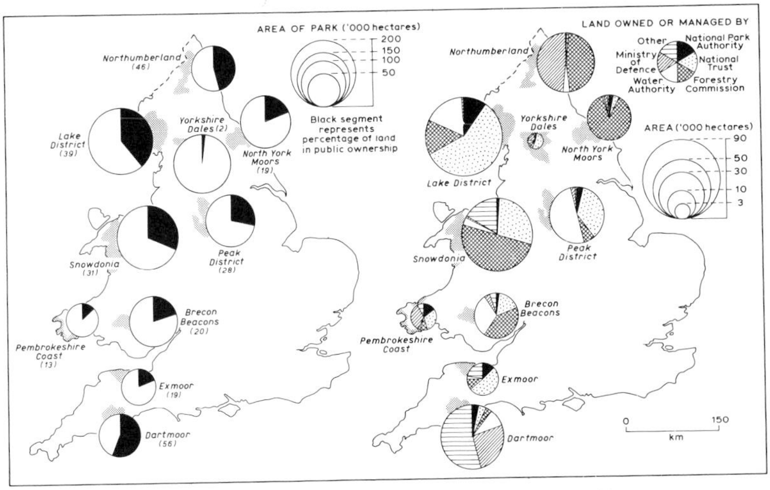

FIGURE 6.4 Land in public ownership in national parks, 1981.
Source: Data from *County Councils Gazette* (November 1981), p. 268

parks is in the ownership of any public body, the proportion ranging from 2 per cent in the Yorkshire Dales to 56 per cent in Dartmoor.

Ownership, however, is only part of the story. Not all public owners fully ascribe to the aims of the national parks. There is a world of difference between, for example, the National Trust on the one hand and the water authorities and the Ministry of Defence on the other in terms of access to land for recreation purposes. Forestry Commission ownership can result in landscape changes that may be directly opposed to the concept of landscape the park seeks to preserve. The two biggest public owners are the Forestry Commission and the National Trust: they own or manage 8.1 and 7.6 per cent respectively of the total area of the parks. The actual national park authorities themselves own a mere 1.3 per cent of the total. Location may be as important as ownership; in the Lake District National Park, for example, the National Trust owns 22.5 per cent of the land, but the impact of that ownership is made all the greater by its concentration in the heart of the area (figure 6.5).

The basic purposes of the parks were spelled out in the formal language of Section 5–1 of the 1949 National Parks and Access to the Countryside Act, which 'shall have effect for the purpose of preserving and enhancing the natural beauty of the areas specified . . . and for the purpose of promoting their enjoyment by the public'. To assist in these purposes, the Act provided for the setting up of a National Parks Commission (appointed in February 1950) and placed responsibility for the planning and management of each designated park on a planning board or a specially constituted committee of the local planning authority. The major

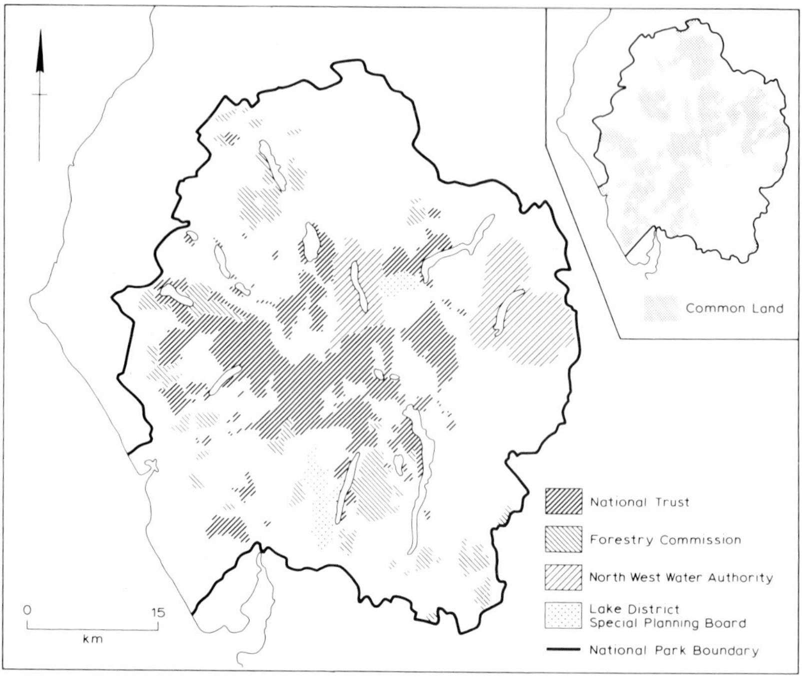

FIGURE 6.5 Land ownership in the Lake District National Park.
Source: based on *Lake District National Park Plan* (Lake District Special Planning Board, 1978), figure 1.4

change in these arrangements (apart from the replacement of the National Parks Commission by the Countryside Commission under the provisions of the 1968 Countryside Act) came in 1974, when each park became the responsibility of a single executive board (in the case of the Peak District and the Lake District) or a separate national park committee. From this date, each park had an executive National Park Officer with his own staff, and each was required to produce a management plan within three years. The individual park boards or committees continued to have two-thirds of their members appointed by the county councils in whose area they lay, and one-third by the Secretary of State.[24]

The administrative arrangements for the parks are important in understanding the ways in which – and the extent to which – their purposes have been achieved. As the Sandford Committee noted, 'the designation of a national park does not alter the ownership of the land within it; nor does designation of itself confer any new rights upon the public . . . The main effect of designation is to define and give national significance to the purposes for which these areas should be planned and managed' (para.

1.7). 'The paradox remains that in the United Kingdom the title "national park" has misled visitors and natives alike for more than 30 years, arousing fears that have little justification and expectations that it has not satisfied.'[25] Finances as well as powers are limited. Not until 1971-72 did expenditure by national park authorities total more than £1 million in a single year: even in 1980-81 the turnover only just exceeded £10 million, and this for 9 per cent of the area of England and Wales with an estimated indigenous population in 1980 of 243,451 (table 6.1).

Within such a restricted budget, the extent to which national park purposes have been achieved is perhaps surprising. In 'preserving and enhancing natural beauty', the prime instrument has been the normal mechanisms of development control with all the limitations as well as the opportunities they provide. These mechanisms evolved primarily to match urban needs, and have been fearsomely inadequate for many rural purposes. Above all, they relate to the built environment and have little impact in consequence on much of the rural landscape. They are, in any event, inherently negative in application, relevant only when there are to be material changes in land – and building – use. It is also difficult to measure the success of a policy whose impact is seen more in what is *not* present in the landscape rather than in the changes that have occurred.

TABLE 6.1 National park financial statistics, 1980-1 outturn

	£ million	*per cent*
Income		
Receipts from users	2.040	20.0
Grants from national exchequer	6.058	59.5
(National Parks Supplementary Grant, and grant aid from Countryside Commission)		
Local authorities	2.083	20.5
	10.181	100.0
*Expenditure**		
Debt charges	0.026	0.3
Information services	1.838	18.0
Recreation	2.356	23.1
Conservation	0.596	5.9
Estate maintenance	0.251	2.5
Administration	3.748	36.8
Capital projects	1.366	13.4
	10.181	100.0

* Of net expenditure, 74.4 per cent came direct from national government: in addition, expenditure by local authorities was subject to rate support grant.
Source: data from *County Councils Gazette* (November, 1981) pp. 268-9

In the present context, a fleeting review must suffice. Pressures for change remain strong. In 1980-81 there were 6188 planning applications determined in the parks, ranging from 1282 in the Lake District (with its population of 44,000) to 62 in Northumberland (population 2000). Of these, only 1256 – 20 per cent – were refused.[26] With the exception of Northumberland, with only 3 refusals, the range of refusals was restricted, varying from 15 per cent in Snowdonia to 27 per cent on the Pembrokeshire Coast. Modest change is both proper and inevitable: with clear policies in management and structure plans, that change can be kept within acceptable limits.[27] The term 'acceptable' is, of course, open to varied interpretation, and the differing parties with an interest in the parks have very varying views. An employment opportunity to a resident may be an eyesore to a visitor. A condition on design and materials may preserve the distinctive character of a village for the visitor but seem an unwarranted constraint on legitimate development to the resident.

However important cumulatively, most decisions cause little wider comment. A few, because of their scale and nature, do attract far greater interest. They fall into three broad categories. In the first are activities and developments that preceded national park designation and which have a continuing impact. The very character of the parks as extensive uplands, frequently built of older, harder rocks, has given them a peculiar significance for water gathering, mineral extraction and military training. In the Peak District, for example, 29 per cent of the area is committed to water catchment; on Dartmoor the Ministry of Defence occupies over a quarter of the high moorland and 78 per cent of the 'wilderness' area of the northern moorland plateau. The problems arise over the extent to which such uses should be allowed to continue.

Mineral extraction is a case in point, not least in the abstraction of the limestone of the Peak District and Yorkshire Dales. In 1949, the then Minister of Town and Country Planning, Lewis Silkin, averred in the House of Commons that

> It must be demonstrated quite clearly that the exploitation of these minerals is absolutely necessary in the public interest. It must be clear beyond all doubt that there is no possible alternative source of supply, and if these two conditions are satisfied then permission must be subject to the condition that restoration takes place at the earliest possible opportunity.[28]

In practice, that support has not been fully forthcoming from government. The draft Structure Plan for the Peak District National Park (1975) declared that

> In deciding planning applications the Board will accept a limited amount of mineral working only if it can be demonstrated conclusively that there is an

> overriding need to work the minerals and that the impact on the National Park can be satisfactorily controlled. The onus of proof of 'overriding need' will rest with the prospective mineral operator.[29]

In the finally approved plan, in 1979, these proposals were modified significantly by successive Labour and Conservative Secretaries of State for the Environment. In essence, the presumption of refusal without conclusive demonstration of 'overriding need' was weakened to a statement that the authority would 'normally' resist mineral workings that constituted 'a major intrusion' or were 'detrimental on a large scale' to national park purposes, and the 'onus of proof' was shifted from the operator to the local planning authority.[30] The practical outworking of such changes in emphasis can be seen in the successive ministerial decisions on ICI's appeal against the Peak Park Board's refusal in 1974 to permit the extension of its Tunstead limestone quarry. After a long public enquiry, the appeal was allowed in 1978, and even after an appeal by the Board to the High Court which ruled in the Board's favour on certain points of law, it was upheld, albeit in modified form, in 1980.

The Peak conflict highlights the second category of decision, where the views of the National Park Committee as the local planning authority are overruled by the minister on appeal. The problem arises not only with continuing activities but also with new activities. Many of these became *causes célèbres:* those that succeeded despite park authority opposition include the Esso oil refinery in the Pembrokeshire Coast (1957), the nuclear power station at Trawsfynydd in Snowdonia (1958), the Fylingdales ballistic missile early warning station in the North York Moors (1960) and the rebuilding of the A66 trunk road in the Lake District (1972). Of the last-named, the Countryside Commission had to 'conclude that the Department got their priorities disastrously wrong. They pursued a simplistic highway solution to a complicated traffic and environmental problem; the result will be a permanent monument to insensitivity towards superb scenery.'[31] Perception of that 'monument', however, is very different by the contemporary visitor: a 'before and after' study found that there was 'no evidence in the surveys to suggest that this road has had any significant detrimental impact on the enjoyment of visitors to the area – whether as pleasure motorists, picnickers or walkers. And there is a suggestion that it has had the advantage of opening up new views of Lake Bassenthwaite. . . .'[32]

Frustrations are even greater in the third category of decision, where landscape changes result from decisions that are largely outside the planning authority's powers to control. This is seen in its most heightened and most widespread form in changes in the agricultural landscape. For all practical purposes, changes in the cultivation of land lie outside the scope of development control: this applies not only to changes in crops, but also to the planting of trees or the removal of field boundaries. As shown earlier in the chapter, this has meant serious changes in the characteristic landscape of some national parks, especially those with large expanses of open moorland on soils that are capable of reclamation.

Aside from informal consultations, the powers of the national park authorities in this context remain extremely limited. The 1968 Countryside Act (Section 14) imposed an obligation on anyone wishing to plough 'any land in a National Park appearing . . . to be predominantly moor or heath' to give six months' notice of intention, but there was no legal constraint to conversion after that period. Pressure for change became extremely strong in the 1970s, and on Exmoor led to the Porchester enquiry,[33] which recommended a system whereby Moorland Conservation Orders, binding in perpetuity, could be made by a national park authority, subject to the payment to the landowner of a lump sum in compensation. Legislation for this was included in the 1978 Countryside Bill, but the bill fell with the general election of May 1979.

The Conservative government's Wildlife and Countryside Act of 1981 adopted, despite stern opposition, a different course. The basic principle was one of voluntary agreement, with no reserve statutory powers. Under Section 41, payment of a capital grant by the Ministry of Agriculture to a farmer for reclamation work in a national park is subject to consultation

8 Disused and ruined field barns in Waldendale, in the Yorkshire Dales. Their modern asbestos sheet successor can be seen adjacent to the farm building in the background.

with the park authority: if in consequence a grant is refused, the authority is required to offer to enter into a management agreement with an annual sum in compensation for the restriction placed on the use of land. The same Act extended the necessary notice for moorland conversion to 12 months (Section 42) and required park authorities to produce a map showing those areas of moor and heath they consider particularly important to conserve (Section 43).[34] These provisions of the Act had yet to be tested in practice at the time of writing, but concern remains over the cumulative annual sum potentially involved in compensation, and the lack of any long-term guarantee of moorland retention by such agreements.

The problems relate not only to the landscape as a whole, but also to the development of agricultural buildings within it. Permitted development rights impose few restrictions on the form or siting of agricultural buildings in national parks, and the charm of traditional groupings of farm buildings in vernacular materials is all too readily displaced by stark erections of asbestos sheet and steel girders. The problem remains of how to fund any alternative structures, and how to use redundant buildings of an earlier farming pattern. The stone field barns, or laithes, of the Yorkshire Dales are a case in point: they characterise the landscape but are largely irrelevant to contemporary agriculture (illustration 8). Conversion to tourist accommodation is an imaginative approach, but applicable only to a tiny minority.[35]

The frustrations of landscape conservation experienced by park authorities stem from both lack of powers and lack of resources. Powers can best be exercised where the authority is landowner, but ownership raises controversial political and economic issues. The North York Moors National Park Committee's decision in 1980 to purchase for £90,000 the 133 ha of Nab Farm in the heart of the Moors at Saltergate was carried by a majority of one, despite the offer of a 50 per cent grant from the Countryside Commission (which would also grant-aid 75 per cent of the remaining capital expenditure).[36]

PARADISE ENJOYED

The problems of resources are even more acute when the second statutory purpose of national parks is considered, and the one more immediately relevant in the present context – that 'of promoting their enjoyment by the public'. In a sense, the whole of landscape conservation is directed at this aim, but more specific recreation-oriented work needs consideration.

Even within the boundaries of national parks, park authorities are very far from the only providers of facilities or the only source of public investment. Indeed, the Countryside Commission, not unfairly, has drawn attention to the great disparity between 'annual levels of public investment, mainly by way of grants, in various rural activities but particularly in agriculture (£300 m) and national park conservation and recreation (£7 m)'.[37]

Direct recreation provision is indeed small, amounting to £2.3 million of national park expenditure in 1980-81. Cumulatively, that provision remains small: by 1981 park authorities could provide 89 picnic sites, 107 public conveniences, 65 information and study centres, and 14,635 car-parking spaces.[38] Only one authority, the Brecon Beacons, had itself developed a country park within its boundaries.

Direct facility provision, however, is only part of the story. The essential aim of national parks is to secure a landscape for quiet enjoyment, and such enjoyment should require little direct intervention. The Dartmoor authority's approach sets out the essence of the problem:

> Looking at recreation positively the situation would appear to a certain extent to be self-regulating. People's tastes do differ and they are mobile, and so, provided that there is a *supply* of recreational opportunities of different types which is more than sufficient to meet the *demand* for those types, then visitors have the opportunity to drive or walk to a place which has both the qualities, and the density of people, of their choice. Problems arise when there is not sufficient of a particular type of resource to meet the demands placed upon it. At present this does not appear to be the case as far as informal recreation in total is concerned. . . .[39]

Such a comment, however, gives no grounds for complacency:

> Some of the present recreational use takes place in areas where it should not, on grounds of landscape, access or ecological sensitivity; some sites are over-used to the point of erosion; traffic queues do form. Nor does this self-regulation mechanism remove conflicts between different activities or between recreation and the local interest. The Authority has a role to play in re-distribution of demand, in management of the landscape and of access systems to minimise environmental impact, in management of sites to ensure that they and therefore the recreational experiences do not suffer; and in reconciliation of visitors and local interests.[40]

Conflict and capacity are themes for the following chapter, but some instances of demand management and site management are relevant here.

While most parks have been concerned not to spread the recreation load unduly, and recognise that the basic 'honeypot' concept has much to commend it, they have rightly sought to ensure that all resources have no undue constraint on accessibility. It will be remembered that one of the prime purposes of national park legislation was to secure effective access to

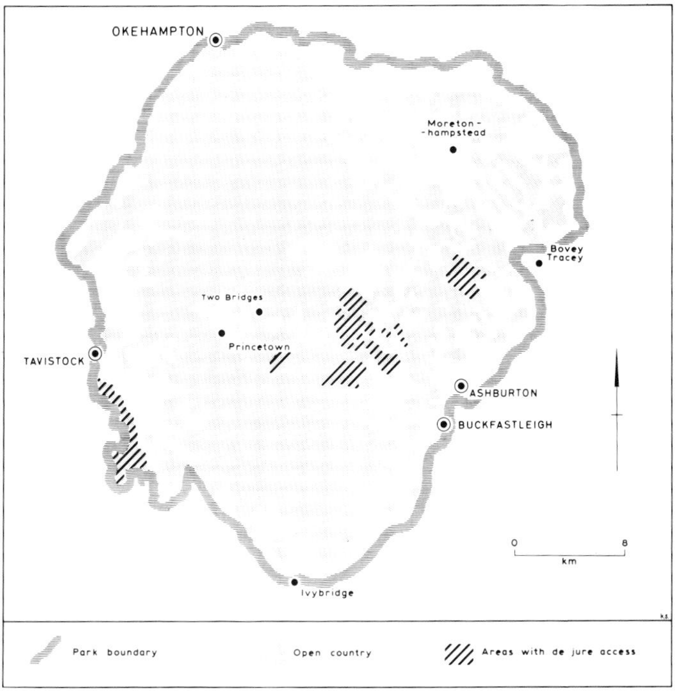

FIGURE 6.6 Access to open country in the Dartmoor National Park.
Source: based on *Dartmoor National Park Policy Plan* (Devon County Council, 1973), map 6

the countryside. This was particularly the case for 'open country', defined melodiously in the 1949 National Parks and Access to the Countryside Act as 'mountain, moor, heath, down, cliff or foreshore'. Little of this land had *de jure* access (figure 6.6); much, however, had long enjoyed *de facto* access. The purpose of the act was to create a means of ensuring access where such informal arrangements were inadequate. In practice, the powers have been used little outside the Peak District, where the access battles of the 1930s were fought (figure 6.7). It was estimated in 1973 that, of the 35,260 ha of access land in England and Wales, 80 per cent were in the national parks and 56 per cent in the Peak District alone:[41] the situation has changed little since that date.

In the long run, of greater significance in securing the continued goodwill of the farming community to both *de facto* and *de jure* access have been the Upland Management schemes. Initiated as experiments in 1969 in the Lake District and Snowdonia, the schemes aimed at funding small-scale works to assist farmers in practical landscape conservation and in reconciling some of the conflicting claims of recreation and farming.[42]

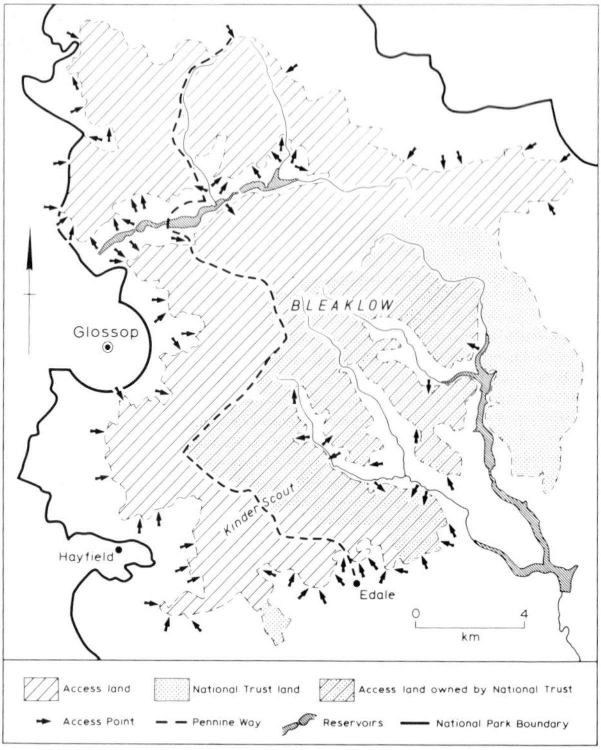

FIGURE 6.7 Access land in the north of the Peak District National Park, 1981. *Source:* data from Peak District National Park

Waymarking, stile construction and stone wall rebuilding were typical activities: the schemes were run by a project officer with access to a modest cash budget. The basic idea has been adopted in other parks, and has proved a successful technique for getting minor recreation works tackled and helping to ease the friction between farmers and visitors.[43] It makes no pretence to solve more deep-rooted problems, but emphasises that small-scale funding can yield high returns in both amenity and goodwill.

At site level, projects in national parks have varied widely in scale beyond the basic provision of visitor facilities already noted and the establishment of ranger services. Sites of major visitor concentrations, the aptly named 'honeypots', have been adapted to enable them to accept more adequately and enjoyably the recreational pressures imposed. The summit of Snowdon and its approach paths, for example, are the subject of a scheme begun in 1979 and planned to continue to 1984. The summit area receives some 200,000 people a year, and some 2500 on a busy summer day:[44] their trampling has reduced it to a mass of unvegetated boulder scree. By 1982 expenditure on rehabilitating the paths to the summit was running at over £200,000 a year, and the Welsh Development Agency joined with the Park Authority, the Countryside Commission and the Wales Tourist Board to purchase and refurbish the summit cafe and its environs.[45]

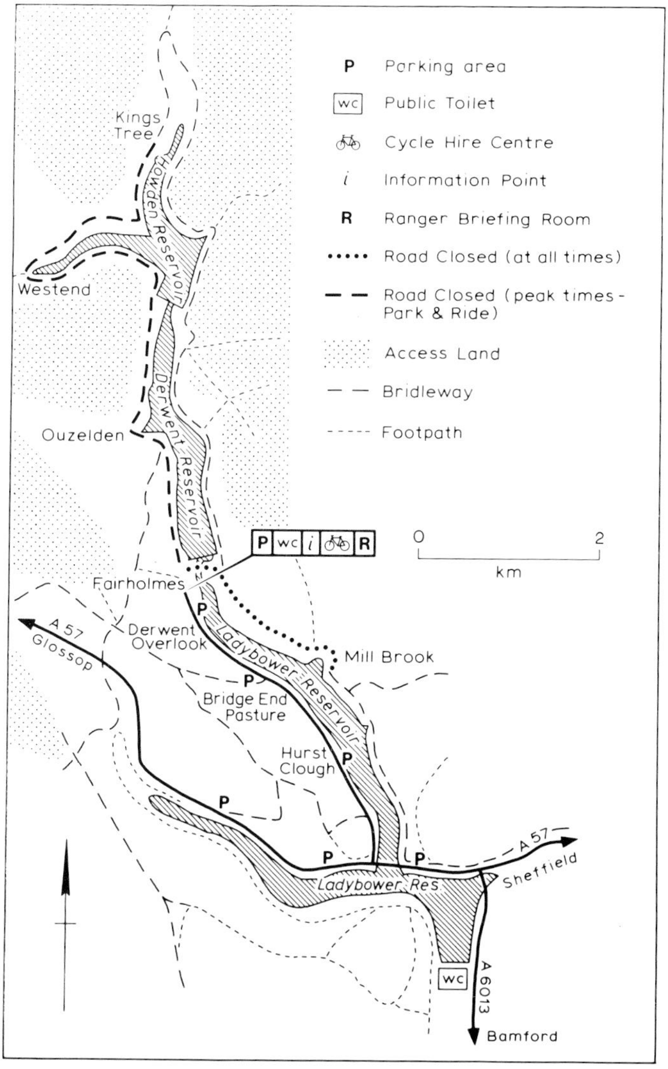

FIGURE 6.8 The Upper Derwent experimental traffic-free scheme, 1982, in the Peak District National Park.
Source: data from Peak District National Park

A scheme of a very different kind was initiated in the Peak Park's Upper Derwent Valley in 1981 (figure 6.8). The valley is the fourth most popular area in the park, with some 500,000 visits in the course of a year and 4000 visitors in 600 cars on peak Sundays. Here the aim was not so much to improve the physical conditions of the site as to permit its unfettered enjoyment in traffic-free conditions. Building on the experience of the earlier Goyt Valley project, the key to the scheme was an enlarged car park at Fairholmes, provided by the Water Authority and accepting up to 200 cars and three coaches at peak periods. Above Fairholmes, the road was made accessible only to users of a public minibus service, and to walkers and cyclists, on summer Sundays and bank holidays.[46]

More modest schemes aim at redistributing visitor pressures at a site. At Tarn Hows in the Lake District, the 20 ha surrounding the 13 ha tarn are visited by some 500,000 people a year, with more than 600 present at peak periods. By 1973, several parts of the site were becoming seriously eroded and unsightly: simple work improved certain paths to accept heavy use, and movement was concentrated on them by the use of signs, temporary barriers and the closure of one car park. The result was the restoration of the most severely damaged areas, and, despite an increase in use, the site was in better condition at the end of the project than at the beginning.[47]

Corridors as well as nodes have received attention. The problems of redistributing traffic are not simple on a multi-purpose public highway network, but a combination of restrictive and positive policies can achieve considerable impact. The classic experiment was the Routes for People scheme in the Peak District between Bakewell and Buxton, implemented in 1973-75.[48] The highway authority (Derbyshire County Council) joined with the planning authority (Peak Park Planning Board) to attempt, with a minimum of resources, to get different types of traffic to use different routes. Three types of traffic were concerned. Heavy lorries were confined to the A roads on the perimeter of the area by a weight restriction order, made more palatable by selective road improvements and advisory signing. For leisure motorists, a scenic route on the most suitable roads was set up, with picnic sites and waymarked walks. For non-motorised traffic – walkers, cyclists and horse-riders – a series of routes was selected from the existing network of public paths and lanes after talks with farmers and landowners. Stiles and gates were restored; the routes waymarked and publicised by leaflets and information boards. While there were some problems in practice, the basic result was a promising redistribution of all kinds of traffic. This scheme was used as a basis for Dartmoor's Functional Route Network, with coloured edgings to signs signifying the capacity of a particular road. Thus a brown edging indicates a road unsuitable for lorries over two tons, coaches exceeding 7.3 m and caravans.[49]

Elsewhere, alternatives to movement by road have been encouraged. In the North York Moors, the park authority has given encouragement and support to the preserved railway between Pickering and Grosmont as it provides an additional scenic route along the main north-south axis of the park. Current usage of the line is in the order of 350,000-400,000 passenger journeys a year. An even more imaginative scheme has been Dales Rail in the Yorkshire Dales National Park. Five disused stations on the Settle and Carlisle railway were reopened from 1975, and charter trains now run on summer weekends, bringing visitors from the West Yorkshire conurbation into the park and giving park residents access to towns. Feeder bus services and guided walks are an integral part of the scheme.[50]

It must not, of course, be imagined that schemes of the kind described are the dominant feature of recreational provision in national parks. Rather, they represent either the response to unusually intense demand, or the seizing of an opportunity to redistribute existing demand and enhance the quality of the recreational experience. Far more typical are the modest additions to site facilities, the minor adjustments to site character, which are barely noticed by the visitor but contribute much to overall enjoyment.

RESOURCE CONSERVATION AND USE

While national parks have attracted the lion's share of attention (and the lion's share of space), they represent only one element in a system of landscape designation. No new parks have been designated since 1955: an attempt to create a Cambrian Mountains National Park in mid-Wales was met by the refusal in 1973 of the Secretary of State for Wales to confirm the order because of 'the number, substance and strength of the objections received by the Welsh Office'.[51] After two decades, a national park was perceived as a threat to local interests by encouraging visitor 'invasions'.

More continuous progress has been made with the designation of a second tier of landscape in Areas of Outstanding Natural Beauty (AsONB). These now cover 14,493 km^2, 9.6 per cent of the area of England and Wales (figures 6.3 and 6.9). From a recreational point of view, however, they have had limited significance. From the beginning, their prime purpose has been to recognise, conserve and enhance 'natural beauty': recreation, in terms of both statutory powers and actual provision, has had little more attention than in the countryside at large.[52]

The problem with AsONB, and to some extent with national parks also, is their sheer scale: however striking their quality of landscape, that very scale inhibits much positive conservation. Most progress can be made

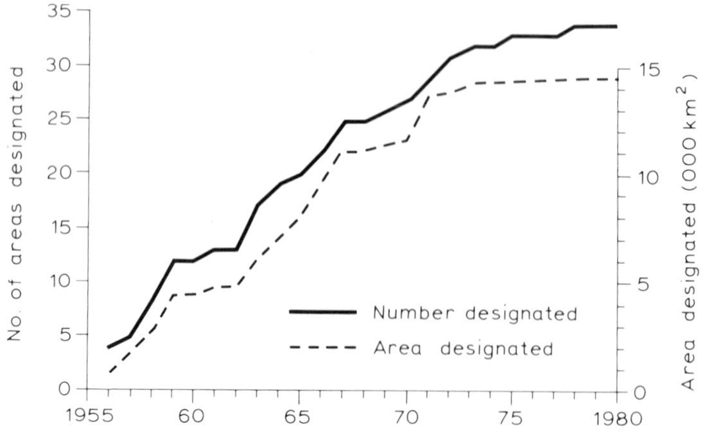

FIGURE 6.9 The growth in number and in area covered of Areas of Outstanding Natural Beauty.
Source: data from *Thirteenth Report of the Countryside Commission for the year ended 30 September 1980* (HMSO, 1981)

when relatively small areas are owned, or managed, specifically for their conservation interest, though that interest may itself inhibit positive recreation use.

The opportunities, and the dilemmas, are well seen in the network of national and local nature reserves (figure 6.10). Nature conservation has long had an enthusiastic following.[53] The Society for the Protection of Birds was founded in 1889 and received a Royal Charter in 1904: it has a current membership of over 300,000.[54] County naturalists' trusts developed between the wars, and began to purchase land for nature reserves. The Yorkshire Naturalists' Trust, for example, has a current membership of over 6000, and manages 46 reserves ranging in size from 0.25 to 253 ha.[55] Translation from private enthusiasm to public concern, however, came after the Second World War, with the foundation of the Nature Conservancy in 1949. The separation of nature and landscape conservation has already been noted: the Conservancy began a vigorous programme of site acquisition, and by 1982 its successor the Nature Conservancy Council managed 123 national nature reserves covering 43,900 ha.[56] To these must be added the 79 local nature reserves covering 10,051 ha,[57] declared by local authorities in consultation with the Nature Conservancy Council under section 21 of the National Parks and Access to the Countryside Act, 1949. The prime purpose of these reserves, however, is conservation as such: while they form a priceless resource, their use for recreation (other than the direct pursuit of natural history) is necessarily limited. Of the national nature reserves in England and Wales, only 17 are open to the public without restriction, though the features of many others can be seen from existing footpaths and other rights of way.

The body that has faced the dilemma of conservation and access most acutely is the National Trust. Founded in 1895 as the National Trust for Places of Historic Interest and Natural Beauty, it was rooted in a period when private initiative rather than paternal intervention by a government

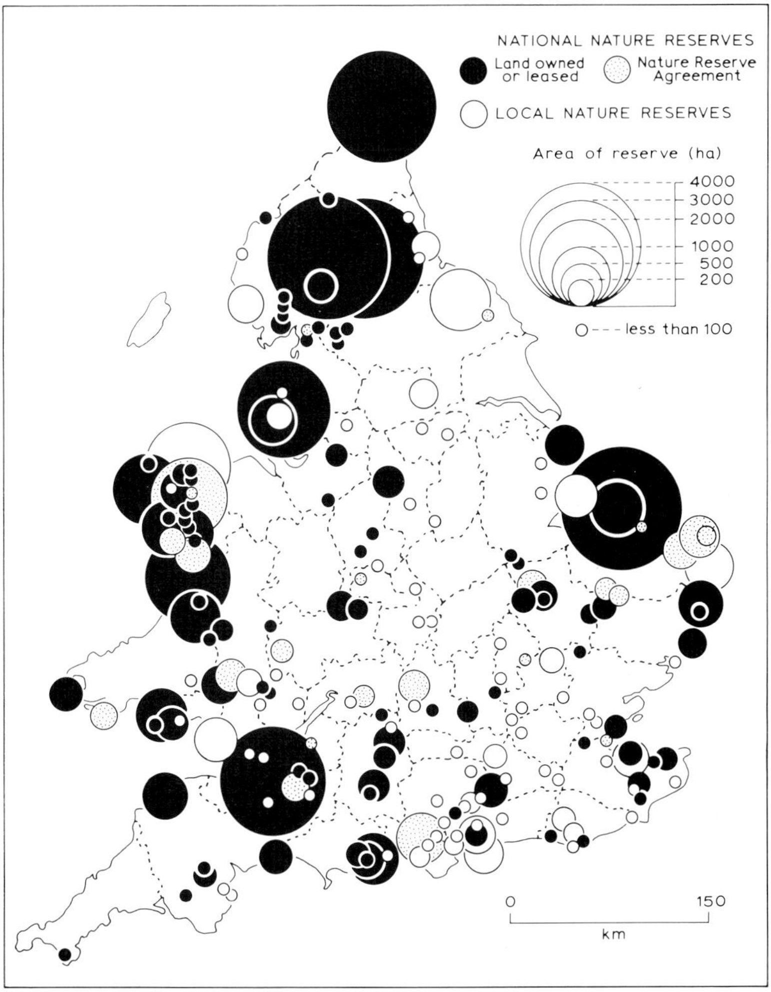

FIGURE 6.10 National nature reserves and local nature reserves, 1982. Where land in a national nature reserve is partly owned or leased and partly held under a Nature Reserve Agreement, it is shown on the map as belonging to the former category.
Source: data from Nature Conservancy Council

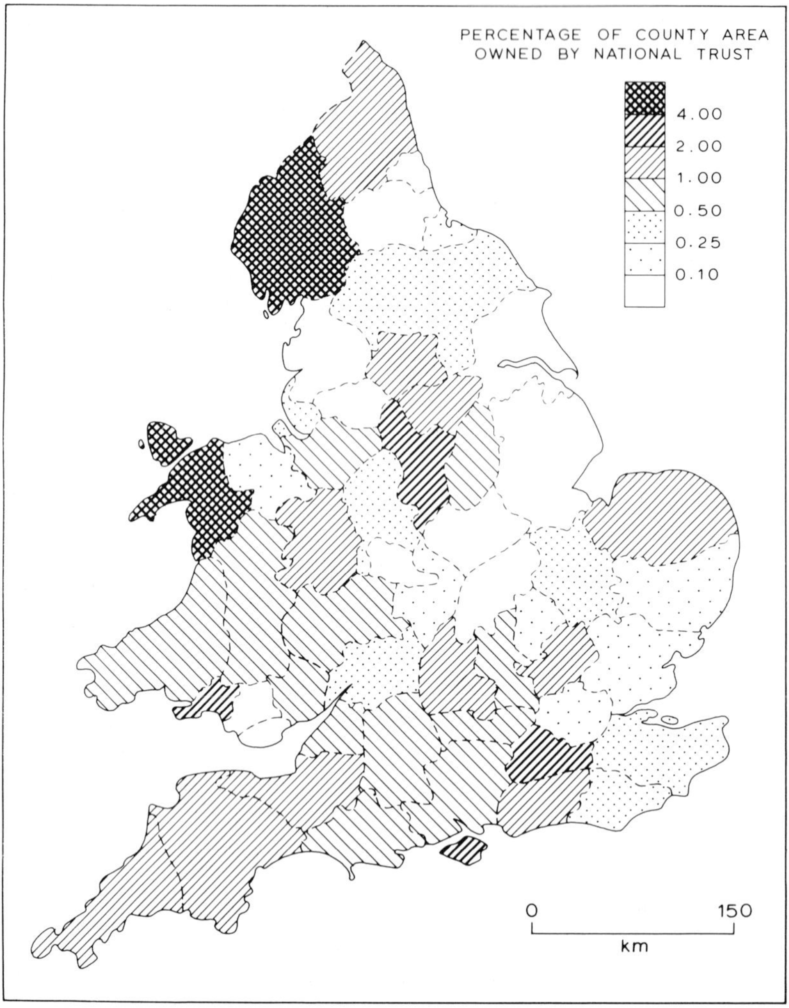

FIGURE 6.11 Land owned by the National Trust, 1980. Covenanted land is not included.
Source: data from *Properties of the National Trust* (National Trust, 1978) and *The National Trust: properties open in 1981* (National Trust, 1981)

agency was seen as the answer to such problems as the despoilation of the country's scenic and architectural heritage. It remains a private body, but is now the largest private landowner in the country, with 184,600 ha in its possession[58] (figure 6.11).

There is no space in the present context to consider its history in detail,[59] but the change in both the scale and the nature of its operations since 1945 needs emphasis. In that year, it had but 7850 members and remained a relatively exclusive group; in 1980 alone it recruited 225,000 new members, and in May 1981 membership passed the 1 million mark. By the end of 1981 membership stood at 1,047,000. This marked the success of a conscious attempt to seek the support of the community as a whole in its work: subscription income amounted to a quarter of its total income in 1981, in a turnover exceeding £31 million, some three times that of the whole national park system. Membership is not, of course, an entirely altruistic gesture: free entry to properties can make it a considerable bargain, as the relatively rapid turnover of members suggests. At many properties, almost half of all visitors are members. Of seven major Yorkshire properties in 1981, they formed between 49 and 58 per cent of visitors at five, and 40 and 15 per cent respectively at the remaining two. This limited evidence suggests the proportion of members is highest at freestanding rural properties, where a more conscious decision to choose a specific destination for a visit is involved.

The Trust's properties have not grown at the same rate as members, though the record is impressive enough. In 1945 it owned some 45,300 ha, less than a quarter of its present holdings. It currently opens to the public nearly 200 historic buildings and 88 gardens. Of these, in 1981 94 had over 20,000 visitors and 13 over 100,000.[60] At properties where a charge is made, a total of 6,229,689 visitors was recorded in 1981.

The spatial distribution of properties reflects a variety of influences. Paramount has been the perceived need of Trust intervention. The concentration in Cumbria is no accident. Concern at the exclusion of visitors from lake shores motivated Canon Rawnsley, one of the 'founding trinity' of 1895. The Trust now owns over 33,500 ha in Cumbria and protects through covenants a further 4800 ha, almost one-fifth of its total holdings (figure 6.5).

Differing thrusts of Trust endeavour have also played a part. The initial concerns were indeed 'places of historic interest and natural beauty'. To these have been added the Country House Scheme, which under the 1937 National Trust Act enables an owner to endow and transfer to the Trust an historic house while allowing him to remain in occupation subject to public access on specified days. The Trust's policy, indeed, is 'to present its historic houses not as empty museums but as homes. . . . The walking sticks in the hall, the flowers, silver-framed photographs, books and papers in the rooms are signs that the house is still loved and lived in and that visitors are welcomed as private individuals just as much as tourists.'[61] Further thrusts have been the Gardens Scheme of 1948, the acquisition of industrial monuments, and coastal protection. The last was the objective of Enterprise Neptune, launched in 1965, though to an initially stormy start. In 1965 the Trust owned 301 km of coast. Between 1965 and 1982 it added 367 km, giving it control over no less than one-eighth of the coastline of England and Wales, or more than two-fifths of what its own survey classified as being of 'outstanding natural beauty'. The major acquisitions have been concentrated in Cornwall and Devon, Dyfed and West Glamorgan: in each of these counties, more than 30 km of coast have been added to the Trust's control since 1965.[62]

The Trust's holdings are obviously a major resource for recreation as well as conservation, though it has never been in any doubt as to where its ultimate priorities lie. Its sheer scale makes easier its task of preservation yet still enables it 'to give enjoyment both to this generation and the ones that come after'.[63] Entry to both land and property is restricted when pressures become unacceptable: the conscious promotion of less popular properties can help divert some of that pressure. A major scheme at Beningbrough Hall, near York, for example, developed a property of modest architectural interest into a major attraction. In 1977, before refurbishing, it received less than 7000 visitors; in 1980, 62,000.

PRESERVATION AND PROFIT: RECREATION ATTRACTIONS

To the casual visitor, National Trust properties are but one of a range of 'attractions' available for enjoyment in both town and country. Even in the countryside, developed resources – stately homes, ancient monuments and safari parks – accounted for the main stop of more than one in six of all countryside visitors.[64] Most of these 'attractions' are resource-based, but their exploitation involves not only a conscious decision to divert from their original function, but often the injection of considerable capital.

Three quite distinct kinds of resource are concerned. The first is simply the opening to the public of an existing resource, usually an historic building or monument. Motives for doing this vary. For bodies like the National Trust and the Ancient Monument branch of the Department of the Environment they are largely altruistic. At many such monuments no charge is made, for their scale or quality would not justify any attempt at commercial operation. There were, for example, no less than 12,616 scheduled ancient monuments in England at the end of 1981, with over a quarter (3375) sited in the area of the West Country Tourist Board.[65] A resource of a rather different kind is the parish church. Of approximately 16,800 Anglican churches, some 8500 are of pre-Reformation age: in England, 11,759 were listed buildings, 2460 Grade A. They are an addition to the wider legacy of historic buildings – 280,195 in England in 1981 – that, though for the most part not open to the public, give so much of quality and character to the built environment in both town and country.

In England in 1981, 1481 historic buildings were regularly opened to the public. Of these, 13 per cent belong to the National Trust, 20 per cent to the Department of the Environment, 22 per cent to local authorities and 45 per cent to private owners. At some, especially in the public sector, no charge is made as a matter of policy – these amounted to 37 per cent of all such properties in 1981. At most, however, there is a price on heritage. For the private owner, 'the only way of keeping a castle nowadays, for most of us, is to share it with them':[66] the attraction-seeking public. The market is certainly worth sharing: there were some 48.5 million visits to historic buildings in England in 1981.

The purely resource-based 'attraction', however, is only part of the range available. At the second kind, the resource has been developed with additional attractions. The distinctions are of degree, rather than of kind. As the Duke of Bedford remarked, 'a Stately home with excellent loos, good teas served at a reasonable price, and sufficient car-parks (near the loos and the tea-rooms) will prosper. If you provide these three commodities, then – according to my computer – 87.3 per cent of your visitors will not notice if you have no house at all.'[67]

That view may be tongue in cheek, but visitor figures show no simple correlation with quality. Modest resources succeed where there is additional advantage, such as association with a major historic figure (Churchill and Chartwell), or a museum display of national reputation (the Motor Museum at Beaulieu, where 'it is easy to forget about the house, sitting quietly on its lawn well away from the sharp end of the business'[68]). Indeed, the additions may soon be of such a scale that the resource moves to the third category, a resource deliberately created with visitor attraction in mind. Lions raised Longleat to the First Division of stately homes, and at Woburn 'the Game Park solved all my problems.'[69]

Created resources are not, of course, inherently rural. Safari parks need space, and space is often available in the estates of stately homes. Others, like steam railways, adapt an existing resource to revised purposes, a resource that may be in an urban as much as a rural setting (figure 2.9). Still others, like many model villages, are developed on sites with no predisposition to tourist development, and again are as likely to be in urban as in rural surroundings.

Visitor figures emphasise the false dichotomy between urban and rural in this context, where the 'attraction' rather than the specific character of its setting is important. The English Tourist Board estimated that about 154 million visits were made to sightseeing attractions in 1981 (table 6.2): this compares with the Countryside Commission's estimate of 82 million countryside visits in England and Wales in a summer month at the height of the season or, perhaps some 350 million in the course of a year.

Visitor attractions are well distributed through the country as a whole,

TABLE 6.2 Estimated visits to sightseeing attractions in England, 1980-81

Type of attraction	*Number of visits (millions)* 1980	1981*
Historic buildings	53.5	48.5
Gardens	7.5	7.0
Zoos and other wildlife attractions	17.0	15.5
Museums and art galleries	52.5	49.0
Other (e.g. model villages, steam railways, workplaces, country and leisure parks, brass-rubbing centres)	36.5	34.0
	167	154

* The 1981 totals are preliminary estimates. Overall, 44 per cent of attractions gave estimated rather than exact visitor totals.
Source: data from *English Heritage Monitor* (English Tourist Board, 1982), p. 27

though the numbers of visitors are highest in the major resort and tourist areas (figure 6.12). London has an obvious advantage. Of the 20 attractions drawing more than one million visits in 1980, 15 were in London. Of the 15, only London Zoo and Kew Gardens were neither cathedrals nor in the 'museum and art gallery' category. Of the 54 attractions with more than 500,000 visits in 1980, 23 were in London. The 54 represent only 2 per cent of the attractions sampled, but account for 38 per cent of all visits.

DESIGNED FOR RECREATION: FORESTS, PARKS AND URBAN FRINGE

The range of visitor attractions highlights not only the irrelevance of an urban-rural distinction in their setting to most visitors, but also the difficulty of drawing a clear divide between resource-based and user-oriented attractions. Clawson's 'intermediate' category saves face but continues to beg the question. In the countryside a useful distinction can be made between a near-ubiquitous resource adapted for recreation use where both resource and demand justify it and a resource identified and developed largely on grounds of demand alone.

Recreation on Forestry Commission properties falls clearly into the former type. The Commission was created in 1919 after the severe shortage of timber during the First World War, its remit the development of a growing stock of timber as quickly as possible against a comparable emergency. By 1981, the Commission's holdings amounted to 1,263,997 ha

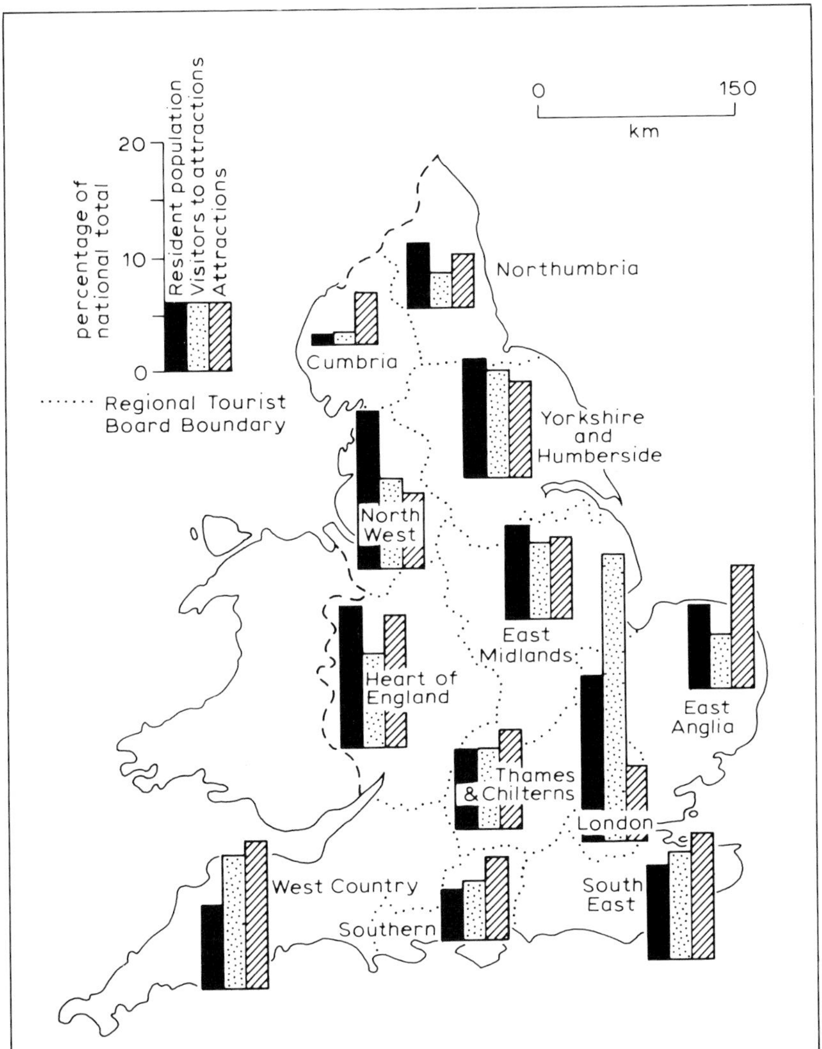

FIGURE 6.12 Numbers of attractions, and numbers of visits to attractions, in relation to resident population, by English Tourist Board Regions, 1980. The number of attractions related only to historic buildings and monuments open to the public, whether in the National Trust, DOE, local authority or private ownership. The number of visits related to a sample of 1281 attractions, including 519 museums, 427 historic buildings, 76 gardens, 68 wildlife attractions and 191 'other' attractions.
Source: data from OPCS, *Census 1981, Preliminary report, England and Wales* (HMSO, 1981); *English Heritage Monitor 1981* (English Tourist Board, 1981), table 14; and *Sightseeing in 1980* (English Tourist Board, 1981), table 1

in Great Britain as a whole, 463,945 ha in England and Wales.[70] While, as even these figures suggest, the concentration of planting has been on more marginal upland areas of the north and west, sporadic forest properties occur throughout lowland as well as upland Britain. The East England Conservancy has 46,077 ha and South East England 56,953 ha, of which the New Forest accounts for slightly less than half.

By the early 1960s, the rapid march of regimented rows of conifers, planted largely regardless of terrain, brought growing protest, a protest only partly quelled by the appointment of Sylvia Crowe as landscape consultant in 1964.[71] The sheer scale of the Commission's holdings also brought growing use for recreation, a use fostered by the designation of 'forest parks' (albeit largely devoid of facilities) on largely unplanted uplands. The Argyll Forest Park was opened in 1935, followed south of the border by the Snowdonia Forest Park (8000 ha) in 1937 and Dean Forest Park (14,000 ha) in 1938. In addition, though not formally designated as such, the New Forest's 25,000 ha of heath and woodland has functioned as a forest park since its management was taken over by the Commission in 1924.[72] The growth of countryside recreation in the 1960s brought increasing numbers of visitors into the forests, and the tentative beginnings of formal provision for their needs. That provision was often the result of the initiative and enthusiasm of individual members of staff, as with Bill Grant at Grizedale in the Lake District, where a Deer Museum in 1956 was followed by a Wild Life Centre in 1968.[73]

The changing situation was acknowledged in the 1968 Countryside Act,

9 Forestry Commission picnic site, Clocaenog Forest, 1972.

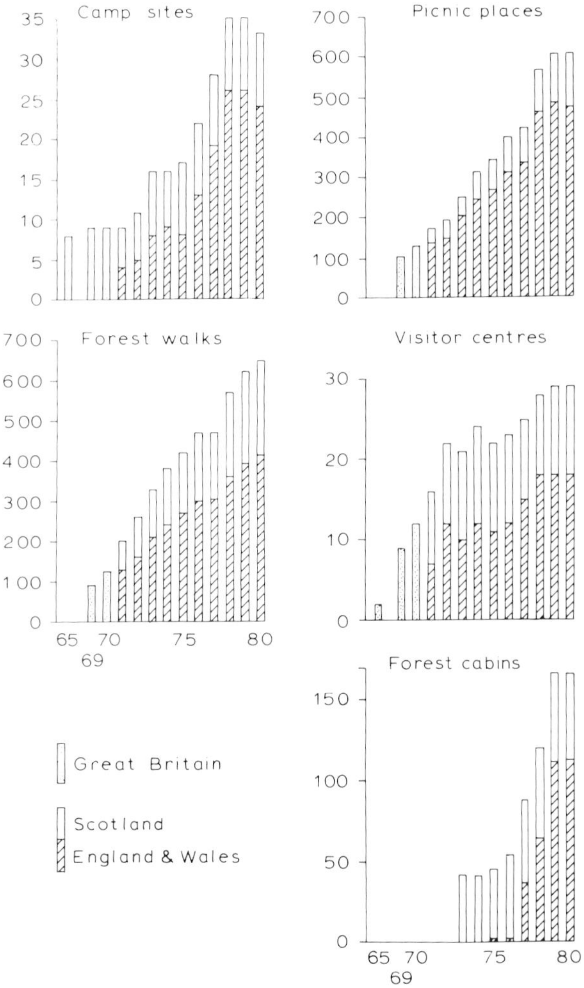

FIGURE 6.13 Forestry Commission recreation facilities, 1965-80.
Source: data from the *Annual Reports* of the Commission

which gave the Commission statutory powers (Section 23) to provide facilities for recreation. The expansion of facilities was rapid in the 1970s (figure 6.13 and illustration 9). Formally, the Commission's policy was 'to welcome visitors and meet the public demand for facilities but not to take the initiative in stimulating demand',[74] but it recognised that

> the unique attraction which the Forestry Commission can offer is the natural environment of woodland; from this it follows that the facilities provided

> should be compatible with and derive their justification from this environment. In order to extend as widely as possible the benefits of recreation in the forest the Commission's main care is for the enhancement of enjoyment and understanding of the value of forests to the nation by day visitors. Major facilities for overnight stays . . . are required to yield an economic return. . . . The scale of expansion of such projects will be governed by the availability of money and manpower.[75]

Visitor numbers responded to improved facilities, rising from an estimated 15 million day visits in 1970 in Great Britain as a whole to 24 million in 1976. The optimism of the period spurred more ambitious schemes. In 1975 a report by Coopers and Lybrand Associates Ltd suggested 'that nearly half the Commission's forests have the right setting and recreational potential to make them attractive places for holiday accommodation' and indicated suitable sites for 7300 self-catering forest cabins and 11 forest lodges offering full hotel service.[76] A modest start was made on this programme, and in 1979 it was reported that existing cabins had a 65 per cent occupancy rate over the year as a whole (illustration 10). Chillier economic winds, however, militated against more sweeping change. By 1980 the Commission had decided 'as part of our contribution to Government expenditure reductions not to fund any new recreational projects for the time being'.[77] In 1981, 'substantial reductions' in the recreation budget had led to concentration 'on the maintenance of existing facilities, with priority being given to revenue-earning developments . . . and to visitor centres and popular day-visitor facilities'.[78]

10 Forestry Commission holiday cabins, Keldy Castle, Cropton Forest, 1979.

The Commission shows the classic response of a government agency subject to external financial control. Initially following rather than leading demand, more heady enthusiasm rapidly wilts in more difficult economic circumstances, and recreation, marginal to the major operations, is an early candidate for cuts. Nevertheless, the Commission's role in recreational provision must not be underplayed. While a 1980 survey showed that visitor numbers had not risen since 1976, that total still represents (albeit for Great Britain as a whole) a substantially greater volume of visitors than to the Peak District National Park or to the Dartmoor and North York Moors National Parks combined.[79] The finance involved is still substantial. In 1980–81, the Commission spent a net £3.385 million on recreation. Camp sites and forest cabins yielded a net surplus of £62,000 on an income of £1.327 million, shooting and fishing a surplus of £123,000 on an income of £477,000. These sums are put in perspective when compared with expenditure by the Peak Park Joint Planning Board. Differing remits and responsibilities preclude direct comparisons, but in that same year the Board had a total expenditure of £2.262 million, and an income from its activities of £544,000.[80]

Country parks represent a different response to the pressures of demand for countryside recreation. They are perhaps the most innovative yet frustrating outcome of the legislation embodied in the 1968 Countryside Act. The need was foreshadowed in the 1966 White Paper, *Leisure in the countryside* (Cmnd 2928). It recognised that many existing beauty spots were overcrowded:

> other areas might do just as well, and might be easier to reach. But at present there is no positive reason for going there, and there may be drawbacks: there is nowhere off the road to park the car, nowhere to picnic or ramble and nowhere for the children to paddle or play games. [para 17].

The solution would be a new generation of country parks, fulfilling three prime roles:

> They would make it easier for town-dwellers to enjoy their leisure in the open, without travelling too far and adding to congestion on the roads; they would ease the pressure on the more remote and solitary places; and they would reduce the risk of damage to the countryside – aesthetic as well as physical – which often comes about when people settle down for an hour or a day where it suits them, somewhere 'in the country' – to the inconvenience and indeed expense of the countryman who lives and works there. [para 18].

With the grant-aid powers conferred by the 1968 Act (Sections 6-8, 33), country parks mushroomed. By 1974 there were 111, covering some 14,974 ha (figure 2.7). Local government reorganisation in that year

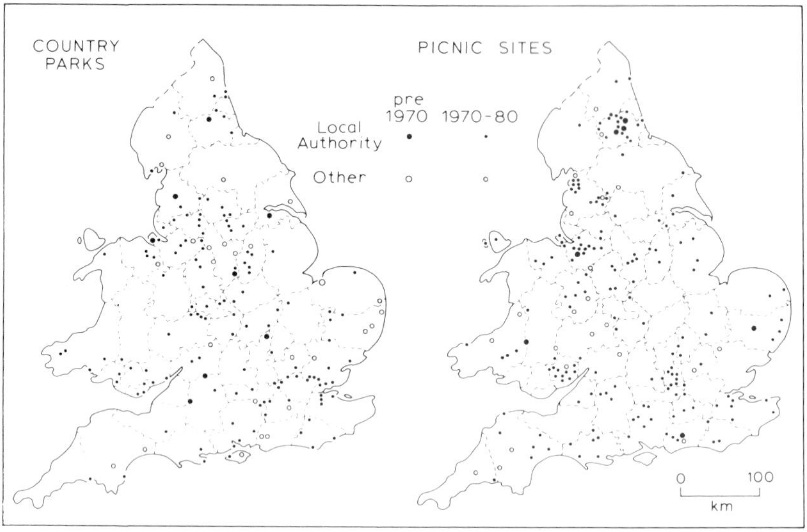

FIGURE 6.14 Country parks and picnic sites supported by the Countryside Commission and approved for grant aid, 30 September 1980.
Source: data from *Thirteenth report of the Countryside Commission for the year ended 30 September 1980* (HMSO, 1981)

brought hesitation in progress, hesitation that was accentuated by growing financial problems in the public sector; but nevertheless, by 1981 there were 167 recognised for grant-aid by the Countryside Commission, 28 being managed by private owners such as the National Trust, and covering some 20,387 ha. In addition there were 212 smaller picnic sites, 23 privately owned.

The facilities are well scattered throughout England and Wales (figure 6.14). They vary widely in size, from the 1273.5 ha of Clumber Park and the 1088 ha of Cannock Chase to the 9 ha of both Hartshill Hayes in Warwickshire and Clare Castle in Suffolk (table 6.3). They vary equally widely in character. Some are great sweeps of open countryside, such as Moel Famau in Clwyd, with 961 ha. Many are the adapted grounds of stately homes, such as Tatton Park or Croxteth Park. Others are ingenious conversions from industrial and transport dereliction, for example Keynes Park in the Cotswold Water Park, utilising the resources of flooded gravel workings, or the pioneer Wirral Country Park, linked to the abandoned West Kirby-Hooton railway. Still others capitalise on the industrial heritage in a more active way, as with the slate quarrying museum in the erstwhile workshops of the Dinorwic quarry in the Padarn Country Park or with the 1784 Quarry Bank mill and other community buildings at Styal.

TABLE 6.3 Country parks in England and Wales, 1981*

	Size (ha)**							
	less than 25	*25-49*	*50-74*	*75-99*	*100-199*	*200-299*	*300-499*	*over 500*
No. of parks	27	32	28	18	30	17	8	6

* The largely linear Battlefield of Bosworth Park has been excluded.
** The mean size of all parks is 122 ha.
Source: data from M. Waugh, *The Shell book of country parks* (David & Charles, 1981)

This network of country parks remains a striking legacy of the concern by the public sector for countryside recreation in the 1965-75 period and is a major addition to user-oriented resources. None the less, the network expresses frustration as well as achievement, a frustration more deep-rooted than simply the level of grant-aid involved (£2.901 million in the period 1978-81). The network is the result of responsive actions by individual local authorities and private owners, rather than of co-ordinated national planning matching resources to expressed demand. While there is inevitably an opportunist element in any programme of this kind, authorities vary widely in the priority they have accorded to provision for countryside recreation. The map is a record of achievement, but it remains a record of sporadic achievement. Country parks cannot be considered in isolation from other recreational provision; none the less, the different patterns north and south of London, or their virtual absence in both the south-eastern and south-western extremities of the country, invites comment. Other anomalies are equally glaring.

Again, comparatively few of the country parks – well under half – offer new, as opposed to improved, facilities. Many of the parks had long been places of resort, and the opportunity of grant-aid was seized to develop them more effectively. The area of the proposed Upper Hamble Country Park in Hampshire, for which a grant was approved in 1981, already attracted some 100,000 visitors a year.[81] The nature of facilities provided might also provoke comment: often, the balance has shifted from enjoyment of the countryside to entertainment within it. In that context, many country parks offer a chance not so much to gain unfettered access to the countryside as to partake of yet another leisure 'attraction' where the countryside element becomes almost incidental.

It would be wrong to underplay the achievement of country parks, but equally wrong to overplay their role in the wider issues of countryside access. They must, however, be seen as one highly important component in a strategic approach to that most crucial area of countryside from a demand-oriented viewpoint, the urban fringe. This role was envisaged from the beginning. The Countryside Act, in giving powers to local authorities to provide, or improve, opportunities for the enjoyment of the countryside by the public, laid down that in exercising these powers the authorities should have regard 'to the location of that area in the countryside in relation to an urban or built-up area' (Section 6-1). More recently that emphasis has been heightened further. Currently, the Countryside Commission aims to 'largely concentrate grant for new country parks and picnic grounds in the urban fringe, making the best possible use of neglected or reclaimed land close to centres of demand'.[82]

Conventional wisdom underpins the logic of this thrust.[83] The previous chapter highlighted the short range of most journeys to the countryside, and the desire to seek satisfaction as close to home as possible. Management for recreation is also a highly attractive visual use for land in the fringe which might otherwise be derelict or degraded. Schemes have received the active encouragement of the Countryside Commission, both in land reclamation, as in the St Helens–Knowsley area, and in recreation provision, as in the schemes for the river valleys of the Greater Manchester fringe; the Croal-Irwell, the Medlock, the Tame, the Mersey, the Bollin and the Goyt-Etherow.[84]

Some research, however, adds a note of caution, not least around the major conurbations. The London Green Belt has been the subject of an intensive study in this regard by geographers from University College, London.[85] Their work highlighted the surprising amount of land in the Green Belt already in *de facto* recreational use – 9.0 per cent for the metropolitan Green Belt as a whole, ranging from 4.1 per cent in the segment in Kent to 14.8 per cent in Surrey. The actual recreational use of the land, however, poses important questions. It was little used by inner-city residents: this research supports the earlier suggestion (figure 5.10) that not only is the fringe relatively inaccessible to such residents, but that, once a journey is undertaken, the fringe is 'leap-frogged' in favour of higher-quality countryside and coast. In contrast, it is much used by local residents, but rather as they might use an urban park and not as a substitute for other countryside visits. The simplicities of location are clearly overlain by the realities of access and function. The potential of the urban fringe as an urban lung and as an interceptor of demand for recreation in more sensitive areas of 'deep' countryside has evident limits, which need careful exploration.

LINEAR RESOURCES: ROADS AND FOOTPATHS

The corridors of countryside movement, the linear resources of roads and footpaths, have not always received the attention they deserve. Yet many people's greatest pleasure is the constantly changing countryside panorama seen from a moving car, and as previously noted, the most popular outdoor recreation by far is simply going for a walk (figures 3.6 and 3.7).

Roads reserved for recreational use – 'scenic drives' – are very much the exception in Britain. The Forestry Commission has developed them to a very limited extent, with only four in England and Wales in 1981. Several upland forests offer great potential in this direction, but pleasure traffic can hamper forest operations and roads to the standard needed for general use are expensive to develop. Elsewhere, schemes have been largely limited to restrictive or advisory signing, as in the Peak District and Dartmoor examples discussed earlier in the chapter.

The present road network in England and Wales extends over 290,033 km, of which 2341 km are motorways.[86] Recreational interest focuses primarily on a small proportion of this, in particular on the routes from major population centres to major resorts and the most popular countryside, and the road networks in the major scenic areas. With a network on this scale, few areas are far from a metalled road, though any extension of the network may be an issue of concern. The increasingly widespread ownership of the motor vehicle led to the metalling of many minor roads in the postwar period and the widening of others which had served for purely local access (figure 6.15). In some remote rural areas, the benefits of the

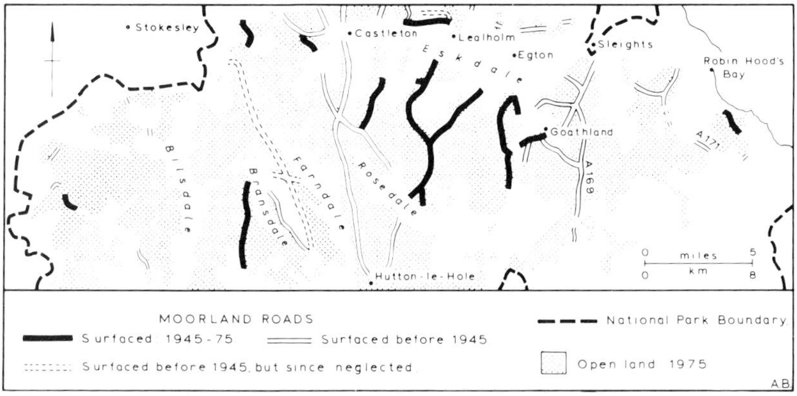

FIGURE 6.15 Changes in road surfaces since 1945 on open land in the North York Moors.
Source: data from North York Moors National Park

improved road network must be weighed against the intrusion into these areas of the motorised visitor. Rural 'wilderness', relatively remote from road access, becomes a recreational resource of growing scarcity.[87]

Away from the roads, the footpath network is one of the most precious recreation resources, much of it greatly underused and substantial portions in a state of desuetude. In its origins it was largely utilitarian. 'Some were deliberately planned, many evolved as simple accommodation routes, from farm or cottage to village, and by usage they have acquired the status of legal rights of way. Others developed as drove roads or pack horse routes and often cover long distances.'[88] Most of these utilitarian purposes have long since faded: the prime use of the network is now recreational, and for this purpose it is often ill-adapted.

As the prime means of direct access into the countryside away from public highways, footpaths were a major concern of the 1949 National Parks and Access to the Countryside Act. First, the Act required county councils, as the highway authorities for rural areas, to survey their areas and produce definitive maps of rights of way – footpaths, bridleways and 'roads used as public paths'. Priority for such work was low, and progress slow. By the time the Footpaths Committee (the Gosling Committee) reported in 1968, nineteen years after the Act, it could comment that there were 'still fourteen counties in England and six in Wales which have not completed the definitive maps for the whole of their areas'.[89] Even by 1980, the Ramblers Association could complain that 'many definitive maps are incomplete and out-of-date. There are still many public rights of way in existence that are not recorded on the maps.'[90] Nevertheless, the appearance of formally defined 'public paths' on Ordnance Survey maps marks a major step forward. A further advance in practical identification came with the 1968 Countryside Act, which required the signing of public footpaths where they leave metalled roads, though in many areas signing is honoured more in the breach than the observance. In 1981 it was estimated that no more than 10 per cent of Gloucestershire's paths were so marked.[91]

The second major feature of the 1949 Act was legislation for the creation of Long Distance Footpaths, a national system of rights of way through some of the most striking upland and coastal scenery. Progress has been slow (figure 6.3), but by the end of 1982 2561 km had been formally opened. These paths, and numerous unofficial additions like the Viking Way and the Peddars Way, helped to stimulate greater interest in, and concern for, the footpath network as a whole. The Local Government Act of 1974, however, gave the Countryside Commission powers to grant-aid expenditure on recreation footpaths other than long-distance routes. In 1976 the Commission decided that:

higher priority should now be given to improving opportunities for the great majority of visitors to the countryside who do not walk long distances or spend more than one day on a walk. More emphasis should be given to well-publicised, signed and waymarked routes designed specifically to meet the needs of the day walker and casual visitor.[92]

The immensely valuable results of this policy have been seen in many parts of the country. Grant-aided footpath officers have led programmes of signposting, waymarking and restoring paths. By 1979 Humberside, for example, had a series of ten leaflets detailing recreational footpaths in areas throughout the county, and the leaflets were linked to extensive, and effective, signing and waymarking on the ground (illustration 11). The success of this approach, not least in giving much pleasure for modest outlay, led the Commission in its 1982 Prospectus to put 'special emphasis on recreational paths: if properly managed, they offer a cheap way of making provision for recreation . . .'.[93]

Such a policy focuses on those paths best suited and best able to carry recreational traffic. They remain but a fragment of the total network. Data for the whole country are incomplete, and not wholly reliable; but excluding the counties of Avon, Greater Manchester, South Yorkshire and Humberside, for which no details are available, there are some 187,000 km

11 Signed bridleway, North Humberside. The small sign reads 'Humberside County Council Circular Walk follow coloured waymarks.' The circular spots are coloured, and link to suggested walking routes on the footpath leaflets.

of footpaths (or 191,000 km, if an independent and more realistic estimate for Gloucestershire is included). Densities vary quite widely from the national mean of 1.35 m per km^2 (figure 6.16). They tend to be

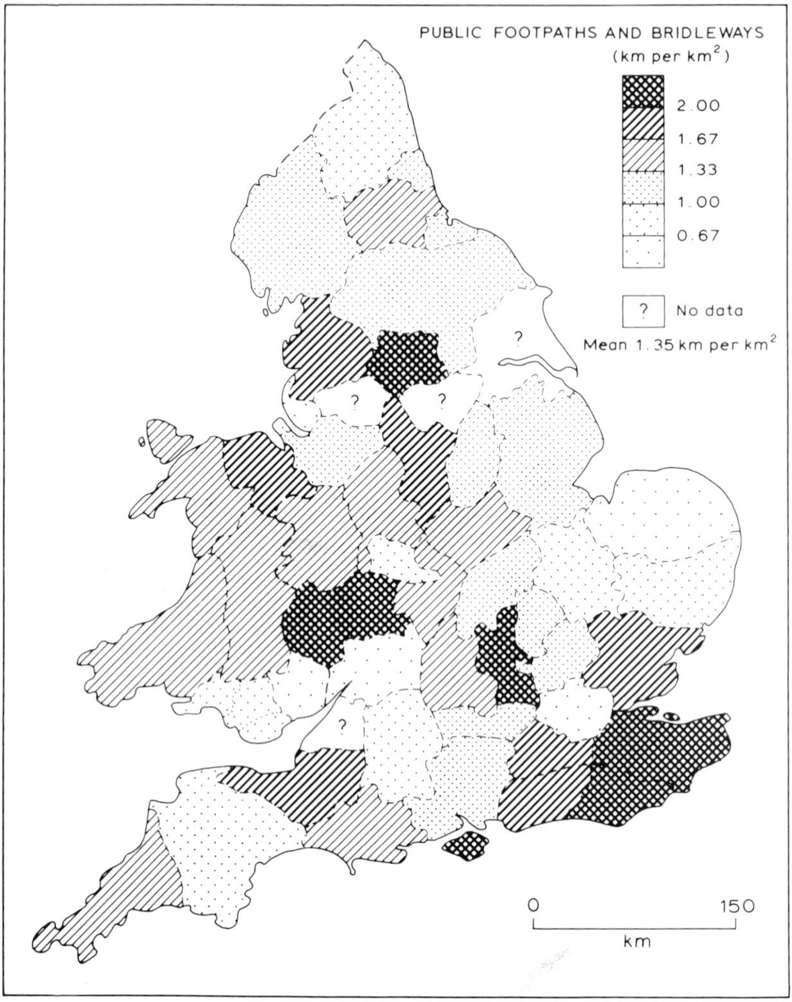

FIGURE 6.16 The density of public footpaths and bridleways in England (1976) and Wales (1981). The data 'are sometimes estimated, or totals of earlier years'. For Greater London and the pre-1974 administrative county of Glamorgan, 1969 returns have been used. The return for Hertfordshire includes unsurfaced roads and green lanes. That for Gloucestershire, at 180 km, appears a serious understatement: the Gloucestershire area of the Ramblers Association estimate some 4700 km, or 1.78 km per km^2.
Source: data from Department of Transport and the Welsh Office

lowest in arable areas of late enclosure, highest in areas of early enclosure, with small fields, as in parts of the Midlands and the South East.

The question remains as to how far a network derived for one purpose should be retained for another. In 1981 it was estimated that 44 per cent of Gloucestershire's 9000 paths were obstructed in some way.[94] In the 1960s it was government policy 'to provide a legislative framework which would permit the development of a system of footpaths and bridleways . . . more suited to modern needs'.[95] A decade later, there was a more cautious view: 'in recommending the promotion of selected recreation footpaths it is not intended that such emphasis should in any way affect the legal responsibilities of highway authorities and landowners for the maintenance of public paths.'[96] To some, even that is a faint-hearted stance. The Ramblers Association, a doughty proponent of walkers' rights, feels that the 'mileage of paths is hardly excessive and, indeed, in those parts of the country (such as Eastern England) where the number of paths per square mile is far lower than the average, the network is clearly inadequate. . . . The path network must be revived and its potential realised.'[97]

WATER RESOURCES

The final resource to be considered in this chapter is for many the sparkle in the jewel of landscape: water. It encapsulates in acute form the perspectives and the problems of resource use as a whole, and deserves far fuller treatment than is possible here.[98]

Even the most cursory review, however, recognises that, as with land resources, it fulfils three broad functions: as landscape, node and corridor. On the first of these, whatever the temptation, we cannot linger, though in the quality of both the most majestic and the most humdrum landscape, water plays an enhancing role.

Water nodes – enclosed lakes and reservoirs – are remarkably scarce, and sustain high pressures for use. The total area of inland water in England and Wales has been estimated at some 84,000 ha,[99] but not all of this is available for recreation. Natural lakes of any size are few in number outside the Lake District and Llyn Tegid in North Wales: for those that do occur, the problems are not only of recreational use; for as Lord Birkett said of the Lake District in 1971, 'it must clearly be discouraging to think that, like so many of our most closely guarded national treasures, it is most often broken into.'[100] The 'thieves', of course, are the water authorities, yet it is their activities that have come to provide so many of the opportunities for recreation on enclosed waters.

For a long time, the provision of water supplies and recreation did not mix. The threat of pollution led most water authorities to try to eliminate it at source by prohibiting public access to both reservoir and gathering grounds. A few permitted limited access to the margins, mainly for bird-watching and angling: fly-fishing was allowed on Blagdon Reservoir in 1904. Changed attitudes date almost entirely from the postwar period, and the explanation is twofold. The first was the growing pressure from recreational interests, not least sailors, searching for enclosed inland waters. As one indication, the number of clubs affiliated to the Royal Yachting Association more than trebled between 1950 and 1970, from 500 to 1500, though remaining little changed since then. The growth of members was even more dramatic, from 1400 in 1950 to over 30,000 in 1970, and to over 65,000 by 1980.[101] Coupled with burgeoning demand were changing technical circumstances. Massive expansion in water demand made many water undertakers have to draw their supplies from already polluted rivers, leading to modern treatment plants capable of dealing effectively, and cheaply, with relatively high levels of pollution. At the same time, the trend has been away from the isolated impounding reservoir towards regulating reservoirs whose prime role is to maintain flows in the rivers now used as natural aqueducts.

New reservoirs invariably include some provision for recreation. The first on a major scale was the 635 ha Grafham Water, completed in 1966. Conditions were also relaxed at many earlier reservoirs. By 1981 there were 531 water supply reservoirs of over 2 ha (5 acres) in extent in England and Wales, covering some 21,239 ha. Of these, 472 (89 per cent) support some form of water recreation on either the water surface or the associated land. Fishing is permitted at 333 reservoirs but sailing at only 81, and in all but eight cases only through membership of a club (figure 6.17). New water sports, introduced mainly since 1974, include sub-aqua (26 reservoirs), canoeing (38), sailboarding (21) and water-skiing (5).[102]

Lakes and supply reservoirs are not, of course, the only areas of enclosed water. Canal feeder reservoirs are a longstanding resource, though individually they tend to be relatively small, with only eight exceeding 40 ha. They provide in total some 1339 ha. Wet mineral workings are an important, and a growing, resource. Gravel workings are found mainly in the valleys of the larger east-flowing rivers of lowland England, especially the Thames and Trent. There has been a rapid expansion of the recreational use of the resultant flooded pits since the mid-1950s: among other schemes, they have permitted the development of the Holme Pierrepont National Water Sports Centre in the valley of the Trent near Nottingham and the Cotswold Water Park in the upper reaches of the Thames.

The major water corridors are rivers and canals. Their potential is threefold: for activities confined to the banks, such as walking; for activities from the banks, such as angling: and for activities in or on the water, including swimming, canoeing, sailing and cruising. Their recreational use must co-exist with other uses, especially drainage, water supply, sewage and waste disposal, and transport. This variety of use leads to frequent and serious conflicts, both between recreational and non-recreational users and between differing kinds of recreation: this theme will be pursued further in the following chapter.

Non-navigable rivers have limited recreational potential, with the very important exceptions of walking and angling. The very presence of a stream heightens the countryside recreation experience for most countryside visitors. Angling is a major sport: the National Angling Survey estimated that, for 1979, 15 per cent of all men and boys aged 12 and over went fishing in the course of the year. The inland waters of England and Wales were fished by some 2.7 million anglers, and sea waters by 1.8 million. The sport is still growing in importance, with an increase in participants of 21 per cent over the past decade.[103] The sheer pressure of such numbers on a finite resource causes frequent problems, not least the high commercial value placed on some waters and the restriction in opportunity this implies.

Navigable streams and canals heighten recreational potential. The

TABLE 6.4 Boat licences and registration on inland waterways, 1973-80

	Powered boats, 1980	*Unpowered boats, 1980*	*Total, 1980*	*Total, 1973*	*% change 1973-80*
Anglian Water Authority					
River Great Ouse	2822	2018	4840	4002	+21
River Nene	—	—	1050	850	+24
British Waterways Board					
Canals and river navigations	20,918	4755	25,673	23,729	+8
Great Yarmouth Port & Haven Commissioners					
Norfolk and Suffolk Broads and rivers	8184	4012	12,196	10,670	+14
Manchester Ship Canal					
Bridgewater Canal	1025	133	1158	800	+45
Thames Water Authority					
River Thames	14,664	11,656	26,320	29,623	−11

Source: data from Water Space Amenity Commission, *Annual Report 1980-1981*, Appendix C

Transport Act of 1968 was a major landmark in Britain's recreational history. Faced with a growing deficit on the canals, the government not only recognised the 'inescapable' nature of the deficit, but determined 'to retain for pleasure cruising substantially the existing network available for

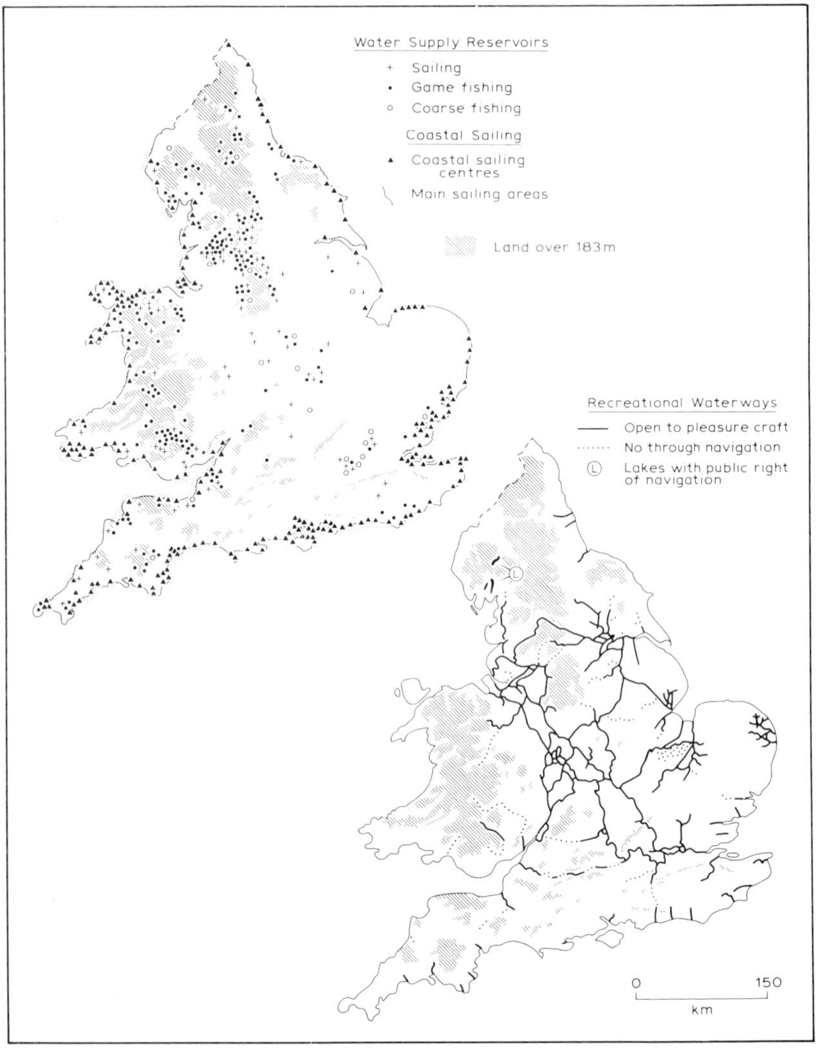

FIGURE 6.17 Coastal sailing, the recreational use of water supply reservoirs and recreational waterways.
Source: data from M. F. Tanner, *Water resources and recreation* (Sports Council, 1973), figure 1; *Amenity use of water-supply reservoirs* (Water Space Amenity Commission, 1976); and *Recreational waterways* (Water Space Amenity Commission, 1976)

this purpose' and believed that 'this recreational purpose of the nationalised waterways should be recognised by public Act of Parliament'.[104] The subsequent Act was important in indicating a creative attitude by government to recreation in general, and for its intention of substantiating that attitude with tangible resources.

Since then, the use of the network has grown considerably (table 6.4), albeit more markedly in earlier years. The net cost of that use is still high. British Waterways Board's cruising waterways showed a net deficit of £11.6 million in 1981, and the 'remainder' waterways a deficit of £4.4 million. Much of the expenditure would, of course, have been incurred whether or not the waterways were used for traffic, but these sums contrast sharply with the gross income from amenity uses of £1.9 million for the cruising waterways and £0.14 million for the remainder waterways.[105] None the less, the waterways are still the home of some 22,000 privately owned boats, and hire boats provided holidays for some 185,000 people in 1981. In addition, some 250,000 anglers regularly fish the canals (though yielding only £75,000 in revenue) and the towpaths provide much pleasurable walking. They remain an important example of a largely moribund commercial resource (with the exception of a few, mainly river, navigations) converted to an attractive recreational resource with a distinctive environment and ready access for large numbers (figure 6.17).

THE COASTAL FRINGE

This chapter began with a vision of a rural paradise held at heart by urban man, however unreal that vision might sometimes be. For most people, beyond the country lies the sea, haunt of day-tripper when accessible, haunt of holidaymaker above all. As a resource, the coast and the sea have been implicit in much earlier discussion, but as the coast is the epitome of the wider problems of recreational resource use, a further brief mention is a fitting conclusion to this chapter.

Coastal recreation is by definition resource-based, yet the coast is within 120 km of every person living in England and Wales. The coast is not one resource, but many.[106] There are variations of opportunity across it – shore, beach and open water – and along it – from developed resort to remote cove: variations matched by equal variations in the intensity and nature of its use. Nor, of course, is that use confined to recreation, for the needs of conservation, industry and commerce pose their own pressures and problems.

For such an extensive resource, it has been little studied in any comprehensive fashion. In 1966–67, the erstwhile National Parks Commission held a series of Coastal Conferences, in preparation for which maps of development and estimates of recreational use were prepared.[107] These have not subsequently been updated in any co-ordinated fashion, though attention has been focused on two specific kinds of problem. The first are the resorts themselves: the Victorian legacy, and still the focus of so much holidaymaking, but with serious economic problems compounded by the short holiday season and the change in emphasis from formal to informal accommodation.[108] Second, in contrast, is the undeveloped coast. The National Trust's response through Operation Neptune has already been noted: the planning response was a new variant of the designation mechanism, the creation of Heritage Coasts (figure 6.3). Heritage Coasts as a concept arose directly from the Coastal Conferences, and the idea was developed, and suggested Heritage Coasts proposed, in the Countryside Commission's report, *The coastal heritage* (1970). In the event, the Secretary of State supported the concept, but left adoption to local authorities rather than to national agencies.[109] By the end of 1981, 1156 km had been defined, 238 km completely, the remainder laterally.

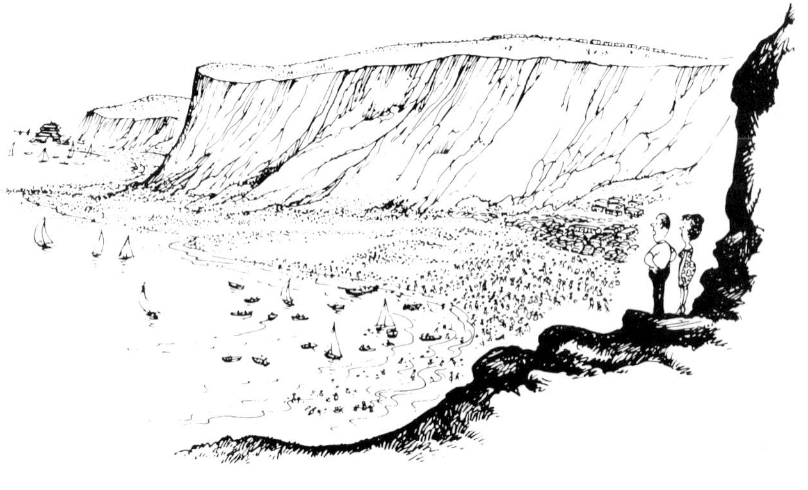

12 'There's talk of trying to acquire it for the nation!' (Thelwell, courtesy *Punch*).

In practice, achievements on many of these coasts have been modest, and in 1982 the Commission could wryly comment that 'in many places the level of management of heritage coast leaves much to be desired.'[110] As with so many recreation resources, of both countryside and coast, the response of the public purse has been too little too late. Perhaps Thelwell best sums it up (illustration 12). Use has long made much of our coasts *de facto* national recreation areas: *de jure* management is often little more than the gilding of a tarnished lily, though recognition of responsibility is better than renunciation.

7 Evaluation, Conflict and Capacity

> Major public attention and much planning has been devoted to the matter of the *area* of land and water used for recreation . . . Area is important, but it is not the whole story, and sometimes it is not even the major one.[1]

Though written in an American context, Clawson and Knetsch's comment has far wider validity. Simply to outline the pattern of demand for recreation and to enumerate the pattern of resources to match that demand ignores much of importance in the relationship between the two. In this chapter three aspects of that relationship will be examined: the evaluation and selection of suitable resources; the conflicts between users of the same resource; and the capacity of resources for recreation use.

RESOURCE EVALUATION

The evaluation of resources for recreation use has two quite distinct facets. The first is concerned with the designation of an area for its landscape quality; the second, the selection of specific sites for development for recreation purposes. The former is of far wider importance in a conservation and planning context and will receive only passing mention here, though it has generated a considerable literature of its own.[2] The latter has more immediate relevance, but, as earlier chapters have often demonstrated, actual selection has tended to be a response to the opportunism of site availability and to fashions in funding rather than to any conscious process of selection.

In England and Wales, the statutory designation of landscape largely preceded the emergence of an objective approach to landscape evaluation. For national parks, there was little dispute as to the areas worthy of that status.[3] The problems centred rather round more pragmatic issues – the need for a national park near London, the administrative practicability of the designation of the Cornish coast and the extent to which the character of the Broads was consistent with the basic definition of a national park. Areas of Outstanding Natural Beauty caused more concern, though in 1980 Himsworth found in his review that 'there seems a surprising satisfaction with the present areas', even if 'one or two designated areas, or substantial parts of them, might be called in question as being of truly national importance.'[4]

The delineation of Heritage Coasts offered another kind of opportunity, but again a subjective appraisal of quality was preferred to a more objective – and more mechanical – approach. To quote the report:

> Those who have visited many different parts of Britain's coastline will have their own ideas of the most beautiful stretches. Some of the better-known parts are so compellingly beautiful in any weather or season that their inclusion in any national list would be readily accepted.
>
> Such a list would probably exclude many superb stretches which are inaccessible except on foot and which will have been visited only by those who have made a special effort to reach them or have had some special reason for doing so. In order to be comprehensive and to include such areas, the most acceptable method would be for a skilled observer to examine critically every mile of coast, irrespective of access, and record his impressions. An assessment of this kind was carried out in 1943–5 by Professor J.A. Steers . . . [and forms] the basis of the present assessment.[5]

In his evaluation, Steers used only three grades of quality, but the simplicity of his work was inappropriate for assessing the worth of more richly varied inland landscapes. More complex approaches, however, tend to confuse rather than clarify. The search for objectivity gives a spurious precision: even the most complex and considered appraisals have given reluctant recognition to 'the inevitability, and indeed desirability, of a subjective element'.[6] Landscape evaluation as a whole has attracted less interest in recent years. No convincing theoretical basis has emerged, and many workers share a concern that 'without a theoretical understanding of what we are attempting, can we be certain that the very process of breaking down landscape into its component parts does not destroy the essence of what we are investigating?'[7]

It would be unjust to dismiss what has been achieved, though often its purpose is only marginal to recreation needs. At county level, not least in the preparation of structure plans in the mid-1970s, landscape appraisals have informed development policy.[8] For Wales, the Welsh Office has completed an assessment of the physical character (though not the quality) of the country's landscapes for 'those required to consider proposed changes and development in the landscape'.[9] These purposes, however, are much wider than the needs of recreation and will not be pursued further in this context.

Landscape, indeed, is only one element in categorising and evaluating recreation resources and in searching for suitable sites for recreation development. There have been surprisingly few attempts at any such categorisation. In fairness, the opportunities to develop a new network of sites have been, to say the least, limited. Even the spate of country park creation following the 1968 Countryside Act relied largely on the development of existing sites or the capitalisation of random opportunities on derelict or degraded land. Nevertheless, if recreation resources are to be fully recognised, and not least if the claims of recreation against other uses of land and water are to be objectively evaluated, some assessment of the recreational potential of an area is worth attempting.

One pioneer approach was that of Duffield and Owen, although it was specifically applied in Scotland (figure 7.1).[10] The basic technique was a simple one and, constrained by finance, depended largely on desk studies. The aim was to identify 'recreation environments', areas with a similar capacity to sustain various forms of outdoor recreation. The method adopted used four separate assessments of land capability for outdoor recreation, and then combined them into a single overall assessment. The four categories were: suitability for land-based recreation; suitability for water-based recreation; scenic quality; and ecological significance. In each case, the criteria adopted were arbitrary, and were often conditioned by the need to use existing sources for each assessment. Thus, for land-based recreation suitability the criteria used were:

(a) Camping, caravanning and picknicking: all countryside within 400 m of a metalled road;
(b) pony-trekking: all upland areas above 300 m with rights of way, or established footpaths and bridleways;
(c) walking and hiking: all upland areas above 450 m with rights of way, or established footpaths and bridleways;
(d) game-shooting: all areas assessed as shooting on valuation rolls;
(e) rock-climbing: all cliff faces over 30 m in height;
(f) skiing: available relief over 280 m with an average snowholding period of more than three months.

The choice of both activities and criteria for activities is obviously arbitrary, and this is equally true of the criteria used for the other three categories.

In each category, the unit for assessment was a 2 km × 2 km square of the Ordnance Survey National Grid, and a simple cumulative score was given on the basis of the number of criteria that could be satisfied in that square. A similar procedure was then adopted for each category, and the scores from each assessment were weighted to give the same possible maximum. All four scores for each square were totalled, and these totals were used to identify a range of recreation environments. The environments so defined can then be used as a basis for a recreation development strategy.

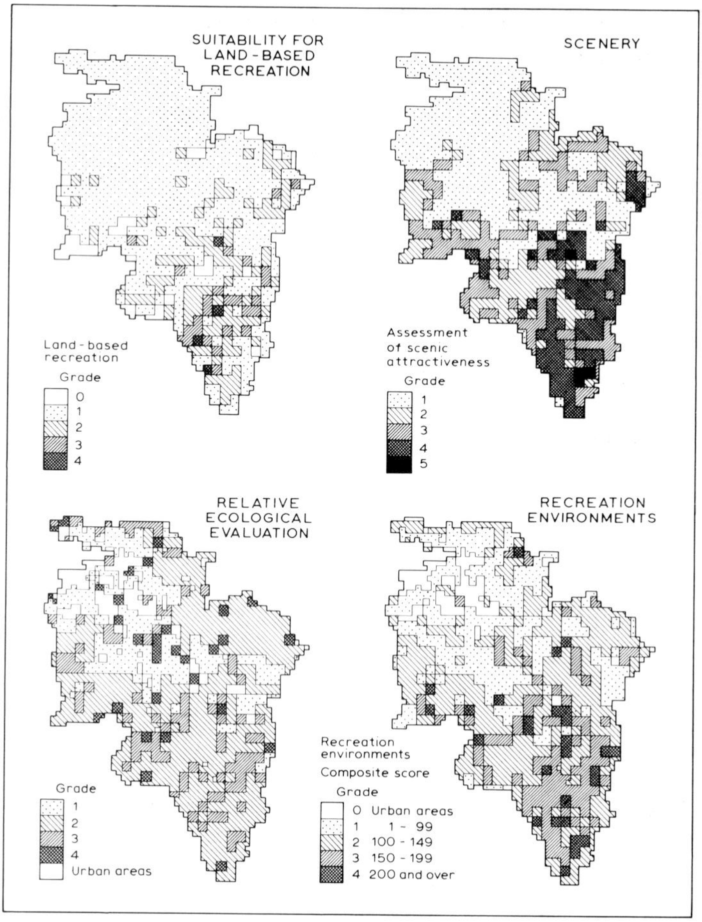

FIGURE 7.1 Resources for countryside recreation in Lanarkshire. The recreation environments (bottom right) are synthesised from assessments of suitability for land-based recreation, water-based recreation (not shown), scenic attractiveness and ecological importance. The unit of assessment is normally 2 km × 2 km squares.
Source: data from B. S. Duffield and M. L. Owen, *Leisure + countryside = : a geographical appraisal of countryside recreation in Lanarkshire* (University of Edinburgh, 1970)

The method has obvious, and acknowledged, limitations. The choice of activities, and the values assigned to them, are arbitrary and debatable: there is the evident danger of a spurious objectivity being given to a series of values subjectively derived. None the less, the method does provide 'a comparative evaluation of resources by which it would be possible to locate and identify all areas suitable for recreational activities on the basis of their physical characteristics',[11] Further, the material is readily handled by computer: differing weights can be given to the differing categories and their component criteria, and the resulting 'environments' readily related to population pressure and other components of demand. This very flexibility in manipulation for specific purposes is a considerable strength.

A similar approach to evaluation was developed for South Wales[12] (figure 7.2). In this case, four indices were used, respectively related to accessibility to population, accessibility to roads, an aggregate of ten recreational attractions, and choice and variety of environmental types. The results were mapped for each kilometre square of the National Grid. Again, the computer was used to vary the scoring method, by giving different weightings to individual indices and to the components used in deriving each. In such a procedure there can be no single 'correct' result, but differing results can be derived according to the perceived importance

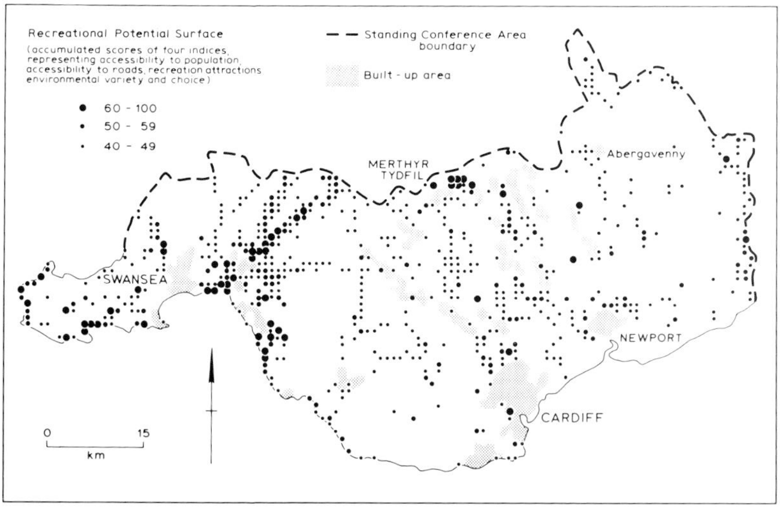

FIGURE 7.2 An evaluation of resources for countryside recreation in South Wales using the potential surface technique. In this example, the four indices were weighted as follows: accessibility to population, 40; accessibility to roads, 35; recreation attractions, 100; environmental variety and choice, 30.
Source: data from *Recreation in South Wales* (Standing Conference on Regional Planning in South Wales and Monmouthshire, 1973), diagram 2

of specific objectives. Thus, if good accessibility to the urban population is of particular importance, greater weight can be given to the first index. For general use, the results should correlate reasonably well with subjective assessments of well-known areas, but with the obvious advantage of being on a uniform basis for the whole area of 3702 km^2.

Figure 7.2 shows the results of the 'preferred' run. Two kinds of area accumulate the highest scores. In the first, the disadvantages of poor accessibility are more than counterbalanced by their exceptional attraction. Prime examples are the Gower Coast, the Wye and Monnow Valleys and the fringes of the Brecon Beacons National Park (the park itself being outside the study area). In the second kind are areas that rate 'fair to good' for both attraction and accessibility. Typical examples are the fringes of the Swansea Bay urban area, and the fringes of Cardiff and Newport.

Analyses of this kind could be much more widely employed with advantage. Their limitations, and their inherent subjectivity, are clear, but they are a much better basis for decision-making than assessments made on individual perceptions and prejudices. Above all, they indicate areas for search, to maximise the impact of investment in accord with acknowledged objectives. They can be adapted to both site and network development, to country parks and recreational footpaths, and they have potential for commercial as well as public sector investment.

RECREATION CONFLICTS

Site selection is only the beginning of site development. One facet of that development that has received little attention in the discussion to date is the conflicts that can arise in site use, both between recreational and other users and between different types of recreational use.

Countryside recreation in Britain contrasts strongly with that in North America, because much of it takes place on land that also serves an agricultural purpose. The seminal report of the US Outdoor Recreation Resources Review Commission, *Outdoor recreation for America*,[13] sought to delineate classes of recreation area based upon the relationship between resource characteristics and recreation needs. Six such classes were described, and their adoption was urged 'to enhance the quality of recreation opportunities, and to facilitate the orderly development of recreation areas' (p. 96). To British eyes, it seems curious that only one of the six – 'natural environment areas' – was envisaged as being 'usually in combination with other uses'. Here, in contrast, 'our densely-populated country does not have room for the luxury of a single-use system of designation.'[14] As the previous chapter emphasised, recreation is but one of the competing claims for rural land. Since the 1960s, the intensifying problems of these rival claims have been alleviated a little by the creation of country parks and numerous new 'attractions' segregating recreational use, but most countryside recreation still has to coexist with other rural activities.

That coexistence inevitably generates friction between the visitor and those who live and work in the countryside. Even the Chairman of the House of Lords Select Committee on Sport and Leisure could comment:

> As a landowner myself and a farmer I am possessed of one of the most lovely parks in the Midlands, which is now half farm. Now, I simply dare not let the public in there at the moment because they will do thousands of pounds worth of damage; they have already done it; they have rolled stones down the hill and all the little monuments have been smashed. I have even had airgun pellets taken out of my bullocks.[15]

Such evidence is only anecdotal, but the causes and consequences of friction remain. Trespass, particularly on farms close to the urban fringe, the worrying of stock and damage to walls and fences are the common and often justified complaints of the farming community (illustration 13).

13 '. . . people simply settle down for an hour or a day where it suits them, somewhere "in the country" – to the inconvenience and indeed expense of the countryman who lives and works there' (Cmnd 2928, 1966) (Thelwell, courtesy *Punch*).

Footpaths are a perennial problem. Memoranda to the House of Lords Select Committee encapsulate the difficulties. From the rambler's point of view,

> The public paths system is extensive enough, but it needs much more vigorous protection by the law if it is to continue to serve a growing recreational demand. . . . The offences are repeated year after year. A deep ploughed path with its furrows is a powerful impediment to most would-be walkers. Standing crops later in the season deter all but the boldest.[16]

In response, the National Farmers Union recognised that

> The simple recreations of walking, riding and cycling in the countryside have a minimal impact upon the use of land for farming, providing the visitors keep to the rights of way. At present however the rights of way provide a somewhat outdated pattern of access which has kept pace with neither the 'leisure boom' nor the 'agricultural revolution' of the last 25 years. The NFU therefore feels that a new look should be taken at rights of way in the context of comprehensive recreation planning. This may well require changes in present legislation and should aim at re-designing the network of public rights of way to meet the needs of today's visitors . . . while at the same time taking into account agricultural changes such as new field boundaries and new methods of crop husbandry.[17]

Since that debate, the problems have intensified, but as the previous chapter indicated, comparatively small injections of funds can ease the consequences if not remove the causes of friction when countryside visitors and other rural land users have, of necessity, to co-exist on the same resource.

The other positive approach is through education, on the grounds that understanding breeds respect. That basic premise may itself be suspect; for much education in this context, through visitor and information centres, reaches principally those in little real *need* of the message, however much they may *enjoy* the 'interpretive experience'. Research indicates that 'the visit to a visitor centre is most effective for those already aware of the countryside':[18] for those unaware, education needs to be part of a far wider community programme of learning for leisure.

Other conflicts, no less acute, exist between differing forms of recreation using the same resource at the same time. Too many activities may overcrowd the space; differing activities may interfere physically with each other; the aural or visual intrusion of one activity may seriously erode the enjoyment of another.

Where the resource can be positively managed for recreation, conflicts can be removed by separating the activities in space or time. In the open countryside, away from country parks or other managed space, the solution may not be so simple. To some extent, there may be a degree of self-management. In her study of the common of Beverley Westwood, Glyptis noted that 'informal games tended to be more isolated, extending away from the roadside to the emptier pastures.' To that spatial segregation was added temporal segregation. Walking was more popular in the morning and later afternoon: 'many of the walkers came from Beverley itself, and there was some indication . . . that local people tend to use the site more at off-peak times.'[19]

Many conflicts are not so readily settled. The most acute generate annoyance out of proportion to the numbers involved. The noisy intrusion of motorcyclists scrambling or trail-riding in the open countryside is a case in point (illustration 14). On sections of the Ridgeway Long Distance Path, for example, where all forms of traffic have an historic legal right of travel on the unmade surface, motorcyclists are a tiny but resented minority. In one survey, they formed only 2 per cent of visitors, but 11 per cent of all interviewed mentioned without prompting the desirability of controlling vehicles, and this proportion rose to 66 per cent when the question was put directly.[20] Minority pleasures, even obtrusive ones, can generally find suitable location, though even then their case may be difficult to make. The Forestry Commission has a 'policy of making forest roads available to a limited number of [car] rallies . . . but we do not plan any extension because of the resulting conflict with one of the bases of our recreational policy, which is to provide facilities for informal recreation and the enjoyment of quiet pursuits.'[21]

14 The peace of the countryside? Motorcyclists scrambling on Mam Tor, in the Peak District.

Some of the most acute conflicts have arisen in the use of water for recreation. Water in itself is a scarce resource, and this scarcity further exacerbates inherent difficulties. In part, the problem is a legal one of access, seen in its most acute form in the extension of canoe touring into rivers where no legal right of navigation exists. When incursions were few in number, objections were equally rare. But the growth of the sport

> has made riparian owners and fishing organisations more conscious of the existence of canoeing. Increasingly there is evidence of action to refuse the use for canoeing of water space that has been used for many years by tolerance or by right by small numbers of canoeists.[22]

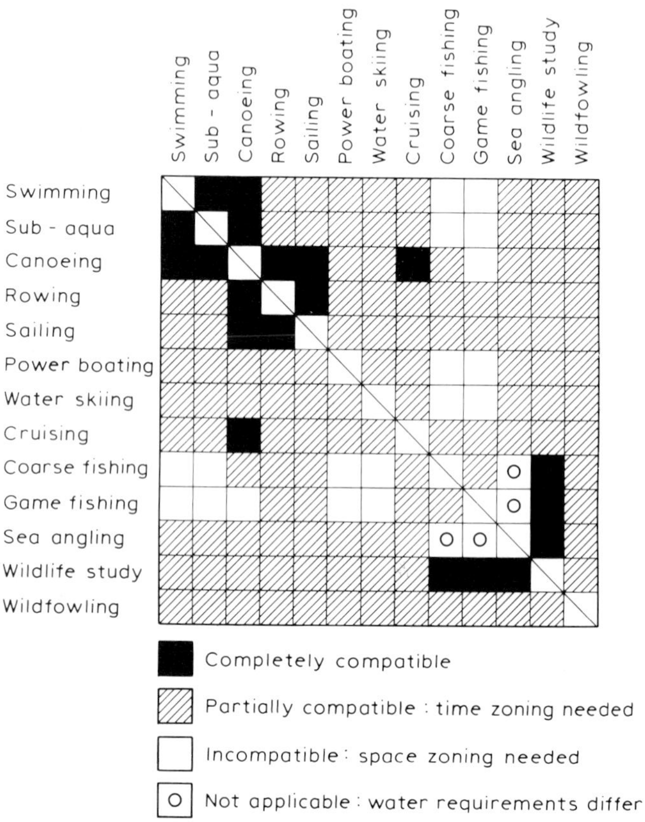

FIGURE 7.3 The compatibility of the use of water by various water-based recreations. Compatible activities can use the same area of water at the same time; partially compatible activities can use the same area of water but not at the same time; incompatible activities cannot use the same area of water.
Source: modified from B. Goodall and J. B. Whittow, *The recreational potential of Forestry Commission holdings: a report to the Forestry Commission* (Department of Geography, University of Reading, 1973), table 2.4

Positions are rapidly entrenched. The fisherman avers that 'on a trout water canoeing and trout fishing are completely incompatible', to which the canoeist replies 'we get along very well where there is a public right of way, but as soon as we meet a situation where the angler is in a position to say no, we apparently become quite incompatible with any fishing at all.'[23]

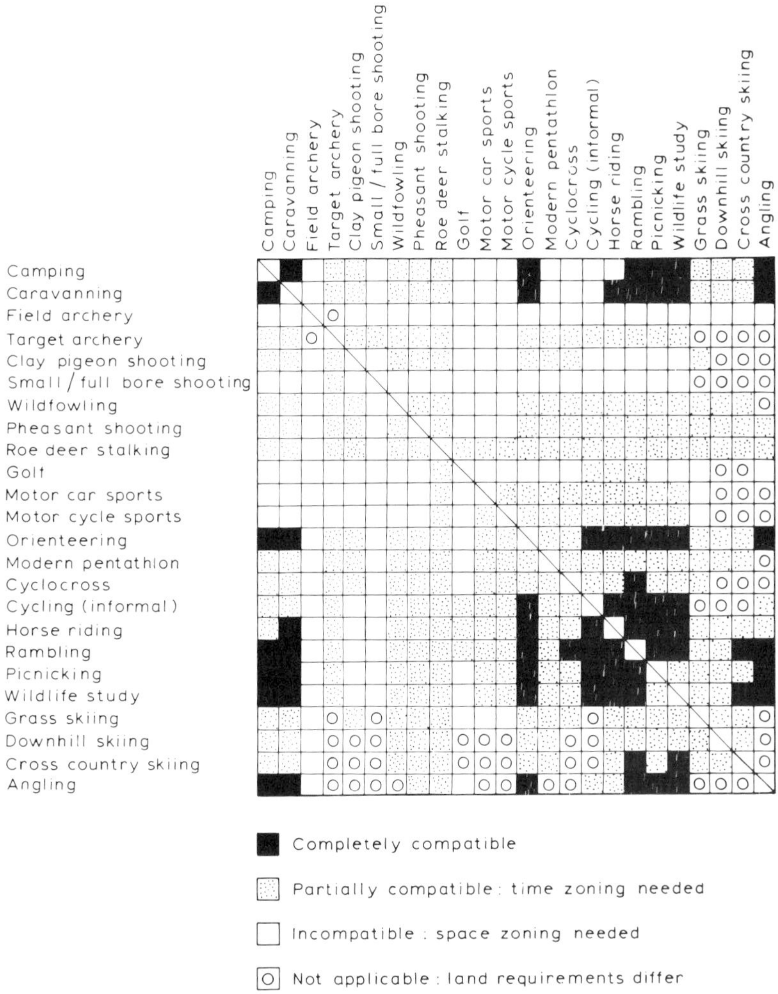

FIGURE 7.4 The compatibility of the use of land by open-air recreation activities. Compatible activities can use the same area of land at the same time; partially compatible activities can use the same area of land but not at the same time; incompatible activities cannot use the same area of land.
Source: modified from B. Goodall and J. B. Whittow, *The recreational potential of Forestry Commission holdings: a report to the Forestry Commission* (Department of Geography, University of Reading, 1973), table 2.3

Even where the legal right of passage is not in question, conflicts occur between anglers and the full range of boat users, but they are 'sporadic in time and space and, by implication, often magnified in reporting and transmission. Most of the time it seems that the presence of one is regarded by the other as a "tolerable nuisance".'[24]

That 'tolerable nuisance' is capable of simple analysis in matrix form (figures 7.3 and 7.4). The concept of segregation by time or space is obvious enough for both water-based and land-based activities: the problem is rarely the fact of segregation but rather its effective management. Difficulties are few when management is independent, as by a local authority in a country park, but are more likely to occur when management is partial to one interest, as in the controversy between fishing and canoeing, or where it is ineffective or non-existent as in many stretches of open country.

THE CONCEPT OF CAPACITY

Site conflicts are exacerbated as use intensifies. It then becomes important to consider the capacity of a particular resource for a specific recreation. In outline, the idea of capacity is simple enough. In terms of the basic demand-supply equation in recreation, capacity is reached when the demand for a resource is just matched by the supply of that resource.

Reality, alas, is more complex. Despite the seeming simplicity of the phrase, recreational carrying capacity is difficult to define, for it has a variety of meanings and may be understood in different situations and by different people in totally different ways.[25] The roots of the concept lie, implicitly at least, in many aspects of land use, particularly in relation to the number of animals a given area can carry.[26] It emerged in a recreation context in the early 1960s as pressure on rural recreation resources increased. One of the early definitions was that of Wagar, of Seattle, who in 1964 saw recreational carrying capacity as 'the level of recreational use an area can withstand while providing a sustained quality of recreation'.[27] Such a definition poses immediate problems. What is meant by 'sustained quality'? Is quality to be measured in physical or aesthetic terms? How is such a measure to be made? The problems remain endemic not only to this particular definition, but to the concept as a whole, but its importance remains such that a more detailed examination is warranted. There is, indeed, no single recreational carrying capacity. Not only does the capacity vary with the activity, but the concept in relation to a specific resource has four distinct facets – physical, ecological, perceptual and economic – and these will be considered in turn.

PHYSICAL CAPACITY

Physical capacity is the simplest in concept and application, and may be defined as the maximum number a site or facility can physically accommodate for a given activity. It is most readily applied to organised, formal activities, and has obvious relevance to spectator events. A theatre or a football stadium, for example, has a finite capacity related to either the number of seats available or the number of people it can safely accommodate: once that number is reached, the physical capacity has been attained.

The idea translates simply to many sports. A soccer pitch, with a playing area and surrounding margin of just under 1 ha, has reached its physical capacity for that game when it is being used by 22 players, together with a referee and two linesmen – 25 in total. That determination of capacity, however, pays no regard to time. In theory, if a game lasts 95 minutes and 5 minutes is allowed for change over, 14 games can be completed on that pitch in a single day and 350 players can take part in a game. On the same basis, over a year, one pitch could provide one game for 127,750 players! Such calculations, of course, reduce the principle to an absurdity, paying no regard to the availability of light, the ability of the pitch to stand such wear, the willingness of the players to participate at what are (to say the least) unsocial hours or the existence of an organisation able to marshal the players as required.

Nevertheless, the idea of physical capacity has relevance in planning sports facilities, in terms both of momentary capacity and of a reasonable multiple of that momentary capacity reflecting practical conditions of use through time. For formal sports with a given size of pitch or court, with a set number of players and a set duration (or readily applied time limit) of game, the calculation can be quite precise. For more informal sports, careful observation can yield practical guidelines. A swimming pool, for example, caters for differing kinds of activity, with a distinction between the true swimmer, requiring a reasonable amount of clear water, and the learner, or those playing or standing in the water whose space requirements are less. In 1962 the Ministry of Housing and Local Government suggested the former needed some 3.3 m^2 (36 ft^2) and the latter 0.9 m^2 (10 ft^2) per person, a mean of 2.1 m^2 (23 ft^2) per person. In 1968 the Sports Council recommended 1.7 m^2 (18 ft^2) as adequate, though by 1978 felt the figure should be 'nearer 2.8 m^2 (30 ft^2)'.[28]

Even here there is a note of caution. Whereas in 1968 the Council thought that the provision of swimming pools should be simply related to population on a 'water area per user' basis, and proposed a suitable formula, they had changed their mind by 1978. 'The deficiencies of the formula and the difficulties of producing a satisfactory alternative to include all the variables suggest that it would be appropriate at this time to abandon the formula approach to the provision of swimming pools. . . .' The alternative suggested was to concentrate on catchment rather than capacity in identifying deficiencies of provision. Even so, the concept if not the precise formulation of physical capacity remained important, with the recognition of the need 'to avoid under-provision leading to overcrowding, frustration and eventually to demand for further pools, and overprovision which would prove expensive in running costs in the short term'.[29]

For most sports, a working approximation of physical capacity can be made, given certain assumptions of the duration of the activity, the willingness of participants to play at varying times and the availability of aids such as lighting to prolong the period during which the facility can be used. The concept is much less readily applicable to informal recreation at the coast and in the countryside; here, the limitation is rarely the physical amount of space available. Thelwell (illustration 15) captures precisely what could happen if the physical capacity of a beach were reached, but on even the most crowded days reality is less dramatic. The limit is not the physical space occupied but the willingness of people to accept intrusions into personal space – the beach *perceived* as full rather than actually full in the physical sense. The limits of perceptual capacity are discussed later in the chapter.

15 Physical capacity – 'ask them to move back – and hurry!' (Thelwell, courtesy *Punch*).

16 At Aberdaron, in the Lleyn peninsula, beach capacity is effectively limited by car park capacity, for no other parking is permitted in the immediate area.

An element of physical capacity may, however, be imposed on an informal recreation site not by the site itself but by its ancillary facilities. The capacity of car parks may be critical: once they are full, the site itself is effectively full even though in strict space terms this may be very far from the case (illustration 16). The manipulation of car park size can be a very effective management tool to regulate the total level of site use at sensitive sites.

ECOLOGICAL CAPACITY

A sensitive site is one where the pressure of human presence leads to its physical degradation. The concept here is of *ecological capacity*, which may be defined as the level of recreational use an area can undergo before irreversible ecological damage is sustained. While it is normally considered in the context of the natural environment, the concept is also applicable to fragile human artefacts. For the National Trust, the problem is depressingly familiar.

> It had taken 60 needlewomen more than two years to repair the eighteenth-century damask curtains at Erdigg, near Wrexham before the Jacobean mansion was opened to the public. After one four-month season, 80,000 visitors had reduced the hanging 'to tatters' because of an irresistible urge to touch everything in reach.[30]

In the wider context, as early as 1958 the Trust's Annual Report could comment that

> At one time the Trust was concerned to expose an indifferent public to the impact of the countryside, to induce thousands from the towns to discover the beauty of the moors, the fens, and the coastland under its protection. The Trust, aided by circumstances and the motor car, has achieved its object only too well. As a result, the Trust is more and more concerned with the reverse process – the impact of the public on the countryside.[31]

That impact is varied and intense. It has an intrinsic interest of its own, and has provoked a substantial literature.[32] Space inhabits an extended review, but its scale and range must be recognised. The prime concern is the repeated impact of human feet. Trampling leads to marked changes in plant growth and to the reproductive performance of plants. Changes in species composition are quick to follow, with a competitive advantage given to the small number of species that are resilient to the effects of trampling. With continued pressure, the percentage of bare ground increases, with the intensity of trampling sufficient to inhibit the growth of even the most resistant species. Decreased vegetation cover and compacted soil lead to accelerated erosion. Paths in hill country, devoid of vegetation and following a direct line up a slope, 'represent ideal channels for water transport. It is difficult to imagine a combination of circumstances more suited to the development of erosion gullies'[33] (illustration 17).

17 Heavily gullied and eroded path on Mam Tor in the Peak District. Management is here restricting use to only part of the path.

Unsurfaced paths, with their concentration of use, can represent recreational impact in its most acute form. The rapidity of wear will depend on local conditions of soil, slope and vegetation. Coastal sand dunes are particularly vulnerable. At Ainsdale, on the coast north of Liverpool, a limit of no more than 4000 people per season on any given trail through the nature reserve is necessary in order to avoid severe wear on the vegetation and subsequent erosion. At Gibraltar Point in Lincolnshire, 7500 people in a season walking over mobile dunes completely eliminated marram, sea couch and prickly saltwort and resulted in considerable dune erosion. Complete recovery of plant life in such areas would require some four years without disturbance.[34]

Many areas bear the scars of popularity. In 1971 the first 1.6 km of the Pennine Way out of Edale, used by an average of 423 walkers a day in summer, had been worn to a mean extent of 12.9 m.[35] An even more striking example was the Lyke Wake Walk across the North York Moors. This 65 km route traverses the highest part of the moors. In 1981 the formal crossing was completed by 7681 people, many in large groups undertaking sponsored walks. Shorter sections were used by at least three times that number. The result was serious erosion on several sections, with large areas of deep peat exposed and removed. On the central 13.8 km section of the walk above Rosedale, no less than 8.65 km, or 62 per cent, was showing progressive damage and erosion.[36] The extent of damage was such that the North York Moors National Park authority, in conjunction with landowners and the Lyke Wake Walk Club, had to initiate a programme aimed at a substantial reduction in the use of the walk as the only feasible alternative to complete closure.

Trampling is far from the only ecological impact of recreation. Erosion from the passage of vehicles on both land and water; pollution by litter, petrol fumes, excrement and noise; the ravages of fire, whether accidental or deliberate; the collecting of botanical and geological specimens; the killing of birds and animals by hunting; even the simple disturbance of birds and animals by sustained human presence, create varying degrees of damage to the natural environment and may permanently affect the capacity of that environment for sustained recreational use.

Environmental damage is not, of course, synonymous with ecological capacity. Much of the damage is relatively trivial and far from irreversible. The initial definition of ecological capacity is concerned with longer-term threats to the ecological status quo – a capacity related to the maximum level of use 'before irreversible ecological damage is sustained'. The definition, however, takes a narrowly ecological view. It assumes no change in the environment other than the level of recreational use. That use, and its ecological impact, can be managed: indeed, ecological capacity is as much a matter of management objective and method as level of use.

Four kinds of management objective may be distinguished in this context. The first is concerned to allow recreational activities to exert a minimal modifying influence, to retain the ecological status quo. This is essentially the nature reserve approach, the use of an area being limited by positive control of visitor numbers or even their complete exclusion. The second seeks to retain the essential characteristics of an area, but otherwise accepts some change. Most open spaces in Britain are managed, implicitly or explicitly, on this basis. Some wear on paths is accepted, some change and simplification of plant communities is tolerated, provided the area still retains a reasonably 'natural' appearance to the lay eye (illustration 18). This shades into the third approach, which creates an ecosystem suitable for the intended use, rather than controlling use to preserve an ecosystem.

18 Stream-side and roadside picnicking at Huccaby on Dartmoor. Sites of this kind are highly attractive for informal recreation, but in consequence suffer rapid erosion of grass and stream banks. Most will recover during the winter and spring, but remedial work, or access restriction, may be necessary in severe cases.

That creation may be partial. Paths may be surfaced to accept visitor impact without damage, while making no change away from the paths themselves. Indeed, simple – and limited – action may greatly increase the effective ecological capacity of the whole area and yet be so unobtrusive as to excite virtually no notice. In the Peak District heavily worn sections of the Pennine Way, where there has been serious erosion of the blanket peat, have been surfaced with a variety of materials to reduce wear to acceptable proportions. The most recent experiment uses a form of chestnut pale fencing top-dressed with bark, chippings and sawdust to produce a relatively cheap yet effective and unobtrusive surface (illustration 19).[37] The problem may be cost rather than capacity. In the earlier example of the Lyke Wake Walk, artificial surfacing was considered as an alternative to reduction in use, but the estimated costs (between £97,000 and £215,000 for the worst sections at 1981 prices) were 'prohibitively expensive'. It becomes a matter of management resources as well as management objectives.

19 Experimental path surfacing of chestnut palings top-dressed with bark, chippings and sawdust, on a wet, peat-based section of the Pennine Way in the Peak District National Park.

In some cases it is not simply paths that need modification, but the whole of an area. Sports grounds, golf courses and urban parks are all instances of seeding and planting to serve a specific use and maintain a high ecological capacity. Even turf cultivated for the purpose may be inadequate for some pressures, and selective replacement with artificial surfaces necessary. In a different context, Blackpool solved the problems of the fragility of a sand-dune coast by the generous use of concrete!

There remains a fourth objective, an essentially *laissez faire* approach. In this, there is no attempt at management, but a simple acceptance of degradation and degeneration through recreational use. By default, this is in practice too common as an implicit objective, through the lack of any explicit consideration of alternatives. Only when problems become acute is a management appraisal made, and by then many options may have already been foreclosed from an ecological point of view.

PERCEPTUAL CAPACITY

For much informal recreation, capacity is conditioned not by the physical dimensions of a site, or by its ability to withstand the physical impact of recreation use, but by the user's own perception. The use must be at a level that permits enjoyment without undue impairment of the recreational experience.

Such a view of capacity is fundamental for many activities, yet is inordinately difficult to assess. It varies between different activities on the same site. The family picnic group on the river bank has a very different perception from the lone fisherman in the same location. The same activity brings differing responses from differing people. To some, no walk is enjoyable unless undertaken with a group: to others of more solitary inclination, even one other person in sight may bring an unwelcome feeling of pressure. Nor are moods and attitudes constant: for any walker there is a time for company and a time for solitude. Even regional distinctions emerge: a beach that seems crowded in the North West of Scotland would be seen as virtually deserted in Cornwall in August.

Tangible measures of perceptual capacity are difficult to derive. Most approaches have been through simple observation, seeing the actual use that people make of the space available to them. These observations can measure the 'activity spaces' evidently needed for particular recreations, creating in essence a measure comparable to those for physical capacity for formal games. An early attempt was that in East Sussex, where a set of minimum standards was derived from the observed behaviour of country-side visitors at differing kinds of site, allowing for both an 'activity area' and space for parking and manoeuvring the attendant car. For car park, roadside verge or lay-by, little more than the car space itself was needed (18-25 m^2). For forest or downland car parks used for picnicking or other activities, but with limited space, some 58 m^2 would suffice, while for similar areas where space was not at such a premium, 93 m^2 was suggested.[38]

Such rule-of-thumb approaches give useful empirical measures, but afford little real understanding of individual needs and satisfactions. Existing techniques are poorly suited to enable perceptions of site crowding and the degree of satisfaction with the experience at a site to be articulated: more promising is the use of methods developed by social psychologists. Of particular importance in this context was the work of Burton at Cannock Chase.[39] Her wide-ranging study explored, among other issues, the level of use at which the visitor first perceives the site as crowded, using the techniques of adjective check-lists and semantic differentials.[40] Some of the results apply to the visitor population as a whole.

The importance of site character is evident. The most heavily wooded zone was far from being the least intensively used, but was persistently perceived as the least crowded, emphasising the value of tree screening in enhancing effective site capacity. There is also an ability to perceive the beauty of the site irrespective of the intrusion of people or cars.

More interesting, though far from conclusive, were the differing perceptions of distinctive groups. In the most crowded zone, Zone 1,

> there may be no limit at which the degree of crowding becomes unpleasant for most of those who chose to use the area, and the final limit may be the purely physical one of the number of cars that can be crammed into the space available. Many people visiting Zone 1 indeed may prefer crowds. . . . The analysis suggests that almost half of those who visit what is already the most crowded part of the Chase would not enjoy their visit any less if the intensity of use increased, and some would even enjoy it more. On the other hand, those who prefer to spend their time in the less crowded areas would appear to be far more sensitive to any increase in the level of recreational use. In brief, visitors sort themselves spatially on the basis of their sensitivity to crowding.[41]

Not only is there 'spatial sorting', but visitors to each kind of area have their own distinct characteristics. Burton suggests that these are closely related to socioeconomic parameters: 'the higher educational and social groups are strongly intolerant of crowding, but the lower educational

20 '. . . high levels of crowding do not detract from their enjoyment of the countryside and may add to it': Easter Monday on Dartmoor.

groups indicate that, on the whole, high levels of crowding do not detract from their enjoyment of the countryside and may add to it' (illustration 20).[42] More experimental work is needed fully to substantiate these findings, work in different recreational environments and among a wider range of people. It remains to be seen whether simple socioeconomic attributes or wider life-style characteristics are the better guide to an understanding of satisfactions in recreation and of the resultant assessment of levels of perceptual capacity.

ECONOMIC AND OPTIMUM CAPACITY

The fourth type of capacity needs no more than passing mention. Economic capacity is simply the level of use of a site or facility that is required to yield a given financial return. It is a fiscal concept, applicable only when a charge is made for the use of a facility. The required return may be measured on a strict profit basis, in the commercial sector, or it may relate to an arbitrary level of financial performance in the public and voluntary sectors. Unlike the other capacities discussed, economic capacity represents a minimum level of use to be achieved rather than a maximum level not to be exceeded.

In practice, these four approaches to capacity are not as distinct as the discussion might suggests. Except in some instances of physical and economic capacity, the concept cannot be simply translated into precise practice, but it remains of value not only for its inherent interest but as a basic management tool. Management affects capacity, through site utilisation and design, and through pricing policy: for many parameters empirical observation gives management guidelines, if only a partial understanding of the mechanisms involved. In Britain there has been a marked reluctance to offer more than fragmented and nebulous guidance from either research or established practice. There is a need for a more co-ordinated and authoritative approach, something akin to the erstwhile US Bureau of Outdoor Recreation's *Guidelines for understanding and determining optimum recreation carrying capacity*.[43] These guidelines are a happy blend of scepticism and realism, and make a shrewd assessment of capacity as a concept and a management tool. They recognise that

> The concept of recreation-carrying capacity is nearly as vague as the concepts of 'beauty' and 'quality of life'. Carrying capacity is a term which is frequently used but not understood. Because of its vagueness, carrying capacity has been widely open to gross generalization on the one hand and theoretical overkill on the other. There has been a tendency to search for

> 'the answers' (often meaning the *only* answers) and a tendency to lose sight of the need to view carrying capacity in an elementary, but comprehensive and systematic way.

Despite the difficulties,

> The blending of factors which determine physical [ecological] capacity of a recreation area with those which determine the social [perceptual] capacity makes it possible to determine optimum capacity guidelines. This blending of the 'physical' and the 'social' aspects of capacity is one of the most critical actions which can be taken to keep our parks and recreation areas from becoming overused and destroyed, and from becoming places where the participants' enjoyment diminishes to the point of frustration.[44]

Such a determination is needed as much as Britain as in the United States, and remains a fruitful area for the active blending of academic interest and practical management.

8 Precept and Practice

PATTERNS

> There can be no greater moral obligation in the environmental field than to ease out the living space and replace dereliction by beauty. Most people will never know true wilderness although its existence will not be a matter of indifference to them. The near landscape is valuable and lovable because of its nearness, not something to be disregarded and shrugged off; it is where children are reared and what they take away in their minds to their long future. What ground could be more hallowed?[1]

Fraser Darling's evocation in his Reith Lectures of the wider concerns of man and environment has equal weight in the narrower vistas of leisure. Of all the paradoxes of leisure patterns with which this book has been concerned, none has been more vivid or more recurring than the dual emphasis on near and far horizons. Leisure movement to distant places gives deep enjoyment and lasting stimulation, yet most of leisure is spent in familiar places, with the constraints as well as the challenges that implies.

That duality shows no signs of abatement, only intensification. Even in recession, travel continues to grow more commonplace. In 1981, for the fourth year running, more Britons than ever went abroad on holiday – 13,250,000 foreign holidays, no less than 27 per cent of all holidays taken, and absorbing spending of £4320 million.[2] Such holidays are not only the prerogative of the affluent, though in 1980 31 per cent of those who took holidays abroad were in social classes A and B, compared with only 15 per cent in these classes in the population as a whole. They have become a particular habit of the young, nurtured with both knowledge and expectation of opportunity. In 1980, 20 per cent of all adult holidaymakers abroad were aged between 16 and 24, compared with 13 per cent of holidaymakers in Britain and 17 per cent of the population as a whole.[3]

Even for the affluent and young, however, long-distance leisure travel still absorbs only a tiny minority of time: the horizons of home are of necessity more familiar. As earlier chapters stressed, 70 per cent of all leisure is spent at home, and for a growing proportion of the population that percentage is increasing. The growing numbers of long-term unemployed, and in the oldest age groups, have little ability for wide-ranging recreation. The evidence suggests that for these perception as well as experience is constrained. As Mercer comments, 'the slum child who has lived all his life in an inner-city environment and whose parents have never had access to a car is likely to find this an exciting environment.' He quotes, in support, Michelson's account of a group of Boston slum children taken on a holiday to Cape Cod on their first trip out of the city:

> They couldn't imagine, after having been there, why anyone would consider it worth visiting, let alone having as home. It was desolate. There was no 'action'. These boys preferred the person-centred life style that was part and parcel of the particular arrangement of their 'hot city streets'.[4]

Such images are a timely reminder that the geographer's descriptions of recreation patterns may, in the accuracy of their observation, miss the underlying perspective of perception and the satisfactions and the values thus involved. Indeed, academic precept is often dulled by the realities of practice, in leisure studies as in many other areas. In this concluding chapter several issues where precept is constrained by practice will be reiterated, for there is little relevance for any geography of leisure that is not rooted firmly in reality.

INFORMATION AND OPPORTUNITY

At an individual level, leisure satisfaction is constrained not only by opportunity but by knowledge of opportunity. Even at the institutional level, that knowledge is still very far from perfect. The regional recreation strategies revealed a lack of much basic information, even for clearly defined, publicly provided sports facilities. Only in 1982 could Lancashire claim to have produced 'a unique breakthrough' . . . 'the first comprehensive survey of tourist facilities of any county of Britain'.[5] While the great majority of local authorities maintain an effective local information service, any individual's knowledge of opportunity is obviously imperfect and incomplete. Knowledge effectively discriminates: the limited research in this field suggests that 'the recreational usage made of an area is in large part a function of the information the visitor possesses.'[6] The basic conclusion is equally true whether referring to a person's home area or to an area visited on a day trip or holiday. In a slightly different context, Hutson writes of her work in Swansea that

> Talking to the organisers of clubs I had the impression that the area was buzzing with activity, jumble sales, bazaars and that the whole area was involved in communal leisure activities. However, when doing house to house interviews, I gained another impression of apathy and lack of activity. . . . In the Lower Swansea Valley, 21 per cent of the sample households were unable to even mention any associations in their area . . . in . . . 37 per cent of households . . . no one in the family attended an association.[7]

From the reverse point of view, of provider rather than visitor, the manipulation of knowledge available to the visitor can be an important tool for management. The National Trust, with a variety of properties, has long been adept at its use.

On Trust land there are

> properties that seem to stir like anthills or that preserve an almost Saxon solitude. The Trust's aim must be to spread the load, alleviating the pressure where it grows intolerable and dispersing it to spaces that may still be called "open". There is little danger in this. Solitude will always remain for those who wish to find it.[8]

Information manipulation can assist programmes of management at site as well as area level. The manipulation may be overt or covert. The interpretive study for Tatton Park had as one objective 'assisting management to disperse visitors throughout the parkland' and suggested in consequence 'the use of interpretive pavilions at various locations in the park . . . to offer options to help in the dispersal of visitors'.[9] Other information deliberately restricts choice. Direction signs channel traffic where routes or surfaces can best withstand it. With greater subtlety, but often no less effect, scarcely perceived physical barriers constrain choice. In Hutton-le-Hole, in North Yorkshire, granite kerbs keep vehicles off the green without disfiguring signs (illustration 21). At Kynance Cove, in Cornwall, serpentine boulder edgings help contain visitors on the new paths, even though the constraint is largely psychological as most of the boulders are small.[10]

Information is only one part of the armoury of site management. The first essential is a conscious management plan with acknowledged objectives. To achieve these objectives, the detailed design of the infrastructure and the price mechanism can be used to underpin the effect of information systems at both site and regional scales. Tried management techniques obtain for a variety of facilities of both a formal

21 Detailed site management at Hutton-le-Hole in the North York Moors. Cars are gently dissuaded from parking on the green by unobtrusive granite kerbs, and from parking on the road by a yellow line, without the use of restriction signs in the village itself. A car park on the edge of the village provides a ready place to stop.

and an informal nature. For countryside areas at least there is much truth in Sidaway's assertion that 'well founded management plans, incorporating effective regulating mechanisms, will enable the countryside to accept substantial increases in recreational use without damage to its characteristics'. Indeed, in a nutshell, 'capacity is after all what we care to make it.'[11]

In a perfect world, information systems would give every consumer of recreation perfect knowledge of opportunity, and effective management at area and site levels would ensure sound – if not perfect – enjoyment. There would then be a convergence of theoretical and actual patterns of recreation. In practice – and for the interest if not precision of geographical study – such perfection is far from being realised. Objectives are blurred, resources fragmented. The problems do not lie simply in the vagaries of consumer knowledge and consumer choice, but in the almost equal vagaries of the systems of provision.

SYSTEMS OF PROVISION

The vagaries of the systems are a response not only to the variety of resources they control, or even to the variety of the providers themselves, with the differing philosophies of the public and private, commercial and voluntary sectors: rather, priorities and even philosophies still need to be articulated, and provision becomes haphazard in an at times alarming way (illustration 22).

22 'Let's enjoy it while we can – this is where they're going to build the new Leisure Centre.' (Hector Breeze, courtesy *Punch*).

Recent research on informal recreation in London's Green Belt underlines how haphazard management can be by any reasonable economic yardstick.[12] The study looked at management expenditure on 32 countryside open spaces in east Surrey and the adjacent London boroughs of Croydon, Bromley and Sutton. Together the sites cover some 2000 ha: with two partial exceptions, all are managed to provide a simple 'countryside experience', a place to roam in peace and quiet, with low-level management and the retention of natural characteristics. They are the responsibility of 12 different public, semi-public and charitable bodies.

While there are some differences in management emphases, these are totally insufficient to account for the wide variation in expenditure. The detailed variations for 12 of the sites are shown in table 8.1. Overall, for the 32 sites studied, the mean expenditure was £153.4 per ha in 1977-78. The range, however, was from £898 per ha at Oaks Park to only £5 per ha at Petridgewood Common. Oaks Park was one of the partial exceptions to the general character of the sites as open countryside. If, however, its 4.3 ha of ornamental gardens and their attendant costs are excluded, expenditure was still £640 per ha, and the overall range more than 120:1.

There is no obvious general, or site-specific, set of explanations for this range. The evidence shows no direct relationship to the scale, character, usage or ownership of individual sites. Even more surprising,

> during the enquiry it became all too apparent that questions were being asked of the managing bodies about their expenditure that they could neither answer in detail nor explain. . . . In most cases the figures . . . are

TABLE 8.1 Informal recreation sites in London's Green Belt: net expenditure and levels of summer use

Site	*Managing body*	*Area (ha)*	*Net expenditure (£/ha)*	*Average weekday use (persons/ha)*	*Average weekend use (persons/ha)*
Oaks Park	London Borough (LB) of Sutton	29.5	898	6	15
Keston Common	LB of Bromley	22.0	556	8	9
Farthing Down	City of London	49.0	360	1	10
Coulsdon Common	City of London	50.5	331	<1	2
High Elms	LB of Bromley	100.2	325	1	3
Tilburstow Hill	Surrey CC	9.3	236	3	7
Epsom & Walton Downs	Epsom & Walton Downs Conservators	181.0	232	1	4
Selsdon Wood	LB of Croydon	79.9	153	<1	2
Happy Valley	LB of Croydon	98.4	127	<1	3
Earlswood Common	Reigate & Banstead DC	52.9	85	6	11
Banstead Downs	Banstead Commons Conservators	87.8	44	<1	<1
Reigate & Colley Hill	Reigate & Banstead DC & National Trust	72.4	23	1	7
Mean (32 sites)		62.2	153.4		

Source: data from R.J.C. Munton, 'Management expenditure on informal recreation sites in the London Green Belt', *The Planner* 67.4 (1981), tables 2 and 4

> new to them. Thus not only do they have but a vague awareness of their true levels of expenditure but also because they do not know what other managers spend, or why they spend it, they have no cost yardsticks by which to judge their own outgoings.[13]

In this case, the degree of variation in expenditure may be extreme, but it points a far more general problem. Much provision, particularly in the public sector, arises from historic legacy rather than conscious contemporary policy. This point was emphasised at the very beginning of this book (figures 1.6 and 1.7) but needs constant reiteration if not only provision for recreation but also many of the patterns of recreation that provision engenders are to be properly understood. Neither diagnosis nor prescription is new. In 1973 the House of Lords Select Committee on Sport and Leisure declared: 'it is time to depart from the traditional practice whereby the facilities for different sports and outdoor activities are supplied without reference to each other. This had led to haphazard provision, with frequent deficiencies and regional inequalities'.[14]

The proposed remedy has an equally familiar ring:

> The provision of facilities adequate to meet demand could be undertaken locally or on a national basis, and the Committee believe that an element of both is needed. The principal requirement is for local facilities, locally provided, so that they reflect local conditions and meet the actual, not the imagined, demands of local people. The second requirement is for national strategic planning and central finance to co-ordinate the action of local authorities, to provide facilities with wider-than-local significance, and to help poorer rural communities to act as hosts to urban visitors.[15]

Since that date, there has been change, though it has been more of degree than kind. At national level, in 1982 the Countryside Commission followed the Arts Council and the Sports Council to greater independence as a public agency outside the civil service. Again in 1982, both the Countryside Commission and the Sports Council published strategic appraisals of their future role. The former looked for 'conservation through co-operation',[16] the latter to a concentration of resources on limited age groups (13-24 and 45-59) and a limited range of sports facilities.[17] More fundamental questions remained unanswered. Responsibility for recreation remains fragmented across government departments (figure 1.8): above all, there is no conscious overall appraisal of the financial resources needed for recreation at national level, or any conscious assessment of priorities in the allocation of those resources between agencies and between programmes.

In one context, more has been achieved at local level, with the necessary rethinking of organisational structures following the reorganisation of local government in 1974. The potential for more coherent thinking came with the emergence of integrated recreation departments,[18] but that process is not only far from complete, but has shown signs of reversal with the curtailment of local authority budgets. Recession tends to bring simple retrenchment, rather than a complete rethinking of programmes. Even a respected recreation planner can feel that recreation themes 'should *not* today be at the top of the planners' agenda – in terms of land, economics or social needs questions!'[19]

While recognising other, more basic, priorities in both the social and the economic environment, there can be no abdication of the need for conscious appraisal. Many eccentricities in facility provision are not so much endearing as exasperating, the unconscious acceptance of an illogical status quo. The London Green Belt site example can be readily replicated elsewhere. In the Yorkshire and Humberside region, for example, estimated net expenditure per head by local authorities on outdoor facilities for sport and recreation in 1978-79 varied from £2.29 to £6.20 in metropolitan districts and from £0.07 to £6.14 in shire districts. For indoor facilities the range was less extreme, but still varied from £2.00 to £3.64 and from £0.68 to £4.67 for metropolitan and shire districts respectively.[20] Some of these variations mirror both the character and the recreation resources of the districts concerned; others reflect conscious policy approaches by particular authorities. But not all variation admits such logical explanation: both the scale and the emphases in expenditure may bear little relation to either patterns of demand or the indications of political philosophies and democratic decisions.

SPATIAL CONCERNS

The vagaries of decision-making and of resource allocation do not negate the continuing importance of a clear spatial perspective. Differing types of resource offer different types of problem and different types of opportunity: continued recognition and understanding of these differences remains vital.

At one end of the spatial spectrum are the precious reserves of open country, of moor and mountains, heath and hills. For recreation, their worth lies in the sheer quality of scenery and the exhilaration of experience they afford. They pose particular problems of conservation, for much of their visual attraction stems from traditional agricultural practices which may yield a poor return in contemporary conditions. As a recent report on the economies of communities within national parks comments, in response,

> an intricate system of support has arisen to offset the natural handicaps that farmers face in these areas. Agricultural policies have largely been geared to securing the economic viability of farms through greater efficiency and productivity . . . in responding to agricultural policies and to change in the economic and technological environment, farmers have adopted practices . . . which have adversely affected the landscapes of the parks. Such changes have undermined an assumption that underlay much of the early thinking about national parks, that agriculture would provide continuing support for the landscapes that existed at the time of designation.[21]

Approaches to the problem have starkly varied, from a simple assumption that economic viability and the production of food must remain the prime goal, regardless of visual consequences, to a cogently argued case for 'regional conservation areas'. Green considers that even within the pressured countryside of England and Wales 'there is ample room for providing a substantially larger area for amenity use without seriously endangering food production, especially if current agricultural support for marginal land were to be redirected to the higher quality areas.' That 'substantially larger area' might, he envisages, include all rough grazing land, which would 'automatically come under the control of an amenity rather than an agricultural agency'.[22] The problem in this context is obviously far wider than that of recreation alone, though the conflicts between amenity use and conservation protection are far from irreconcilable. Indeed, in open country, recreation and conservation are concerned with the same basic resources: 'it is in their mutual interest that these resources are maintained, whether they be wildlife or landscape'.[23]

Aside from the maintenance of landscape quality, the prime problems remain those of access. But access for recreation has a double connotation. On the one hand, there is the need to ensure adequate access not only in the legal sense, or in the practical sense of maintaining an uninterrupted waymarked network of paths, but in removing the discrimination in access that the growing contraction of public transport in rural areas implies. The private car may serve most needs, but it does not serve all. Schemes like Dales Rail in the Yorkshire Pennines, the Mountain Goat buses in the Lake District, the Snowdon Sherpa buses in Snowdonia and Coastlink on Exmoor not only help to reduce the number of cars in their respective areas, but also provide an invaluable service for those without cars and for whom the residual patterns of public transport for local needs are often ill-attuned for recreational access.[24]

Paradoxically, there may also be a need to restrict access. While the crowded countryside may be at best a relative concept, 'solitude' and 'wilderness' are still rare and priceless assets. Remote areas of the uplands need to preserve that very remoteness and to be protected from burgeoning tracks and trails. Not without reason does the Dartmoor Preservation Association see the military range roads of northern Dartmoor, with their growing recreational use, as 'a poisoned dagger aimed at the heart of Dartmoor's northern wilderness'.[25] There must be areas that hard physical endeavour alone can realise: the right of access must not be confused with the encouragement of access. Such protection is no more than horizontal segregation. The summits of Snowdon and the Carneddau serve widely different, if complementary, needs.

Much of the countryside is neither wild nor distant, yet its problems are no less acute than those of more remote areas. The processes of agricultural change have been even more intense, and with greater justification. Much remains a landscape of good husbandry, even if a different landscape from that of a generation ago. Access at least has a legal charter, if not always unfettered range. Growing networks of recreational paths bring wide enjoyment at little cost to the public purse: the path network is still extensive enough for solitude, if not wilderness, to be readily attainable with comparatively little persistence.

The problems in this intermediate area are, indeed, more conceptual than spatial. Recreation pressure has been matched by a growing recreation segregation. Countryside 'attractions' may make a virtue of a rural setting, but offer very often an urbanised experience – an entertainment in, rather than an enjoyment of, the countryside. Country parks are welcome, and largely as free as their urban precursors, but many offer a tamed, sanitised experience, the freedom of open rather than rural space. For many activities, and for a majority of countryside users, that experience is more than adequate. Perhaps few town children ever did 'know what it is to go tadpoling, to fashion little houses out of the hedgerows, to run over springy chalk downs or to frolic in fields of buttercups',[26] but there can only be justifiable regret, and anger, at the widening gulf between many urban dwellers and the experience of real countryside.

Improved access is only a tiny part of the answer: earlier chapters have shown the growing isolation of the inner city from even the nearest countryside of the urban fringe. The conscious retention of odd scraps of uncultivated land, with 'hedgerows, spinneys, woods, rough lanes, marshes or streams',[27] may help conserve an increasingly scarce and precious resource and give continuing opportunity, but that opportunity is in danger of remaining the prerogative of the few. Far more important is a programme of effective education in the joy and the love of the countryside, an education not confined to the set-piece, in its largely artificial setting, of the urban farm, the demonstration farm or the interpretative centre, but embedded in the whole of the school curriculum, and needing the much wider thrust of a fuller education for leisure both in and far beyond the years of schooling.

The schoolroom is an apt reminder that most leisure is local, and that local for most is an urban setting. As chapter 4 emphasised, urban leisure behaviour and urban leisure provision remains poorly documented, a comment that gains even greater force when applied to the micro-geography of home and garden where so much of leisure is spent. The divorce between precept and practice is little marked, for precept is scarce, and practice riddled with preconceptions or lingering traditions. There is a growing literature on many types of facility, the sports centre and the swimming pool not least, but insufficient literature that looks at geographical and social inequalities in participation, and identifies those inequalities that result from inadequacies in the supply of facilities and those that relate rather to people's own images and aspirations. Recreation deprivation is an obvious yet elusive concept. It is perhaps the greatest paradox of all in recreation studies that many of those who suffer the greatest degree of deprivation in recreation are those with the greatest amount of leisure time and who live nearest the greatest range of leisure facilities and opportunities.

The resolution of that paradox is a matter of both precept and practice. Insights into its understanding must be high on any academic agenda; the translation of understanding into opportunity must be the concern of any practitioner, whatever his innate political philosophy. In wider fields of leisure, too, as this book has tried to show, an understanding of patterns is of no mere academic interest: the lessons of precept for practice are vital if all the resources of the economic, social and physical environment are to be effectively harnessed for the fulness of human satisfaction. For leisure at least, 'the good life for a larger proportion of any country is not an illusion but an ideal capable of being achieved. Indeed, we should never lose sight of it or be in any way content with the half-lives so many are compelled to lead.'[28]

Notes

The book includes no detailed bibliography, for two reasons. First, the notes to each chapter deliberately contain a good deal of bibliographical material and are designed to be used for this purpose: a formal bibliography would be largely repetitive. Second, good bibliographies have already been published, the most recent being J. Knight and S. Parker, *A bibliography of British publications on leisure, 1960-77* (Leisure Studies Association, 1978); from 1977 to 1982, *Progress in Human Geography* (Edward Arnold) contained annual reviews of progress in recreation and leisure studies by the author and M. F. Collins which effectively update the Knight and Parker volume.

INTRODUCTION

1 J. T. Coppock, 'The recreational use of land and water in rural Britain', *Tidjschrift voor Economische en Sociale Geografie*, 57 (1966), pp. 81-96; J. A. Patmore, *Land and leisure in England and Wales* (David & Charles, 1970), revised edition produced as *Land and leisure* (Penguin, 1972); I. Cosgrove and R. J. Jackson, *The geography of recreation and leisure* (Hutchinson, 1972); I. H. Seeley, *Outdoor recreation and the urban environment* (Macmillan, 1973); P. Lavery (ed.), *Recreational geography* (David & Charles, 1974); J. T. Coppock and B. S. Duffield, *Recreation in the countryside: a spatial analysis* (Macmillan, 1975); and I. G. Simmons, *Rural recreation in the industrial world* (Edward Arnold, 1975).

2 See, for example, M. Chubb and H. R. Chubb, *One third of our time? An introduction to recreation behaviour and resources* (John Wiley, 1981). This is avowedly interdisciplinary in approach, but is an apt illustration of the general point that theoretical understanding in the whole field of leisure is still at a very elementary stage.

3 The problems of extending data and ideas across international boundaries, even in Western Europe, are illustrated in H. B. Rodgers, *Sport in its social context: international comparisons* (Council of Europe, 1977).

4 Coppock and Duffield, *Recreation in the countryside*.

CHAPTER 1: LEISURE AND SOCIETY

1 *First report from the Select Committee of the House of Lords on Sport and Leisure* (HMSO, 1973).

2 Department of the Environment, *Sport and recreation* (HMSO, Cmnd 6200, 1975), para. 5.

3 *Ibid.*, para. 67.

4 C. Jenkins and B. Sherman, *The collapse of work* (Eyre Methuen, 1980).

5 Central Statistical Office, *Social Trends 12* (HMSO, 1982), tables 4.7 and 4.9.

6 For a fuller, recent account see K. Roberts, *Contemporary society and the growth of leisure* (Longman, 1978).

7 N. & J. Parry, 'Theories of culture and leisure', in M. A. Smith (ed.), *Leisure and urban society* (Leisure Studies Association, 1977), p. 81.

8 S. R. Parker, *The sociology of leisure* (George Allen & Unwin, Studies in sociology, 9, 1976), chapter 1.

9 Countryside Recreation Research Advisory Group, *Countryside Recreation Glossary* (Countryside Commission, 1970), p. 5.

10 *Ibid.*, p. 7.

11 *Ibid.*

12 See, for example, Parker, *Sociology of leisure*, p. 22 and S. DeGrazia, *Of time, work and leisure* (Twentieth Century Fund, 1962), pp. 13-14.

13 Used as a text by the Catholic, Josef Pieper in *Leisure: the basis of culture* (Pantheon Books, 1962).

14 J. A. R. Pimlott, *Recreations* (Studio Vista, 1968), p. 13. The following section owes much to this source.

15 *Ibid.*, p. 15.

16 B. Jewel, *Sports and games* (Midas Books, 1977), p. 22.

17 *Ibid.*, p. 70.

18 Pimlott, *Recreations*, Plate 23.

19 Parker, *Sociology of leisure*, p. 21.

20 Pimlott, *Recreations*, p. 39.

21 For fuller account see E. Dunning, *Soccer: the social origins of the sport and its development as a spectacle and profession* (Sports Council and Social Science Research Council, 1979); and J. Bale, *The development of soccer as a participant and spectator sport* (Sports Council and Social Science Research Council, 1979).

22 Quoted in C. Hill, *Society and Puritanism in Pre-Revolutionary England*, (Secker & Warburg, 1964), p. 125.

23 See J. Walvin, *The people's game: a social history of British football* (Allen Lane, 1975), and J. R. Bale, 'The geographical diffusion and the adoption of professionalism in football in England and Wales', *Geography*, 63 (1978), pp. 188-97.

24 These and subsequent figures on employment come from Central Statistical Office, *Social Trends* (HMSO, especially 10 (1980), p. 32 and 12 (1982), table 4.11).

25 *Ibid.*, 10 (1980), p. 32.
26 *Ibid.*, 12 (1982), table 6.15. In 1970, 65 per cent of households had washing machines and 30 per cent central heating.
27 This refers to all over school-leaving age: *Ibid.*, 12 (1982), tables 4.4 and p. 63.
28 J. A. R. Pimlott, *The Englishman's holiday* (Faber and Faber, 1947), p. 211. This invaluable book remains the standard account.
29 Chairmen's Policy Group, *Leisure policy for the future* (Sports Council, 1981), table 3.7.
30 *Social Trends, 12* (1982), table 3.16.
31 H. Smith, *The job crisis: increasing unemployment in the developed world* (Economist Intelligence Unit, Report no. 85, 1981).
32 *Employment Gazette* (Department of Employment, December 1981). In Northern Ireland, the level was 19.0 per cent.
33 *Social Trends, 12* (1982), p. 72.
34 C. Vereker, 'Leisure', in H. Thomas (ed.), *The quality of life* (British Association for the Advancement of Science, 1979), p. 17.
35 See J. Long and E. Wimbush, *Leisure and the over 50s* (Sports Council and Social Science Research Council, 1979); and *Perspectives on leisure around retirement: an interim report* (Tourism and Recreation Research Unit, University of Edinburgh, 1981).
36 *Social Trends, 12* (1982), table 1.2.
37 *Planning for social change* (Henley Centre for Forecasting, 1981).
38 M. Talbot, *Women and leisure* (Sports Council and Social Science Research Council, 1979).
39 J. I. Gershuny and R. E. Pahl, 'Britain in the decade of the three economies', *New Society* (3 January 1980), pp. 7-9.
40 *Social Trends, 12* (1982), table 5.1.
41 Chairmen's Policy Group, *Leisure policy for the future*, table 4.9. See also R. W. Vickerman, *Personal and family leisure expenditure* (Sports Council and Social Science Research Council, 1979).
42 See W. H. Martin and S. Mason, *Broad patterns of leisure expenditure* (Sports Council and Social Science Research Council, 1979); A. S. Travis, *The state and leisure provision* (Sports Council and Social Science Research Council, 1979); A. J. Veal and A. S. Travis, 'Local authority leisure services – the state of play', *Local Government Studies*, 5.4 (1979), pp. 5-16; and R. Rapoport and M. Dower, 'Local authority leisure provision – relating to people's needs', *Local Government Studies*, 5.4 (1979), pp. 17-30.
43 G. F. Chadwick, *The park and the town* (Architectural Press, 1966).
44 *Ibid.*, p. 36.
45 *Ibid.*, p. 44.
46 Minister of Land and Natural Resources and the Secretary of State for Wales, *Leisure in the countryside: England and Wales* (HMSO, Cmnd 2928, 1966), para. 5.
47 *Ibid.*, para. 18.
48 Veal and Travis, 'Local authority leisure services', table 2.

49 R. Fedden, *The continuing purpose: a history of the National Trust, its aims and work* (Longmans, 1968), pp. 3-6.
50 H. C. Darby, 'British National Parks', *The Advancement of Science*, 20 (1963), p. 307.
51 *Report of the National Park Committee* (HMSO, Cmnd 3851, 1931), para. 84.
52 National Parks Commission, *Third report* (HMSO, 1952).
53 *Use of reservoirs and gathering grounds for recreation,* Ministry of Land and Natural Resources circular 3/66, Department of Education and Science circular 19/66.
54 Department of the Environment, *Sport and recreation,* para. 16.
55 J. Roberts, *The commercial sector in leisure* (Sports Council and Social Science Research Council, 1979). The literature on the commercial sector is remarkably sparse. One recent leisure bibliography has only 9.3 per cent of its entries overtly connected with it: J. Knight and S. Parker, *A bibliography of British publications on leisure, 1960-1977* (Leisure Studies Association, 1978).
56 Centre for Contemporary Cultural Studies, *Fads and fashions* (Sports Council and Social Science Research Council, 1980), pp. 13-20.
57 *Social Trends, 11* (1981), table 11.4.
58 Centre for Contemporary Cultural Studies, *Fads and fashions,* pp. 39-44.
59 A. Tomlinson, *Leisure and the role of clubs and voluntary groups* (Sports Council and Social Science Research Council, 1979).
60 *Ibid.*, p. 1.
61 S. Hutson, *A review of the role of clubs and voluntary associations based on a study of two areas in Swansea* (Sports Council and Social Science Research Council, 1979).
62 Royal Horticultural Society, 1804; Royal Society for the Prevention of Cruelty to Animals, 1824; Grand National Archery Society, 1841; and National Chrysanthemum Society, 1846.

CHAPTER 2: LEISURE PATTERNS AND PLACES

1 M. Dower, *The challenge of leisure* (Civic Trust, 1965), p. 5.
2 R. H. Best, *Land use and living space* (Methuen, 1981), especially chapters 3 and 4 and tables 8 and 12.
3 T. L. Burton and G. P. Wibberley, *Outdoor recreation in the British countryside* (Wye College, 1965), table 1. This pioneer study included the following categories of land in its definition: Statutory Access Areas in national parks; nature reserves; National Trust properties; common land and woodland. Since 1965 there have been increases in some of these categories (especially National Trust properties) and other categories, such as country parks, should now properly be added. The overall order of land available, however, remains a valid indication, and the range in the calculation highlights the effective problem of definition. The proportion compares with the 12.5 per cent of England and Wales classed as rough grazing in 1971, and the 7.4 per cent as woodland (Best, *Land use,* table 8).

4 D. C. Nicholls, unpublished estimate, 1966, prepared for the abortive National Land Data Handbook.

5 J. A. Giles, *History of the parish and town of Bampton* (1847); quoted in R. W. Malcolmson, *Popular recreations in English society, 1700-1850* (Cambridge University Press, 1973), p. 21.

6 H. Fielding, *An enquiry into the causes of the late increase of robbers* (1751), p. 7; quoted in Malcolmson, *Popular recreations*, p. 157.

7 J. A. R. Pimlott, *The Englishman's holiday* (Faber and Faber, 1947), p. 68.

8 B. S. Duffield and S. E. Walker, 'People and the coast – current demands and future aspirations for coastal recreation', in Countryside Recreation Research Advisory Group, *Recreation and the coast* (Countryside Commission, CCP127, 1979), p. 62.

9 R. H. G. Thomas, *The Liverpool & Manchester Railway* (Batsford, 1980), p. 195.

10 M. Robbins, *The railway age* (Routledge & Kegan Paul, 1962), p. 57.

11 H. Cholmondeley-Pennell, 'How we got to the Brighton Review', in K. Hopkins, *The poetry of railways* (Leslie Frewin, 1966), pp. 212-14.

12 E. W. Gilbert, *Brighton, old ocean's bauble* (Methuen, 1954), p. 152.

13 C. H. Grinling, *The history of the Great Northern Railway* (Methuen, 1903), p. 103.

14 R. Christiansen and R. W. Miller, *The North Staffordshire Railway* (David & Charles, 1971), p. 192.

15 Quoted in S. Margetson, *Leisure and pleasure in the nineteenth century* (Cassell, 1969), p. 82.

16 'Manifold', *The Leek & Manifold Valley Light Railway* (J. H. Henstock, 1955).

17 T. B. Maund, *Local transport in Birkenhead and district* (Omnibus Society, 1959), p. 5.

18 H. Cunningham, *Leisure in the industrial revolution* (Croom Helm, 1980), p. 135.

19 A. Howkins and J. Lowerson, *Trends in leisure, 1919-1939* (Sports Council and Social Science Research Council, 1979), p. 21.

20 Central Statistical Office, *Social Trends 12* (HMSO, 1982), table 9.7.

21 *British Home Tourism Survey, 1980* (British Tourist Authority, 1981), p. 6.

22 G. Young, *Tourism, blessing or blight?* (Penguin, 1973), p. 28.

23 *Tourism Intelligence Quarterly* (British Tourist Authority, 4, 1981), p. 9.

24 British Waterways Board, *Annual Report and Accounts* (HMSO, 1967; 1980).

25 J. H. Appleton, *Disused railways in the countryside of England and Wales* (HMSO, 1970); J. Grimshaw and associates, *Study of disused railways in England and Wales: potential cycle routes* (HMSO, 1982).

26 See map by M. L. Bazeley in H. C. Darby (ed.), *An historical geography of England before 1800* (Cambridge University Press, 1951), p. 177.

27 Quoted in Malcolmson, *Popular recreations* p. 108.

28 *Ibid.*

29 The pythogenic theory, or the theory of miasma, evolved in the late eighteenth century, held that all disease was due to bad air; hence the belief that access to fresh air could reduce the incidence of disease. See

S. E. Walker and B. S. Duffield, *Urban parks and open spaces: a review* (Tourism and Recreation Research Unit, University of Edinburgh, 1982) for a full account of park development.

30 Quoted in Cunningham, *Leisure in the industrial revolution*, p. 96.

31 J. C. Scott, 'The providers of Birmingham's parks', *Parks and Sports Grounds* 40.10 (1975), pp. 18-30.

32 *Survey of existing facilities for sport and physical recreation: preliminary report* (Lancashire County Council, 1967).

33 A. Demangeon, *The British Isles* (Heinemann, 2nd ed, 1949), pp. 380-81.

34 The classic works are E. W. Gilbert, 'The growth of inland and seaside health resorts in England', *Scottish Geographical Magazine* 55 (1939), pp. 16-35, and Pimlott, *Englishman's holiday*. See also J. A. Patmore, 'The spa towns of Britain', in R. P. Beckinsale and J. M. Houston (eds), *Urbanization and its problems* (Basil Blackwell, 1968), pp. 47-69; and J. Walvin, *Beside the seaside: a social history of the popular seaside holiday* (Allen Lane, 1978).

35 T. Short, *History of mineral waters* (2 vols, 1734-40).

36 Quoted in Pimlott, *Englishman's holiday*, p. 43.

37 Quoted in W. Addison, *English spas* (Batsford, 1951), p. 103.

38 *The Times*, 30 August 1860.

39 A. Smith and J. Southam, *The good beach guide* (Penguin, 1973), p. 63.

40 Duffield and Walker, '*People and the coast*', pp. 68-70.

41 *Resorts and spas in Britain* (British Tourist Authority, 1975), p. 8.

42 C. T. Goode, *The railways of East Yorkshire* (Oakwood Press, 1981), p. 73.

43 The initial rail link was opened in 1848 to Poulton (as Morecambe was then known), by the North Western Railway, later absorbed by the Midland: G. O. Holt, *A regional history of the railways of Great Britain. Volume 10, the North West* (David & Charles, 1978), pp. 233-4.

44 D. St J. Thomas, *A regional history of the railways of Great Britain. Volume 1, The West Country* (Phoenix, 1960), p. 161.

45 K. Hoole, *North Eastern Railway buses, lorries and autocars* (Nidd Valley Narrow Gauge Railways Ltd, 1969), pp. 15-16.

46 G. E. Cherry, *National parks and recreation in the countryside: Environmental planning, 1939-1969, Vol. II* (HMSO, 1975), p. 17.

47 *The reshaping of British Railways* (British Railways Board, 1963).

48 Middleton Railway, 1960, a former industrial railway; Bluebell Railway, 1960; Keighley & Worth Valley Railway, 1968; and Dart Valley Railway, 1969.

49 *Sport in the community: the next ten years* (Sports Council, 1982), p. 20.

CHAPTER 3: THE USE OF LEISURE

1 K. Roberts, *Contemporary society and the growth of leisure* (Longman, 1978), p. 26.
2 Countryside Recreation Research Advisory Group, *Countryside recreation glossary* (Countryside Commission, 1970), p. 23.
3 *Outdoor recreation for America* (Outdoor Recreation Resources Review Commission, 1962). This report was based on the results of 27 studies, including the National Recreation Survey, a nationwide survey of outdoor recreation habits and preferences of Americans aged 12 and over. Four separate samples, each involving some 4000 interviews, were carried out.
4 Full references are as follows: *Outdoor leisure activities in the Northern Region* (North Regional Planning Committee, 1969); H. B. Rodgers and J. A. Patmore (eds), *Leisure in the North West* (North West Sports Council, 1972); J. G. Settle, *Leisure in the North West: a tool for forecasting* (Sports Council Study no. 11, Sports Council and North West Council for Sport and Recreation, 1977); *Greater London Recreation Study:* Part 1, *Demand Study;* Part 2, *Participant profiles;* Part 3, *Supply study* (Research Report 19, Greater London Council, 1975-76); *SIRSEE: study of informal recreation in South East England; The Demand Report; Appendices to the Demand Report* (2 vols); *Summary report for the site studies; County site studies* (4 vols) (Countryside Commission Working Papers, 1977). Techniques and initial results of the Greater London survey had been published in Greater London Council, *Research Memoranda*, 383, 407, 411 and 435 in 1972-74.
5 A. J. Veal, *Sport and recreation in England and Wales: an analysis of adult participation patterns in 1977* (Research Memorandum 74, Leisure and Tourism Unit, Centre for Urban and Regional Studies, University of Birmingham), Appendix 1.
6 Interviewing continues throughout the year and the results are made available in four quarterly sets as well as an annual total. This is particularly important in generating effective data about seasonal activities.
7 *People in sport* (The Sports Council, 1979) and *Leisure and the countryside* (Countryside Commission, CCP 124, 1979).
8 *The people's activities* British Broadcasting Corporation, 1965); *The people's activities and use of time* (British Broadcasting Corporation, 1978). In 1961, 2363 usable diaries were obtained, in 1974-75, 2635.
9 For a full commentary on these surveys and an accurate comparison between them, see J. I. Gershuny and G. S. Thomas, *Changing patterns of time use: UK activity patterns 1961 and 1975. Data preparation and some preliminary results* (Science Policy Research Unit, University of Sussex, 1980).
10 *Ibid.*, p. 58.
11 M. Young and P. Willmott, *The symmetrical family* (Routledge & Kegan Paul, 1973; Penguin Books, 1975).
12 R. Rapoport, R. N. Rapoport and Z. Strelitz, *Leisure and the family life cycle* (Routledge & Kegan Paul, 1975).

13 *National Angling Survey, 1970* (Natural Environment Research Council, undated).

14 S. Glyptis, *National Angling Survey, 1980* (Water Research Centre, 1980).

15 Veal, *Sport and recreation*, pp. 79-80.

16 See, for example, Rodgers and Patmore, *Leisure in the North West*, Appendix E, and B. S. Duffield and J. A. Long, *Large-scale recreation participation surveys: lessons for the future* (Working Paper 16, Countryside Commission, 1979).

17 This discussion is based wholly on Gershuny and Thomas, *Changing patterns of time use*.

18 Rodgers and Patmore, *Leisure in the North West*, p. 26.

19 *Anual Report, 1980-81* (The Sports Council, 1982), p. 25. In addition to 64 sports, the Council grant-aided a further 18 sports-related bodies, such as the Ramblers Association.

20 J. E. Thornes, 'The effect of weather on sport', *Weather*, 32 (1977), pp. 258-69.

21 J. E. Thornes, 'Rain starts play', *Area*, 8 (1976), pp. 236-45.

22 Sports Council, *Planning for sport* (Central Council of Physical Recreation, 1968), p. 25.

23 Of activities with a smaller sample not included on the diagram, horse-riding shows far greater female participation – 0.8 per cent as against 0.4 per cent for men.

24 M. Talbot, *Women and leisure* (Sports Council, Social Science Research Council, 1979).

25 H. B. Rodgers, *Sport in its social context: international comparisons* (Council of Europe, 1977), p. 16.

26 Unpublished data from the General Household Survey. The figures relate to the third quarter of the year, and to participation in the four weeks prior to survey. The changes in definition previously discussed mean that comparisons between 1973 and 1977 in particular must be viewed with some caution, though less in a relative than in an absolute sense. The absolute participation rates in sport (third quarter) are as follows:

	1973		*1977*		*1980*	
	Indoor	*Outdoor*	*Indoor*	*Outdoor*	*Indoor*	*Outdoor*
	%	%	%	%	%	%
Male	12.5	31.8	31.0	47.0	30.5	44.6
Female	5.5	17.4	13.0	31.0	16.1	32.0

27 K. K. Sillitoe, *Planning for leisure* (HMSO, 1969), table 10.

28 Young and Willmott, *The symmetrical family*, table 36. The data relate to married men and women aged 30-49.

29 J. Boothby, M. Tungatt, A. R. Townsend and M. F. Collins, *A sporting chance? Family, school and environmental influences on taking part in sport* (Sports Council, Study 22, 1981).

30 M. Hillman and A. Whalley, *Fair play for all: a study of access to sport and informal recreation* (PEP, Broadsheet no. 571, 1977), p. 26.

31 M. F. Tungatt, 'Leisure patterns of non-car owners in Hull' (unpublished MA thesis, University of Hull, 1979), p. 53.

32 *British Home Tourism Survey, 1980* (British Tourist Authority, 1981). In this survey, tourist trips include all stays of one or more nights away from home: business and conference visits account for 15 per cent of such trips in both Britain and abroad.

33 Boothby, Tungatt, Townsend and Collins, *A sporting chance?* pp. 20-3 and Appendix 2.

34 H. B. Rodgers, *Pilot National Recreation Survey Report No. 2* (British Travel Association, University of Keele, 1969), p. 38.

35 H. B. Rodgers, 'The leisure future: problems of prediction', in J. G. Settle, *Leisure in the North West: a tool for forecasting* (Sports Council, Study no. 11, 1977), p. 7.

36 *Ibid.*, p. 7.

37 Roberts, *Contemporary society and the growth of leisure*, p. 37.

38 M. Baxter, B. S. Duffield and J. Blackie, *A research study into recreation activity substitution in Scotland* (Tourism and Recreation Research Unit Research Report no. 32, University of Edinburgh, 1977). This study is particularly valuable for its critical approach to its own conventional, activity-based, methodology. It concludes that there is a need 'to look at leisure systems as a whole and not, as hitherto, at only limited parts . . . Only when progress has been made in understanding motivations and satisfactions of recreationists . . . will it be possible to establish whether . . . pursuits . . . can be substituted with similar, or at least, acceptable levels of satisfaction' (p. 113).

39 S. A. Glyptis, 'Leisure life-styles', *Regional Studies*, 15 (1981), pp. 311-26.

CHAPTER 4: RECREATION AND THE CITY

1 Quoted in Asa Briggs, *Victorian cities* (Penguin, 1968), p. 10.

2 Office of Population Censuses and Surveys, *Census 1981: preliminary report for towns* (HMSO, 1981), para. 23. For this Census report, the Registrar General counts as 'towns' those areas included in the boroughs and urban districts prior to local government reorganisation in 1974 together with new towns and some urban overspill into pre-1974 rural districts. Such a definition has acknowledged limitations, but serves for an easy comparison of trends.

3 *Ibid.*, para. 43.

4 J. T. Coppock, 'Geographical contributions to the study of leisure', *Leisure Studies*, 1.1 (1982), pp. 1-27.

5 Two recent reviews have been of particular help in this section: S. A. Glyptis and D. A. Chambers, 'No place like home', *Leisure Studies* 1. 3 (1982), pp. 247-62; and A. S. Travis and G. E. Cherry (eds), *'Leisure and the home'*

(unpublished report to the Sports Council and Social Science Research Council Panel on Leisure and Recreation Research, 1981).

6 S. A. Glyptis, 'Leisure life-styles', *Regional Studies,* 15.5 (1981), pp. 311-26.

7 Chairmen's Policy Group, *Leisure policy for the future* (Sports Council, 1981), table 4.9.

8 Central Statistical Office, *Social Trends 10* (HMSO, 1980), p. 29.

9 *Ibid.*, pp. 28-9.

10 Central Statistical Office, *Social Trends 12* (HMSO, 1982), table 8.13.

11 Ministry of Housing and Local Government, *Homes for today and tomorrow* (HMSO, 1961).

12 I. P. B. Halkett, 'The recreational use of private gardens', *Journal of Leisure Research,* 10.1 (1978), pp. 13-20.

13 R. H. Best, *Land use and living space* (Methuen, 1981), pp. 105-8.

14 J. A. Cook, 'Gardens on housing estates', *Town Planning Review,* 39 (1968-9), pp. 217-34.

15 H. Thorpe, 'A new deal for allotments: solutions to a pressing land use problem,' *Area,* 3 (1970), p. 1. See also *Report of the Departmental Committee of Inquiry into Allotments* (HMSO, Cmnd 4166, 1969).

16 Travis and Cherry, 'Leisure and the home', pp. 203-5. The estimate of 600 garden centres is made by the International Garden Centre Association: a centre is defined as having an outdoor sales area for plants of at least 500 m^2, a covered area, and a shop of at least 100 m^2.

17 I. Opie and P. Opie, *Children's games in street and playground* (Oxford University Press, 1969), p. 10.

18 Department of the Environment, Design Bulletin 27, *Children at play* (HMSO, 1973), p. 15.

19 *Ibid.*, figures 20 and 23.

20 *Ibid.*, p. 48.

21 K. R. Balmer, *Open space in Liverpool* (Liverpool Corporation, 1973).

22 Department of the Environment, *Recreation and deprivation in inner urban areas* (HMSO, 1977).

23 M. Hillman and A. Whalley, *Fair play for all: a study of access to sport and informal recreation* (PEP, Broadsheet no. 571, 1977).

24 See, for example, G.C.B. Mitchell and S. W. Town, *Access to recreational activity* (Transport and Road Research Laboratory, Supplementary Report 468, 1979), tables 5 and 6.

25 A. J. Veal, *New swimming pool for old* (Sports Council Study 18, 1979).

26 See, for example, J. Boothby and M. Tungatt, *Urban recreational facilities and organisations: compilation of an inventory of Cleveland County* (North East Area Study, University of Durham, Working Paper 38, 1976).

27 *Provision of facilities for sport* (Ministry of Housing and Local Government, Circular 49/64, and Department of Education and Science, Circular 11/64, 1964).

28 For a list of these 'Initial appraisals' and a discussion of the data see J. A. Patmore, *Land and leisure in England & Wales* (David & Charles, 1970), pp. 78-82.

29 At the time of writing, not all strategies had been published. A full list of all regional strategies and their constituent reports is included as Appendix 2 to the Sports Council's national strategy proposals, *Sport in the community: the next ten years* (Sports Council, 1982). It is the Council's ultimate intention to complete a national inventory, on a common data base, of major sports facilities.

30 For an indication of this variety, even at relatively modest levels, see A. J. Veal, *Six examples of low cost sports facilities* (Sports Council Study 20, 1979).

31 R. Rees, 'The organisation of sport in nineteenth century Liverpool', in R. Renson, *The history, evolution and diffusion of sport and games in different cultures* (Fourth HISPA Conference, Catholic University of Leuven, 1976).

32 *Sport in the community: the next ten years*, figure 15 and table 16.

33 *Ibid.*, and *Provision for swimming* (Sports Council, 1978), table 1.

34 The most recent comprehensive study dates from a survey of 46 pools in 1967-68, and the report in M. F. Collins, *Indoor swimming pools in Britain* (Sports Council Research Working Paper 1, 1977). This paragraph is derived from this source and from M. F. Collins, 'Large or local – some geographical issues in the planning and management of indoor sports centres and swimming pools in Britain', *Wiener Geographische Schriften*, 53-4 (1979), pp. 73-86.

35 Public Attitude Surveys Ltd, *Leisure pools: a study of pools at Bletchley, Whitley Bay and Rotherham* (Sports Council Study 19, 1979). The survey data relate to 1975: all three pools were opened in early 1974.

36 Veal, *New swimming pool for old.*

37 *Sport in the community: the next ten years*, p. 25. In this context, 'centres' excludes small sports halls and those not open to general public use.

38 Summarised in A. J. Veal, *Sports centres in Britain: a review of user studies* (Sports Council, forthcoming). Among the more important studies are the following: Sports Council Studies: 1, J. G. Birch, *Indoor sports centres* (HMSO, 1971); 13, Built Environment Research Group, *The changing indoor sports centre* (Sports Council, 1977); 14, Built Environment Research Group, *Sport in a jointly provided centre* (Sports Council, 1978); 15, Built Environment Research Group, *Sport for all in the inner city* (Sports Council, 1978); 20, A. J. Veal, *Six examples of low cost sports facilities* (Sports Council, 1979); *Sports centre users – a comparative study* (Sports Council for Wales, 1978); *The impact of a new sports centre on sports participation and sporting facilities: a case study of the Atherton area, 1976-81* (North West Council for Sport and Recreation, 1982); J. Atkinson and M. F. Collins, *The impact of neighbouring sports and leisure centres* (Sports Council Research Working Paper 17, 1980).

39 *Sports halls: a new approach to their dimensions and use* (Sports Council, 1975), pp. 15-17.

40 B. Whaley, 'Sports centre planning and provision in England and Wales (unpublished PhD thesis, University of Birmingham, 1980).

41 *Sport in the community: the next ten years*, p. 25.

42 *Ibid.*, p. 37.

43 S. E. Walker and B. S. Duffield, *Urban parks and open spaces: a review* (Tourism and Recreation Research Unit, University of Edinburgh, 1982). In England and Wales, there are major user studies for London, Liverpool and Leicester. See Greater London Council Planning Department, *Surveys of the use of open spaces*, vol. 1 (GLC Research Paper no. 2, Greater London Council, 1968) and Greater London Council, Department of Planning and Transportation, *Surveys of the use of open spaces*, vol. 2 (GLC Research Memorandum No. 381, Greater London Council, 1972); Balmer, *Open space in Liverpool;* and I. R. Bowler and A. J. Strachan, *Parks and gardens in Leicester* (Recreational and Cultural Services Department, Leicester City Council, 1976). For a useful comparative study see also Tourism and Recreation Research Unit, *A study of four parks in and around Glasgow: report of surveys carried out in 1977 and 1978* (TRRU Research Report no. 44, University of Edinburgh, 1980).

44 Walker and Duffield, *Urban parks and open spaces*, p. 39.

45 A. J. Strachan and I. R. Bowler, 'The development of public parks and gardens in the City of Leicester', *East Midland Geographer*, 6 (1976), pp. 275-83.

46 J. A. Patmore, 'Recreation', in J. A. Dawson and J. C. Doornkamp (eds), *Evaluating the human environment* (Edward Arnold, 1973). pp. 234-5.

47 This, and other detailed statistics in this paragraph, from B.S. Duffield, J. P. Best and M. F. Collins (eds), *Digest of sports statistics* (Sports Council, 1983).

48 *Golf in the Northern Region* (Northern Council for Sport and Recreation, 1978), p. 79.

49 *Ibid.*, p. 31.

50 Duffield, Best and Collins, *Digest of sports statistics*. There are no current figures for the number of *courses* in England, and it is not therefore possible to construct an accurate map on a county basis.

51 *Outdoor playing space requirements: review of NPFA playing space target, 1971* (National Playing Fields Association, 1971), p. 3.

52 *Ibid.*, p. 7.

53 *Sport in the community: the next ten years*, p. 27.

54 *Towards a wider use: a report of an inter-association working party on joint provision and dual or multiple use of facilities for recreational use by the community* (Association of County Councils, Association of District Councils, Association of Metropolitan Authorities, 1976), p. 5.

55 See, for example, P. Prescott-Clarke, *Joint provision, the school leaver and the community* (Social and Community Planning Research, 1977); Coopers and Lybrand Associates, *Sharing does work: the economic and social costs and benefits of joint and direct sports provision* (Sports Council Study 22, 1980); M. F. Collins (ed.), *Integrated facilities* (Sports Council, for Council of Europe Committee for the Development of Sport, 1980).

56 I. Emmett, quoted in *Second report from the Select Committee of the House of Lords on Sport and Leisure* (HMSO, 1973), p. civ.

57 *A survey of shared and extended use of schools, 1978/9* (Department of Education and Science, Statistical Bulletin 1/82, 1982).

58 J. Roberts, *A review of studies of sport and recreation in the inner city* (Sports Council Study 17, 1978).

59 Sports Council, *Provision for sport* (Department of the Environment, 1972), p. 6.

60 J. Bale, 'Football clubs as neighbours', *Town & Country Planning* (1980), pp. 93-4.

CHAPTER 5: RECREATION PATTERNS IN COUNTRYSIDE AND COAST

1 Countryside Review Committee, *Leisure and the countryside: a discussion paper* (HMSO, 1977), p. 4.

2 J. T. Coppock, 'The geography of leisure and recreation', in E. H. Brown (ed.), *Geography, yesterday and tomorrow* (Oxford University Press, 1980), pp. 263-79.

3 M. Shoard, 'Children in the countryside', *The Planner*, 65 (1979), pp. 67-71.

4 M. Dower, *The challenge of leisure* (Civic Trust, 1965), p. 5.

5 A. M. H. Fitton, 'The reality – for whom are we actually providing?', in Countryside Recreation Research Advisory Group, *Countryside for all? A review of the use people make of the countryside for recreation* (Countryside Commission, CCP 117, 1978), p. 39. This paper is the fullest published account of the 1977 National Survey of Countryside Recreation, but see also 'Participation in informal countryside recreation', *Digest of countryside recreation statistics 1979* (Countryside Commission, CCP 86, 1979), unpaged.

6 'Trends in informal countryside recreation participation', *Digest of countryside recreation statistics 1979*.

7 R. Stoakes, 'Oil prices and countryside recreation travel', *Digest of countryside recreation statistics 1979*.

8 R. Sidaway, personal communication.

9 *Patterns of informal recreation in the North York Moors National Park* (North York Moors National Park, 1981), p. 6. Specific fuel shortages may have depressed the total slightly in early 1979.

10 S. Lucarotti, 'Our visitors are stable', *Peak Park News* (Spring 1981), p. 4.

11 Department of Transport, *Transport Statistics Great Britain 1970-1980* (HMSO, 1981), table 2.28.

12 *Countryside issues and action: prospectus of the Countryside Commission 1982* (Countryside Commission, CCP 151, 1982), p. 4.

13 Countryside Review Committee, *Leisure and the countryside*, p. 6.

14 The exact length depends on the definition adopted. The Nature Conservancy, including all areas along the high-water mark to the first bridge or ferry, derived a length of 6191 km; the National Parks Commission, concerned with direct frontage to the sea and including inlets only where they could properly be regarded as 'arms of the sea', made a more modest estimate of 4413 km. See A. Patmore and S. Glyptis, 'The coastal resource', in Countryside Recreation Research Advisory Group, *Recreation and the coast* (Countryside Commission, CCP 127, 1979), pp. 5-6.

15 B. S. Duffield and S. E. Walker, 'People and the coast – current demands and future aspirations for coastal recreation', in *Recreation and the coast*, table 7.

16 G. Wall, 'Socio-economic variations in pleasure-trip patterns: the case of Hull car-owners', *Transactions of the Institute of British Geographers*, 57 (1972), p. 50 and figure 2.

17 J. C. Miles and J. N. Hammond, *A survey of routes taken by motor vehicles in the Lake District* (Transport and Road Research Laboratory, Supplementary Report 264, 1977), table 2.

18 *Ibid.*, table 3. More than one reason was allowed, and totals therefore exceed 100 per cent.

19 R. Colenutt, 'An investigation into the factors affecting the pattern of trip generation and route choice of day visitors to the countryside' (unpublished PhD thesis, University of Bristol, 1970), p. 302.

20 M. J. Elson, *Countryside trip-making* (Sports Council and Social Science Research Council, 1979), p. 39. See also J. C. Miles and N. Smith, *Models of recreational traffic in rural areas* (Transport and Road Research Laboratory, Supplementary Report 301, 1977); and *Models of recreational travel* (Tourism and Recreation Research Unit Research Report no. 33, University of Edinburgh, 1980).

21 *Models of recreational travel*, p. 66.

22 The remaining 4 per cent were business visitors and local people resident within the park: *Dartmoor National Park – policy plan* (Devon County Council, 1973). The data refer to Sunday, 23 July 1967, and were derived from cordon surveys. Later surveys suggest a slightly higher proportion of holiday visitors, but this may be related to site-based survey methods as well as changes over time. See n. 51.

23 See, for example, J. Wager, 'Outdoor recreation on common land', *Journal of the Town Planning Institute*, 53 (1967), pp. 398-403. Variations at a number of sites are recorded in C. A. J. Jacobs, *Countryside recreation site survey*, vol 1 (Clwyd County Council, 1976), table 8.

24 Wager, 'Outdoor recreation'. See also J. R. Duffell, 'Further studies in recreational trip generation, 2: Recreational indices of use – meteorological factors', *Traffic Engineering and Control* 14.6 (1972), pp. 285-8.

25 It was suggested in 1968 that, in the East Hampshire Area of Outstanding Natural Beauty, some 400 ha of land would suffice for *all* envisaged informal recreation in the area by the 1980s, almost exactly 1 per cent of the total area. See *East Hampshire AONB, a study in countryside conservation* (Hampshire County Council, 1968), p. 6.

26 Most such studies are concerned with the car-borne visitor and with locating parking patterns. One early study was concerned with the total recreational use of land in Snowdonia and gives a better indication of the full impact of recreation, though the basic generalisation still holds good. See J. A. Patmore, 'Recreation', in J. A. Dawson and J. C. Doornkamp, *Evaluating the human environment: essays in applied geography* (Edward Arnold, 1973), figure 10.3, p. 238.

27 P. A. K. Greening and P. G. Smith, *A survey of recreational traffic in the Yorkshire Dales* (Transport and Road Research Laboratory, Supplementary Report 539, 1980), pp. 4-5.

28 *Lake District National Park: National Park Plan* (Lake District Special Planning Board, 1978), p. 92, paras. 6.13 and 6.14.

29 J. A. Patmore, 'Routeways and recreation', in P. Lavery, *Recreational Geography* (David & Charles, 1974).

30 *Snowdon Management Scheme: Management Plan 1981* (Snowdonia National Park, 1981), pp. 27 and 30.

31 Data from J. Alcock, 'The footpath network in an area of N. Lancashire' (unpublished BA dissertation, University of Liverpool, 1971).

32 See, for example, M. J. Elson, *A review and evaluation of countryside recreation site surveys* (Countryside Commission, 1977) and *A research study into monitoring the use of informal recreation sites* (Tourism and Recreation Research Unit Research Report no. 46, University of Edinburgh, 1981). Practical advice in survey design is available in *Outdoor recreation information: suggested standard classifications for use in questionnaire surveys* (Countryside Commission, 1970) and *Outdoor recreation surveys: the design and use of questionnaires for site surveys* (Countryside Commission, 1970).

33 The most useful studies are R. J. C. Burton, *The recreational carrying capacity of the countryside* (University of Keele Library, Occasional Publications no. 11, 1974); Jacobs, *Countryside recreation site survey;* S. A. Glyptis, 'Room to relax', *The Planner,* 67.5 (1981), pp. 120-2; and 'People at play in the countryside', *Geography,* 66.4 (1981), pp. 277-85.

34 Wager, 'Outdoor recreation'.

35 Glyptis, 'Room to relax', p. 121.

36 Glyptis, 'People at play', figure 2.

37 Jacobs, *Countryside recreation site survey,* p. 42.

38 P. Downing and M. Dower, *Second homes in England and Wales* (Countryside Commission, CCP 65, 1973), p. 7. This section leans heavily on this study, but see also C. L. Bielckus, A. W. Rogers and G. P. Wibberley, *Second homes in England and Wales* (Wye College, Studies in rural land use no. 11, 1972) and J. T. Coppock, *Second homes: curse or blessing?* (Pergamon Press, 1977). Among studies of specific regions are C. A. J. Jacobs, *Second homes in Denbighshire* (County of Denbigh Tourism and Recreation Research Report 3, 1972); C. B. Pyne, *Second homes* (Caernarvonshire County Planning Department, undated, c. 1973); R. de Vane, *Second home ownership: a case study* (University of Wales Press, 1975); South West Economic Planning Council, *Survey of second homes in the South West* (HMSO, 1975); C. Bollom, *Attitudes and second homes in rural Wales* (University of Wales Press, 1978); A. L. Ray, *Second homes in North Norfolk* (A. L. Ray, 1979); and P. V. Sarre, *Second homes: a case study in Brecknock* (Open University, 1981).

39 Sarre, *Second homes,* pp. 2-3.

40 *Annual survey of holiday development* (Devon County Council, 1978), table 7.

41 D. C. Gill, *Coastal caravans and camping subject plan* (Humberside County Council, 1978), p. 16.

42 These figures relate to the early 1970s, but there is no reason to doubt their continuing significance in a relative sense. See Downing and Dower, *Second homes in England and Wales,* pp. 7-8.

43 The Abersoch total relates to houses empty in winter in 1970. See Pyne, *Second homes,* p. 8.

44 *Lake District National Park: National Park Plan,* pp. 154-5.

45 In Gwynedd in 1974, only 2 per cent of second home owners had their primary home in Wales. See de Vane, *Second home ownership,* table 3.7.

46 Bielckus, Rogers and Wibberley, *Second homes in England and Wales,* p. 32.

47 *Ibid.,* p. 36. There is no recent study to enable the impact of the completion of the M4 motorway to be examined, but the overall evidence suggests it is unlikely to have made a substantial change in the pattern.

48 *Digest of Tourist Statistics No. 9* (British Tourist Authority, 1981), table 51. Unless separately acknowledged, data in the following paragraphs are from this source.

49 *Tourism in the UK – the broad perspective* (British Tourist Authority, 1981), p. 13.

50 Unlike their counterparts in other countries, British geographers have been inclined to divorce the study of tourism from the study of recreation: apart from studies of individual resorts and resort areas, tourism tends to have been more the preserve of the economist. For a refreshingly different view, see D. G. Pearce, 'Towards a geography of tourism', *Annals of Tourism Research,* 6.3 (1979), pp. 245-72; and D. G. Pearce, *Tourist development* (Longman, 1981).

51 *Dartmoor National Park Plan* (Dartmoor National Park Authority, 1977), p. 7. The data relate to 1975.

52 The figures, from the annual British National Travel Survey of the British Tourist Authority, relate to holidays of four nights and more, and to holidays taken by both adults and children.

53 *Annual survey of holiday development,* table 4.

54 See J. A. Patmore, *Land and leisure* (David & Charles, 1970), figure 45, for a map of inter-regional holiday movement in 1960.

55 *South East 1980* and *Cumbria 1980* (English Tourist Board, Tourism Regional Fact Sheets, 1981): data derived from British Home Tourism Survey.

56 C. P. Cooper, 'Spatial and temporal patterns of tourist behaviour', *Regional Studies,* 15.5 (1981), pp. 359-71.

57 *Ibid.,* p. 366.

CHAPTER 6: COUNTRYSIDE RESOURCES

1 P. Hall, 'Britain 2000: speculations on the future society', in M. Chisholm (ed.), *Resources for Britain's future* (Penguin, 1972), p. 179.

2 M. Shoard, *The theft of the countryside* (Maurice Temple Smith, 1980), p. 9.

3 The literature on specific themes will be noted subsequently, but the following are essential reviews of general problems, putting recreation into a wider context: G. E. Cherry (ed.), *Rural planning problems* (Leonard Hill, 1976); J. Davidson and G. Wibberley, *Planning and the rural environment* (Pergamon, 1977); A. W. Gilg, *Countryside planning: the first three decades, 1945-76* (David & Charles, 1978); H. Newby, *Green and pleasant land? Social change in rural England* (Penguin, 1979); and M. Blacksell and A. Gilg, *The countryside: planning and change* (George Allen & Unwin, 1981). See also the invaluable *Countryside Planning Yearbooks,* edited by A. W. Gilg; Volume One (Geo Books, 1980); Volume Two (Geo Books, 1981); Volume Three (Geo Books, 1982).

4 M. Clawson and J. L. Knetsch, *Economics of outdoor recreation* (Johns Hopkins Press, 1966), pp. 36-8.

5 Quoted in J. H. Appleton, *The experience of landscape* (John Wiley, 1975), p. 31. Gilpin was writing in 1786.

6 V.Cornish, *The scenery of England: a study of harmonious grouping in town and country* (Council for the Preservation of Rural England, 1932), p. 89.

7 D. Lowenthal and H. C. Prince, 'English landscape tastes', *Geographical Review,* 55 (1965), p. 205.

8 Technically, the Commission was created by the Act, but the Conservancy secured its royal charter in 1949 prior to the passing of the Act, the Act conveying its statutory powers. See J. Sheail, *Nature in trust: the history of nature conservation in Britain* (Blackie, 1976), pp. 215-16.

9 Lowenthal and Prince, 'English landscape tastes', p. 192.

10 These figures, and those in succeeding paragraphs, from Shoard, *Theft of the countryside,* pp. 34 et seq.

11 *Ibid.,* p. 10.

12 Quoted in H. Cunningham, *Leisure in the industrial revolution* (Croom Helm, 1980), p. 80.

13 *Countryside issues and action: prospectus of the Countryside Commission 1982* (Countryside Commission, CCP 151, 1982), p. 7.

14 *The future of the moorland* (North York Moors National Park Committee 1982), p. 3. The information in the following paragraph is derived from this source except where noted.

15 M. L. Parry, A. Bruce and C. E. Harkness, *Changes in the extent of moorland and roughland in the North York Moors* (Surveys of moorland and roughland change no. 5, Department of Geography, University of Birmingham, 1982).

16 The two essential general reviews are Department of the Environment, *Report of the National Park Policies Review Committee* (better known as the Sandford Report) (HMSO, 1974); and A. MacEwen and M. MacEwen, *National parks: conservation or cosmetics?* (Allen & Unwin, 1982).

17 IUCN, *World directory of national parks and other protected areas* (International Union for the Conservation of Nature and Natural Resources, 1975).

18 For a full history of the emergence of National Parks in Britain see G. E. Cherry, *Environmental Planning 1939-1969. Volume II, National Parks and recreation in the countryside* (HMSO, 1975).

19 MacEwen and MacEwen, *National parks,* p. 6.
20 J. Dower, *National Parks in England and Wales* (Cmnd 6628, HMSO, 1945), para. 4.
21 *Report of the National Parks Committee (England and Wales)* (Cmnd 7121, HMSO, 1947).
22 *The management of enclosed agricultural land* (North York Moors National Parks Committee, 1981), para. 1.2.
23 *National Park Plan* (Brecon Beacons National Park, 1977), Appendix 1.
24 Section 46 of the Wildlife and Countryside Act, 1981, makes statutory provision for the appointment of district council representatives to each committee as of right, rather than by the county councils allocating seats to the district councils.
25 MacEwen and MacEwen, *National parks,* p. 6.
26 These data from 'General statistics of national parks, 1980-81', *County Councils Gazette* (November 1981), pp. 268-9. When successful appeals are included, the proportion of refusals drops to 19 per cent.
27 Structure plans are the responsibility of the appropriate county council, with the exception of the area of the Peak Park Joint Planning Board.
28 House of Commons, *Official report,* 31 May 1949.
29 *The Peak District National Park Draft Structure Plan* (Peak Park Joint Planning Board, 1975), p. 66, para. 11.19.
30 See MacEwen and MacEwen, *National parks,* pp. 232-8.
31 *Sixth report of the Countryside Commission for the year ended 30 September 1973* (HMSO, 1974), p. 16.
32 P. Prescott-Clarke, *People and roads in the Lake District: a study of the A66 road improvement scheme* (Transport and Road Research Laboratory, Supplementary Report 606, 1980), p. 29.
33 Lord Porchester, *A study of Exmoor* (HMSO, 1977).
34 For the Exmoor precursors, see L. F. Curtis and A. J. Walker, *Moorland conservation on Exmoor. The Porchester maps: their construction and policies* (Exmoor National Park Authority, 1981).
35 *Bunkhouse barns: a new use for redundant farm buildings* (Countryside Commission, CCP 131, 1980).
36 *A draft management plan for Nab Farm* (North York Moors National Park Committee, 1981), Appendix 1.
37 *Fourteenth report of the Countryside Commission for the year ended 30 September 1981* (HMSO, 1982), p. 8.
38 'General statistics of national parks', p. 268.
39 *Dartmoor National Park Plan* (Dartmoor National Park Authority, 1977), p. 14, para. 4.11.
40 *Ibid.*, para. 4.13.
41 R. S. Gibbs and M. C. Whitby, *Local authority expenditure on access land* (Agricultural Adjustment Unit, University of Newcastle upon Tyne, 1975).
42 *Upland management experiment* (Countryside Commission, CCP 82, 1974); *The Lake District upland management experiment* (Countryside Commission, CCP 93, 1976); *The Snowdonia upland management experiment* (Countryside Commission, CCP 122, 1979).

43 *Eleventh report of the Countryside Commission for the year ended 30 September 1978* (HMSO, 1979), pp. 5-6.

44 *Snowdon Management Scheme: Management Plan, 1981* (Snowdonia National Park, 1981).

45 T. Heath, 'Snowdon gets £¼m facelift with new deal for peak cafe', *The Guardian* (5 August 1982).

46 J. Thompson, *The Upper Derwent experiment – how it worked* (Peak Park Joint Planning Board leaflet, 1982).

47 I. Brotherton, O. Maurice, G. Barrow and A. Fishwick, *Tarn Hows: an approach to the management of a popular beauty spot* (Countryside Commission, CCP 106, 1977).

48 *Routes for people: an experiment in rural transport planning* (Countryside Commission, CCP 108, 1977).

49 *Roads and traffic* (North York Moors National Park Committee, 1982), Appendix B.

50 *Dales Rail: a report of an experimental project in the Yorkshire Dales National Park* (Countryside Commission, CCP 120, 1979); A. O. Grigg and P. G. Smith, *An opinion survey of the Yorkshire Dales Rail service in 1975* (Transport and Road Research Laboratory, Report 769, 1977).

51 *Sixth report of the Countryside Commission for the year ended 30 September 1973* (HMSO, 1974), p. 8.

52 K. H. Himsworth, *A review of Areas of Outstanding Natural Beauty* (Countryside Commission, CCP 140, 1980); *Areas of Outstanding Natural Beauty: a policy statement* (Countryside Commission, CCP 141, 1980); M. A. Anderson, 'The land patterns of Areas of Outstanding Natural Beauty in England and Wales', *Landscape Planning*, 7 (1980), pp. 1-22, 'Planning policies and development control in the Sussex Downs AONB', *Town Planning Review*, 52 (1981), pp. 5-25, and *Historical perspectives on the role for AONBs: recreation or preservation?* (Wye College, University of London, Department of Environmental Studies and Countryside Planning, Occasional Paper no. 3, 1981).

53 For fuller accounts see Sir Dudley Stamp, *Nature Conservation in Britain* (Collins, 1969), and Sheail, *Nature in trust*.

54 *Aspects of leisure and holiday tourism* (English Tourist Board, 1981), table 4.

55 For a full list of County Naturalists Trusts' reserves, see *Nature reserves handbook* (Royal Society for Nature Conservation, 1981). For a map of the situation in 1974, see Sheail, *Nature in trust*, figure 15. At that date, there were 850 such reserves in Great Britain, covering 23,562 ha.

56 Personal communication from Nature Conservancy Council. Data correct to 31 January 1982, and relate to England and Wales.

57 As at 31 March 1981.

58 From this total should be excluded the 1853 ha owned in Northern Ireland. Scotland is the concern of the separate National Trust for Scotland, founded 1931.

59 See R. Fedden, *The continuing purpose: a history of the National Trust, its aims and work* (Longmans, 1968) and *The National Trust, past and present* (Jonathan Cape, 1974). For a more geographical approach, see

J. E. Tunbridge, 'Conservation trusts as geographic agents: their impact upon landscape, townscape and land use', *Transactions of the Institute of British Geographers*, new series, 6.1 (1981), pp. 103-25. Data in this section are drawn from these sources, and successive *Annual Reports* and newsletters of the Trust.

60 In addition, two in Northern Ireland had over 20,000 visitors. Those with over 100,000 were St Michael's Mount (168,000), Stourhead Garden (167,000), Chartwell (159,000), Tatton Park Garden (150,000), Bodnant Garden (129,000), Bodiam Castle (128,000), Housesteads (121,000), Sheffield Park Garden (117,000), Tatton Park House (114,000), Brownsea Island (108,000), Wakehurst Place (106,000), Polesden Lacey Garden (105,000) and Sissinghurst Castle Garden (102,000).

61 *Properties open in 1982* (National Trust, 1982), p. v.

62 For a map of acquisitions, see A. Patmore and S. Glyptis, 'The coastal resource', in Countryside Recreation Research Advisory Group, *Recreation and the coast* (Countryside Commission, CCP 127, 1979), figure 8.

63 *Annual Report 1980* (National Trust, 1981), p. 23.

64 A. M. H. Fitton, 'The reality – for whom are we actually providing?', Countryside Recreation Research Advisory Group, *Countryside for all?* (Countryside Commission, CCP 117, 1978), table 20. Data from 1977 National Survey of Countryside Recreation, relating to 'main stop on trip'.

65 In the following paragraphs, several English Tourist Board sources are used for data, most notably *English heritage monitor* (1981 and 1982), *Sightseeing in 1980* (1981) and *Aspects of leisure and holiday tourism* (1981).

66 Duke of Bedford, *How to run a stately home* (André Deutsch, 1971), p. 43.

67 *Ibid.*, p. 15.

68 N. Burton, *RAC Historic Houses Handbook* (Macmillan, 1981), p. 163.

69 Duke of Bedford, *How to run a stately home*, p. 114.

70 *Sixty-first annual report and accounts of the Forestry Commission for the year ended 31 March 1981* (HMSO, 1982), table 7. Subsequent data are from this source unless otherwise noted. The actual areas planted are 895,717 ha for Great Britain, 387,702 ha for England and Wales. Commission land now occupies 5.5 per cent of Great Britain, 3.1 per cent of England and Wales.

71 For a recent statement of the case against the Commission's activities, see *Afforestation: the case against expansion* (Ramblers Association, 1980).

72 *British forestry* (Forestry Commission, 1974), pp. 30-1. In addition to three other forest parks in Scotland, the 50,000 ha Border Forest Park, designated in 1955, straddles the border.

73 *Forty-ninth annual report and accounts of the Forestry Commission for the year ended 31st March 1969* (HMSO, 1970), p. 14, para. 46.

74 *Forestry policy* (HMSO, 1972), p. 10, para. 23.

75 The objectives of the Commission, as set out in the *Fifty-fourth annual report and accounts of the Forestry Commission for the year ended 31st March 1974* (HMSO, 1974), p. 12, para. 8d.

76 *Fifty-fifth annual report and accounts of the Forestry Commission for the year ended 31st March 1975* (HMSO, 1975) p. 10, para. 20. See also Coopers &

Lybrand Associates Ltd, *Forestry Commission potential for permanent tourist accommodation: planning and policy report* (Forestry Commission, 1974).

77 *Sixtieth annual report and accounts of the Forestry Commission for the year ended 31st March 1980* (HMSO, 1980), p. 23, para. 55.

78 Forestry Commission, *Sixty-first anual report*, p. 14, para. 23.

79 The Peak District National Park had an estimated 16.8 million day visitors in 1973, Dartmoor 7.9 million visits in 1975 and the North York Moors 11.3 million in 1973 and 11.14 million in 1979.

80 'General statistics of national parks'.

81 Countryside Commission, *Fourteenth report*, p. 34.

82 *Countryside issues and action*, p. 8.

83 See, for example, J. Davidson, 'The urban fringe', *Countryside Recreation Review*, 1 (1976), pp. 2-7; Countryside Review Committee, *Leisure and the countryside: a discussion paper* (HMSO, 1977), pp. 11-12; M. J. Elson, *The leisure use of green belts and urban fringes* (Sports Council and Social Science Research Council, 1979).

84 See *Countryside management in the urban fringe* (Countryside Commission, CCP 142, 1981); Countryside Commission *Fourteenth report*, pp. 25-8.

85 See especially M. J. Ferguson and R. J. C. Munton, 'Informal recreation sites in London's Green Belt', *Area*, 11 (1979), pp. 196-205; C. Harrison, 'A playground for whom? Informal recreation in London's Green Belt', *Area*, 13 (1981), pp. 109-114; R. J. C. Munton, 'Management expenditure on informal recreation sites in the London Green Belt', *The Planner*, 67.4 (1981), pp. 93-5. See also the following Working Papers from the Department of Geography, University College, London: no. 7, M. J. Ferguson, *The evolution of a recreational role for London's Green Belt: towards countryside recreation for all?* (1980); no. 8, C. Thompson, *Substitution in recreation: a review and results of a survey at sites in London's Green Belt* (1980); and no. 9, C. M. Harrison, *Preliminary results of a survey of site use in the South London Green Belt* (1981).

86 Department of Transport, *Transport Statistics Great Britain 1970-1980* (HMSO, 1981), table 2.37.

87 G. E. Ballantine, 'Planning for remoteness', *Journal of the Town Planning Institute*, 57 (1971), pp. 60-4.

88 Ministry of Housing and Local Government, Welsh Office, *Report of the Footpaths Committee* (HMSO, 1968), p. 3. This is usually referred to as the Gosling Committee after its chairman, Sir Arthur Gosling.

89 *Ibid.*, p. 5. County borough councils had discretionary powers to survey their (largely urban) areas.

90 *A policy for footpaths* (Ramblers Association, 1980), p. 4.

91 *Survey of the public paths of Gloucestershire, July 1981* (Ramblers Association, Gloucestershire area, 1981), pp. 7-8.

92 *Footpaths for recreation: a policy statement* (Countryside Commission, CCP 99, 1976), p. 3.

93 *Countryside issues and action*, p. 8.

94 *Survey of public paths of Gloucestershire*, p. 7.

95 Minister of Land and Natural Resources, *Leisure in the countryside, England and Wales* (HMSO, Cmnd 2928, 1966), pp. 11-12, para. 47.

96 *Footpaths for recreation*, p. 4, para. 15.

97 *A policy for footpaths*, p. 3.

98 For a full geographical study of both demand and supply see M. F. Tanner, *Water resources and recreation* (Sports Council Study 3, 1973). Though dated in detail, the basic appraisal remains valid. The problems of specific kinds of resource were subsequently treated in a series of sample studies, all undertaken by the Dartington Amenity Research Trust, and published by the Sports Council: Study 4, *Rickmansworth gravel pits* (1973); Study 5, *River Hamble* (1973); Study 6, *Southampton Water* (1973); Study 7, *Canals around Braunston* (1975); Study 8, *Yorkshire Ouse* (1974); Study 9, *Llandegfedd and Siblyback Reservoirs* (1975).

99 An Ordnance Survey estimate, used in T. L. Burton and G. P. Wibberley, *Outdoor recreation in the British Countryside* (Wye College, 1967), p. 17. There are obvious problems of definition which makes any precise calculation difficult.

100 Quoted in G. Berry and G. Beard, *The Lake District: a century of conservation* (Bartholomew, 1980), p. 71.

101 B. Duffield, J. P. Best and M. F. Collins (eds), *Digest of sports statistics* (Sports Council, 1983), p. 92.

102 *Annual report 1980-1981* (Water Space Amenity Commission), Appendix A. See also M. F. Tanner *The recreational use of water supply reservoirs in England and Wales*, and *Permit sailing on enclosed waters* (Water Space Amenity Commission Research Reports 3 and 4, 1977).

103 S. Glyptis, *National Angling Survey, 1980: summary report* (Water Research Centre, 1980).

104 Ministry of Transport, *British waterways: recreation and amenity* (HMSO, Cmnd 3401, 1967), p. 3.

105 *Annual report and accounts for the year ended 31st December 1981* (British Waterways Board, 1982), Appendix V.

106 A. Patmore and S. Glyptis, 'The coastal resource', in Countryside Recreation Research Advisory Group, *Recreation and the coast* (Countryside Commission, CCP 127, 1979), pp. 5-61.

107 Summarised in cartographic form in J. A. Patmore, *Land and leisure* (David & Charles, 1970), figures 67-70. See also the study and summary reports prepared by the Countryside Commission: *Coastal recreation and holidays* (HMSO, 1969); *Nature conservation at the coast* (HMSO, 1969); *The planning of the coastline* (HMSO, 1970); *The coastal heritage* (HMSO, 1970).

108 *Resorts and spas in Britain* (British Tourist Authority, 1975).

109 *The planning of the undeveloped coast* (Department of the Environment, Circular 12/72, 1972).

110 *Countryside issues and action*, p. 12. See also, W. Le-Las, 'Heritage coasts', *Heritage outlook*, 2.2 (1982), pp. 40-1.

CHAPTER 7: EVALUATION, CONFLICT AND CAPACITY

1 M. Clawson and J. L. Knetsch, *Economics of outdoor recreation* (Johns Hopkins Press, 1966), p. 143.
2 For summaries of approaches and problems see E. C. Penning-Rowsell, *Alternative approaches to landscape appraisal and evaluation* (Middlesex Polytechnic, 1973, and *Supplement*, 1975); J. A. Patmore (ed.), 'Landscape evaluation: a symposium', *Transactions of the Institute of British Geographers*, 66 (1975), pp. 119-61; D. G. Robinson, I. C. Laurie, J. F. Wager and A. L. Traill (ed.), *Landscape evaluation: the landscape evaluation research project, 1970-75* (University of Manchester, 1976); *A landscape classification of Wales* (Planning Services, Welsh Office, 1980), pp. 9-24.
3 G. E. Cherry, *Environmental planning 1939-1969, Volume II, National parks and recreation in the countryside* (HMSO, 1975), especially pp. 42-4 and 52-6.
4 K. H. Himsworth, *A review of Areas of Outstanding Natural Beauty* (Countryside Commission, CCP 140), p. 84.
5 Countryside Commission, *The coastal heritage: a conservation policy for coasts of high quality scenery* (HMSO, 1970), p. 11. See also J. A. Steers, 'Coastal preservation and planning', *Geographical Journal*, 104 (1944), pp. 7-27.
6 Robinson, *et al.*, *Landscape evaluation*, para 9.16.
7 J. H. Appleton, 'Landscape evaluation: the theoretical vacuum', *Transactions of the Institute of British Geographers*, 66 (1975), p. 122.
8 Penning-Rowsell, *Alternative approaches, Supplement* p. 4, records appraisals in 30 counties of England and Wales.
9 *Landscape classification of Wales*, p. 89.
10 First developed in B. S. Duffield and M. L. Owen, *Leisure+countryside=: a geographical appraisal of countryside recreation in Lanarkshire* (University of Edinburgh, 1970) and *Leisure+countryside=: a geographical appraisal of countryside recreation in the Edinburgh area* (University of Edinburgh, 1971). See also J. T. Coppock and B. S. Duffield, *Recreation in the countryside, a spatial analysis* (Macmillan, 1975), pp. 106-122.
11 Coppock and Duffield, *Recreation in the countryside*, p. 119.
12 *Planning for informal recreation at the sub-regional scale: the application of potential surface analysis to the assessment of resources for informal recreation* (Countryside Commission, CCP 71, 1974).
13 US Government Printing Office, Washington, 1962.
14 Countryside Review Committee, *The countryside – problems and policies* (HMSO, 1976), para. 53.
15 Lord Cobham, in *Second Report from the Select Committee of the House of Lords on Sport and Leisure* (HMSO, 1973), Minutes of Evidence, p. 420, para. 1480.
16 *Ibid.*, pp. 392-3.
17 *Ibid.*, p. 425.
18 Dartington Amenity Research Trust, *Interpretation in visitor centres* (Countryside Commission, CCP 115, 1978), p. 66.

19 S. A. Glyptis, 'People at play in the countryside', *Geography*, 66.4 (1981), pp. 280 and 283.
20 *The Ridgeway Path: report of survey 1975* (Oxfordshire County Planning Department, undated), pp. 29-30.
21 *Fifth-seventh annual report and accounts of the Forestry Commission for the year ended 31st March 1977* (HMSO, 1978), p. 15, para. 14.
22 *Second report from the Select Committee of the House of Lords*, p. 264 (British Canoe Union evidence).
23 *Ibid.*, oral evidence, pp. 275 and 279.
24 T. O'Riordan and G. Paget, *Sharing rivers and canals: a study of the views of coarse anglers and boat users on selected waterways* (Sports Council, Study 16, 1978), p. 5.
25 J. P. Barkham, 'Recreational carrying capacity: a problem of perception', *Area*, 5.3 (1973), pp. 218-22.
26 J. Tivy, *The concept and determination of carrying capacity of recreational land in the USA* (Countryside Commission for Scotland, Occasional Paper no. 3, 1972), p. 1.
27 Quoted in *ibid.*, p. 3.
28 *Provision for swimming* (Sports Council, 1978), p. 27.
29 *Ibid.*
30 E. Grice, 'Counting the scars of success', *The Sunday Times* (26 April 1981).
31 Quoted in R. Fedden, *The continuing purpose: a history of the National Trust, its aims and work* (Longmans, 1968), p. 48.
32 For useful reviews, see R. J. Lloyd, *Countryside recreation: the ecological implications* (Lindsey County Council, 1970); and M. C. D. Speight, *Outdoor recreation and its ecological effects: a bibliography and review* (University College, London, Discussion Papers in Conservation no. 4, 1973).
33 Speight, *Outdoor recreation*, p. 9.
34 Lloyd, *Countryside recreation*, p. 60.
35 *Pennine Way Survey* (Countryside Commission, CCP 63, undated), p. 48.
36 Data from North York Moors National Park.
37 M. Ingham, *Access to the countryside* (Peak District National Park, National Parks Conference excursion notes, 1982).
38 J. Furmidge, 'Planning for recreation in the countryside', *Journal of the Town Planning Institute*, 55 (1969), pp. 62-7.
39 R. J. C. Burton, *The recreational carrying capacity of the countryside* (Keele University Library Occasional Publication no. 11, 1974).
40 *Ibid.*, pp. 124-40 for a discussion of these, and of alternative techniques.
41 *Ibid.*, pp. 153 and 155.
42 *Ibid.*, p. 168.
43 Urban Research and Development Corporation. *Guidelines for understanding and determining optimum recreation carrying capacity* (US Department of the Interior, Bureau of Outdoor Recreation, 1977).
44 *Ibid.*, pp. 1.3 and 2.1.

CHAPTER 8: PRECEPT AND PRACTICE

1 Sir Frank Fraser Darling, *Wilderness and plenty* (Ballantine, 1971), p. 110.
2 'Holidaytaking by the British in 1981', *Research Newsletter*, no. 29 (British Tourist Authority, 1982), p. 5.
3 *Digest of Tourist Statistics*, no. 9 (British Tourist Authority, 1981), table 54.
4 D. Mercer, 'Perception in outdoor recreation', in P. Lavery (ed.), *Recreational geography* (David & Charles, 1974), p. 57.
5 'Lancashire inventory', *Tourism in Britain*, 41 (1982), p. 27.
6 Mercer, 'Perception', p. 64.
7 S. Hutson, *A review of the role of clubs and voluntary associations based on a study of two areas in Swansea* (Sports Council and Social Science Research Council, 1979), p. 8.
8 R. Fedden, *The continuing purpose: a history of the National Trust, its aims and work* (Longmans, 1968), pp. 90-1.
9 United States National Park Service, *Tatton Park Interpretive Study* (Countryside Commission, undated), pp. 19, 23-4.
10 F. B. O'Connor, F. B. Goldsmith and M. Macrae, *Kynance Cove: a restoration project* (Countryside Commission, CCP 128, 1979), p. 37.
11 R. M. Sidaway and F. B. O'Connor, 'Recreation pressures in the countryside', in Countryside Recreation Research Advisory Group, *Countryside for all?* (Countryside Commission, CCP 117, 1978), pp. 131 and 139.
12 R. J. C. Munton, 'Management expenditure on informal recreation sites in the London Green Belt', *The Planner*, 67.4 (1981), pp. 93-5.
13 *Ibid., p. 95.*
14 *Second report from the Select Committee of the House of Lords on Sport and Leisure* (HMSO, 1973), para 352, p. cxxvii.
15 *Ibid.*, para. 354.
16 *Countryside issues and action: prospectus of the Countryside Commission 1982* (Countryside Commission, CCP 151, 1982). This was envisaged as a prelude to the drawing up of a strategy for the period 1983-88.
17 *Sport in the community: the next ten years* (Sports Council, 1982). Specific financial proposals were put forward in *A case for sport: bid for resources 1983/4* and *A forward look: rolling programme 1983-88* (Sports Council, 1982).
18 A. J. Veal and A. S. Travis, 'Local authority leisure services – the state of play', *Local Government Studies*, 5.4 (1979), pp. 5-16.
19 A. S. Travis, 'Recreation at the urban fringe', *Planner News* (July 1982), p. 3.
20 *Strategic issues in sport and recreation* (Yorkshire and Humberside Council for Sport and Recreation, 1979), tables 12 and 13. The tables are derived from CIPFA estimates for 1978-79.
21 J. T. Coppock, B. S. Duffield and R. Vaughan. *National Parks: a study of rural economies* (Countryside Commission, CCP 144, 1981), pp. 63-4.

22 B. Green, *Countryside conservation* (George Allen & Unwin, 1981), p. 220.
23 *Ibid.*, p. 215.
24 In 1978 Dales Rail carried 6425 passengers, in 1980 Mountain Goat 23,750, Snowdon Sherpa 84,280 and Coastlink 5750. For these, and other schemes, see *Public transport* (North York Moors National Park, 1982), Appendix A.
25 *Newsletter*, no. 71 (Dartmoor Preservation Association, August 1976).
26 M. Shoard, 'Metropolitan escape routes', *London Journal*, 5.1 (1979), p. 97.
27 *Ibid.*, p. 96.
28 Darling, *Wilderness and plenty*, p. 13.

Index